# GOD, POWER, AND EVIL: A PROCESS THEODICY

Books by David Ray Griffin

*Published by The Westminster Press*

God, Power, and Evil: A Process Theodicy

A Process Christology

*In collaboration with John B. Cobb, Jr.:*

Process Theology: An Introductory Exposition

# God, Power, and Evil: A Process Theodicy

*by*

DAVID RAY GRIFFIN

THE WESTMINSTER PRESS
*Philadelphia*

*Book Design by Dorothy Alden Smith*

Published by The Westminster Press®
Philadelphia, Pennsylvania

PRINTED IN THE UNITED STATES OF AMERICA

---

Grateful acknowledgment is made for use of excerpts from copyrighted material:

The Bobbs-Merrill Company, Inc., from James F. Ross, *Philosophical Theology.* 1969.
James Clarke & Company, Ltd., from Martin Luther, *On the Bondage of the Will,* tr. by J. I. Packer and O. R. Johnson. 1957.
T. & T. Clark, Ltd., from Karl Barth, *Church Dogmatics,* III/3, *The Doctrine of Creation,* tr. by G. W. Bromiley and R. J. Ehrlich. 1960.
Harper & Row, Publishers, Inc., from John H. Hick, *Evil and the God of Love.* 1966.
Macmillan Publishing Co., Inc., from Alfred North Whitehead, *Process and Reality,* copyright 1929 by Macmillan Publishing Co., Inc., renewed 1957 by Evelyn Whitehead.
Routledge & Kegan Paul, Ltd., from G. W. Leibniz, *Theodicy,* tr. by E. M. Huggard. 1952.
The Westminster Press, from *Calvin: Institutes of the Christian Religion,* Vols. XX, XXI (The Library of Christian Classics), ed. by John T. McNeill and tr. by Ford Lewis Battles. Copyright MCMLX by W. L. Jenkins.

---

**Library of Congress Cataloging in Publication Data**

Griffin, David, 1939–
God, power, and evil.

Includes bibliographical references and index.
1. Theodicy—History of doctrines. 2. Theodicy.
3. Process theology. I. Title.
BT160.G74 231'.8 76-21631
ISBN 0-664-20753-7

In Memory of
Michael Bartell (1946–1968)

who died in the Vietnam war,
one of the great evils of this world,
of which he wanted no part

# Contents

# Formal Statement of the Problem of Evil

NOTE: The premises of this formal statement of the problem of evil are referred to by number many times throughout the book. The statement is placed here for easy reference.

1. God is a perfect reality. (Definition)
2. A perfect reality is an omnipotent being. (By definition)
3. An omnipotent being could unilaterally bring about an actual world without any genuine evil. (By definition)
4. A perfect reality is a morally perfect being. (By definition)
5. A morally perfect being would want to bring about an actual world without any genuine evil. (By definition)
6. If there is genuine evil in the world, then there is no God. (Logical conclusion from 1 through 5)
7. There is genuine evil in the world. (Factual statement)
8. Therefore, there is no God. (Logical conclusion from 6 and 7)

# Preface

THIS is a book on the theoretical problem of evil as it appears in the Western philosophical and theological traditions. The problem, briefly stated, is this: If there is a providential God who is perfect in both power and moral goodness, why is there evil in the world? More precisely, is belief in the existence of such a deity made incredible by the apparent fact that the world is not as good as it could have been?

There have been many discussions of this problem. The justification for the appearance of the present book is twofold: First, there has not previously appeared a full-scale treatment of the problem written from the perspective of the "process" philosophical and theological thought inspired primarily by Alfred North Whitehead and Charles Hartshorne. Whereas members of this movement have indicated its solution of the problem many times in writing, this has been done in passing or at most a journal article. Partly for this reason, this potential solution has been largely ignored and/or misrepresented in the best-known literature on the subject. For example, in the most comprehensive historical-constructive book in English on the problem of evil thus far, John Hick's four-hundred-page *Evil and the God of Love,* the Whiteheadian position is not even mentioned, except for the false suggestion that it is essentially the same as that of E. S. Brightman.[1]

The second part of the justification for this book is that there have been remarkably few historical studies of the problem. Most of the treatments of the problem of evil tackle the transmitted problem directly, without careful analysis of the various elements that were brought together historically to make such a knotty problem, a problem that many have held to be insoluble in principle. An examination of the historical formation of a problem and the necessary consequences of combinations of certain traditionally accepted assumptions often frees one from taking all the traditional notions as equally belonging to the given elements of the problem. In the present case, a historical examination may help one to see that certain assumptions about the nature of God's power that made the problem so intractable are not necessarily inherent in the idea of perfect power and do not necessarily belong to the essence of the Judeo-Christian idea of deity.

These two aspects of the justification for the present book, which is both historical and constructive, finally merge. For a historical overview of a problem is never neutral, but emphasizes those aspects of previous positions which the author thinks to be crucial, positively or negatively, to the possibility of an adequate solution. Hence, the historical critiques in the present book will differ considerably from those found in books written from other perspectives. For example, John Hick retains precisely those traditional ideas about divine power that I think must be rejected if any viable solution is to be forthcoming. Hence his historical critiques by and large have a different slant from mine.

The book follows this plan: In the Introduction the importance and the central elements of the problem of evil are discussed. In Part I, some of the central influences on the problem deriving from the Biblical tradition and Greek philosophy are discussed. Part II is an examination of variations on the traditional position that emerged from the attempted synthesis of these traditions. The purpose of this lengthy discussion is to suggest not only that no satisfactory solution has been articulated by any of the representatives of this position, but also that this is not simply a contingent failure which we might expect to be remedied in the future, i.e., that no adequate solution is possible within the context of this traditional idea of God. In each chapter, a somewhat different aspect of the traditional position will be stressed; these critical chapters will thereby point out more or less explicitly several of the changes that I believe need to be made if an adequate theodicy is to be constructed. Part III is an attempt to construct an adequate theodicy on the basis of a Whiteheadian-Hartshornean process perspective. As the title of the book indicates, the critical issue is taken to be the nature of power. Specifically, the question is: If an actual world necessarily has power, is it possible for God to have the type of power in relation to the world which was ascribed to God by the traditional doctrine of omnipotence?

I have incurred many debts in the preparation of this book. Several colleagues have offered helpful suggestions: Marjorie Suchocki read the entire manuscript; Jack Verheyden read Parts I and II; Lewis Ford and John Cobb read earlier versions of Part III; Rolf Knierim read Chapter 1; Charles Young read Chapters 2–5; June O'Connor read Chapters 6 and 7; Jane Douglass read Chapter 6; Frank Kirkpatrick read Chapters 7, 8, and 17; Tad Beckman read Chapter 11; Alvin Plantinga read Chapter 17. My student assistants, Nelson James Howard and Jack Keller, made several valuable suggestions as well as doing much of the mechanical work. Everyone who has prepared a manuscript knows what a blessing it is to have a fast and accurate typist. I had three: Earlyne Biering, Mar Goman, and Kathy Wilson. Finally, beyond all these particular debts, any attempt to formulate in words my general indebtedness to John Cobb would necessarily be an understatement.

Chapter 14 is a slightly revised version of "Divine Causality, Evil, and Philosophical Theology: A Critique of James Ross," which appeared in the *International Journal for Philosophy of Religion,* Vol. IV, No. 3 (Fall 1973), pp. 168-186.

D. R. G.

# Introduction

Why did Mommy die? Why can't I walk? Why do we have to go to bed hungry every night? Such are some of types of questions that reflect some of the earliest encounters of human beings with the experience of evil. Later on, with the growth of our generalizing power and our capacity imaginatively to share the experiences of others, we ask such questions as: Why did six million Jews die? Why did innocent children in Biafra die such tragic deaths? Why is there so much suffering in the world? The inadequacy of simple answers in terms of just rewards for vice and virtue is quickly suggested by one ancient way of posing the question, i.e., Why do the wicked prosper? Likewise we quickly realize that earthquakes, tornadoes, and many diseases as well as totalitarian dictators and droppers of napalm and atomic bombs are not respecters of persons, but equally strike down those deemed good as well as those deemed evil by any moral criteria we employ.

How are we to respond to these questions? Some writers argue that the problem of evil is an existential, practical problem, so that it is wrong to attempt to give any theoretical answers. The proper way to meet a practical problem is with a practical solution. That is, the question is not how we explain evil—for by definition it is an absurdity, and hence inexplicable—but how we overcome it. In fact, preoccupation with theoretical questions only adds to the evil, since it prevents one from exerting all one's energy to overcoming evil.

I reject this line of reasoning. In the first place, a great amount of the evil we human beings experience is caused or at least greatly aggravated by the thoughts and feelings that we have by virtue of our rational capacity for generalizing and comparing what is with what might have been. Accordingly, it is false to say that the problem of evil is a purely "existential" or "practical" problem, if this is meant to deny that it has a theoretical dimension.

Second, the questions people raise about evil always implicitly contain theoretical affirmations. In contexts where people have been decisively shaped by the Jewish and/or Christian traditions, the question generally means, "Why did God cause (or permit) this to happen?" And behind this question stands the more or less explicit belief that "God (if there be a God) causes (or permits) everything that happens." This is a very theoretical belief! And it is one that can lead to all sorts of psychic distress, even to the point of viewing one's ultimate environment, the universe, as an alien place because controlled by an alien God or because totally devoid of divinity altogether.

Accordingly, if human theoretical beliefs are central to the human experience of evil, then the effort to overcome human evil cannot omit the theoretical dimension of the problem. In other words, the theoretical side of the problem of evil is a significant aspect of the existential problem to be met, and a theoretical problem can only be met with a theoretical solution.

Much of the so-called existentialist thought of this century has maintained that it is inappropriate to discuss passionate issues of ultimate concern such as the relation of God and evil in a detached, philosophical manner. I maintain just the opposite. It is precisely in regard to issues of ultimate concern—issues with which we are most passionately engaged as concrete, living, loving, hating human beings—that we must try the hardest to achieve a properly philosophic state of mind, in which we consider every conceivable position on its merits as unbiasedly as possible. It is precisely where truth is most important that we must not take the chance of missing it by caricaturing some proffered position, or dismissing it without consideration by attaching some convenient disreputable label to it because of its apparent similarity to some previously rejected position. In fact, even the old heresies must constantly be reevaluated for the element of truth they may contain.

In short, I hold that it is in regard to the issues that raise the greatest passion that we must try to be the most dispassionate. With this apologia for the importance of the topic and the method of approach, I now turn to the issue.

A central, and perhaps the central, notion in the traditional idea of

God in Western thought has been the notion that God controls, or at least could control, every detail of the events in the world. This has been taken as belonging to the defining essence of "God"—a being would not be God, it is said, if it did not have this power. In popular thought and piety this notion has generally been held in a less rigorous form than articulated by the theologians. The theologians, for reasons that we will see later, held that God actually controlled every detail of every event. No matter how much some of them tried to soften the impact of this doctrine by subtle distinctions and definitions, this was the common teaching of Augustine, Thomas Aquinas, Martin Luther, John Calvin, Gottfried Leibniz, Friedrich Schleiermacher, Jonathan Edwards, and Karl Barth. Popular theistic faith has generally not held this doctrine in such rigorous form, but has been content with the belief that, although most events are due to "natural causes" and "free will," God *can,* at any chosen time, totally determine what will happen. "Miracles" give evidence of this power on God's part. Recently some philosophers and theologians have stated a position that strikes something of a balance between this popular theism and the traditional philosophical-theological theism. They hold that, although God *could* have created a world which is completely controlled, God in fact has chosen to create some creatures with genuine freedom. These free creatures (usually restricted to human beings, at least among earthly creatures) have the bestowed ability to act contrary to God's will, so that God is not finally the real "doer" of "their" deeds (as was ultimately the case in traditional theistic systems). According to the theodicy based upon this third position, which in this book will be called the "hybrid free-will defense," some events happen that God would prefer not to have happen. In some versions of this theodicy, God does not even know in advance exactly what is going to happen, so that the events can surprise God.

Despite important differences among these three positions they all have one crucial point in common. They hold that God is "omnipotent" in the sense that nothing happens which God does not either cause or at least permit. "Permission" is used here in the sense of allowing something to happen when one has the power to prevent it. For, even in the hybrid free-will defense, it is maintained that the freedom is bestowed to the creatures, not inherent in them as creatures, so that this bestowed autonomy vis-à-vis God could be withdrawn without the creatures' losing their reality. Accordingly, God, knowing the intention of some creature to cause some great harm, could withdraw that creature's power to act autonomously and "cause it to act" in a manner different than had been intended. Or, alternatively, God could interfere in the chain of cause and effect resulting from the potentially harmful act, causing some consequence other than that which would normally have occurred.

In other words, these positions all accept the *traditional* doctrine of divine omnipotence, according to which everything that happens is either directly caused by God or at least permitted when it could have been prevented. The word "omnipotent" literally means "all-powerful," but, as we will see, this "literal" meaning is filled with ambiguity. There is no one right way to understand its meaning. In traditional theism the term has this meaning: "actually or potentially having all the power there is." This definition can be seen as strictly correlative with the meaning indicated above. For if God actually has all the power there is, then God by definition causes or does everything that happens, for there are no other beings with any iota of power to whom agency could meaningfully be attributed. Or if the only reason there are beings with power besides God is that God freely chose to create beings and to give power to at least some of them, then God potentially has a monopoly on power—perhaps God did once, and could again. Hence, to say that divine omnipotence means that God actually or potentially has a monopoly on power is identical with saying that everything that happens happens because God causes it or at least permits it while having the power to prevent it.

It is this traditional doctrine of divine omnipotence which provides one of the two key premises for the problem of evil. For it seems to imply that if God wanted to prevent all evil, God could. The other key premise is, of course, the doctrine that God is perfectly good. And the "goodness" that is relevant here is *moral* goodness, which can somewhat adequately be defined as the desire to promote good and prevent evil. Accordingly, if God is *perfectly* good morally, this seems to imply that God would want to prevent all evil. From these two premises it would seem that, if God exists, evil would not. But if a third premise is accepted, that evil does exist, it seems to follow that God as thus defined cannot exist. Hence, either God's omnipotence or moral perfection (or both, or the belief in any God at all) must apparently be given up, if one wishes to retain fidelity to the logical principles of rationality. Of course, this "if" suggests another solution: one *can* say, "Then so much the worse for logic."

The problem of evil is generally formalized as a syllogism using only the above three premises, as follows:

A. If God is omnipotent, God could prevent all evil.

B. If God is perfectly good, God would want to prevent all evil.
C. There is evil.
D. Therefore [an omnipotent, perfectly good] God does not exist.

This will be called the "simple statement" of the problem of evil. It has proved useful for generating much debate. But for analyzing the positions of those who have written on the problem, I have found, for reasons that will become clearer as we proceed, that an expanded version of the statement is more helpful. This eight-step version, which is the statement of the theoretical problem of evil that will be referred to throughout the book, is as follows:

1. God is a perfect reality. (Definition)
2. A perfect reality is an omnipotent being. (By definition)
3. An omnipotent being could unilaterally bring about an actual world without any genuine evil. (By definition)
4. A perfect reality is a morally perfect being. (By definition)
5. A morally perfect being would want to bring about an actual world without any genuine evil. (By definition)
6. If there is genuine evil in the world, then there is no God. (Logical conclusion from 1 through 5)
7. There is genuine evil in the world. (Factual statement)
8. Therefore, there is no God. (Logical conclusion from 6 and 7)

I believe this argument is valid, which means that the final conclusion follows from the premises. That is, 6 follows from 1 through 5, while 8 follows from 6 and 7. The question then is whether the argument is *sound,* which requires that, besides being valid, all its premises must be acceptable. (Normally one speaks of premises as being true or false, rather than acceptable or unacceptable. But many of the premises are definitions, rather than reputed statements of fact, and it is problematic to talk of definitions as being either "true" or "false.") To reject the soundness of the conclusion, all one need do is reject at least one of the premises. The question then is, Which one of the premises, if any, can the theist consider unacceptable? Which one can he reject and still be a theist, a believer in a reality justifiably termed "God"?

I will now discuss the above premises briefly, specifying their meanings more precisely, considering the possibility of their rejection by the theist, and suggesting some of the virtues of this expanded form of the argument for indicating the various issues involved. Could a theist reject premise 1? It is difficult, but it has been done. I take "perfection" formally to involve this meaning: "Nothing less than the greatest (consistently, i.e., genuinely) conceivable." This means that a "perfect reality" would not necessarily be limited to that which we are capable of conceiving, but that we cannot consider something as perfect if we can conceive of something else that would be greater. (The qualification "consistently, i.e., genuinely" is placed parenthetically in front of "conceivable" to stress that one is talking about genuine concepts, not mere verbal statements that perhaps *sound* as if they are referring to some truly superior possible reality but are in fact referring to nothing, since it is impossible to understand how the various notions suggested by the statement can be related.) Accordingly, for a theist to deny that the word "God" denotes a perfect reality would be to imply that the God which in fact exists is not as great as another reality which could exist but happens not to exist. And this would seem to ignore the central context from which the word "God" derives its meaning, i.e., the context of worship. Included in the formal essence of the meaning of the word "God" is the idea of "a reality worthy of worship." And can one really worship, or give unconditional devotion to, a reality that is less than perfect? This is the central basis for saying that premise 1 is a definition.

Accordingly, I think it would be impossible for the theist to solve the problem of evil by saying that God has "less" of some estimable attribute than "a God" conceivably might have. Hence, if both power and moral goodness are estimable attributes, it is impossible for the theist to solve the problem of evil by denying that God is less powerful or less moral than "a deity" might have been. For this would be in effect to deny that there is a being worthy of worship, and hence a God.

Premises 2 through 5 are said to be "by definition." This slight distinction from premise 1, which was strictly a definition, indicates that the subjects and predicates are not interchangeable. For example, the characteristic of being an omnipotent being is only one of the characteristics of a perfect reality, and is not an adequate definition thereof.

This is perhaps a good point at which to emphasize the extent to which the problem of evil is constituted by definitions. Those who say that the problem of evil is not primarily a logical problem are right in the sense that the crux of the problem is constituted by a set of definitions that are not matters of logic or illogic at all, but are essentially matters of *valuation,* and these are matters that are at least in part historically contingent, being influenced by the particular historical tradition(s) in which one stands. The purely formal idea that "deity" and "perfection" are identical is transcultural. But when one begins to spell out the content of what is involved in perfection, the cultural conditioning becomes paramount. The idea that a perfect reality, to be perfect, must exert power upon the world of space and time is an idea not shared by all the religio-philosophico-theological traditions of humanity. And the idea that the perfect reality must be morally good is probably about equally provincial. This is the reason why the problem of evil is primarily a problem for Western thought, as it has been decisively influenced by the Biblical vision of reality in which God is understood to be both morally good and providentially active in history.

This reflection upon the historical conditionedness of many of the elements constituting the problem of evil is not included for the purpose of suggesting that the theist can solve the problem by simply giving up on either God's moral goodness or his power to act in our world. For (I maintain) these ideas are essential to the meaning of the term "God" in our tradition. Or, to put the issue more personally: As one who has been centrally conditioned by this tradition of thought about deity, I believe, even after recognizing the contingency of this conditioning, that moral goodness and power in the world are two characteristics that cannot be given up without giving up God's perfection, and hence giving up God.

But I do mean this reflection upon the historical conditioning of our valuations to suggest that the precise *form* given to the traditional statements of these characteristics may be questionable and hence revisable. That is, even we who have been conditioned by the tradition of theological reflection that created these traditional formulations may decide that our idea of perfection does not entail precisely the same conclusions about divine power and/or goodness.

I now return to the discussion of the premises. One difference between the simple statement of the problem and the expanded statement is that in the latter the word "genuine" is inserted before the word "evil." This is done to prevent the oscillation between various meanings of the word "evil" that occurs in many discussions. That is, many defenders of theism claim to deny premise B of the simple statement. That is, they deny that a morally perfect being would want to prevent all evil. However, whereas the critics of theism are referring to "genuine evil," these defenders are referring to "only apparent evil." This ambiguity camouflages the fact that the defenders are really denying premise C of the simple statement, i.e., the assertion that there is evil, here taking evil to mean genuine evil.

In order to make this point clear, I need to define the notions of "genuine evil" and "only apparent evil," as well as a third possible meaning for the term "evil" which this distinction presupposes, i.e., "*prima facie* evil." By "genuine evil," I mean anything, all things considered, without which the universe would have been better. Put otherwise, some event is genuinely evil if its occurrence prevents the occurrence of some other event which would have made the universe better, all things considered, i.e., from an all-inclusive, impartial perspective. "*Prima facie* evil" is anything that may be judged evil at first glance, superficially, i.e., when considered from a partial perspective, and/or within a limited context. Some *prima facie* evils may be considered, upon reflection, to be genuine evils. But other *prima facie* evils may be judged to be "only apparent evils." That is, when considered in a larger context than originally, they may be judged not to be genuinely evil, since their badness may be regarded as compensated for by the goodness to which they contributed.

This notion of "compensation" presupposes a distinction between "intrinsic" and "instrumental" value. Something is "intrinsically" good if it is good in itself, i.e., apart from any consideration of its usefulness to something else (e.g., to some other being, or to a later moment in the life of the being in question). Something is intrinsically evil if it is bad or evil in itself, apart from considerations of utility to some other being, or to a later moment in the life of the being in question. Something is "instrumentally" good if it is useful for something else, i.e., if it contributes to the intrinsic good of something else. And something is instrumentally evil insofar as it is destructive of the potential intrinsic good of something else.

The instrumental goodness or badness of something is obviously a relative matter. Whereas some event may be perceived as instrumentally good from Jones's point of view, it may be regarded as instrumentally evil by Smith. The tennis player may curse the rain, while the farmer gives thanks. This relativity is reflected in proverbs, such as: "One man's blessing is another man's bane."

It is this relativity of instrumental value that requires that *prima facie* evils be divided into those which are considered genuinely evil and those which are only apparently evil. This applies both to intrinsic and instrumental *prima facie* evils. Some events that are *prima facie* considered intrinsically evil, such as sin or suffering, may be regarded as really being good "in the long run." For example, it may be judged that the suffering a young woman experienced helped make her much more sympathetic to others than she would have been otherwise, so that it was really good, all things considered, that she underwent the suffering. Or the sins committed by a man may be thought to have led to a compensating good, e.g., by deepening his own understanding of the nature of humanity, or by providing others with an opportunity to exercise patience and offer forgiveness, or by providing a chance for retributive justice to be manifested. Or it may be that, while the man intended to do something evil to someone else (and it is this evil intention that makes the deed a sin), the actual result of his deed was instrumentally good for the other person.

Also, events that are judged instrumentally evil in a limited context may be judged instrumentally good in a larger context. While a heavy rain may prevent many people from taking a vacation that would have been enjoyable, the rain may save food crops in the region that are necessary for the continued health of all the people; and the fact that millions of people stayed home may mean that the depletion of the earth's resources and the pollution of its air was less than it would have been otherwise. A minor catastrophe may provide a stimulus for other people to take precautions, so that major catastrophes are avoided in the future. Hence, when the larger context is considered, the small catastrophe may be regarded as having been a "blessing in disguise."

Because of the distinction between intrinsic and instrumental value, and because of the relativity of the latter, it is possible in principle for one to claim that every instance of *prima facie* evil is to be understood as only apparently evil. Hence, there would be no instances of genuine evil. And this is the claim that is really being made when defenders of theism appear to be denying premise B of the simple statement, or premise 4 or 5 of the expanded statement. In other words, the controversy is not really about the meaning of a "morally perfect being"—everyone agrees that such a being would want to prevent all genuine evil. Hence, the insertion of the word "genuine" into the statement of the problem helps prevent confusion as to the point of controversy.

I believe that once this ambiguity in the meaning of evil is cleared up, it is not possible for the theologian to solve the problem by rejecting either of the premises dealing with God's moral perfection, i.e., premises 4 and 5—that is, not if the theologian wants the "solution" to be relevant to the Christian (or Jewish) community of worship. Nor do I believe one should reject the logical canons of rationality, which is what would be entailed by rejecting statement number 6. Nor do I find it plausible, or consistent with Christian (or Jewish) faith, to deny the reality of genuine evil (premise 7), even though this is what most of the traditional theologians of these faith communities have done, as Part II will show. This means that the only possibilities left for me to consider unacceptable are premises 2 and 3. Part III of this book will be devoted largely to the argument for rejecting either one or the other of them. (The issue as to which one to reject depends upon the arbitrary decision whether to redefine "omnipotence" or to use it only in its traditional sense.)

Comment should be made at this point about another novel element in this expanded statement of the problem of evil, the phrase in premises 3 and 5, "bring about an actual world." This language is included to help prevent two possible ambiguities. In the first place, it points to a distinction between an actual world and another kind of world with which it might be contrasted, such as a merely ideal or imaginary world. By so doing, it forces reflection upon the issue as to what might be the crucial difference between the two. By anticipation I will say that I have found the failure to reflect upon the metaphysical question of the nature of actuality qua actuality to be the single most serious failure in discussions of the problem of evil, and the failure which has been most central in the failure to arrive at a satisfactory resolution.

In the second place, the phrase "bring about an actual world without any genuine evil" makes this statement of the issue much clearer than do premises A and B of the simple statement of the problem, which speak simply of "preventing all evil." For there are many theists who hold that God could have avoided the existence of an actual world altogether. Accordingly, God could have prevented all evil simply by not creating a world. And, in the light of this and the totally negative criterion of goodness given in premise B, one could well conclude that God simply would avoid creating a world. For if the essence of moral goodness is the prevention of evil, the easiest way to prevent evil is not to allow a situation in which it could occur. But these kinds of reflections distract one from the real complaint of most of the critics of theism, which is: Granted that the creation of a good world would be a good thing, why did God apparently create such a bad one? Accordingly, premise 3 specifies the relevant question about omnipotence by raising to explicitness the question as to whether an omnipotent being could prevent all genuine evil in bringing about an actual world. And premise 5 places the negative criterion of moral perfection, i.e., the desire to prevent evil, within the context of the positive act of creating an actual world. (Furthermore, once "genuine evil" is defined, it will be seen that the criterion of the desire to prevent genuine evil is negative in form only, and that in content it has a wholly positive meaning.)

One final novel element in the expanded statement should be pointed out at this time, the insertion of the word "unilaterally" in premise 3. This insertion clarifies what has always been intended, e.g., in premise A of the simple statement of the problem. For the argument would not be valid if "could" were taken as meaning that deity could prevent all evil in an actual world *if it were lucky*. For in this case the fact of evil in this world would not disprove God's omnipotence (assuming God's moral perfection), but might only mean that God had been unlucky. The argument is only valid if the assertion is taken as meaning that deity could unilaterally prevent all genuine evil, if it so wished. Hence, in one sense the insertion of the word "unilaterally" only renders explicit what has always been implicit. However, inserting "unilaterally" also helps focus attention on presuppositions about divine and worldly power that are contained in the argument. This will be the central topic of Chapter 17.

In Part II, this eight-step argument will be used to clarify the attempted solutions given to the problem of evil by traditional theists, and the reasons why these solutions are inadequate. In Part III, a solution will be offered which I believe to be more adequate. But first, in Part I, I will discuss some dimensions of the Greek and Biblical traditions that provided much of the historical conditioning for the valuations that account for so much of what we have come to call the problem of evil.

However, before we launch into this historical study, something further should be said about the perspective from which this book is written. It was stated in the Preface that it is written from the perspective of the process philosophical and theological thought inspired primarily by Whitehead and Hartshorne. But one might ask whether I am writing as a theologian or a philosopher; i.e., am I writing on the basis of certain faith commitments, or am I intending not to let any ideas and evaluations derived from a particular community of faith influence my approach and conclusions?

In an earlier book I indicated my rejection of this either-or attitude toward theology and metaphysical philosophy.[1] On the one hand, every metaphysical philosophy presupposes some prerational vision of reality. Insofar as one argues from rather than to this way of seeing things, it functions as a faith perspective. On the other hand, it is possible (and desirable, I hold) to understand the faith perspective with which the theologian begins as not differing formally from that of the philosopher. Also, it is possible (and desirable, I hold) to understand this faith perspective not as something to which theologians are "committed," so that they intend to hold to it regardless of any and all evidence that may be marshaled against it, but as something of which they are "convinced." In the latter case, they hold it because they find that it leads to the most consistent, adequate, and illuminating account of reality available at the time. Accordingly, the nature of the theologian's faith perspective, the way it is held, and the reason for holding it, are not such as to make the approach of the "theologian" different in kind from that of the "philosopher." In fact, the force of this way of understanding the approach of the two professions is to make the distinction between them one of self-understanding and degree rather than one of kind. That is, they differ in that those called "theologians" understand themselves to be explicating and defending a vision of reality that they have received from a particular community of faith, while those termed "philosophers" do not normally see themselves in these terms. (This formal difference in self-understanding can lead to radically different concentrations, because theologians tend to devote much attention to those events which are seen as decisive for the existence of the community to which they belong.) And philosophers and theologians differ in degree in that the latter tend to focus primarily upon matters of "ultimate concern," i.e., issues directly related to questions about deity and the origin, meaning, and destiny of life, especially human life, while the former tend to spread their attention over a much wider span of concerns. However, this is only a generalization dealing with a question of degree. Also, there is much overlap between the subject matters treated by "philosophers" and "theologians."

This area of overlap has traditionally been labeled "natural theology." It was seen as "theology" because it obviously dealt with the questions of ultimate concern that constituted the subject matter of the theologian. But it was seen as part of "philosophy," because it was supposedly approached from the viewpoint of "natural" reason, i.e., reason uninfluenced by the perspective of a community of faith, the latter allegedly being derived from "revelation." However, if all constructive philosophies in fact (even if the philosophers themselves do not explicitly recognize this fact) presuppose some such faith perspective, the distinction between theology based upon natural reason and theology based upon faith in a "revelation" breaks down. Accordingly, rather than there being one or more natural theologies and then several theologies based upon faith, there are in reality only a number of theologies based upon various visions of reality, or faith perspectives. Rather than speaking simply of "philosophy," therefore, one needs to put some prefix before the word "philosophy" in order to distinguish it from other philosophies that approach the same issues from different visions of reality. Likewise, if the term "natural theology" is to be retained to indicate that aspect of philosophy which deals directly with matters of ultimate concern, a similar prefix needs to be used.

In these terms, the present treatment of the problem of evil is intended to be an example of "Christian philosophy" or "Christian natural theology." It is intended to be "philosophy" or "*natural* theology" in that I mean the constructive position to be advocated because of its ability to satisfy, better than competing views, the normal criteria of philosophic excellence, i.e., self-consistency, adequacy to the facts of experience, and illuminating power. This treatment of the problem of evil is intended to be "Christian" in that I see my basic convictions regarding the central elements of the problem (e.g., deity, world, freedom) as decisively influenced by the Christian community of faith. For example, I indicated above that I could not regard as adequate any solution to the problem of evil that involved the rejection of God's perfect exertion of power in our world, or God's moral perfection. Accordingly, there will be an appeal to the Christian "revelation" in this sense: I intend the advocated position to be in harmony with the formal claim of Christian faith that the nature of deity is best revealed in Jesus of Nazareth. In short, there is no appeal to revelation to support the *truth* of the position advocated—this would be contrary to the nature of philosophical argumentation. The discussion of revelation is rather for the purpose of arguing the compatibility of the position advocated here with the basic formal claim of Christian faith concerning the place from which one can best derive concepts about the nature of deity. This argument is necessary to show that the proffered position is not only possibly true but also relevant to the piety of that community of faith whose ideas about deity were primarily responsible for the formulation of the theoretical problem of evil in Western thought in the first place.

## NOTES ON TYPES, DEFINITIONS, AND EXAMPLES OF EVIL

One other distinction which is relevant to the problem of evil, but which did not belong in the above discussion, is the distinction between "natural" and "moral" evil. The use of these terms is widespread, although the distinction between them is made differently by different writers. Some (e.g., John Hick) base the distinction upon the type of agent involved. Hence, "moral evil" refers to all evil that is due to the misuse of rational freedom; hence it refers not only to *evil intentions* but also to any *bad effects* of these intentions. Hence, all suffering that is due to human agency would be classified under moral evil. "Natural evil" is used to refer to all evil that is due to nonmoral agents. Authors who use the distinction in this way are usually dualists who posit an absolute difference between those creatures who do and those who do not have some measure of self-determining freedom. Other authors use the terms to distinguish between evil that is *intended* and evil that is *undergone.* Accordingly, "moral evil" is used only for the evil intention itself, not also for its bad consequences; often the term "sin" is used synonymously. "Natural evil" is used to refer to all forms of suffering, regardless of the kind of agent that caused the suffering. Writers who make the distinction along these lines often speak of "physical" rather than "natural" evil. Insofar as I use these terms, I will use them in the latter way, unless I specify otherwise, as in the discussions of Augustine and Hick.

I should add at this point that I do not deal with the material definitions of evil offered by various philosophers and theologians. For example, I do not make integral to the discussion of Augustine's theodicy the fact that he defines evil as a "privation of being." This would be an important consideration in regard to some issues. But the key question in regard to the logical statement of the problem of evil is whether the theologian, regardless of how he defines evil, believes there is any *genuine* evil in the universe. For example, if the theologian says that evil is a privation of being, and believes that some instances of such privation have occurred, the key question is whether he thinks that the universe would have been better off in the long run if these instances had not occurred. If he does not think so, then he has denied that there is any genuine evil, and the problem of evil does not exist for him. But if he does think there is genuine evil in this sense, then the issue as to whether evil is defined as something positive or as a mere privation is irrelevant to the formal question as to why God allowed something without which we would have all (God knows) been better off. (However, in Chapter 7 I do briefly examine Jacques Maritain's contention that this privative definition of evil *is* relevant to the formal problem of evil.)

Furthermore, I do not give any account of the kinds of things I would consider genuine evil. There is no necessity that the reader and I agree on which things are genuine evils. All that is necessary is that we both, given our own value judgments, believe that at least one thing has happened without which the world would have been better. That genuine evil in this sense has occurred is, of course, incapable of proof. But I also take it to be unnecessary to prove. It is one of those basic presumptions in terms of which we all live our lives, in spite of what we might verbally affirm.

# PART I

## *Biblical and Greek Sources*

---

## 1
## The Biblical Tradition

THE BIBLE has been, both in theory and in fact, the dominant influence upon ideas about God and evil in the Western world. However, its witness is quite ambiguous. It can be cited by defenders of absolute divine determinism as well as advocates of creaturely freedom vis-à-vis God. The passages that are relevant to the topic are legion.[1] I will refer only to a few; most of them will be ones which have figured prominently in the later debates.

If one were to count the passages that explicitly deal with the question of whether God is omnipotent and in fact determines all things, those giving an affirmative answer would surely be in the majority. Gen. 18:14 asks rhetorically, "Is anything too hard for the LORD?"[2] Job 42:2 states: "I know that thou canst do all things, and that no purpose of thine can be thwarted." These affirmations are repeated in the New Testament: "For with God nothing will be impossible" (Luke 1:37). "With God all things are possible" (Matt. 19:26).

Besides God's having the *power* to do all things, it is often implied or stated that God in fact *does* all things that are done. James 1:17 says: "Every good endowment and every perfect gift is from above." In a statement that has been cited countless times against "synergists" who believe that we, through the exercise of our freedom, contribute something to our salvation, Paul says: "What have you that you did not receive? If then you received it, why do you boast as if it were not a gift?" (I Cor. 4:7.)

If God does all things, the implication would be that God causes those things which are evil (at least in our estimation) as well as those things which are good. And many passages affirm this. I Sam. 16:14–23 says that God sent an evil spirit to torment Saul. Amos 3:6 asks rhetorically: "Does evil befall a city, unless the LORD has done it?" Lam. 3:38 reads: "Is it not from the mouth of the Most High that good and evil come?" Job asks: "Shall we receive good at the hand of God, and shall we not receive evil?" (Job 2:10.) Isa. 45:7 has God say: "I form light and create darkness, I make weal and create woe, I am the LORD, who do all these things." One corollary of this doctrine would be that earthly rulers are appointed by God. And this is stated: "By me kings reign, and rulers decree what is just; by me princes rule, and nobles govern the earth" (Prov. 8:15–16; cf. Dan. 2:21; Hos. 13:11). The political implication of this notion is stated explicitly by Paul in a fateful passage: "Let every person be subject to the governing authorities. For there is no authority except from God, and those that exist have been instituted by God. Therefore he who resists the authorities resists what God has appointed, and those who resist will incur judgment." (Rom. 13:1–2.)

The passages stating that God causes evil could be interpreted as meaning that God inflicts suffering as a punishment for sin. However, there is a strand in the Bible which indicates that human disobedience to God is due to the fact that God blinds people, and hardens their hearts. For example, Josh. 11:20 says of the enemies of Israel: "For it was the LORD's doing to harden their hearts that they should come against Israel in battle, in order that they should be utterly destroyed, and should receive no mercy but be exterminated, as the LORD commanded Moses." Isaiah reports hearing the voice of the Lord saying: "Go, and say to this people: 'Hear and hear, but do not understand; see and see, but do not perceive.' Make the heart of this people fat, and their ears heavy, and shut their eyes; lest they see with their eyes, and hear with their ears, and understand with their hearts, and turn and be healed." (Isa. 6:9–10.) This passage is quoted with approval in the New Testament (Acts 28:26–27). And Jesus is quoted as making reference to it to explain why he speaks in parables: "To you has been given the secret of the kingdom of God, but for those outside everything is in parables; so that they may indeed see but not perceive, and may indeed hear but not understand; lest they should turn again, and be forgiven" (Mark 4:11–12). Perhaps the strongest statement of this theme is found in Paul's letter to the Romans. In Rom. 9:15 Paul cites the statement attributed to God in Exodus: "I will be gracious to whom I will be gracious, and will show mercy on whom I will show mercy"

(Ex. 33:19). Paul then includes the element of hardening within the scope of this divine arbitrariness: "So then he has mercy upon whomever he wills, and he hardens the heart of whomever he wills" (Rom. 9:18). Furthermore, Paul draws out the implications for human cooperation: "So it depends not upon man's will or exertion, but upon God's mercy" (Rom. 9:16).

Furthermore, there are many passages suggesting that both good and evil deeds are done because they were predestined by God. Acts 2:23 indicates that Jesus was delivered up for crucifixion "according to the definite plan and foreknowledge of God." Acts 4:25–28 indicates that the actions of Herod, Pilate, and the others responsible for the crucifixion were in accord with what God's plan had predestined to take place. In Rom. 8:29–30, Paul states: "For those whom he foreknew he also predestined to be conformed to the image of his Son, in order that he might be the first-born among many brethren. And those whom he predestined he also called; and those whom he called he also justified; and those whom he justified he also glorified." Paul compares the "vessels of wrath made for destruction" with the "vessels of mercy, which he has prepared beforehand for glory" (Rom. 9:22–23).

How could God be regarded as just, on this basis? One major doctrine was that the good would prosper, while the wicked would suffer. Deut. 30:15–20 has Moses state that if the Israelites walked in the ways of the Lord, they would live longer in the land, multiply, and be blessed, but if they disobeyed God they would be cursed and perish. It is a strong theme in the Old Testament that God blesses the righteous, punishes the wicked, and that, accordingly, suffering is punishment for evil (e.g., Ps. 5:5–6, 12; 9:5; Lam. 1:8). This doctrine could be maintained as long as there was a strong corporate sense, so that evils suffered by relatively righteous people could be understood as punishment for the sins of their fathers (e.g., Lam. 5:7). However, as individualism grew, it seemed that a just God would reward and punish each individual according to his or her own deserts. Ezekiel says: "The word of the LORD came to me again: 'What do you mean by repeating this proverb concerning the land of Israel, "The fathers have eaten sour grapes, and the children's teeth are set on edge"? As I live, says the Lord GOD, this proverb shall no more be used by you in Israel. Behold, all souls are mine; the soul of the father as well as the soul of the son is mine: the soul that sins shall die.' " (Ezek. 18:1–4; cf. Jer. 31:29–30.) In this more individualistic context, the observed fact that the wicked often prosper (Jer. 12:1; Job 21:7) became a source of greater tension. The Book of Job constitutes a dramatic repudiation of the Deuteronomic view that earthly prosperity is proportionate to righteousness. In Ecclesiastes, it is recognized that "there are righteous men to whom it happens according to the deeds of the wicked, and there are wicked men to whom it happens according to the deeds of the righteous" (Eccl. 8:14). Furthermore, "one fate comes to all, to the righteous and the wicked, to the good and the evil" (Eccl. 9:2). In the New Testament the repudiation of a correlation between righteousness and earthly prosperity is continued. Jesus says that God "makes his sun rise on the evil and on the good, and sends rain on the just and on the unjust" (Matt. 5:45). And, after being told of an event involving some Galileans, Jesus replies: "Do you think that these Galileans were worse sinners than all other Galileans, because they suffered thus? I tell you, No." (Luke 13:1–3.)

The earlier expectation of a correlation between righteousness and prosperity on the one hand, and sin and suffering on the other, led to questioning about the existence of God, or at least about divine providential concern. Psalm 10, in discussing the oppression of the poor by the wicked, says that the wicked man thinks, "There is no God," while the oppressed man thinks, "God has forgotten, he has hidden his face, he will never see it." The preacher in Ecclesiastes, after having tried to understand God's work, concludes that "man cannot find out the work that is done under the sun" (Eccl. 8:17).

This questioning was based on the idea that God should reward the just and punish the wicked. The earlier doctrine that God rewarded and punished nations and/or individuals in this life could not be maintained in the face of experience. But the growth of the belief in a meaningful future life allowed the basic notion of divine justice to be maintained. The rewards and punishments would take place after death. This irrefutable doctrine allowed one to reconcile belief in God's power and justice, on the one hand, with the experienced fact that the good often suffer while the wicked often prosper.

However, another dimension to the solution was needed, in view of the doctrine that those who did good and evil were predestined to do so by deity itself. Why is it just to reward some persons for doing good, if they were caused to do good by God, and to punish others for doing evil, if they were caused to do evil by God? There is a strand in the Bible which suggests that this question should not be raised. In Isa. 45:9–11, we find these words attributed to God: "Woe to him who strives with his Maker, an earthen vessel with the potter! Does the clay say to him who fashions it, 'What are you making'? or 'Your work has no handles'? . . . Will you question me about my children, or command me concerning the work of my hands?" Likewise, God answers Job out of the whirlwind with these words: "Who is this that darkens counsel by words without knowledge. . . . Where were you when I laid the foundation of the earth? Tell me, if you have understanding." (Job 38:2, 4.) And, after raising many more questions, God concludes: "Shall a faultfinder contend with the Almighty? He who argues with God, let him answer it." (Job 40:2.) One of God's key points is stated in these words: "Who has given to me, that I should repay him?" (Job 41:11.) This theme is picked up by Paul in Romans. His statement that God "hardens the heart of whomever he wills" evokes the question as to why God should judge anyone, if no one can resist God's will (Rom. 9:19). Paul replies: "Who are you, a man, to answer back to God? Will what is molded say to its molder, 'Why have you made me thus?' Has the potter no right over the clay, to make out of the same lump one vessel for beauty and another for menial use?" (Rom. 9:20–21.) Paul includes in this discussion an exclamation that would be repeated many times by defenders of divine predestination: "O the depth of the riches and wisdom and knowledge of God! How unsearchable are his judgments and how inscrutable his ways!" (Rom. 11:33.) Paul concludes (Rom. 11:34–35) by referring to passages in Isaiah and Job which state that no one knows the mind of God, and that God owes nothing to anyone. (It should be remarked here that Paul does not believe that God's plans are totally inscrutable, and that the severity of Paul's doctrine is mitigated by his belief that God hardened some of the Jews for the purpose of saving all [Rom. 11:26, 32]. But these ideas could be used by later theologians to support the idea of God's predestination of some persons to eternal punishment.)

The notion that God determines all things in advance would fit together well with the doctrine that deity does not change. Only if things happened in the world which God did not expect would there be any reason for a change in the content of divine knowledge, a change in God's emotions and/or plans. There are a few passages that have been used as Biblical support for the doctrine (of traditional theism) that God is unchangeable in all respects. In Mal. 3:6 we read: "For I the LORD do not change." James 1:17 states that in God "there is no variation or shadow due to change." And God's statement in Ex. 3:14, "I AM WHO I AM," has been interpreted as meaning that God is unchanging Being.

Thus far I have discussed the Biblical material that has been used to support traditional theism. However, there is also material in the

Bible which stands in tension with this position. I will begin with the question of unchangeability. This doctrine's support in the Bible is very weak. Most present interpreters agree that the Exodus passage does not support the doctrine. The passage in Malachi is immediately followed with these words by God: "Return to me, and I will return to you" (Mal. 3:7). This exhortation implies, first, that God does not determine all things and, second, that a change in the world will be followed by a change in God. The context of the statement that God does not change shows the meaning to be that God does not break covenants (cf. Mal. 2:4). God is also quoted in Malachi as saying, "I have no pleasure in you." The reason given is not that God has no emotional reactions to the world, but that the Israelites are offering polluted food on the altar. The notion that God and the world interact is implied by the promise that, if they are faithful with their tithes and offerings, God will pour out blessings upon them (Mal. 3:10). The statement in James is made in the context of the idea that God will give gifts to those who ask (James 1:5; cf. 4:2–3; 5:16). Also, in this same book it is said that God does not tempt us (James 1:13); since we are tempted, this implies that God does not do all things. Also, it is said that God will give the crown of life to those who endure trial, which again suggests that real interaction occurs between God and the creatures. Further, in James 4:8 the idea from Malachi is repeated: "Draw near to God and he will draw near to you." However, the ambivalence of the Biblical witness is shown by the fact that the book of James also contains one of the main passages which contributed to the idea that God controls all things: "We should say, 'If the Lord wills, we shall live and we shall do this or that' " (James 4:15).

There is obviously much more support for God's predestinating omnipotence than there is for divine immutability. However, the evidence is also ambivalent here. For example, in the same chapter in Isaiah which employs the analogy of the potter and the clay, God is quoted as saying: "Turn to me and be saved, all the ends of the earth!" (Isa. 45:22.) This seems to imply that the pots, once created, have some freedom. Likewise Paul, in the same book in which he uses the potter-clay analogy, says that those who do not obey God are "without excuse" (Rom. 1:20). Further, he exhorts Christians: "Do not become proud, but stand in awe" (Rom. 11:20). He says that they will be cut off from the tree of salvation if they do not remain steadfast, and that others will be grafted on if they do not persist in their unbelief (Rom. 11:22–23). These exhortations seem to presuppose some human freedom in relation to God.

The correlative ideas that God determines all things, knows all things in advance, never changes plans, and never has changes in emotion, stand in considerable tension with much of the Biblical witness. One passage that has always been particularly difficult for traditional theists is Gen. 6:5–7: "The LORD saw that the wickedness of man was great in the earth, and that every imagination of the thoughts of his heart was only evil continually. And the LORD was sorry that he had made man on the earth, and it grieved him to his heart. So the LORD said, 'I will blot out man whom I have created.' "

Countless other passages could be cited which support the idea that God genuinely interacts with the world and has emotional reactions, and that persons are free in relation to God and hence responsible for their actions. The existence of these passages is not disputed by traditional theists. They only insist that those which suggest change in God must be regarded as metaphorical, and that in some mysterious way human freedom is compatible with God's determination of all events. Hence, there are two strands within the Biblical tradition: one which supports traditional theism and one which *prima facie* stands in tension with it. There is no dispute about this point. The issue is: What should the theologian who wishes to restate the "essential message" of the Biblical tradition do in the face of these two strands? Should one simply restate both of them, with no attempt to reconcile the contradiction? This is the answer of some theologians, represented in this book by Brunner and Fackenheim. If not, which of the strands should be subordinated to the other? Most of the theologians in Part II subordinate the assertions of creaturely freedom to those affirming God's all-controlling power. In Part III a theodicy will be presented which understands divine power within the context of an unequivocal assertion of creaturely freedom.

# 2
# Plato

WHEREAS the Biblical record is quite inconsistent in regard to the issue of whether God determines all things, there is no such ambiguity in Plato. In his project to demythologize theology, Plato makes clear that the chief purpose of this project is to represent deity as it truly is, which means stating that God is the cause not of evil, but only of good. This means unambiguously stating that God is not the cause of all things. Plato's summary statement is:

> Then God, if he be good, is not the author of all things, as the many assert, but he is the cause of a few things only, and not of most things that occur to men. For few are the goods of human life, and many are the evils, and the good is to be attributed to God alone; of the evils the causes are to be sought elsewhere, and not in him. (*Republic* II. 379)[1]

Elsewhere Plato develops a less anthropocentric theodicy, no longer so simply equating genuine evil with misfortunes suffered by individual human beings but rather thinking in terms of the good of the whole (*Laws* X). But he never relinquishes the position that, while on the one hand there is real evil in this world (even though this is the "fairest of creations" [*Timaeus* 29]), on the other hand God is not the cause of this evil.

Plato can consistently maintain this, since there are other beings in reality with genuine power besides God. For one thing, there are the souls. They are created by God, but once created, they have the power to initiate activity. They are self-moving movers. And they are a source of evil (*Laws* X). Both in the *Timaeus* (39e–42) and the myth of Er (*Republic* X. 614–621) Plato stresses that we are responsible for our own lives. Although a general plan is provided before our life begins, our qualities or characters are determined by our individual choices (*Laws* X. 904; *Republic* X. 618). And he stresses the theodical implication—"God is justified" (*Republic* X. 617; cf. *Timaeus* 42).

There is an even prior source of the fact that, although God wanted to create a world that would be as good "as possible" (*Timaeus* 46), it is not perfect. This is the fact that God's creation of the world did not involve an eliciting of an actual world out of nothing, but a bringing of an ordered cosmos out of a "chaos," a sphere which was "moving in an irregular and disorderly fashion" (*Timaeus* 30). This chaotic sphere exerts one of the types of causation in the world, that type referred to by Plato as "necessity," or the "errant cause" (*Timaeus* 46–48, 68–69). Hence, even apart from the creation of souls, God's power in the universe is not absolute. God is not the sole power in reality. The creation of the world involves a victory of persuasion over necessity (*Timaeus* 47–48), and as such is not a total determination of all the details of the world. Describing the way in which the creation of the world was accomplished requires reference also to the "errant cause" (*Timaeus* 48).

The early Christian theologians adopted much from Plato. Had they also adopted the idea that God's creative activity involved bringing order persuasively out of a chaotic realm which had its own "movement" and hence could not be completely coerced, and had they generalized this idea so as to conceive of God's *modus operandi* in general as persuasion of partially self-determining entities rather than as unilateral determination, the history of Christian thought and of Western thought and sensibility in general would have been greatly different, especially in regard to the problem of evil. And this particular borrowing from Plato would have been compatible with the creation story in Gen., ch. 1, which can be understood (and is understood by most modern scholars) as reflecting the idea of creation out of chaos. Furthermore, this understanding of creation and the general idea of divine activity that could have been drawn therefrom would have provided a context for holding consistently to that strand in the Biblical tradition which presupposes that the creatures, at least the human ones, are free vis-à-vis God. Of course, one could reply, this idea could have been explicated philosophically without the Platonic notion of creation but simply in terms of Plato's idea that souls, once created by God, are self-moving. However, that idea by itself can be understood as meaning that the question as to whether to have an actual world with self-moving creatures or one without them is a free choice on God's part. And this entails theodical problems not burdening a theory which holds that self-movement is in actuality as such. (This issue will be discussed in Chapters 13 and 17.)

The early Christian theologians did mean to agree with the Platonic idea that created souls are self-determining, or "possessed of free will," and to account for much or all of the world's evil on this basis. However, the "orthodox" ones were not able to hold this view consistently, because of other, contradictory commitments. And one of these came in part from another facet of Plato's thought. This is the idea that God cannot change. Plato argues in the *Republic* (II. 380–381) that deity, being perfect, cannot be changed either by other things or by itself. Plato goes from the particular and valid notion that "the bravest and wisest soul" will be "least confused or deranged by any external influence" to the general and questionable principle that the better anything is, the less it is "liable to suffer change from without." And since deity is perfect, it cannot be susceptible to change from without at all; therefore if it is to change, the change will have to be a self-transformation. But this is also ruled out. For the change would have to be for the better or the worse. But deity would not be willing to change itself for the worse. And the change cannot be for the better, since God is already the "best that is conceivable," not being "deficient either in virtue or beauty." Hence God must remain "absolutely and for ever in his own form."

It is not entirely clear that Plato means to be saying that God must be beyond change in *all respects.* Perhaps he is talking only about the general form, structure, or character of God, which would be compatible with change in the *content* of the divine experience. For example, God could remain equally virtuous, while continually exemplifying this constant virtue in different ways. But, regardless of what Plato actually meant here, traditional Christian theologians used this argument to support the idea that a perfect being must be unchanging in all respects, whereas they rejected Plato's argument that the only way to protect God's moral perfection is to say that God is not the total cause of all things. Being supported by Plato (apparently) and other philosophers, the idea that God cannot change in any respect took on the status of a dogma (as evidenced, for example, by the fact that it became heretical to hold a view that would imply "Patripassianism," the idea that God the Father can suffer). And the charge of arbitrariness in this selective adoption cannot be overcome by reference to compatibility with the Bible. I have already suggested that the Platonic idea of creation would have been in accord with one strand of Biblical thought. And the passages in the Bible that can be taken as support for God's impassibility (inability to be affected from without) and immutability (inability to be changed by any source) are very few in comparison with those which suggest that God genuinely interacts with the world, being affected by its events—sometimes getting angry, sometimes rejoicing—and making new decisions based upon the world's responses to previous divine decisions. Traditional Christian thought relegated all these passages to the status of "metaphors for unsophisticated minds" in order to bring these passages into line with the Greek idea that perfection, and hence deity, must be unchangeable in all respects.

The importance of this idea of divine immutability for the problem of evil is incapable of exaggeration. The central point, briefly stated, is this: If God knows the world (which the Biblical tradition clearly implies), and if God is unchangeable in all respects, so that even the content of divine knowledge cannot change, then God must know all the events of the world unchangeably, nontemporally, eternally. This idea by itself makes the notion of contingency, including genuinely free decisions, difficult to say the least. And if to this complex of ideas is added the idea that God influences the world (which the Biblical tradition also implies), then the thought lies near that God completely determines all things. This idea puts the blame for any genuine evil clearly upon God. This set of ideas will be discussed more fully later.

There is one important strand in Plato's thought which is in tension with the doctrine that the best must be unmoved. In Bk. X of the *Laws* he says that, of the various types of motion, the superior type is that which moves itself and other things. He explicitly says this is superior to the kind that moves other things but cannot move itself (which Aristotle took to be characteristic of the superior being). Plato says that this self-moving motion, which is the defining essence of "soul," is the first type of motion both in generation and in power: Soul is the "oldest of all things," and the beginning of all change (*Laws* X. 894–896). Although Plato does not explicitly draw the conclusion, this line of thought would suggest that the creator-father God discussed elsewhere would be the supreme soul. Hence this line of thought is in tension with the idea that the superior being would be incapable even of changing itself.

Another dimension of Plato's thought should be mentioned, since it is a dimension much discussed in present-day discussions of the problem of evil. In view of the fact that some theologians tend to call "Manichaean" any doctrine which suggests that there is any power in the universe that is not totally determinable by God, which would include Plato's view of creation, the relationship between his view and that which is properly called "Manichaeanism" should be examined. According to Manichaeanism, the reason there is evil which opposes the will of the supramundane good power is that reality contains also a supramundane evil being who is not merely a creation and finally an instrument of the good being, but is equally primordial and stands in genuine opposition. In one place Plato seems to suggest such a view. After the discussion of souls mentioned above, in which Plato concluded that soul must be the cause of all things, he posits that there cannot be "less than two—one the author of good, and the other of evil" (*Laws* X. 896, 897). And he refers to this latter as an "evil soul." However, it would be rash to label Plato "Manichaean" on the basis of this passage. For one thing, he explicitly says elsewhere that we must not say that two opposed divinities move the universe, but that evil is due to the universe's "moving itself" (*Politicus* 270a). And it is possible to consider this evil soul not as a being on the same level as the creator God, but as only one of the creations. Also, Plato holds that things are intrinsically good insofar as they have being. It is precisely upon the basis of this Platonic principle that Augustine will rule out the possibility of the existence of any intrinsically evil being or beings.

In summary, there is no good basis for labeling Plato's views "Manichaean." The one statement in which he suggests the existence of an evil soul as the cause of evil is not sufficient basis. And the more general doctrine that creation involves the ordering of a chaotic realm cannot meaningfully be called Manichaean, since the unordered beings are not intrinsically evil, but only instrumentally so, insofar as their disorderly movement thwarts the achievement of the highest possible values.

# 3
# Aristotle

ARISTOTLE'S GOD is not the creator of the world, even in the sense that Plato's God is. And Aristotle's God is not an efficient cause actively bringing about effects in the world. Hence there was no need for Aristotle to construct a theodicy. Nevertheless, the elements of his thought about God that were appropriated by Christian theologians, when combined with ideas from the Biblical tradition, have been of tremendous importance for the problem of evil.

Aristotle's God is an "unmoved mover." It moves other things, but without moving itself (*Physics* VIII, 5). It moves others simply by being the object of desire and thought (*Metaphysics,* Lambda, 6). Hence God can function as a "final cause" for worldly activities while being completely impassible and unchangeable in every respect. Aristotle echoes Plato's argument, saying that since God is the best substance, any change would have to be change for the worse (*Metaphysics,* Lambda, 9).

The only activity in God is the immobile activity of contemplation or thought (*Nicomachean Ethics* VII. 14). But the object of this thought is not the world, but is simply deity itself, i.e., thought itself (*Metaphysics,* Lambda, 7). For, to say that deity thought about something other than itself would imply that it were dependent upon this other something (*Metaphysics,* Lambda, 9). And this would undercut God's superiority, for the more superior a being is the more independent it is. A superior being will need nothing, such as friends, for its happiness (*Eudemian Ethics.* VII. 12).

Accordingly, to describe Aristotle's God as the "unmoved mover" and as "self-thinking thought" is to stress the absolutely positive valuation of the characteristics of unchangeability and independence in every respect. For Christian theology to incorporate the Aristotelian notion of perfection into the Christian idea of deity meant attempting the *prima facie* impossible task of synthesizing these characteristics with the Biblical notion of God, which seemed to suggest that God is affected by what happens in the world, and that God's happiness is not completely independent of these happenings.

There is another element in Aristotle's thought that, had it been consistently appropriated by Christian theologians and then by Western thinkers in general, would have made the problem of evil much less of a theoretical problem than it has been. This is Aristotle's argument that the determinateness of truth does not imply the lack of genuine contingency in the world. Many have argued that every proposition must be either true or false. Hence a proposition about the future, e.g., "There will be a revolt in twenty years in Athens," must *now* either be true or false. Accordingly, if when that day comes there is a revolt, this cannot be considered a contingent happening, i.e., one that might have failed to occur. Aristotle rejects this argument, saying that statements about the future need not be either true or false. There is a third possibility—they may as of now be indeterminate (*On Interpretation* 9).

Aristotle could hold this view consistently with his doctrine that God is unchangeable because he held that God does not know the world. But when the Aristotelian unchanging God was combined with the Biblical God who knows the world, it became necessary, in order to achieve a self-consistent position, to deny all genuine contingency. However much some of the traditional Christian theologians wanted to assert the reality of contingency, i.e., the possibility that events could have occurred other than those which actually do occur, they could not finally affirm this. For if God knows everything that occurs in the world, and knows this infallibly and unchangeably, without any additions to the content of divine knowledge, then the total truth about reality, including what is future for us temporal beings, must be completely determinate. Accordingly, the Aristotelian position on the indeterminateness of propositions about the future, which would have been consistent with the Platonic suggestion that worldly beings have some degree of autonomous activity even vis-à-vis God, could not be appropriated by traditional Christian theologians because of the other elements of Platonism and Aristotelianism that they did accept. It is important to note here that it was not simply a matter of adopting "Greek philosophy" as "natural theology" but of accepting certain ideas from the Greeks and rejecting other ones.

# 4
# Plotinus

As WAS THE CASE with the Bible, Plato, and Aristotle, there are various strands of thought in Plotinus that are relevant to the problem of evil. And again, some strands were appropriated by traditional Christian theology while others were not. Three major strands of Plotinus' thought will be examined here. One deals with the nature of deity, and the other two involve the question as to whether there is genuine evil in the world and, if so, what its source is. In Plotinus these three elements could fit together consistently. But because of the doctrine of God that resulted from the way the traditional theologians combined Greek and Hebrew notions of deity, the third element of Plotinus' thought to be examined below, that which affirms the presence of genuine evil in the world and attributes it to nondivine agents, could not be more than verbally appropriated by these theologians.

In Plotinus' idea of deity, which involves a reworking of Plato's views with some influence from Aristotle, there are three aspects. The highest element of the Supreme is the One; below it is the Intelligence; and below it is the Soul.

The One, which is the most divine aspect of the Supreme, can also be called the Good. It is completely unmoved; it does not act (I. 7. 1).[1] Everything else depends upon it, while it is absolutely self-sufficient and independent (I. 8. 2). And it is absolutely simple; for anything that has constituents is dependent upon them (II. 9. 1).

These are descriptions of deity that Christian theologians would take over. In the light of these descriptions, it is worthy of note that in Plotinus' thought, as in Aristotle's, the absolutely simple, unmoved, independent being is not an efficient cause of the universe. So there was no problem in understanding how that which does not move (e.g., in the sense of moving from a state of potentiality in some respect to a state of actuality in that respect) could act as an efficient cause. Activities that Plotinus could attribute to other aspects of the Supreme, especially the Soul, which is not simple or unmoving, the Christian theologians would attribute to the being they had said was simple and immutable in all respects. And since Plotinus did not attribute efficient causation to the totally independent principle, the fact that it was not affected by the activities of the worldly agents did not prejudice their capacity for self-movement and hence their genuine agency. But if one says that the totally independent principle is an efficient cause, it seems to be implied that this causation will be total determination, since the causation cannot be a series of responses to now this and now that activity of the beings acted upon, but must be decided independently of any such activities. This raises the question as to whether any room can remain for genuine activity on the part of these other beings.

A second strand in Plotinus' thought that has been greatly influential in Christian theodicies is his defense of the goodness, in fact the perfection, of the world when considered as a whole (III. 2. 3). The criterion of perfection employed is essentially aesthetic. This world is considered a reflection of the Intelligible Realm; and Plotinus considers it the most beautiful representation possible (II. 9. 4, 7). The central notion of this defense is what has come to be called the "principle of plenitude," or the "great chain of being," the notion that perfection of the whole requires that every possible level of existence be represented. As Arthur Lovejoy points out, this idea can be found earlier, especially in Plato, but it is first fully and exclicitly stated by Plotinus.[2] Since Plotinus equates the descent from higher to lower on the chain of being with the move from a lesser to a greater mixture of evil with goodness, he can say that this principle of plenitude necessitates the existence of things that are in themselves evil for the sake of the perfection of the whole (II. 9. 13; III. 2. 11). The analogy used, in keeping with the aesthetic criterion of goodness, is the artistic one. For the painting as a whole to be beautiful, it is not necessary that the colors be beautiful in every place considered in isolation; in fact the ugly portions are necessary for the perfection of the whole. Nor should a drama contain only heroes; the low characters are an integral part of its power (III. 2. 11).

The upshot of this line of argumentation, considered by itself, would be that there is no genuine evil in the universe, if by genuine evil we mean something without which the world would have been better, all things considered, i.e., if some other possibility had been actualized instead. This line of thought suggests that, while many things are evil when considered in isolation or within a limited context, they are not really evil when all things are considered, i.e., when "the whole," or the ultimate context is considered. In this context, the instrumental good that each of the individually bad things contributes to the whole scheme of things is such as to cancel out its badness. This, I will attempt to show, is the position finally held, more or less comfortably, by traditional Christian theologians, insofar as they do not eschew logic.

But this was not quite the position taken by Plotinus himself. For there is a third strand in his thought relevant to theodicy, a strand that could not really be appropriated by traditional theologians. Whereas Plotinus believes that the general structure of the world is perfect, he allows for evil in the details of life. And he can hold this without impugning the perfection of deity, since he allows worldly beings to have their own agency.

Plotinus is very clear on this point. He says that the soul must have its individual movement (III. 2. 7), and that human beings contain a principle of freedom (III. 3. 4). And he explicitly makes the connection that, since human beings are agents, one need not attribute evil to deity (III. 2. 10). (Here Plotinus has in mind the kind of evil that I call "genuine evil," not the kind that is necessary for the good of the whole.) Although Plotinus thinks of life as a kind of play, with parts assigned by the author, he does not believe that the author is the "source of all that exists," or that the author inspires our "precise conduct" (III. 2. 18). Rather, we express our qualities through actions, the details of which are decided by us at the moment. (Furthermore, as a believer in reincarnation, Plotinus can hold that even our qualities were decided by us, in a previous existence [III. 3. 4].)

Critics have often charged that those who believe in divine providence give all credit to God for good, thereby robbing humanity of all dignity, and then inconsistently assign to humanity all the blame for evil. But this is certainly not true of Plotinus. He says that right is done *in accord with* providence, but is not done *by* providence (III. 3. 5). And, since he does not hold that deity has all the power, Plotinus need not introduce the kinds of distinctions employed by traditional Christian theologians to say that evil is loathed by God in one sense, and yet willed and even caused by God in another sense. Plotinus can say simply that evil is that which is done neither by providence nor in accord with it *(ibid.)*.

In agreement with the Platonic principle that power is of the essence of being, Plotinus says that if we assigned all agency to the author of the play, thereby taking all power away from the souls, this would make them *mere parts* of the author (III. 2. 18). Elsewhere, in response to the question as to why the wicked rule over the good, he answers simply: because, although the wicked are inferior in virtue, they are generally superior in strength. Plotinus is saying that these are matters decided not by providence, but by worldly agencies. Those who say that providence should reverse the situation are talking nonsense, as he implies in a statement worthy of quotation:

> Providence cannot be something reducing us to nothingness: to think of Providence as everything, with no other thing in existence, is to annihilate the Universe; such a providence could have no field of action; nothing would exist except the Divine. As things are, the Divine, of course, exists, but has reached forth to something other—not to reduce that to nothingness but to preside over it. (III. 2. 9)

In other words, to say that deity has a monopoly on power is to imply both that deity is the only reality that exists, and also that deity really has no providential power, since this is a relational concept—providential power can only be exerted over other beings with some power of their own.

Furthermore, Plotinus agrees with Plato in attributing some kind of agency to nonhuman things. He speaks of other agents, both living and lifeless (III. 3. 5). And he refers to both "accident" and "necessity" as other agencies besides the author (II. 2. 7). The term "necessity" is an explicit reference to Plato's idea that the world is a joint product of Intelligence and Necessity (I. 8. 7). When Plotinus says that evil exists "from necessity" (III. 3. 5), he apparently means that it is necessary that there be this realm of not-totally-rationalized movement, and that evil (here again, genuine evil) arises from this chaotic movement. This interpretation would fit with the previous quotation supporting the equation of power and being, and with the following answer as to why evil is not driven out of the universe:

> In a word, those that would like evil driven out from the All would drive out Providence itself. What would Providence have to provide for? Certainly not for itself or for the Good:

> when we speak of a Providence above, we mean an act upon something below." (III. 3. 7)

This means that, since anything actual will have some power of its own which will not be completely controllable by the providential power, the only way to preclude the possibility of evil in the world would be to annihilate all worldly beings. Besides the fact that this would be impossible, it would mean destroying providence itself, for the reason given in the earlier quotation (from III. 2. 9).

This type of reflection, if sound, is of tremendous importance for the problem of evil. Christian theologians have assumed they were increasing the power of deity beyond that attributed to it by Plato and Plotinus. But Plotinus had already suggested that the attempt to increase God's power by completely subordinating the power of the creatures to it might mean conceptually destroying the creatures altogether and, paradoxically, thereby conceptually destroying the divine power by rendering it literally nonsensical.

This third element of Plotinus' thought, in which he asserts the reality of genuine evil in the details of the world (as opposed to the perfection of its general outline) and attributes this evil to nondivine agencies, could not be appropriated by traditional Christian theologians, since they combined the notion of deity as absolutely simple, independent, and immutable with the Hebrew idea of God as efficient cause in such a way as to imply a divine determinism. This meant that the Plotinian defense of the perfection of the general structure of the world logically had to be turned into a justification of every last detail, if the goodness of God were to be defended. I will in Part II turn to various representatives of traditional theism, beginning with Augustine, who was most instrumental in appropriating Plotinian themes into Christian theology.

# 5
# Summary

BEFORE I BEGIN the analysis of traditional Christian theists, it may be helpful to review the formal statement of the problem of evil and to consider the response that would have been made to it by the Biblical writers and the three Greek philosophers considered above. The formal statement was as follows:

1. God is a perfect reality. (Definition)
2. A perfect reality is an omnipotent being. (By definition)
3. An omnipotent being could unilaterally bring about an actual world without any genuine evil. (By definition)
4. A perfect reality is a morally perfect being. (By definition)
5. A morally perfect being would want to bring about an actual world without any genuine evil. (By definition)
6. If there is genuine evil in the world, then there is no God. (Logical conclusion from 1 through 5)
7. There is genuine evil in the world. (Factual statement)
8. Therefore, there is no God. (Logical conclusion from 6 and 7)

Plato, Aristotle, and Plotinus could each avoid the conclusion (8) by rejecting premise 2 or premise 3. In Aristotle's case, God is not thought of as an efficient cause at all, and hence, not thought of as a creator. So Aristotle would have denied premise 2, if "omnipotence" were clarified so as to include efficient power. Or, if "omnipotence" were said to mean simply "perfect power," then Aristotle could have affirmed premise 2, explaining that perfect power is the power eternally to contemplate contemplation. He would accordingly have denied premise 3, saying that perfect power has nothing to do with the ability to create a world at all, let alone one without evil.

Plato would have denied premise 2, if "omnipotence" were clarified to mean "having a monopoly on power," or any other meaning which would entail premise 3. However, if "omnipotence" were said simply to mean "perfect power," i.e., "the greatest power conceivable for a being to have," Plato would probably have affirmed premise 2. He would then have clearly rejected premise 3, since he held that evil exists "from necessity." This would hold true regardless of which of the possible candidates for the "perfect reality" in Plato's thought was chosen. (If one were thinking of "The Good" as the perfect reality, then Plato's position on this issue would be similar to Aristotle's.)

Plotinus would have rejected either premise 2 or premise 3, following the same logic as Plato. This would hold true whether simply "the One" were being considered the perfect reality, or whether "the Supreme" as a whole were in view, since the lower two aspects of the Supreme are said to emanate necessarily from the One.

In regard to the Biblical tradition, it is impossible to say which premise "the Bible" would reject, since the Biblical record is the product of many authors over many centuries. From different segments of the Bible one could find passages that could be read as implying a rejection of any of the premises. Especially in earlier traditions one could find implicit denials of premises 2 and 4, and many would find that (by their own criteria) premise 1 was denied. Also, one must admit that statement number 6 is denied in portions, i.e., that the necessity of holding to the rules of logic in matters concerning God is in effect denied. However, in those portions of the Bible that reflect the rise of what has been called with some justice "ethical monotheism," the greatest number of relevant passages can most reasonably be taken as implying a rejection of either 5 or 7. The rejection of premise 5 would be implied in those passages that stress the mystery of God, and the inability of humans to use their own standards to judge God. Those sections which imply a rejection of premise 7 would primarily be those in which future rewards and punishment are stressed, and the assumption is made that "all's well that ends well." One of these two positions, or some somewhat vague combination of them, probably represents the dominant explicit Biblical answer to the problem of evil, insofar as there is one. But I would hold that equally central to the Biblical tradition is an implicit rejection of premise 3, insofar as it is assumed that creatures, at least human ones, by virtue of being created, have the power to disobey the will of their creator.

If this is true, then a revision of Christian theodicy along the lines suggested in this book need not be seen as a rejection of "the Biblical viewpoint" in favor of some non-Biblical viewpoint. Rather, the change from the traditional Christian theodicy, in which premise 5 or premise 7 was rejected, to a Christian theodicy in which premise 2 or premise 3 is rejected, can be regarded as a change from the attempt consistently to develop the more explicit of the two major lines of the Biblical tradition to the attempt consistently to develop the other major line. And the development of this new Christian theodicy can be regarded as formally the same as the development of the traditional Christian theodicy, inasmuch as ideas suggested by Greek philosophers are employed in the attempt to achieve philosophical consistency. Substantively the attempt differs, of course, in that it is a different set of ideas suggested by these Greek philosophers that is employed.

I turn now to an examination of several representatives of the traditional position.

# PART II

## *Traditional Theodicies*

---

# 6

# Augustine: The Traditional Free-Will Defense

Augustine repeatedly affirmed God's omnipotence and goodness. And he was acutely aware of the problem of evil that is occasioned by this combination of divine attributes and the apparent existence of evil. In his early Christian writings against the Manichaeans, he stressed that God created all natures, and that all natures are good, insofar as they are—i.e., whatever is, is good (e.g., *C* VII. 18).[1] There is no nature that is evil, even the devil's. Evil is due to will, not to nature (*CG* XII. 3). All evil can be accounted for in terms of the misuse of free will (*FW* III. 17, 48). Hence, although God is the creator of all natures, God is absolved from the responsibility for evil.

In his later writings Augustine retracted some of his statements about free will that were used by the Pelagians. And he emphasized predestination much more, insisting that predestination is not based upon God's prevision of faith and good works, but that faith and good works are the result of grace which follows from eternal predestination to salvation. But he never explicitly gave up the free-will defense of God's goodness. He continued to maintain that evil ultimately comes from the free choice of creatures, so that God is not responsible for sin and hence is justified in inflicting evil as a punishment for sin. In this chapter, I will examine whether the tracing of evil to creaturely free will is compatible with Augustine's doctrine of God's power, and hence whether his defense of God's goodness is tenable.

## THE SUPERNATURALISTIC FRAMEWORK OF AUGUSTINE'S THEODICY

In regard to the question as to why good people suffer and seem to get the same rewards and punishments in this life as sinful people, Augustine states flatly that good and evil persons are treated the same way by God in regard to material goods. There are several reasons for this evenhandedness. It will encourage us not to covet material goods and not to cultivate religion for rewards in this life (*CG* I. 8; XXII. 22). It will help us realize that there are future rewards and penalties as well as present ones (*CG* I. 8). Whereas suffering is punishment for bad persons, it helps good ones prove their perfections or correct their imperfections (*CG* I. 29). For example, when virgins are raped this helps destroy their pride, actual or potential (*CG* I. 28). Furthermore, the good people in a community, as well as the bad, love this present life, and thus deserve punishment (*CG* I. 9). And in losing temporal goods, the good really lose nothing important, for they do not thereby lose their faith and their godliness (*CG* I. 10 and 28). God even permits baptized infants, who are unsurpassed in innocence, to be tormented, in order to teach us to bewail the calamities of this life and desire the life to come (*CG* XXII. 22). However, God does sometimes interfere, delivering present rewards and punishments, so that we will believe in his providence (*CG* I. 8).

From these statements one can see that Augustine's view of the meaning and end of life is almost totally supernatural, so that the question of the balance of goods and evils that we experience in this life is not really very important. They can all be justified in terms of their relation to the supernatural end of life. However, although he offers many possible justifications for the way things happen, he admits that God's judgments are finally unsearchable. But, he says, speaking of the day of judgment,

> we shall then recognize the justice of all God's judgments . . . and . . . we shall also recognize with what justice so many, or almost all, the just judgments of God in the present life defy the scrutiny of human sense or insight, though in this matter it is not concealed from pious minds that what is concealed is just. (*CG* XX. 2)

Faced with this answer to the question as to why evil has been caused or allowed by an omnipotent God, many people would want to stand with Ivan in the chapter entitled "Rebellion" in Dostoevsky's *The Brothers Karamazov.* Ivan admits that at the end of the world a "higher harmony" may be realized, and that if he is there, he may then cry aloud with the rest, "Thou art just, O Lord, for Thy ways are revealed." But, both in spite of this possibility and because of it, he wants to get his protest on the record in advance. He announces that he hopes he will not join that chorus, for he cannot accept the idea that any "higher harmony" could justify the evils that were allegedly necessary for this harmony, such as the suffering of innocent children.

However, whether or not we can share Augustine's faith that it will be revealed to us some day that the distribution of good and evil in this life reflects wholly just judgments on God's part, this does provide a possible answer to the problem of evil. That is, although one might not believe it, or might rebel against it, there is nothing necessarily self-contradictory in the answer. In a context where belief in an omnipotent God and a future life is already accepted on other grounds, it is possible consistently to maintain that all presently unanswerable questions as to why God caused or at least permitted certain things will be answered in and by this future life. Later I will argue that today one cannot simply assume the existence of an omnipotent God and a future life when dealing with the problem of evil. But it would be anachronistic to criticize Augustine on these grounds.

Accordingly, this examination of Augustine's theodicy must be primarily concerned with the problem of evil as it emerged in terms of his own central ideas. This means dealing with his attempt to reconcile the doctrine of supernatural rewards and punishments for this life with the assertion of God's absolute goodness. Whereas this discussion will not directly be of much interest to those who do not believe in a future life (especially one understood in terms of rewards and punishments), or to those who at least do not believe that a future state should be the primary focus of the religious life, this examination of Augustine's position will be indirectly relevant to the possibility of "justifying God's ways to humanity" simply in terms of the good and evil in our present existence. For, this discussion will be relevant to the possibility of reconciling the belief in a good and omnipotent God with the reality of any type of genuine evil whatsoever.

## THE FREE-WILL DEFENSE

One absolutely clear teaching of Augustine regarding the future life is that it will not be a pleasant experience for all persons. In fact, a majority will be condemned to eternal punishment (*CG* XXI. 12; *E* XXIV. 97). And equally clear, at least in his later writings, is the teaching that the question as to who will be saved is settled entirely by God (*GFW* XLV; *PS* XI, XIX, XXXIV). In regard to how it can be just of God unilaterally to elect some for salvation and to condemn the rest to punishment apart from any question of merit, Augustine has a two-part response: On the one hand, in reference to the question as to why God chooses the particular persons chosen for salvation, Augustine refers to Paul's statement in Rom. 9:20 about the potter and the clay, saying that this statement reminds us to consider the limits of our capacities (*E* XXV. 99; *PS* XVI). The other half of Augustine's answer deals with the more general question of the justice of saving some and not the rest. The answer to this is that all people have freely sinned, and therefore all people deserve punishment (*CG* XII. 8). God would be perfectly just if all of them were condemned to eternal punishment. The fact that God graciously chooses to save some simply shows that God is merciful as well as just (*E* XXV. 99; *PS* XVI).

Augustine's entire theodicy hinges on this argument. If he cannot consistently claim that all people (except the God-man, of course) deserve eternal punishment, his theodicy fails.

The context for this argument is his doctrine of original sin and its effects. The first people had the possibility of not sinning *(posse non peccare)* and yet sinned. As they were our parents, we all sinned "in" them. Because of this, we do not have the possibility of not sinning *(non posse non peccare)*. We can do no good unless we are freed from our bondage to sin by God's grace, which returns us to Adam's state of having the ability not to sin. (The third possible state, that of not having the ability to sin [*non posse peccare*], will characterize those who attain eternal life.)

There are three crucial aspects of Augustine's argument that all people deserve eternal punishment. First, he must argue that the punishment is just in the sense of being proportional to the crime. And this he does, arguing that Adam's sin was very heinous, partly because it was such an easy sin to avoid (*CG* XIV. 12). Second, he must argue for the intelligibility of the idea that the rest of humanity sinned "in" Adam, and hence is responsible for this first sin. Both of these arguments have seemed weak to many. But the debate about these issues does not have relevance to the more general problem of reconciling omnipotent goodness and genuine evil. Hence I will not rehearse this debate, but will move to the third crucial step in the argument, the idea that we could be said to have sinned freely. In order to broaden the issue, so that the rather archaic and questionable idea of humanity's sinning in Adam can be ignored, I will examine the question as to whether anyone could sin freely in the Augustinian universe, be they angels, humans before the fall, humans after the fall but before receiving grace, or humans after grace.

Augustine certainly means to affirm the reality of free choice. He sees that the whole idea of precepts would be nonsensical unless we had freedom to choose to obey them (*GFW* II, IV), and that unless sin is voluntary, it would not be sin (*TR* XIV. 27). Furthermore, he sees that unless there is volition that does not come from God, God would be the author of sin (*SL* LIV). For Augustine, the evil will is the one thing in the universe that God did not create (*CG* V. 8, 10). The devil's wicked will came from the devil himself, not from God (*NOG* 32). And the original sin of humanity resulted from human free will (*NAG* III).

It cannot be overstressed how central to Augustine's thought is this affirmation of free will. In his early writings he was especially concerned with Manichaeanism, and stressed that all beings are created by a good God and are therefore good. Evil is not to be explained on the basis of any being whose nature is bad, whether this being be created or uncreated. In order to account for evil, then, Augustine distinguished between the created "nature," which all beings have, and the "will," which free beings have. The will as such is also created. But God does not create its evil volitions; in fact, these evil volitions have no efficient cause at all, but only a "deficient" cause (*CG* XII. 6, 7).

Only upon this basis could Augustine simultaneously reject Manichaean dualism and yet avoid suggesting that his own monotheistic God was responsible for the world's evil. He saw evil willing as the source of all evil; he said that there is no evil other than sin and its punishment (*TR* XII. 23).

But is this affirmation of free choice on the part of some of God's creatures compatible with Augustine's doctrine of God? *Prima facie* it seems incompatible with his doctrine that God is both immutable and omniscient. And it seems incompatible with his doctrine of God's omnipotence. I will first examine the compatibility of creaturely free will with an immutably omniscient God and then turn to the problem raised by Augustine's doctrine of omnipotence.

## FREE WILL AND DIVINE OMNISCIENCE

By itself the doctrine of an immutable being would not be prejudicial to the freedom of worldly beings, if this immutable being did not know the world, as was the case with Aristotle's God. And by itself, the doctrine of an omniscient being would not be prejudicial to worldly free choice, since this doctrine could simply mean that this being knows all things that are knowable, and one could maintain that a free choice is not knowable until after it is made. In other words, the omniscient being would not know the future (except insofar as some more or less abstract characteristics of the future are already settled in the present). But Augustine holds that God is both omniscient and immutable; and he explicitly points out that this entails that God is not affected by anything, so that there can be no increase in the content of the divine knowledge (*CG* XII. 17; XI. 21). Accordingly, omniscience includes prescience. In fact, Augustine takes this characteristic to belong to the defining essence of deity, saying that "one who is not prescient of all future things is not God" (*CG* V. 9). This makes the reality of free choice on the part of the creatures quite dubious.

Augustine argues that God's prescience of all things does not mean that our wills are not genuine causes, since God, in foreknowing all things, foreknows the causes of all things. Human wills, which are genuine causes of human actions, are included in that order of causes which God foreknows (*CG* V. 9). And in foreknowing what will be in the power of our wills, God does not foreknow simply nothing (*CG* V. 10).

This reconciliation seems purely verbal. The meaning of the "freedom" that is thereby allowed to us is not such as to make us responsible in the sense that Augustine's theodicy requires. The word "freedom" can be defined in many ways, of course, and different meanings can be relevant in different contexts. But when one is asking whether an action is "free" in a context in which the issue is whether the agent could justifiably be held responsible in the sense of being liable to incur blame, one must be asking whether the agent *could have done otherwise.* Or, since some people (such as Augustine) distinguish between willing and doing, one could be asking whether a person's *willing* is blameworthy. One would then have to be asking whether the individual could have willed something different from what he in fact did will.

Free choice in this sense is not compatible with an omniscient being who knows the details of what is still the future for us. If this being knows infallibly that next year I will do A, instead of B or C, then it is necessary that I will do A. It may seem to me then as if I make a real choice among genuine alternatives, but this will be illusory. I really could not do otherwise. If I were to do otherwise, God's immutable, infallible knowledge would be in error, and this is impossible. So in what meaningful sense will I be responsible for that choice? The response often made here is that, although I will not have been able to choose B or C, I will choose A because I *want* to choose A. And if A is a wicked deed, then I am blameworthy for wanting to do something wicked. But here we only need to focus on willing or wanting instead of doing, or to see willing as a type of doing. In any case, we can ask whether I shall be able at that future moment to *will* to do either B or C (even though I shall actually have to *do* A). Here the answer must be: If God knows that I shall will to do A, then I shall necessarily will to do A. And how can I be blameworthy for willing something when there was absolutely no possibility that I could have willed otherwise? If at this point the response is made that I shall necessarily will A at that future moment because of my character, and that I am in part responsible for forming my own character, the same objection must be stated. That is, to the extent that we form our own characters we do this by the choices we make, especially those kinds which we reinforce by frequent repetition. But if there is a being who eternally knows all things, then every single "choice" in my life prior to wicked deed A and the desire to do it is as devoid of real alternatives as the wicked deed A itself. Hence I am not responsible for my character any more than I will be for that particular decision.

If this analysis is correct, then an immutably omniscient God (who would certainly know that it is correct) would be unjustified in condemning anyone to punishment for sinning. For, from the moment of conception, a person's life could not have been one iota different from its actual course. So the person exercises no freedom in any sense that would justify blame. This conclusion follows merely from the definition of God as an omniscient being who is also immutable in all respects.

## FREE WILL AND DIVINE OMNIPOTENCE

When Augustine's notion of omnipotence is brought into focus, the self-contradictory character of his reconciliation of God's goodness with worldly evil becomes even more apparent. The previous discussion about omniscience was based upon allowing tentative validity to

Augustine's claim that God could foreknow some things, i.e., evil wills, without causing them (*PS* XIX). But now it will become apparent that this claim cannot be maintained.

For Augustine, omnipotence belongs to the defining essence of deity as fully as does immutable omniscience. He stresses that the first sentence of the creed is a confession of faith in God the Father Almighty. Then he adds: "For he is called Almighty for no other reason than that he can do whatsoever he willeth and because the efficacy of his omnipotent will is not impeded by the will of any creature." To deny this, he says, would be to undermine our confession of faith (*E* XIV. 96). Elsewhere he says that "he who denies that all things, which either angels or men can give us, are in the hand of the one Almighty, is a madman" (*CG* X. 14).

However, one meaning of "omnipotence" that might be suggested by these statements (that all things are in God's hands and that nothing can impede the divine will) is not the full Augustinian meaning. That is, these statements could be compatible with the following sketch of the world, which Augustine sometimes suggests: God created the world, willing that everything be good. God included beings with free will in this good creation. Some of these beings (some of the angels, and all of the humans, except the God-man) use their free will to sin, which means willing in a way that is contrary to God's will (*E* XXVI. 100). Of course, God foresees this sin, and builds appropriate responses to it into the divine eternal plan. On the one hand, God includes a plan of mercy:

> But since he did foreknow that man would make bad use of his free will—that is, that he would sin—God prearranged his own purpose so that he could do good to man, even in man's doing evil, and so that the good will of the Omnipotent should be nullified by the bad will of men, but should nonetheless be fulfilled. (*E* XXVIII. 104)

On the other hand, God includes punishments for the sin:

> Unbelievers indeed do contrary to the will of God when they do not believe His gospel; nevertheless they do not therefore overcome His will. . . . God's will is forever invincible; but it would be vanquished, unless it devised what to do with such as despised it, or if these despisers could in any way escape from the retribution which He has appointed for such as they. (*SL* LVIII)

These passages suggest that God's ideal plan, in which there would be no evil, is upset by the free will of creatures who go contrary to the divine will, and that God, foreseeing this misuse of free will, forms the plan so as to bring good out of evil. On the one hand, to some of the sinful creatures God returns good for evil, thereby manifesting the divine mercy, which is a good thing to do. On the other hand, God plans a punishment for the rest of the sinful creatures, thereby manifesting the divine justice, which is also a good thing to do.

Essential to this account is the idea that creatures can really will and act contrary to the divine will. That idea is suggested in each of the preceding quotations as well as in the following one: "But, however strong the wills either of angels or of men, whether good or evil, whether they will what God willeth or will something else, the will of the Omnipotent is always undefeated" (*E* XXVI. 102). And Augustine defines humanity's sin as doing what it willed, not what God had willed (*E* XXVI. 100). God's will is always undefeated because deity can arrange things in such a way that its will concerning the creatures will be done whether the creatures act according to it or contrary to it (*E* XXVI. 100; XXVII. 107).

However, although this is the sense that Augustine often gives to the notion that creatures cannot impede the divine will, and although this is the sense which he must suggest if his statement that creatures are justifiably punished for their actions is to have some plausibility, this is not the stronger sense which he gives to the notion elsewhere, and which his doctrine of God requires. According to this stronger sense, *nothing* happens other than what God wills to happen. For example, Augustine stresses "how certain, immutable, and effectual is the will of God," and that God "willeth nothing he cannot do." In regard to the Psalm which states that God has done all things that he would (composed inexactly from Ps. 115:3 and 135:6), Augustine says:

> This obviously is not true, if there is anything that he willed to do and did not do, or, what were worse, if he did not do something because man's will prevented him, the Omnipotent, from doing what he willed. Nothing, therefore, happens unless the Omnipotent wills it to happen. He either allows it to happen or he actually causes it to happen. (*E* XXIV. 95)

And, whether God is said to "cause" something or merely to "allow" it, if it happens this is because God wills it: "For it would not be done without his allowing it—and surely his permission is not unwilling but willing" (*E* XXVI. 100).

Not leaving any ambiguity, Augustine insists that we are not on any account "to underrate the fully omnipotent will of God." For, "if he willeth, then what he willeth must necessarily be." And, after offering his interpretation of a Scriptural passage that seems to cast doubt on this view, Augustine says: "We could interpret it in any other fashion, as long as we are not compelled to believe that the Omnipotent hath willed anything to be done which was not done." He then adds: "There must be no equivocation on this point" (*E* XXVII. 103). (The Scriptural passage in question is I Tim. 2:4, which states that God "desires all men to be saved." Augustine's interpretation of this is that it does not really mean "all men" but "all kinds of men," i.e., some from every class of human beings, e.g., rich and poor, rulers and subjects, etc.)

This would seem to imply that even sinful choices are willed by God. And Augustine does not flinch from making this application. Whereas he had insisted that God does not *create* evil wills, he does say that God *rules* them (*CG* XI. 17). He states that those wills "which follow the world are so entirely at the disposal of God, that He turns them whithersoever He wills, and whensoever He wills" (*GFW* XLI). God "does in the hearts of even wicked men whatsoever He wills" (*GFW* XLII).

Some passages suggest that the wicked willing is done independently by the creatures, and that God only then uses this self-determined wicked will. For example, Augustine says:

> It is not unjust that the wicked should receive power to harm so that the patience of the good should be proved and the iniquity of the bad should be punished. By the power given to the devil Job was proved that his justice might be made apparent; Peter was tempted so that he might not think too highly of himself. . . . God himself . . . did all things justly by the power he gave to the devil. Not for performing these just actions, but for the wicked will to do hurt, which came from the devil himself, will he in the end be awarded punishment. (*NOG* 32)

However, this element of autonomy cannot be granted. The previous statements about omnipotence do not allow it. Also Augustine elsewhere says explicitly that even the willing is done by God: "The Almighty sets in motion even in the innermost hearts of men the movement of their will, so that He does through their agency whatsoever He wishes to perform through them" (*GFW* XLII). And further: "God works in the hearts of men to incline their wills whithersoever

He wills, whether to good deeds according to His mercy, or to evil after their own deserts" (*GFW* XLIII).

Augustine recognizes, of course, that this idea that sinning is willed by God and thereby necessitated seems to negate the creatures' freedom and responsibility, and hence to throw God's justice for punishing them into question. Accordingly, he makes a distinction between two kinds of sin. Some sins are penalties for previous sin. God causes these "by a counsel most secret to Himself, indeed, but beyond all doubt most righteous" (*GFW* XLI). It is righteous because these sins that are caused by God are brought about in us because of previous sin on our part:

> [God's judgment is] sometimes manifest, sometimes secret, but always righteous. This ought to be the fixed and immovable conviction of your heart, that there is no unrighteousness with God. Therefore, whenever you read in the Scriptures of Truth, that men are led aside, or that their hearts are blunted and hardened by God, never doubt that some ill deserts of their own have first occurred, so that they justly suffer these things. (*GFW* XLIII)

This first wickedness on their part "was not made by Him, but was either derived originally from Adam, or increased by their own will" (*ibid.*).

But can this be? Can there have been an original sin, by the wicked angels, the first humans, and/or by each human being, i.e., some act or even desire that was contrary to the will of God? Not in light of what has already been reviewed about the divine omnipotence. Nothing happens but what God wills to happen; and what God wills necessarily happens. So there is no way to distinguish between those sins which Augustine admits that God causes and those which he sometimes implies that God does not cause.

Augustine's way of overcoming the apparent contradiction—that we are responsible for evil willing and acting even though God causes them—is simply to *assert* that God's causation does not take away our free agency. For example, he says that faith and works are commanded and also shown to be God's gifts to us so that "we may understand both that we do them, and that God makes us to do them" (*PS* XXII). And in regard to the Biblical statement that God "hardened" Pharaoh's heart and then punished him, Augustine says: "Thus it was that both God hardened him by His just judgment, and Pharaoh by his own free will" (*GFW* XLV). But is this both-and position tenable? If God "makes" us do something, then do "we" do it at all? In a statement quoted previously, Augustine said that God sets in motion even the movement of people's wills, "so that He does through their agency whatsoever He wishes to perform through them" (*GFW* XLII). But if God "does" the act, do the people really have any "agency" at all? Is it not self-contradictory and therefore simply nonsense to say that an act is B's act, if the act was totally determined by A? Most theists have held that God cannot do the self-contradictory, e.g., make a round square. Is it not saying that the self-contradictory is done when it is said that *God* performs certain acts without causing these acts not to be *our* acts?

The argument against this doctrine of double causation, which was suggested by Augustine and later developed as the doctrine of "primary and secondary causation," will be continued later, especially in the chapter on the theodicy of James Ross. For the present I will simply state somewhat dogmatically that the doctrine is not intelligible, and hence does not help absolve God from the charge of injustice, if people are punished for sins which God causes "them" to commit.

## SIN AND THE DIVINE WILL(S)

Furthermore, how can there even be any sin in the Augustinian universe? Augustine's definition of sin includes the idea of going contrary to the will of God. And yet Augustine has so defined God's omnipotence that nothing can happen which God does not will. He tries to overcome this contradiction by making a distinction between two "wills" in God. Whereas we go against God's will in one sense when we sin, Augustine says, we nevertheless fulfill God's *eternal* will. This distinction is suggested in a passage in which Augustine says that the fall of the wicked angels was ordained although not approved by God (*CG* XI. 19–20). Elsewhere he states that God inspires people to pray for things which God then does not grant. Regarding this, Augustine states that we can say:

> God wills and does not perform—meaning that He Who causes them to will these things Himself wills them. But if we speak of that will of His which is eternal as His foreknowledge, certainly He has already done all things in heaven and on earth that He has willed. (*CG* XXII. 2)

This same distinction is seen in the following passage, in which Augustine is speaking about those angelic and human creatures who have sinned:

> For, as far as they were concerned, they did what God did not will that they do, but as far as God's omnipotence is concerned, they were quite unable to achieve their purpose. In their very act of going against his will, his will was thereby accomplished. . . . In a strange and ineffable fashion even that which is done against his will is not done without his will. (*E* XXVI. 100)

It is in terms of this distinction between two meanings of "God's will" that all those passages in Augustine must be interpreted which seem to say that the creatures have some freedom vis-à-vis God by which they can go contrary to the divine will, and hence be genuinely responsible. With this distinction made explicit, it becomes clear that nothing happens that is not willed and thereby necessitated by God's eternal will. Accordingly, there is no original sinful free choice on the part of the creatures by which they can then be justly caused to commit further sins, and then justly punished for both types of sin.

## ANALYSIS OF AUGUSTINE'S POSITION

What, then, is Augustine's position on the problem of evil? He clearly would not reject either premise 1 or premise 2 (i.e., that God is perfect, and that this perfection includes omnipotence). Could Augustine reject premise 3, which says that God could have created a world without evil in it? There is, indeed, one passage in which Augustine seems to foreshadow those who will suggest that evil, or at least the possibility of evil, is metaphysically necessary, since the world is made out of nothing, and the "nothingness" in it has some power to resist God's power:

> Now, nature could not have been depraved by vice had it not been made out of nothing. Consequently, that it is a nature, this is because it is made by God; but that it falls away from Him, this is because it is made out of nothing. (*CG* XIV. 13)

However, Augustine's numerous statements on God's omnipotence show that this condition of being made out of nothing is not a sufficient (or even a necessary) condition for the occurrence of evil. And he explicitly says elsewhere that "it is undoubtedly as easy not to allow to exist what he does not will, as it is for him to do what he does will" (*E* XXIV. 96). And he asks rhetorically: "For who will dare to believe or say that it was not in God's power to prevent both angels and men from sinning" (*CG* IV. 27)? Furthermore, the fact that the "nothing" out of which God created the world is "absolute nothingness" (*ouk ōn*), rather than "relatively nothing" (*mē ōn*) with some kind of autonomy, is indicated by Augustine's rejection of the idea that evil is necessitated by the fact that God created the world out of some pre-existent stuff (*C* VII. 5).

What about premise 4, which asserts that perfection includes moral perfection? There is indeed a strain in Augustine's position which could be taken as a denial that God is moral in any sense that corresponds with our ideas of morality. Augustine refers approvingly to Paul's statement that the clay cannot criticize the potter. One could take this to mean "might makes right." And in one passage Augustine even says that "there is a very great difference between what it is fitting for man to will and what is fitting for God" (*E* XXVI. 101). However, the passages quoted four paragraphs above, plus numerous similar passages (e.g., *PS* XVI), including the passage quoted in the fourth paragraph of this chapter, clearly show that Augustine would not consider rejecting the idea that perfection includes moral goodness and that this is a moral goodness that we will be able to recognize as good when we can see things from a larger perspective. And, of course, the defense of God's moral goodness is the main point at issue in theodicy.

To reject statement number 6 would mean to reject the validity of logic when thinking about God and the world. Some of Augustine's statements might be so interpreted, as he often appeals to the mystery of God's ways, and the inability of the human mind to fathom God's "unsearchable" judgments (*PS* XVI). However, I do not believe Augustine means to be making the formal point that logic has to be suspended in these matters. Rather, his intention is that now we often cannot understand how the content of God's judgments is compatible with God's righteousness. He has no doubt that at the day of judgment we will understand the compatibility of omnipotent goodness and worldly evil. And just as there is no suggestion that this will involve seeing that God is "beyond good and evil," there is no suggestion that this will involve transcending the formal laws of thought.

This leaves premises 5 and 7 to be considered. In the "simple statement" of the problem of evil (given in the Introduction), the equivalent of premise 5 is stated as follows: "If God is perfectly good, he would want to prevent all evil." In concluding this discussion of Augustine, I will argue that, although he would reject this premise, the insertion of the qualifier "genuine" before "evil" in the expanded statement of the problem requires that we see the rejection of premise 7 ("There is genuine evil in the world") as the Augustinian solution.

## THE DENIAL OF GENUINE EVIL

What kind of evil does Augustine think there is in the universe? He specifically says that there is no "natural evil" (*CG* XI. 22). According to his use of this term, this means in the first place that there is nothing whose "nature" is evil, nothing that is "naturally" bad. Whatever is, is good. For all natures are created by God, and were created good (*NOG* 1). And there is no uncreated being, as the Manichaeans supposed, whose nature is evil. The devil is a creature; and even the devil's nature is good. Accordingly, nothing is by nature intrinsically evil.

In denying all "natural evil," Augustine also means that there is no genuine evil in the universe below the level of creatures with freedom. As was stated in the previous paragraph, there is no intrinsic evil in this realm. Things such as fire, frost, and wild beasts are excellent in their own natures (*CG* XI. 22). All things are good, even though we may not like all things (*C* VII. 22). Augustine also believes there is no genuine instrumental evil arising from this realm. Some sufferings caused in us by this realm, which are *prima facie* evil, are in reality punishments from God, and as such are just *(ibid.)*. And the things that cause these sufferings are actually useful to us, and hence are instrumentally good; we should believe this even when we do not yet see their utility (*CG* XI. 22). Furthermore, the irrational beings that sometimes cause suffering in us contribute grace and beauty to the universe as a whole; although we cannot see this from our limited perspectives, we should believe it (*CG* XI. 22; XII. 4). In short, in the realm of subhuman nature everything is intrinsically good; everything has positive instrumental value for us; and everything contributes to the good of the whole, so that there is no genuine evil in this realm.

What about the suffering that is caused in us by the sin of other people? It is not genuinely evil, for the suffering inflicted is just:

> Nor can any other nature which is less than divine be hurt unjustly. No doubt some people by sinning do harm unjustly. Their will to harm is counted against them, but the power by which they are permitted to do the harm comes only from

> God, who knows, though they do not, what those ought to suffer whom he permits them to harm. (*NOG* 11)

Augustine explains more fully: "It is not unjust that the wicked should receive power to harm so that the patience of the good should be proved and the iniquity of the bad should be punished" (*NOG* 32). Accordingly, suffering due to the sin of other people is not genuine evil, for it does not make the universe a worse place than it would otherwise be. To put it otherwise, sin, considered in regard to its instrumental effects on other beings, is not genuinely evil.

The only possible candidates for genuine evil, then, are moral evil, or sin, and its penalty. The penalty is caused by God, and hence, by definition (since there is no unrighteousness in God), cannot be genuinely evil. That is, once sin has occurred, it is better that it be punished than that it go unpunished. Accordingly, it is only sin itself that might be genuinely evil. And when Augustine speaks of evil, it is almost exclusively sin that he has in mind. He considers it intrinsically evil. But the question is whether this judgment of evil is a *prima facie* judgment only, or whether he thinks that sin is genuinely evil, so that the universe would have been a better place without it.

The answer to this must be that he sees it as only apparently evil. He constantly repeats the theme that God, who could have prevented all evil, allowed it only because he could bring good out of it. Assuming that the good that God brings out of the evil were perfectly balanced by the resulting good, then the *prima facie* evil would be neither good nor bad, all things considered, but simply neutral. But if the resulting good more than compensates for the *prima facie* evil which was a necessary condition for the resulting good, then the *prima facie* evil is not simply neutral, but is instrumentally good. And this is what Augustine holds. He says that the beauty of the world is achieved by the opposition of contraries. God is thereby able to use the wickedness of humans and angels for good, "thus embellishing the course of the ages, as it were an exquisite poem set off with antitheses" (*CG* XI. 18). "To the eye that has skill to discern it, the universe is beautified even by sinners, though, considered by themselves, their deformity is a sad blemish" (*CG* XI. 23).

Several other passages indicate that God not only compensates for *prima facie* evil, but more than compensates for it, so that it is really good that the *prima facie* evil occurred. Augustine says that God allowed man to be tempted by the devil "because He foresaw that by the man's seed, aided by divine grace, this same devil himself should be conquered, to the greater glory of the saints" (*CG* XIV. 27). "In this universe, even what is called evil, when it is rightly ordered and kept in its place, commends the good more eminently, since good things yield greater pleasure and praise when compared to the bad things" (*E* III. 11). "God judged it better to bring good out of evil than not to permit any evil to exist" (*E* VIII. 27). "If it were not good that evil things exist, they would certainly not be allowed to exist by the Omnipotent Good" (*E* XXIV. 96).

In summary, Augustine's position is that there is only one thing that is clearly evil intrinsically, and this is sin, or evil willing. But this *prima facie* evil is only apparently evil, for the universe is a better place with sin than it would have been without it. The one other thing that might be considered intrinsically evil, i.e., suffering, is never genuinely evil, for it is always a just punishment for sin and/or an aid toward achieving eternal life, which is such a great good that it more than compensates for any suffering. And those things which seem instrumentally evil within a limited context or from a partial perspective are not evil within the context of the universe as a whole. Accordingly there is no genuine evil in reality.

This is a possible position to hold in the sense that it is not necessarily inconsistent (even though each person holding such a position may have inconsistencies in his thought). But two questions can be asked: First, is this position adequate to our experience? Or do we have intuitions about the reality of genuine evil which should be given higher credibility than at least one of the traditional Christian premises about the nature of a "perfect reality"? Second, is this conclusion that there is no genuine evil in the world adequate to Christian faith itself?

I believe we must answer these questions differently from the way Augustine did. His position, that there is no genuine evil, was necessitated by the particular way in which he tried to combine Greek and Hebrew ideas of deity. The idea of divine power that resulted from affirming God's knowledge of and influence upon the world, on the one hand, and divine immutability and impassibility, on the other, implied that God caused all things. This belief, added to the idea that God is morally perfect, implied that there is no imperfection in the universe. Only a thoroughgoing revision of the idea of God can allow one consistently to affirm the virtually universal intuition that not everything is as good as it could have been.

# 7
# Thomas Aquinas: Divine Simplicity and Theological Complexity

THOMAS AQUINAS accepted most of Augustine's doctrines summarized in the previous chapter. There are some differences in the overall theologies of the two men, but few if any important differences in regard to the nature of God, the nature of evil, or the relation of God and evil. Of course, Thomas stressed the Aristotelian idea of God as the "unmoved mover"; but no one could have insisted upon God's immutability and impassibility more than Augustine had. The main difference between the two men, insofar as theodicy is concerned, is the greater detail in which Thomas worked out the implications of the traditional Christian synthesis of Greek and Hebraic ideas of deity, and the greater explicitness with which he dealt with the objections to God's alleged goodness which this synthesis, combined with the apparent evil in the universe, suggested.

In this chapter, I will first summarize seven characteristics which Thomas attributes to God and point out how these characteristics are interconnected. I will refer to this set of interconnected attributes as the "essential core of Thomistic theism." I will then argue that, given this essential core, it is impossible to hold both that genuine evil exists and that God is morally perfect. Accordingly, the argument and the conclusion will not differ significantly from that of the chapter on Augustine.

However, I have thought it important to include this chapter on Thomas for several reasons. First, the hold that traditional theism has had upon those who have framed theodicies, whether systematically or off-handedly, has been so long-standing and tenacious that the repetition involved in the present chapter is justified if the most it does is to add a little reinforcement to the case against the possible truth of traditional theism. Second, since Thomas explicitly considers most of the objections to traditional theism that revolve around the problem of evil, a review of his answers provides the opportunity to consider the validity of the rebuttals given by one of the most ingenious and influential defenders of traditional theism. Third, the "essential core of Thomistic theism" is really only a more systematic explication than one finds in Augustine and most other traditional theists of what is implied in the traditional synthesis of divine immutability with divine knowledge of and causal influence upon the world. Accordingly, it is also a statement of the essential core of traditional theism in general.

Hence, a look at Thomas' views helps one to see better what options are and are not open for theodicy within the context of traditional theism. In particular, most of the distinctions commonly made by traditional theists (Thomas included) to save God's moral goodness are ruled out in principle by the doctrine of divine simplicity, a doctrine which Thomas explicates most clearly, but which is implied by traditional theism in general.

It should be stressed that, while I will often use Thomas' own statements to make the case against his theodicy, the question of what Thomas' "true position" is on some particular issue on which he apparently says contradictory things is not to be settled by counting his explicit statements on both sides. Rather, the crucial matter is what the essential core of his theism allows him consistently to say, not what he actually says here and there in a possibly *ad hoc* way when considering a particular objection.

The thrust of my argument is that all of Thomas' statements which apparently reconcile both God's goodness and genuine worldly evil with the essential core of his theism are *ad hoc* assertions, inconsistent with that essential core. (This analysis is concluded in Chapter 5.)

## THE ESSENTIAL CORE OF THOMISTIC THEISM

It is to this essential core that I now turn. I will briefly explain the meaning of seven attributes of deity, and suggest some of the ways in which each one is implied by (or, in the case of the last two, at least implies) the others. God is said by Thomas to be:

1. *Eternal,* or *Nontemporal:* This means not simply that God always exists, but also that there is no temporal process, no "before and

after," within the divine reality (*ST* I. 20. 1, ans. and ad 4; *SCG* I. 15. 3).[1]

2. *Immutable* and *Impassible* (*SCG* I. 16. 6): The latter term stresses that God cannot be affected by any other realities. "Immutable" is a more general term, meaning that God cannot be changed in any way, even from within. This notion is implied by nontemporality, for a change from one state to another would imply a temporal distinction.

3. *Actus purus:* This means that God is pure act or actuality, in the sense that there is no unrealized potency or potentiality in God (*ST* I. 3. 1, ans; *SCG* I. 16. 1). This notion is implied by nontemporality and immutability, for unactualized potency would imply that God could change from one state (potency) to another (actualization). And had there ever been some potency which was subsequently actualized, this would entail a "before and after." Also *actus purus* is equatable with impassibility, for it implies that God does not have passive power, the power of being acted upon (*ST* I. 25. 1, ans.).

4. *Simple:* This notion is, paradoxically, the most complex, and really provides the clearest insight into the core of Thomistic theism. It has three verbally different formulations.

A. An often-used phrase is that "God's essence is his existence" (*SCG* I. 22. 1). But the term "existence" is ambiguous. It could mean simply the bare fact that the divine essence is instantiated, in which case the phrase would mean that "God's essence *includes* his existence," so that the divine essence is necessarily instantiated. But the term "existence" is used by Thomas to mean the full actuality of God, so that the phrase also means that there are no "accidents" in God, no elements in God's actuality that go beyond the divine eternal essence (*SCG* I. 23. 1). (There is more to the meaning of the phrase than this; but this additional meaning, very important in some contexts, is not relevant to the issues to be discussed here, at least as far as I can see.)

This and the previous doctrines mutually imply each other. The denial that there is any change or temporality in God means that there can be no successive states of God's experience which embody the divine essence as a partial and abstract element, along with some other non-essential, i.e., "accidental," elements. Likewise, having "accidental" experiences would imply having had the potentiality for these.

B. The doctrine of simplicity also means that there is no distinction between God's essence and any of God's attributes. The full implications of this can be brought out by comparing this doctrine with a temporalistic view. In the latter, God's perfect "knowledge" would belong to the divine essence, and one would distinguish between it as an abstract characteristic ("the capacity to know everything knowable"), and God's concrete acts of "knowing." These concrete acts of knowing would not belong to the divine essence, since God could have known different things (if different things had occurred) and still have been God. But in the nontemporalistic view, there is no distinction between God's knowledge as an abstract capacity, and God's concrete knowing. Hence God's actual knowing belongs to the eternal essence of deity, and in fact is said to be identical with it (*SCG* I. 65. 5). The same is true for God's other attributes, e.g., God's will is identical with the divine essence (*SCG* I. 73. 1). And there can accordingly be no distinction between God's "will" as an abstract characteristic and God's concrete willing. And, by the same logic, God's power and God's actual causation are one and the same.

C. If each attribute is identical with the divine essence, then every attribute is identical with every other one. So, if God has power, will, knowledge, and love, these are all identical. (*ST* I. 14. 4, o.c.; I. 14. 8, ans.; I. 14. 15; I. 19. 1, ans.; I. 25. 1, ad 2, 4.)

5. *Necessary:* God is eternal, and that which is eternal is necessary (*SCG* I. 83, 3). That God is the "necessary being" does not only mean that God exists necessarily. Rather, the doctrine of simplicity entails that *everything* about God is necessary. Since the divine essence is necessary, and there is nothing "in" God other than this essence, then God as a concrete whole is necessary.

The preceding five doctrines are derived primarily from the Greek heritage, and are all mutually implicatory. There are two other doctrines that belong to the essential core of Thomism—omniscience and omnipotence. They presuppose the Biblical heritage, with its assumptions that God knows and acts on the world. But they are defined in such a way as to harmonize with the preceding views. Although they are not implied by the previous doctrines, they do imply them.

6. *Omniscient:* This means that God knows everything knowable, and the "knowable" must include not only everything past and present, but also everything that for us temporal beings is future. Since God knows the world, the doctrines of eternity and immutability imply that God must know all things eternally, since there can be no succession and no changes in the content of the divine knowledge (*SCG* I. 66. 7; *ST* I. 14. 15, ad 2). The doctrine of *actus purus* means that God cannot pass from a state of potentially knowing something to a state of actually knowing it. The doctrines of God's necessity and simplicity entail that

there can be no distinction between a necessary essence and a contingent knowing which would have to wait for events to occur to know them.

7. *Omnipotent:* This means not only that God *can* do all things which are not self-contradictory (*ST* I. 25. 3, ans.), but finally must mean that God actually *does* everything that is done, that God causes everything that occurs. This stronger interpretation, in which "all-powerfulness" literally means that God really has *all* the power, follows from reflection upon the implications of divine omniscience combined with simplicity: since God knows all things, and his knowing cannot be distinct from God's power or causation (*ST* I. 25. 1, ad 2, 4), it follows that God causes all things (*ST* I. 14. 8, ans.). This is the difference between God's knowledge and ours that is due to the fact that we are composite while God is simple: our knowledge is caused by the causal impact of things on us, while God's knowledge is the cause of all things (*SCG* I. 65. 7; I. 67. 8).

This doctrine of God's omnicausality, implying God's monopoly on power, is consistent with the combination of immutability and omniscience: there is no danger that any of the creatures will do anything unforeseen, which would cause an addition to the content of God's knowledge, since none of the creatures really have any power to do anything.

Whereas the description of the first six attributes would be accepted by most Thomists, this interpretation of the meaning of "omnipotence" is controversial. Thomists will rightly point out that Thomas repeatedly says that God's omnipotence does not prevent the creatures from exercising causation. My reply is that this attribution of genuine causal power to the creatures is only verbal, that they cannot be regarded as exercising any agency in any meaningful sense of the term. The principal doctrine in question, that of primary and secondary causation, I take to be devoid of any meaning, at least any meaning that is relevant to the relation between a creator and a genuine creation. I mean to make this case somewhat in this chapter, but to develop it more fully in the later discussion of James Ross's position.

Now, with the essential core of Thomistic theism stated in advance, and with the warning that the most crucial aspect of it (the doctrine of omnipotence as omnicausality) is controversial, I will proceed to examine the various suggestions of Thomas as to how to understand the presence of evil in the world, given the belief in a God who is all-good as well as all-powerful. The conclusion will be that all the attempts to defend this God either violate the core of Thomistic theism, deny the ultimate reality of evil (i.e., deny genuine evil) or implicitly deny the perfect moral goodness of God.

## DIVINE OMNISCIENCE AND WORLDLY CONTINGENCY

Whereas Augustine, in those contexts where he apparently affirmed the reality of genuine evil, rested his case on a "free-will defense," Thomas rests his case more broadly upon what might be called a "contingency defense," since he does not follow Augustine in finding the source of all evil in creatures endowed with free will. The chief question to raise is whether Thomas can self-consistently assert the reality of contingent events, given his doctrine of God and the world's relationship to this God. Contingent events are ones that can either be or not be, i.e., they are not necessary (*SCG* I. 67. 3). Events of free choice by rational creatures would be a species under the genus of contingent events. Accordingly, if there is no contingency in the created universe, there is no free choice.

Thomas recognizes that the very fact of God's immutable omniscience throws into question the reality of all contingency. He argues that God's knowledge of events which are still future to us is not incompatible with the contingency of those events.

However, we must remember that, because of the divine simplicity, God's knowledge is identical with the divine essence. And God's essence, being eternal, is necessary—it could not be otherwise. Accordingly, God's knowledge must be equally eternal, and hence equally necessary. Now, Thomas asserts that God can have necessary knowledge of contingent things (*SCG* I. 67. 5). But this cannot be, if "contingent" means that an event could have failed to occur. If God's knowledge of event X (Smith's killing Jones with a butcher knife in New York City at 3:46 P.M. on January 18, 1967) is necessary, then it is impossible that the event itself could be merely contingent. For if event X failed to occur, then God's eternal and necessary knowledge would be wrong. And if something else instead of X occurred, God, being omniscient, would know that it occurred; accordingly, something new would come into God's knowledge. This would violate the divine immutability, impassibility, and nontemporality. Worse yet, since the knowledge and the essence of God are identical, God's essence would be changed—God would no longer be God, or at least not the same God. Of course, all of this is nonsensical. But this means that the idea that events which are eternally and therefore necessarily known can in themselves be contingent is nonsensical.

Another aspect of the doctrine of divine simplicity, the identity of all the divine attributes, makes the idea of contingent events even more difficult. For this doctrine means that God's knowledge, will, and causation are identical, so that for God to know events is for God to will and to cause those events. And since the events are known necessarily, they are willed and caused necessarily. Reflection upon this aspect of Thomism means that the Thomists' attempt to support freedom despite omniscience by an appeal to the analogy of a man looking down on a road from a great height (suggested by Thomas himself, *ST* I. 14. 13, ad 3) is illegitimate. The argument by analogy is based upon the fact that, although the man can foresee that a traveler is going to be robbed, his foreknowledge does not mean that he wills the robbery or causes it and thereby does not destroy the responsibility of the thieves. But the analogy only has force insofar as it depends upon violating the differences between God and humans upon which Thomas usually insists. That is, we human beings are complex, so that our knowledge, will, and causation are different. Hence, insofar as we can foresee an event, we do not thereby will or cause it. Human knowledge is caused by the events, whereas divine knowledge causes the events. Also our so-called "foreknowledge" of an event is not necessary, but only probable; e.g., one of many possible things might occur which would prevent the predicted robbery—the thieves might themselves be attacked by other robbers, a landslide might bury them, the intended victim might overpower them, etc. Accordingly, the fact that we can to some extent foreknow events does not mean that the Thomistic God can foreknow them without also willing and causing them. The analogy thereby provides no basis for seeing the events as contingent, or for avoiding God's responsibility for them.

In contexts where Thomas recognizes that God necessarily knows and wills all things that occur and as such is the necessary cause of those things, he tries to save the contingency of some things by distinguishing between the "remote" and "proximate" causes. God, the remote cause, is a necessary cause. But the things can be contingent by virtue of the fact that they have contingent proximate causes (*SCG* I. 67. 6; I. 85. 4). Thomas' definition is: "A contingent cause has relation to opposite things" (*ST* I. 14. 13 ans.). This means that a cause, A, is contingent if it could have more than one effect, i.e., if A could cause either B or C. Now this is a good definition of a contingent cause, and it is the one that is needed if the kind of contingency relevant to saving the creator's goodness is to be allowed into one's conceptual universe. But this type of contingent cause is impossible in

Thomas' universe. For God eternally and necessarily knows whether A will be followed by B or C. So A, the cause, does not *really* have "relation to opposite things." This could only be the case if one prescinded from the relation to God. But this is precisely the relation that cannot be prescinded from when one is asking whether contingency is possible in the universe *if there be* an omniscient, immutable, simple, omnipotent being.

Another argument Thomas makes is that, precisely because the divine will is perfectly efficacious, it can determine not only *what* will be done, but also the *manner* in which it is done. Hence, God can determine that some things will be done necessarily, but that other things will be done contingently. (*ST* I. 19. 8, ans. and ad 2; *SCG* I. 85. 2.) But this is sophistry. Thomas agrees with most theologians that God cannot bring about that which is self-contradictory. God cannot make a round square, since this is self-contradictory. But neither (I claim) can God cause an event to occur which is both contingent and necessary, i.e., which occurs necessarily and yet could fail to occur. If the Thomistic God wills an event to occur, then that event occurs necessarily. By Thomas' own principle, i.e., that not even omnipotence can do that which is impossible because self-contradictory, even his God cannot make a necessary event to be also a contingent event.

Thomas admits as much, in that he shifts from the distinction between "necessary" and "contingent," to the distinction between "absolute necessity," on the one hand, and "conditional necessity," or "necessity of supposition," on the other. (*ST* I. 19. 8, ad 3; *SCG* I. 67. 10; I. 85. 5.) Worldly events are said to be necessary only conditionally, i.e., upon the condition that God wills them to occur. They are not absolutely necessary, since God did not have to will that they occur—God could have created another world, or no world at all, since God creates voluntarily, not by necessity of the divine nature. I will argue later that even this claim of God's free creation of the world cannot stand. But even if it could, it should be noted that Thomas has now admitted that, supposing that God wills something, then that thing is a *necessity.* And he agrees that it is necessarily true that "if God wills something, it will be" (*SCG* I. 85. 6). Thomas' claim that it is only "absolute necessity" that would exclude contingency from events (*SCG* I. 85. 5) is not true in the sense that would be relevant to the point at issue. For the issue is whether any events can be contingent *in relation to* the will and causation of God, so that God might be absolved from the charge of having willed and caused evil. The statement that the events are "only" necessary by supposition, i.e., on the supposition that God wills and causes them to happen, obviously does not provide the kind of contingency that is needed for a theodicy.

## DIVINE PRIMARY CAUSATION AND DEFICIENT SECONDARY CAUSATION

Although the foregoing discussion, if correct, has shown the impossibility of any contingent events in Thomas' universe and hence of a "contingency defense" for God's goodness, the central doctrine in his attempt to absolve God of blameworthiness for the world's evil should be examined. This is the doctrine that evil is due to deficient secondary causes.

According to Thomas, every event (except for miracles) has two different kinds of efficient causes. On the one hand, God is the primary efficient cause of every event. On the other hand, each nonmiraculous event has a finite cause, which Thomas calls the secondary cause. The relation between the primary and secondary causation is not one of partly-partly, but of wholly-wholly. That is, the effect is not achieved partly by God and partly by the natural cause, but wholly by God and wholly by the secondary cause (*SCG* III. I. 70. 8). This seems to mean that there are two *sufficient* causes for the effect (an idea which will be examined in detail in the discussion of James Ross). Thomas concedes that it seems difficult to understand how there can be two agents for an action, that one or the other seems superfluous (*SCG* III. I. 70. 1–4). But he says that the idea is understandable if we distinguish between the thing that acts and the power by which it acts. The secondary causes are genuine causes; but they are able to produce their effects only by virtue of the power that God provides. An analogy is provided by comparing the secondary cause to an instrument and the primary cause to the artisan who gives motion to the instrument and is thereby the principal agent (*SCG* III. I. 70. 5–8).

Thomas insists that the "secondary causes" really are causes: "The causality of the lower type of effects is not to be attributed to divine power in such a way as to take away the causality of lower agents" (*SCG* III. I. 69. 12). He gives several reasons why we should believe that the creatures are active in producing effects. For one thing, it would be contrary to the divine rationality for there to be anything which is useless, and the creatures would be useless if God did everything immediately without using their agency. Also, if the divine likeness has indeed been communicated to actual beings, it has been communicated in regard to acting, so that they may have their own actions. Furthermore, the greater a power is, the greater its effects; God, being the perfect agent, must have created beings which could be active in producing effects, since this kind of creature is better than those without this ability (*SCG* III. I. 69. 13–16).

So, there is no doubt that Thomas verbally affirms that God does not exert all the causation in the universe. And this is his basis for absolving God of responsibility for evil. He says that God has imparted the dignity of causality to creatures in general, and free will to humans in particular. (*ST* I. 23. 3, ad 2, 3; I. 22. 3, ans.) Evil is attributable to defects in these secondary causes. (*SCG* III. I. 10. 7; III. I. 71. 2; *ST* I. 49. 2, ad 2.) For example, Thomas says that, insofar as bad actions possess something of action and being, they are from God; but "bad actions, according as they are defective, are not from God but from defective proximate causes" (*SCG* III. I. 71. 13).

However, there is doubt that this attribution of causality to creatures can be any more than merely verbal, at least causality in a sense that would be helpful in the attempt to defend God against full responsibility for the world's evils. The discussion of so-called defective secondary causes would only be relevant to protecting the goodness of God's will if these secondary causes could exert some activity of their own, or at least some passive resistance, which would prevent God's will from being perfectly fulfilled. But the very analogy used by Thomas, that of the artisan and his instrument, suggests that all the activity is God's, while the so-called secondary causes are merely instruments employed by God. And, to the extent that the analogy does suggest that there is some given stuff with which God must do the best that is possible, this suggestiveness is due precisely to that aspect of the analogue which cannot be retained in regard to the relation between God and the secondary causes. There is nothing which is "given" with which God must work; the so-called secondary causes are themselves creatures which are created *ex nihilo.* Any "defects" in them are there because God willed them. Accordingly, it is illegitimate to suggest that any evil in the effects produced by means of these secondary causes can be attributed to any defects which are not themselves due to God's will, and which therefore prevent God's will from being perfectly fulfilled.

Furthermore, Thomas himself explicitly says this. He states that there is really no such thing as "chance" in the universe, for nothing escapes the universal (divine) cause. And, he says that the secondary causes execute God's orders (*ST* I. 22. 3, ad 3), and that God's will is always fulfilled and cannot be hindered by a defect in a secondary cause (*ST* I. 19. 6, ans. and ad 3; I. 19. 8, ans.). In regard to moral evil, the "defective secondary cause" is, of course, the sinful human will. And Thomas says that God is the cause of our acts of free choice (*ST* I. 22. 2, ad 4). In regard to the relation of God and secondary causes in general, Thomas says: "The supreme agent does the actions of all inferior agents by moving them all to their actions and consequently, to their ends" (*SCG* III. I. 17. 7). Again it must be asked how these can be *our* actions if *God* is the one who *does* them. But, regardless of what one thinks about the meaningfulness of there being two sufficient causes for effects, it is clear that Thomas has not described the relation of "secondary causes," including acts of human "free choice," to God's causation in such a way as to introduce the slightest qualification in the conviction that all events, evil as well as good, happen because God wills them to happen and causes them to happen.

## THE DISTINCTION BETWEEN CAUSING AND PERMITTING

At this point the common Thomist teaching that God does not cause evil but only permits it (*ST* I. 19. 9, ad 3; I. 23. 3, ans.) should be examined. In the first place, the uselessness of the distinction for denying God's responsibility for moral evil has already been established by Thomas' own admission that even so-called acts of free choice are caused by God.

Second, Thomas says that God foreknows sinful acts, but permits them without causing them. But this implies a distinction between God's knowing and causing, and hence implies a violation of the divine simplicity. If God knows our thoughts and the motions of the will, as Thomas says (*SCG* I. 68. 1), then it follows that God causes them.

Third, Thomas himself says that permitting is not simply foreknowledge, but "something more" (*ST* I. 23. 3, ans.). And to indicate what this "something more" is, he refers back to a passage which points out that in God, will and intellect are identical (*ST* I. 22. 1, ad 3), which in turn refers to a passage which states that God's will-intellect is the cause of all things (*ST* I. 19. 4, ad 4). Hence a meaningful distinction between permitting and causing is ruled out not only by the implications of the essential core of Thomas' theism, but also explicitly by Thomas himself.

Fourth, Thomas, like Augustine, teaches that God is justified in punishing sinners because they sin freely, since God does not cause but only permits their sin. And Thomas follows Augustine's doctrine that being as such is good, and that a deficiency in being and a deficiency in goodness are one and the same thing. An immoral being is an example of a deficiency of being and hence of goodness. But Thomas also says that the reason some things have more good than others is that God loves them more, willing a greater good for them (*ST* I. 20. 3, ans.; cf. *SCG* I. 91. 10–11). This conclusion follows, of course, from the doctrine of divine simplicity, since in God will and love must be identical. This will-love is the cause of the being and thereby the goodness of things (*ST* I. 20. 2, ans.). This implies that any lack of moral goodness in a man would be due to the fact that God loved him less, and thereby caused less moral goodness in him. Accordingly, since God's relatively low degree of love for a particular man and God's decision to condemn him to eternal punishment are the cause rather than the result of that man's sin, Thomas has the same problem as did Augustine in justifying the goodness of God in relation to the predestination of some to eternal punishment. Thomas' God, even more clearly than Augustine's, does not simply "permit" angels and human beings to sin freely, but causes them to do so necessarily.

## THE DISTINCTION BETWEEN GOD'S ANTECEDENT AND CONSEQUENT WILLS

As stated above, Thomas in some contexts clearly states that all things that happen happen because they are willed by God. But he has another distinction which might be used to absolve God from blameworthiness for consigning some people to eternal punishment. As we saw in the previous chapter, Augustine suggested a distinction between two wills in God in order to handle the apparent contradiction between his own doctrine that God consigns most people to eternal punishment and the doctrine suggested both by Scripture and the doctrine of divine love that God wills all persons to be saved. Thomas develops this distinction between two wills, in the context of the same embarrassing contradiction, labeling them the "antecedent" and the "consequent" wills. The former is a qualified willing, since it considers something only in itself, and is antecedent to taking all relevant considerations into account. The consequent willing is absolute, since it is what is willed after taking these facts into account. Thomas suggests an analogy: a just judge may antecedently will that all men should live, because they are men. But he may consequently will that certain men be killed, after considering the additional fact that they are murderers. "In the same way God antecedently wills all men to be saved, but consequently wills some to be damned, as His justice exacts" (*ST* I. 19. 6, ad 1). But Thomas is again employing an analogy that is ruled out by his essential core of ideas. The distinction cannot be transferred to God precisely because of the differences between God and humans. First, the distinction of "antecedent" and "consequent" smacks of temporality, and there was said to be no "before" and "after" in the divine experience. Second, the analogy is vitiated by the crucial difference between human complexity and God's simplicity. The human judge can know that a man is a murderer and perhaps rightly condemn him, for the judge's knowledge is caused by prior facts. But God's knowing is creative, so any "additional circumstances" that God "takes into account" are factors caused by deity itself. So there is nothing left to the analogy to vindicate God's justness. Third, any distinction whatsoever in God is ruled out by the divine simplicity. Thomas himself admits this, saying that the distinction of antecedent and consequent applies not to the divine will itself, "but to the things willed" *(ibid.)*. And this qualification undercuts the whole argument.

## THE DENIAL OF GENUINE EVIL

If we were to conclude the analysis of Thomas' position on God and evil at this point, we would have to conclude that he holds that God freely decided to create a world with much natural and moral evil in it, even though God could have created a world totally devoid of such evil, and that God unilaterally decided which of the rational creatures would commit which sins, and likewise decided which of these rational creatures to subject to eternal punishment because of these sins. Faced with this picture, one might conclude that Thomas' theodicy implicitly involves a rejection of premise 1, that God is a perfect reality, or premise 4, that a perfect reality is a morally perfect being. But of course Thomas would not explicitly countenance either suggestion. Accordingly, one might suppose that Thomas would reject statement number 6, i.e., that he would appeal to the translogical mysteriousness of God and his ways. However, one would find little support in Thomas for constructing a defense of God, who is Reason and Truth itself, by rejecting the ultimate validity of logic.

This would leave us without any solution to the problem of evil that Thomas would recognize as his own. However, Thomas does not leave his analysis at this point. As was the case in Augustine, the affirmation that there is evil in the world is ambiguous. There are natural and moral evils in a *prima facie* sense, i.e., things which seem evil when the world is looked at from a limited perspective and when events are considered only within a limited context. But Thomas believes that in relation to the whole of reality there is no genuine evil, since nothing occurs which detracts from the perfection of the whole. The *prima facie* evils are only apparently evil; in reality they contribute to the perfection of the whole.

This position is clearly stated in the following passage:

> Since God, then, provides universally for all being, it belongs to His providence to permit certain defects in particular effects, that the perfect good of the universe may not be hindered, for if all evil were prevented much good would be absent from the universe. (*ST* I. 22. 2, ad 3)

Where Thomas speaks of "evil" in this statement, we should read "*prima facie* evil." For the term "permit" we should read "cause." And in contexts where Thomas is affirming this "greater good" argument, he has no need to try to disguise the fact that *prima facie* evils are willed and caused by God, since they are only apparently evil. For example, in a discussion of corruptible beings, he says:

> They can suffer a defect in their natural beings, yet such a defect works to the advantage of another being. For, when one thing is corrupted, another comes into being. Likewise, in their proper actions they may fall short of the natural order, yet such a failure is balanced by the good which comes from it. Thus, it is evident that not even those things which appear to depart from the order of the primary rule do actually escape the power of the First Ruler. Even these corruptible bodies are perfectly subject to His power, just as they are created by God Himself. (*SCG* III. I. 1. 6)

Thomas, like Augustine, affirms the Plotinian "principle of plenitude," that the perfection of the whole requires that every possible level of existence be actualized: "It pertains to divine providence that the grades of being which are possible be fulfilled" (*SCG* III. I. 72. 3). And he also agrees that things are good insofar as they are, so that the degree of being which something has is its degree of goodness. Accordingly, he affirms that perfect goodness in the creation requires that all possible grades of goodness be realized, and this means that some beings must be better than others (*SCG* III. I. 71. 3). He then concludes that this means that there must be some beings with the power to fall from the good *(ibid.)*. But this statement, that they merely have the power of falling from the good, and the assertion that "evil is the consequence of this power, because what is able to fall does fall at times" *(ibid.)*, is not the full implication of the principle of plenitude within the context of omnipotence. Within this context the principle must be understood as meaning that the perfection of the whole requires that things actually *do* fall from the good. And, as we saw earlier, all events must be attributed to God, since no creature has its own inherent power, even to fall from the good.

Accordingly, Thomas gives several justifications for the occurrence of *(prima facie)* evils: Since what is intrinsically good for an individual is instrumentally evil for others, because of the incompatibility of things when acting according to their own natures, preventing this form of evil would mean preventing much good (*SCG* III. I. 71. 4–5). Also, many goods could not occur unless there were evils; for example, the patience of the just is logically dependent (to use the modern terminology) upon the malice of their persecutors. Hence to prevent the evil would also mean preventing the good (*SCG* III. I. 71. 6). Furthermore, the presence of evil helps us both to know the good better by comparing it with evil, and also more ardently to desire the good (*SCG* III. I. 71. 8). Finally, the same aesthetic argument that we found in Augustine is clearly stated in the following passage:

> The good of the whole takes precedence over the good of a part. It is proper for a governor with foresight to neglect some lack of goodness in a part, so that there may be an increase of goodness in the whole. . . . But if evil were removed from some parts of the universe, much perfection would perish from the universe, whose beauty arises from an ordered unification of evil and good things. (*SCG* III. I. 71. 7)

No clearer statement could be desired for the idea that the *prima facie* evils of the world are only apparently evil when considered in the context of the whole of things. For in this context, far from detracting from the greatest possible good that could have been actualized, they are necessary to this greatest good.

Hence, Thomas Aquinas' own answer to the question as to why a good and omnipotent God permits and even causes evil is that God does not—there is no genuine evil. In the eighteenth century, Alexander Pope wrote:

> All discord, harmony not understood;
> All partial evil, universal good;

And, spite of pride, in erring reason's spite,
One truth is clear, Whatever is, is right.

Carl Becker has rightly commented that "Pope was merely repeating St. Thomas."[2] I have already suggested in the Introduction that I do not consider this answer viable. This issue will be explored more fully later.

However, I do not believe that Thomas' own final position is the position which the essential core of his theism implies. But before turning to this argument, it seems appropriate to examine the developments by contemporary Thomists of a couple of ideas suggested by Thomas.

## MARITAIN ON GOD'S PERMISSION OF EVIL

Although Thomas' own distinction between causing and permitting has already been rejected as inconsistent with the essential core of this theism, it should not be ruled out in advance that someone could modify the Thomistic position in such a way that this distinction could be meaningful. If so, then one might be able to defend God's moral goodness without the drastic step of denying the ultimate reality of evil in the universe. Jacques Maritain is one who has particularly emphasized the idea that God permits evil without causing it. This emphasis is shown by the title of his major work on theodicy, *God and the Permission of Evil.*[3]

Maritain believes that it is possible to remain true to the essentials of Thomism and yet make a more than verbal distinction between God's permitting and causing. He holds that one can maintain that "moral evil is permitted by God without being in absolutely any way willed or caused by Him" (*GPE* 1 n. 2; cf. *STPE* 37),[4] since it is possible to make sense of Thomas' assertion that "the first cause of the absence of grace comes from us" (*GPE* 5, citing *ST* I–II. 112. 3, ad 2). The key is to emphasize the *dyssymmetry of good and evil,* to which Thomas pointed (*GPE* 9).

This dyssymmetry is based on the principle that being is good, and that evil is a privation of due good, and hence really non-being. In the line of good, it is true that God is the first cause of our free decisions, "because there is not a fibril of being which escapes the causality of God." And God's knowledge is the cause of all being (*GPE* 10). But in the line of evil, the human being is the first cause, and evil is "known by God . . . without having been created by him" (*GPE* 10). In short, Maritain attempts to reconcile God's noncausation of evil with the doctrine that God's knowledge is the cause of all things by exploiting consistently the notion that evil is not a "thing" but a mere absence of being.

But if God is not the cause of evil, what is? Maritain rejects the view of some Thomists that the cause of moral evil is a privation (an absence of a due good), for this would be to say that evil is the cause of evil. This theory would not only involve a vicious circle (*GPE* 34); it would also make God the indirect cause of evil, for it implies that God withdraws the grace that would prevent this privation (*GPE* 30). What is needed is the insight that prior (at least logically) to the morally defective act is a "non-consideration of the rule," in which one is not reflecting upon rational and divine laws (*GPE* 34; *STPE* 25). This act is really a non-act, and as nonbeing it cannot be traced to God's causality. But it is not yet a privation of a due good, but a mere negation; for in a moment when a moral decision is not being made, it is not a sin not to be considering the rule. Hence, this moment in which the creature "dis-acts," or "nihilates," is not evil, but it is the cause of moral evil, in that the person in the next moment acts without having considered the moral rule (*GPE* 35, 45, 47, 48, 50 n. 5).

Maritain then explicates the difference between God's total causation of the good and God's mere permission of evil. Moral evil is possible where God gives a "shatterable motion," i.e., one "which causes the free agent to tend to a morally good act, but which includes . . . the possibility of being shattered" (*GPE* 37). This motion implies a general permission that the creature may opt for evil, if it takes the first initiative to do so (*GPE* 39). Hence the creature is responsible, for God's permissive decree does not cause the evil, but only involves the decision not to prevent it (*GPE* 63).

Coming from a Thomist, this is all rather startling. It seems to say that some creatures, at times at least, have genuine freedom to act either in a moral or an evil manner. But this raises the problem as to how evil can be known by God. Maritain seems to face a dilemma. If God is not the cause of evil, and yet knows it, the creature would seem to have an effect on God, violating God's impassibility (*GPE* 68 f.). The alternative seems to be that God knows evil in the same way as good, i.e., God's knowledge of it causes it. But this would bring us back to making God responsible for it.

Maritain admits that this is "the most difficult problem," yet he says: "It does not worry me excessively, since I know in any case, with certain knowledge, that God is absolutely not the cause of evil" (*GPE* 67). He suggests that reflecting upon the divine transcendence will lead to seeing that God can know evil without causing it, and without its having a causal effect on God. Although the things God created are truly known by God, there would be nothing changed in the divine act of knowledge (which is simply God) had God not created anything. Maritain refers to this as a "mystery" (*GPE* 69). But this is surely one of those places where "contradiction" would be the more appropriate term.

He further asks, rhetorically, how evil, which is nonbeing, could affect the divine knowledge, when even created *being* cannot affect it (*GPE* 74). But the answer here is that being is infallibly *caused* by the divine knowledge, whereas nonbeing allegedly is not. Maritain concludes by saying that we are speaking here of things which are entirely above our own comprehension, so that we can only hope to find the slenderest thread of intelligibility (*GPE* 75). It may seem ungenerous to say so, after he has conceded so much, but it is hard for me to find even the slenderest thread of intelligibility in all this.

The difficulty is increased by the fact that Maritain, in line with the idea of shatterable motions, says that everything in the world is "adventure and improvisation," that God takes real risks, and even that the creatures invent forms of horror that "astonish the Author himself" (*GPE* 80, 85). This seems a clear violation of divine nontemporality and impassibility. But then we learn that the suggestion of temporality involved in such speaking is not to be taken literally (*GPE* 91 f.), and that in God's eternal plan everything is infallibly established—there is no event with the slightest indetermination (*GPE* 91). Everything is established in a single and indivisible flash of the divine will to which is present every detail, nihilations and all (*GPE* 94). Now we have returned to essential Thomism. But when we do so, the whole idea that there are shatterable motions which allow the creatures to be the first causes of some acts (or "non-acts") is undercut. Maritain tries to reconcile the two sets of statements by saying that God's eternal plan takes account of all that happens, including the nihilatings of created liberty (*GPE* 98, 113; cf. *STPE* 38 f.). He says, for example, that if Judas had not taken the initiative that led to the betrayal of Jesus, a different eternal plan would have been immutably established by the divine will (*GPE* 97). But this implies an illegitimate distinction between God's knowing and his causing, not to mention the difficulty in the idea that Judas had some type of decision-making reality "prior" to the divine decision to create this particular world.

Furthermore, even if some slender thread of intelligibility were granted all this, Maritain has not supported "God's absolute innocence of all moral evil," for he says that God could give unshatterable motions to all persons. This would protect them against any nonconsideration of the rule, and thereby from all moral evil (*GPE* 38 f., 110 n. 30). Hence, despite what Maritain usually maintains, it is God who takes the first initiative in regard to moral evil, by withholding unshatterable motions. If one asks why, the answer is: "God gives unshatterable motions to whom he will. This is the mystery of the divine free predilections" (*GPE* 39). This also seems to imply that might makes right, so that Maritain would be throwing in doubt premise 4 (that God is a morally perfect being), since "might makes right" is unacceptable to most people formed by the Judeo-Christian tradition as a statement of what is involved in moral perfection.

However, this does not adequately reflect what Maritain believes. Another Thomistic idea central to his thought is the idea that "God permits evil only in view of a greater good" (*GPE* 62). God does what is best for the whole, not for the parts taken separately (*STPE* 6, ref. to I. 48. 3). Hence, the reason all persons have not been given unshatterable motions is that "doubtless" the perfection of the whole required fallible beings (*STPE* 17). In other words, Maritain, like Thomas himself, must finally give up the attempt to use the distinction between permitting and causing to save God's goodness in the face of genuine evil in the universe, and deny that there is any genuine evil, on the principle that the apparent evils in the world are necessary for the perfection of the whole.

## JOURNET AND THE DENIAL OF A BEST POSSIBLE WORLD

Charles Journet, in his attempt to work out a contemporary Thomist theodicy in his book *The Meaning of Evil*,[5] picks up on a different suggestion made by Thomas, the suggestion that God could have created a better world. The position which Journet develops out of this suggestion is in some tension with the idea that the universe is perfect by virtue of its apparent evils. He does state that every evil is the occasion for a greater good than would have been realized otherwise; and he even speaks of the perfection of the universe (*ME* 80, 83). However, he rejects the Leibnizian suggestion that the universe is perfect in the sense of being the "best of all possible worlds."

Journet, expanding on Thomas' suggestion that God could have created a better world (*ST* I. 25. 6, ad 3), says that God could have created a universe in which there would be no evil (*ME* 91, 104 f.). This introduces an apparent dilemma. On the one hand, if God did not "do his best," God's moral goodness seems to be doubtful. On the other hand, Journet wants to protect God's freedom, and he agrees that, if this were the best possible world, God would have been obliged to create it (*ME* 110). His solution is to deny that it is meaningful to talk about God's "doing his best," for there is no "best possible world."

The argument is as follows: (A) If God creates, it is to give outward expression to the infinite good that deity is in itself (*ME* 110). (B) But any created world will be finite, and as such will be infinitely removed from being an adequate expression of God's goodness (*ME* 111). (C) Hence, even if God had created a world many times better than this one, there would still be an infinite number of better worlds (*ME* 110). (D) Accordingly, it is meaningless to indict God for not having done better, for no matter how much better God might have done, it would have been possible to do still better. (E) This shows the falsity of the principle: "If God could have created a world totally devoid of evil, he ought to have done so." All that can be claimed is that, if God creates, God is "bound to create a world of which the sum total will be good" (*ME* 104).

However, there is a nonharmless shift in this argument from one meaning of "better world" to another, and a correlative shift in the meaning of "evil." One meaning of "evil" and "better world" is the meaning probably suggested to most people by the statement that "God could have created a better world than this, in fact one devoid of evil." But Journet's argument uses another meaning of "evil" and hence another meaning of "better world."

This other meaning presupposes the Plotinian-Augustinian universe in which there are degrees of being which are also degrees of goodness. Evil is the privation of good. Accordingly, since being and goodness are identical, evil is a privation of being. God is infinite being and hence infinite goodness. The universe is a reflection of the infinite goodness. There are an infinite number of possible universes. But any particular universe must be finite. And the gap between the finite and the infinite is an infinite gap. Accordingly, the universe can never be an adequate reflection of God, who is infinite being-goodness.

From this complex of ideas it can be deduced that a universe will necessarily be evil. For, if being and goodness are identical, and good and evil are opposites, the statement that evil is a privation of being can be reversed, so that a privation or lack of being is evil. Since any possible universe will necessarily have a lack of being in comparison with infinite being, any possible universe will necessarily be evil. This is the kind of evil which some authors (e.g., Leibniz) have called "metaphysical evil." It is simply the evil (if such be regarded as evil) of being finite rather than infinite. Accordingly, any world will be evil, even if there is no sin or suffering (moral or physical evil) in it. And, since there are an infinite number of possible worlds, any particular possible world will have an infinite number of better possible worlds above it, i.e., ones with less metaphysical evil.

It is this notion that Journet uses to argue that it is meaningless to speak of God's "doing his best" in the sense of creating the "best possible world." And if this argument is sound and relevant, it undercuts the premise which Journet rightly sees to be necessary to argue that God is morally indictable for not creating a world that would be better because devoid of natural and moral evil, i.e., the premise that "a morally perfect being will always do its best."

However, this whole procedure involves a shift to a meaning of "evil" and "better world" that is not generally assumed when people ask why omnipotent goodness did not create a better world, one with less evil and more good. In asking such a question, few if any critics are asking why the world is not infinite, i.e., why it is not God. Rather, they are asking about the moral and physical evil, i.e., the sin and suffering; more specifically, they are asking about the apparently great excess of sin and suffering over that amount which could reasonably be considered necessary as the occasion for some of the higher forms of good.

Furthermore, there does not seem to be any close connection between physical and moral evil on the one hand, and so-called metaphysical evil on the other. In the first place, there is probably little connection between them in the minds of most people who think about the problem of evil. Those things which are lower on the scale of being (by whatever criteria this is measured) are considered more evil metaphysically by those philosophers and theologians who use this category. For example, most would say that a flea has less being than a dog or a human. Accordingly, it would be metaphysically more evil. But how many people have this lesser being in mind when they regard fleas as evil? Rather, they are probably thinking of the fact that fleas cause discomfort to both dogs and human beings. The question of the fleas' lower status may enter into the picture, but only in the sense that the nuisance value of the flea for dogs and people seems more evil in the light of the fact that the flea has so little intrinsic value. Those beings with low intrinsic value which are not thought to be harmful to humans and the things humans care about, and which are not regarded as aesthetically repulsive, are probably not included on most people's informal list of evils in the universe. In other words, introducing the subject of so-called metaphysical evil diverts the discussion to issues that are quite unrelated to the forms of evil most people have in mind when wondering about the reason for evil in God's world.

In the second place, there seems to be no necessary connection between metaphysical evil and physical and moral evil which would allow both to be understood in terms of the idea of "privation of being." On the one hand, the idea of various levels of being, to the degree that it makes sense, seems to apply to the differences *between* various species. For example, one can somewhat intelligibly say that living beings have more being than nonliving ones; and that among living beings mammals with a central nervous system have more being than plants and other animals. On the other hand, moral and physical evils represent defects *within* a species, therefore a distortion of the perfection proper to a certain level of being, not a mere privation of being in comparison with some other species. For example, a deformed baby is evil, not because it is a human and not a conceivable superhuman being, but because it does not have all the characteristics that are proper to the human species. A dog with rabies is evil because it has rabies, not because it is not a human. A morally evil person such as Hitler is considered evil not because he was not God but because he was a grotesque distortion in some respects of what we think a human life should be. In short, there is a great difference between physical and moral evils on the one hand and so-called metaphysical evil on the other, a difference which is blurred by subsuming them both under the notion of "privation of being."

In summary, when someone suggests that God, to be omnipotent and morally perfect, should have created the best world possible, the person means that God should have created a world devoid of all unnecessary moral and physical evil, or sin and suffering—unnecessary for the production of higher goods that compensate for the *prima facie* evils in question. And Journet has said that a world devoid of moral and physical evil is a possible world, and that God could have created it (*ME* 91, 104 f.). Accordingly, there would seem to be an intelligible meaning to the idea of a "best possible world," as long as the discussion of good and evil is limited to the moral and physical forms of evil. But Journet then denies that we can say God should have created such a world. He does this by introducing another, quite different and unrelated notion of "best world," one that he himself admits, indeed insists, is devoid of meaning. He rightly says that, since this notion of a best of all possible worlds is meaningless, one cannot, on the basis of this notion, say that God should have done "his best," since this would be meaningless. But what Journet has failed to do, and could not in principle do, is to show how the fact that there is a meaningless notion of "best world" and of "God's doing his best" can cancel out the principle that God should do "his best" by creating the "best possible world" in the sense in which this *does* make sense! The existence of statements that have the verbal form of moral principles but are not in reality moral principles because they contain words or phrases that are devoid of meaning can never negate the validity of genuine moral principles. Accordingly, Journet has not given any good reason why God did not create a world without genuine moral and physical evil in it.

And in fact, Journet finally follows Thomas Aquinas and Jacques Maritain in asserting that there is no genuine evil in the world. For he endorses the idea of "O felix culpa," saying that God "only allowed the corruption of the evil of sin into this first universe because he foresaw the setting up of a universe of redemption which as a whole would be better" (*ME* 124; cf. 259). However, although this rejection of premise 7 is the solution that Thomas and Thomists seem finally to affirm, it is questionable whether this is the premise which the essential core of Thomism requires be rejected. In the following chapter, I will argue that there is a sense in which it is premise 4 that must be rejected.

## CONCLUSION

I take Thomas simply to have stated more clearly than others what is involved in the traditional synthesis of Hebrew and Greek ideas of deity. In particular, Thomas stated with utmost clarity (even though he sometimes tried to avoid its implications) the doctrine of divine simplicity which is required by the assumption that deity must be totally devoid of process. With no change of any kind in God, there can be no distinction between an (eternal) essence and (changing) actualizations of this essence; nor can there be any way in which God's various "attributes" could be different from each other. Hence, although I have spoken in this chapter primarily of the "essential core of Thomistic theism," the attributes discussed belong in fact to the "essential core of traditional theism."

One of the purposes of stressing the interconnections among these attributes is to point out that the problem of evil cannot be solved by "tinkering" with the traditional concept of God, i.e., by modifying only one or another of the attributes. This set of attributes forms a coherent whole such that one cannot be rejected without rejecting the rest. As stated earlier, this applies strictly to the first five. It applies to the last two (omniscience and omnipotence) in a qualified sense: one could not give up the first five without giving up the last two, i.e., in their traditional meanings, since the last two presuppose the first five. But since the first five do not presuppose the last two, these two could be given up without giving up the first five, by rejecting divine causation on and knowledge of the world altogether. Of course, this would mean giving up the Biblical aspects of the doctrine of God, leaving something like Aristotle's Self-thinking Thought or Plotinus' One. So this move is not possible in the development of a theodicy relevant to the religious faiths based upon the Biblical traditions. Accordingly, for the purposes of constructing such a theodicy, the statement can stand that a change in one of the attributes requires a change in all of them. In other words, if traditional theism is rendered untenable by the problem of evil it engenders, then a solution will be found not by a slight modification here or there in the traditional idea of God, but only, if at all, by completely reconceiving the idea of a perfect reality.

# 8
# Spinoza: Everything Is Simply Divine—Unorthodox Conclusion from Orthodox Premises

BENEDICT (BARUCH) SPINOZA (1632–1677) argued that God creates this world in all its details from necessity, not from free choice, and in fact that all the individual things in the world are in God as mere modes of God's attributes. This implies that the world is divine. But it also implies, as Charles Journet points out, that God would be neither moral nor immoral, but simply amoral.[1] Journet rejects this position. But it is questionable whether traditional theists, and especially Thomists (since Thomists particularly stress the divine simplicity), can avoid Spinoza's conclusion if they reason consistently from their premises. Spinoza says they cannot, and I believe he is right.

Spinoza defines substance as that which exists independently of everything else (I, Def. 3),[2] and in agreement with traditional theism he defines God as an infinite substance (I, Def. 6). He believes that if God is really infinite, there can be no other substances (I, Prop. 14). It follows from this that whatever is, is in God (I, Prop. 15). What we call individual things are mere modes of God's attributes (I, Prop. 25). Therefore, since there is no contingency in God (as all traditional theists agree), there can be no contingency in the world (I, Prop. 29, Demonst.). From this basis Spinoza can conclude that everything is as it eternally had to be, so that either praise or blame of either God or humans is inappropriate.

This argument rests upon taking "infinite" literally, so that an infinite being would have to be all-inclusive. If there were anything "outside" of God, God would by definition not be infinite. However, most traditional theists have insisted that deity's infinity is compatible with a world external to God, as long as this world does not "limit" God. And, of course, their doctrines of omnipotence and impassibility entailed that the world did not limit God in any way. They went on to argue that lack of contingency in God was compatible with the world's contingency, so that creation and providence were understandable as free acts on God's part. Accordingly, although I believe there *is* a problem of consistency in holding both that God is infinite and that there is a world external to God, we need to see whether there is an argument for the world's divinity and God's lack of freedom vis-à-vis the world that does not depend upon the literal meaning of "infinite being."

One of Spinoza's arguments depends upon the strict meaning he assigns to "substance." A substance is that which does not depend upon anything else. On the basis of this definition Descartes had said that God was the only substance in the proper sense of the term, but that finite bodies and minds were substances in a secondary sense, in that they fulfilled the definition except for their dependence upon God as their creator and sustainer. Spinoza simply refuses to allow this qualified type of substance, saying that by definition one substance cannot produce another (I, Prop. 6), and concludes that bodies and minds can only be modes of the one infinite substance. On this basis he states that whatever is, is in God, since there can be no other substance, and modes can exist only in a substance (I, Props. 15, 25). And from this he draws his conclusions about the noncontingency of all things.

However, the traditional theist can still regard this as an external criticism, dependent upon an arbitrary definition of "substance" or "actual thing" which he does not share. The traditional theist holds that the idea of a "dependent (upon God) substance" is perfectly legitimate, and on this basis he maintains that there is a real world of substances or actualities dependent upon but external to God. Spinoza's position need not be taken very seriously by traditional theists unless his unorthodox conclusion can be deduced from premises which traditional theists themselves accept.

Spinoza points to the crucial premise. He states that the doctrine that the divine intellect is the cause of all things is "a truth which seems to have been understood by those who have maintained that God's intellect, will, and power are one and the same thing" (I, Prop. 17, Schol.; cf. II, Prop. 7). In other words, the crucial premise is that of the divine simplicity. Spinoza himself rejects the idea that deity in itself has "will" or "volition" in any but an equivocal sense (I, Prop. 17, Schol.; I, Props. 31, 32). But he says that, even if will be granted to God, the conclusion that God created this world by necessity still follows from the perfection (by which he primarily means the unchangeableness) of God. His argument can be constructed out of his own words in the following five steps:

A. Traditional theists agree that "it depends upon the decree and will of God alone that each thing should be what it is."
B. "It is also admitted that all God's decrees were decreed by God himself from all eternity, for otherwise imperfection and inconstancy would be proved against Him."
C. "But since in eternity there is no *when* nor *before* nor *after,* it follows from the perfection of God alone that He neither can decree nor could ever have decreed anything else than that which He has decreed; that is to say, God has not existed before His decrees, and can never exist without them."
D. "If God had decreed something about nature and her order other than that which He has decreed—that is to say, if He had willed and conceived something else about nature—He would necessarily have had an intellect and a will different from those which He now has."
E. "But since His intellect and His will are not distinguishable from His essence, as all admit, it follows from this also that if God had had another intellect and another will, His essence would have been necessarily different . . . , which is absurd." (I, Prop. 33, Schol. 2.)

I see no way that one can avoid this conclusion, given the premises. If God's nature is eternal and necessary, and God's will is identical with God's essence, then God's will must be equally eternal and necessary. This, plus the doctrine that nothing can prevent God's will from being perfectly fulfilled, leads to Spinoza's conclusion: all things flow necessarily from God's nature. Accordingly, the world is not a free creation, but is as fully necessary as God. And from this it is difficult to see how one can resist the further conclusion that all things are parts or "modes" of God. If God's necessary existence does not distinguish God from all worldly beings, what basis is there for insisting upon a distinction? It seems that Spinoza is right—one can say "God or Nature." Hence, if God be simple, then all of reality must be included in this simple divinity.

Let us look now at the distinctions made by Thomas Aquinas to avoid the conclusion that God creates the creation necessarily, so that the world is as necessary as God and hence divine. Thomas says that "from the fact that God wills from eternity whatever he wills, it does not follow that he wills it necessarily, except by supposition." This means that, "supposing that he wills a thing, then he is unable not to will it, as his will cannot change." That is, being "necessary by supposition" is to be distinguished from being "absolutely necessary" (*ST* I. 19. 3; *SCG* I. 83. 1–3). But this is a distinction without a difference. For just as one cannot meaningfully say "supposing God exists," since God exists necessarily, one cannot meaningfully say "suppose God wills so and so," since God's existence, essence, and will are all identical, so that whatever God wills is willed necessarily. As Spinoza says, God "acts by the same necessity by which he exists" (IV, Preface).

Equally invalid is Thomas' much-used distinction between what is "natural" to God and what is "voluntary" (*ST* I. 19. 3, ad 2; I. 20. 10, ans.; *SCG* I. 82. 9; III. I. 1. 1), since God's nature (essence) and God's will are identical. The statement that God could "make more than He makes," even though "He cannot know more than He knows" (*ST* I. 14. 15, ad 2), implies an illegitimate distinction between God's knowledge and causation. The statement that God necessarily knows other things but does not necessarily will them (*SCG* I. 81. 7) implies an illegitimate distinction between God's knowing and willing. Nor can Thomas legitimately say that, since the present order of creation does not adequately express the divine wisdom, God can do things other than those that are done (*ST* I. 25. 5, ans.). This again implies a distinction between God's knowing and causing. Finally, the famous distinction between God's absolute and ordained power (*ST* I. 25. 5, ad 1) implies a denial of God's simplicity, and suggests some unactualized potency in this *actus purus.*

Accordingly, all statements made by traditional theists which suggest that God was free to create or not create, or to create one world instead of another, are based upon *ad hoc* distinctions that are incompatible with the essential core of traditional theism, and this incompatibility is especially evident when the doctrine of simplicity is stressed, as it is by Thomas. Spinoza is correct that his necessitarianism is simply a more consistent statement of the implications of the traditional Jewish-Christian idea of God. And if this is correct, then the premise that is in effect denied by traditional theists is number 4—not because God is immoral, but because God is amoral, since all beings which are devoid of free choice are beyond good and evil. This unorthodox conclusion follows, as Spinoza shows, from premises held by orthodox theologians.

Of course, on this basis God is absolved from responsibility for evil. But this "solution," which few major philosophers and theologians have been willing explicitly to accept, involves a rejection of divine attributes which have been widely accepted as belonging to "perfection" because of the impact of the Biblical suggestions about God, namely, freedom and moral goodness. Spinoza's rejection of these attributes, in the name of perfection understood as infinity, absolute independence, and immutability in all respects, points to the fact that traditional theism has been an attempt to join together two incompatible notions of perfection. A solution that does not involve an at least implicit denial of Biblically inspired notions of perfection will have to involve a rejection of some of the notions inspired by Greek thought.

# 9
# Luther: The Explicit Denial of Creaturely Freedom

IN MANY RESPECTS the writings of the Protestant reformers differ significantly from those of the medieval scholastic theologians, such as Thomas Aquinas. But it is one of the purposes of this and the following chapter to argue that Luther and Calvin do not differ substantively from other traditional theists, such as Augustine and Aquinas, in regard to those doctrines which are central to the problem of the relationship between God and evil. The only significant difference is the greater clarity with which they admit—indeed insist upon—the fact that the God in whom they believe is responsible for all that occurs.

The analysis of Luther's position will be based solely upon his *On the Bondage of the Will.*[1] Luther addresses himself in this work directly to the issues with which we are concerned, and himself brings together the various considerations that are relevant to the problem of evil.

## THE IMPORTANCE OF BELIEFS

Luther's name has been associated with theological positions in which the importance of the intellectual content of faith *(fides quae creditur)* is played down in favor of the subjective form of faith *(fides qua creditur)* to such an extent that faith as trust is sometimes seen as rendering faith as belief unnecessary (and perhaps even detrimental). It is perhaps necessary to point out that this was not Luther's own understanding of faith. Early in his book he considers Erasmus' statement that "it is irreligious, idle and superfluous to want to know whether our will effects anything in matters pertaining to eternal salvation, or whether it is wholly passive under the work of grace." He first criticizes Erasmus for being inconsistent, since Erasmus makes assertions which do imply a position on this issue (609–614).[2] Then Luther asserts that it is "in the highest degree wholesome and necessary, for a Christian to know whether or not his will has anything to do in matters pertaining to salvation." In fact, he says, if we know nothing of "what ability 'free-will' has, in what respect it is the subject of Divine action and how it stands related to the grace of God . . . we shall know nothing whatsoever of Christianity" (609–614). He continues:

> For if I am ignorant of the nature, extent and limits of what I can and must do with reference to God, I shall be equally ignorant and uncertain of the nature, extent and limits of what God can and will do in me—though God, in fact, works all in all (cf. I Cor. 12:6). Now, if I am ignorant of God's works and power, I am ignorant of God himself; and if I do not know God, I cannot worship, praise, give thanks or serve Him, for I do not know how much I should attribute to myself and how much to Him. We need, therefore, to have in mind a clear-cut distinction between God's power and ours, and God's work and ours, if we would live a godly life. (609–614)

Reinforcing this further, Luther says that where these things are not known, "there can be no faith, nor any worship of God. To lack this knowledge is really to be ignorant of God—and salvation is notoriously incompatible with such ignorance" (614–620).

Clearly, Luther's distinction between saving faith and mere *fides historica* does not mean that he was not seriously interested in the noetic side of faith, or that he understood faith to be a "practical" or "existential" matter in such a way as to exclude concern for "theoretical" issues. I will now proceed to examine his position on the theoretical problem of evil.

## THE EXPLICIT DENIAL OF FREE WILL

The chief verbal difference between Luther, on the one hand, and Augustine and Thomas Aquinas, on the other, is that Luther rejects any attempt at a "free-will defense" of God's justice in the light of the adversity of the good and the prosperity of the wicked in this life, and God's decision to punish some while rewarding others in regard to the future life. Luther begins his critique of the notion by saying that those who would speak about free will should first decide whether it exists. He then offers his "bombshell" which "knocks 'free-will' flat, and utterly shatters it." This is the bombshell: "that God foreknows nothing contingently, but that He foresees, purposes, and does all things according to His own immutable, eternal and infallible will" (614–620).

Without using the word "simplicity," Luther presupposes the doctrine in arguing that, if God's nature remains unchanged to all eternity, this must be true of all the divine attributes, and that this implies that God must foreknow by necessity. He then asks:

> Do you suppose that He does not will what He foreknows, or that He does not foreknow what He wills? If He wills what He foreknows, His will is eternal and changeless, because His nature is so. From which it follows, by resistless logic, that all we do, however it may appear to us to be done mutably and contingently, is in reality done necessarily and immutably in respect of God's will. For the will of God is effective and cannot be impeded, since power belongs to God's nature. (614–620)

Having stated the conclusion which one would not find stated with such clarity in either Augustine or Thomas Aquinas, Luther then attacks one of the distinctions used by scholastics (Luther called them "Sophists") to obscure this conclusion:

> They maintained that *all things take place necessarily, but by necessity of consequence* (as they put it), *and not by necessity of the thing consequent.* By this distinction they eluded the force of their own admission—or rather, *de*luded themselves! I shall not find it hard to show how unreal the distinction is. By *necessity of consequence,* they mean, roughly speaking, this: If God wills something, then it must needs be; but that which thus comes to be is something which of itself need not be; for only God exists necessarily, and everything else can cease to be, if God so wills. . . . So their absurd formula . . . amounts merely to this: everything takes place by necessity, but the things that take place are not God Himself. But what need was there to tell us that? . . . So our original proposition still stands and

> remains unshaken: all things take place by necessity. There is no obscurity or ambiguity about it. (614–620)

Luther then cites statements made by "heathen poets" about Fate, and common remarks made by "ordinary people," such as "God so willed," to argue that "the knowledge of predestination and of God's prescience has been left in the world no less certainly than the notion of the Godhead itself" (614–620). In other words, Luther does not consider the ideas of divine foreknowledge and predestination to be matters uniquely derived from "special" (Biblical) revelation, but to belong to the "general" revelation given to all peoples. (As one who rejects both of these ideas, I must insert as an aside: Would that Luther had rejected "natural theology" as completely as some of his exponents claim that he did!)

One possible misinterpretation of Luther's position on free will should be precluded at this point. It is sometimes said that Luther in *The Bondage of the Will* is not interested in the abstract, philosophical problem as to whether we are free in general, e.g., in regard to whether we have coffee or tea for breakfast, but only in the particular, theological question as to whether we have, apart from God's freeing grace, the ability to *do good.* In other words, some claim that Luther is thinking concretely and theologically about men and women in the fallen state of original sin and is only saying that, although we can choose between this and that, whatever we do will be evil; and in particular that we can do nothing to earn our own salvation.[3]

Luther certainly is saying this. And this is certainly the question in which he is most interested. But this is not all he is saying. His "bombshell" is that God does *all things* according to God's infallible will. And part of Luther's reasoning is that the necessity of all things follows from the fact that God surely wills and does what God foreknows—and this includes all things. Luther does seem to give sanction in one place for the interpretation which I am rejecting, as he says that, if Christians are to speak of our "free-will," it must not be in respect of what is above us (matters of salvation or damnation) but only in respect of what is below us (money and possessions). However, Luther quickly adds that even "that very 'free-will' is overruled by the free-will of God" (634–639). Furthermore, at the end of the book Luther summarizes his arguments against free will. One of them is indeed that "original sin has ruined us to such an extent that . . . in a man who lacks the Spirit nothing is left that can turn itself to good, but only to evil." But this is the third of five arguments. The first one is:

> If we believe it to be true that God foreknows and foreordains all things; that He cannot be deceived or obstructed in His foreknowledge and predestination; and that nothing happens but at His will (which reason itself is compelled to grant); then, on reason's own testimony, there can be no "free-will" in man, or angel, or in any creature. (784–786)

This argument is summarized prior to any mention of the effects of original sin, and the particular problem of the human inability to do good. And it is concerned with *all* creatures, including angels, not just humans; hence the lack of free will cannot be due solely to Adam's sin, nor can it be simply the inability to do good.

Luther differs from Augustine and Thomas Aquinas, then, in that they preferred to ascribe "free will" to us verbally, while denying it in effect, while Luther does not even ascribe it to us verbally. He says that " 'free-will' is obviously a term applicable only to the Divine Majesty. . . . If 'free-will' is ascribed to men, it is ascribed with no more propriety than divinity itself would be—and no blasphemy could exceed that!" (104–107.) There is only one sense in which the term would not be inappropriate:

> If we meant by "the power of free-will" the power which makes human beings fit subjects to be caught up by the Spirit and touched by God's grace, as creatures made for eternal life or eternal death, we should have a proper definition. And I certainly acknowledge the existence of *this* power, this fitness, or "dispositional quality" and "passive aptitude" (as the Sophists call it), which, as everyone knows, is not given to plants or animals. As the proverb says, God did not make heaven for geese! (104–107)

But Luther thinks that theologians should refrain from using the phrase "the power of free-will" for speaking of human ability, since "the mass of men are sadly deceived and misled by this phrase." The false idea of free will "is a real threat to salvation" (104–107).

This leads to what is probably the major reason (besides his antipathy toward "sophistical distinctions") why Luther states without qualification that God necessitates all things, while Augustine and Thomas Aquinas had hedged this logical conclusion around with qualifications. Augustine and Aquinas were most concerned to justify the prescriptions to do good works, and to protect God's goodness by insisting that God does not cause sin. But Luther was most concerned about the certainty of salvation. His lack of concern for the problem of exhortation in relation to God's sole efficacy is expressed in this passage:

> Who, you say, will take pains to correct his life? I answer: No man will and no man can, for God cares nothing for your correctors without the Spirit, since they are hypocrites. But the elect and the godly will be corrected by the Holy Spirit, while the rest perish uncorrected. . . . Who will believe, you say, that he is loved by God? I answer: No man will or can believe this; but the elect will believe while the rest perish in unbelief, indignant and blaspheming as you are here. So some will believe. (630–634)

And his primary concern for the certainty of salvation is expressed in the following passage:

> If you hesitate to believe, or are too proud to acknowledge, that God foreknows and wills all things, not contingently, but necessarily and immutably, how can you believe, trust and rely on His promises? When He makes promises, you ought to be out of doubt that He knows, and can and will perform, what He promises; otherwise, you will be accounting Him neither true nor faithful, which is unbelief, and the height of irreverence, and a denial of the most high God! And how can you be thus sure and certain, unless you know that certainly, infallibly, immutably and necessarily, He knows, wills and will perform what He promises?. . . . If, then, we are taught and believe that we ought to be ignorant of the necessary foreknowledge of God and the necessity of events, Christian faith is utterly destroyed, and the promises of God and the whole gospel fall to the ground completely; for the Christian's chief and only comfort in every adversity lies in knowing that God does not lie, but brings all things to pass immutably, and that His will cannot be resisted, altered or impeded. (618–620)

Luther states further on this subject:

> I frankly confess that, for myself, even if it could be, I should not want "free-will" to be given me, nor anything to be left in my own hands to enable me to endeavour after salvation. (783)

Since salvation is totally under the control of God's will, and God has promised to save not by our works but by his own mercy,

> I have the comfortable certainty that He is faithful and will not lie to me, and that He is also great and powerful, so that no devils or opposition can break Him or pluck me from Him. (199)

## A THEODICY OF REASONABLE FIDEISM

However, although it is not his first concern, Luther is not unaware of the problems of theodicy. He remarks:

> You may be worried that it is hard to defend the mercy and equity of God in damning the undeserving, that is, ungodly persons, who, being born in ungodliness, can by no means avoid being ungodly, and staying so, and being damned, but are compelled by natural necessity to sin and perish. (784–786)

Since Luther has emphatically rejected the free-will defense, and has openly admitted, even insisted, that God necessitates the unbelief of sinners as well as the faith of believers, how can he defend God's righteousness? His position is essentially fideistic—we should show deference "by believing Him just when to us He seems unjust" (784–786). In fact, Luther comes close to justifying the appearance of divine injustice as a necessary condition for genuine faith:

> This is the highest degree of faith, to believe him merciful when he saves so few and damns so many, and to believe him righteous when by his own will he makes us necessarily damnable, so that he seems . . . to delight in the torments of the wretched and to be worthy of hatred rather than of love. If, then, I could by any means comprehend how this God can be merciful and just who displays so much wrath and iniquity, there would be no need of faith. (632–633)

However, Luther does give grounds for considering this fideism reasonable:

> If His justice were such as could be adjudged just by human reckoning, it clearly would not be Divine; it would in no way differ from human justice. But inasmuch as He is the one true God, wholly incomprehensible and inaccessible to man's understanding, it is reasonable, indeed inevitable, that His justice also should be incomprehensible. (784–786)

Also, nature and reason teach us that our wisdom, power, and substance are nothing compared with God's, and that God is incomprehensible in all respects. So it is very perverse for us to presume to comprehend and evaluate God's judgment (784–786).

Furthermore, Luther gives justification for his fideistic position by making a distinction between two divine wills. On the one hand, there is the "revealed will." This is God as offered to us, preached in the Word, and worshiped; this is the will of God with which we should be concerned. On the other hand, there is the "hidden will" of God.

> This will is not to be inquired into. . . . Wherever God hides Himself, and wills to be unknown to us, there we have no concern. (684–686)

This is "God as He is in His own nature and Majesty." And in this respect God "is to be left alone; in this regard, we have nothing to do with Him, nor does He wish us to deal with Him" (684–686).

It is in terms of this distinction that Luther answers the kinds of questions that Thomas Aquinas answered with the distinction between the "antecedent" and "consequent" wills of God. Like the "antecedent" will, the "revealed" will desires that all persons be saved. And, like the "consequent" will, the "hidden" will determines all things. Accordingly, Luther says that God as revealed desires that all persons be saved, and hence does not will the death of a sinner. But deity in its inscrutable will does will it. Deity hidden in its majesty has all things under its powerful hand, and works all in all, including the death of sinners; and God does not deplore this death. But we are not to try to live by this inscrutable will; this would be impossible, since it is inscrutable. "It is enough simply to know that there is in God an inscrutable will." It is unlawful to ask such questions as to why God does not remove the faulty will of people who do not receive God, since only God has the power to remove it; "or why He lays this fault to the charge of the will, when man cannot avoid it" (684–686).

Whereas there is some similarity to Aquinas' distinction, the primary effect of Luther's talk of God's "hidden" will is to point to the necessity of faith in God's inscrutable justice. There is no attempt, as there is in Thomas' employment of the idea of God's "consequent will," to suggest that God's efficacious will is subsequent to foreknowledge of creaturely free will. Luther does, to be sure, come close to indulging in cant in his discussion of God's hardening of hearts, as he speaks of the evil will which is "already" in us and which God "finds there" when God works in us. And he says that "God works evil in us (that is, by means of us) not through God's own fault, but by reason of our own defect, we being evil by nature." And he says that God "cannot but do evil by our evil instrumentality." Worst of all, Luther says that when God causes a man to do evil, he is made to act by his own willing, so that "no violence is done to his will; for it is . . . impelled to will naturally, according to what it is (that is, evil)." (711–714.) This discussion is reminiscent of scholastic attempts illegitimately to suggest that we have some power of our own by which we have determined our own nature. Hence, Luther is here guilty of speaking as if his own insistence that God necessitates *all* things were not strictly true.

However, he quickly raises the questions that are suggested by his own doctrine of omnipotence and his insistence that God in majesty has set no "bounds to Himself by His Word, but has kept Himself free over all things" (684–686). This statement is evidently a rejection of the doctrine of some nominalist theologians that God, who has the absolute power to do anything that is not self-contradictory, has made a commitment to follow certain divinely ordained laws. Luther asks why God does not simply alter the evil wills that God moves; why God let Adam fall when this could have been prevented; and why God created us all tainted with Adam's sin, when God could have created us out of other material, or from seed that had been cleansed. To these questions Luther says:

> It is not for us to inquire into these mysteries, but to adore them. If flesh and blood take offence here, and grumble, well, let them grumble; they will achieve nothing; grumbling will not change God! (711–714)

## ANALYSIS OF LUTHER'S POSITION

What, then, is Luther's answer to the theoretical problem of evil? Which premise would he reject? It is not immediately clear. In terms of the heavy stress on inscrutability in the discussion thus far, one might suppose that Luther denies statement number 6, which assumes the validity of logic in matters pertaining to deity. However, he severely chastized Erasmus for his inconsistency in such issues. And further considerations suggest that Luther's position lies elsewhere.

There is a sense in which one might plausibly say that he rejects premise 4, i.e., that God must be a morally perfect being. One could reasonably maintain that we cannot *meaningfully* say that God is morally good unless we believe God to be good according to the principles that *we recognize* as moral principles. And, as we saw, Luther says that divine justice, by definition, must be different from human justice, and not recognizable as just by our reckoning. On this basis, one could claim that Luther is using terms such as "just" and "morally good" equivocally, and hence is in effect denying God's moral perfection. Furthermore, Luther says:

> God is He for Whose will no cause or ground may be laid down as its rule and standard; for nothing is on a level with it or above it, but it is itself the rule for all things. If any rule or standard, or cause or ground, existed for it, it could no longer be the will of God. What God wills is not right because He ought, or was bound, so to will; on the contrary, what takes place must be right, because He so wills it. (711–714)

On the basis of this type of statement a critic might claim that Luther is saying that "might makes right" and that this is, from the critic's point of view, a denial in effect that God is a moral being.

The question as to how the right (or the good) is related to the will of God is, of course, an old and hoary problem. Can some principle that is not inherently right morally be made so simply by God's will? That the two (right and God's will) are not strictly identical is suggested by the fact that we can always ask whether we should obey the will of God. On the other hand, others like Luther argue that, if God wills something because it is right, this implies that there is some higher standard logically antecedent to the will of God, and that the belief in some higher standard than God's will is self-contradictory, for its undercuts God's divinity.

However, we do not need to resolve this problem now in order to decide how to characterize Luther's theodicy (although I will later return to this problem). For Luther points to a solution to the problem of evil which shows that he does not reject God's moral goodness, even by equivocation. For he, like Augustine, says that, although for the time being we cannot see that God is just but must simply *believe* it, "when He reveals His glory we shall all clearly *see* that He both was and is just!" (784–786.)

In order to give us some reason for believing that the eschaton will show that God is just in showing mercy to some and condemning others, Luther suggests a "parallel case." He distinguishes three lights —the light of nature (natural reason), the light of grace, and the light of glory. God governs the external affairs of the world in such a way that by the light of nature one must conclude that there is no God, or that God is not just. For it is inexplicable by natural reason that the good should be afflicted while the wicked prosper (784–786). But this aspect of the problem of evil "is most easily cleared up" by the gospel, the light of grace, for it gives us this explanation:

> *There is a life after this life; and all that is not punished and repaid here will be punished and repaid there; for this life is nothing more than a precursor, or rather, a beginning, of the life that is to come.* (784–786)

This answer which the light of grace provides creates a new problem, of course.

> By the light of grace, it is inexplicable how God can damn him who by his own strength can do nothing but sin and become guilty. Both the light of nature and the light of grace here insist that the fault lies not in the wretchedness of man, but in the injustice of God; nor can they judge otherwise of a God who crowns the ungodly freely, without merit, and does not crown, but damns another, who is perhaps less, and certainly not more, ungodly. (784–786)

However, Luther asks, since the light of grace so easily swept away the problem that was insoluble by the light of nature, is it not reasonable to believe "that the light of glory will be able with the greatest ease to solve problems that are insoluble in the light of the word and grace"? The light of glory "will one day reveal God, to whom alone belongs a judgment whose justice is incomprehensible, as a God Whose justice is most righteous and evident" (784–786).

Accordingly, Luther is saying that, although God's justice and therefore moral perfection is incomprehensible to us now, this is *not* because it is a justice that is incomprehensible to creatures as such, so that the word "justice" must necessarily be used equivocally by finite beings when discussing divinity. Rather, it is only incomprehensible to us now because the full story has not yet been revealed to us. And Luther would surely affirm with Augustine that on judgment day it will be revealed to us "with what justice so many, or almost all, the just judgments of God in the present life defy the scrutiny of human sense or insight" (*CG* XX: 2).

Luther's intended answer is therefore best regarded not as an implicit denial of the validity of logic or of the moral perfection of God, but as the rejection of premise 7. That is, Luther follows Augustine and Aquinas in denying the reality of any genuine evil. God's judgment controls every detail of the external matters of this world and of the internal matters of belief and unbelief, and every detail of the future life. And it is evident from a more inclusive perspective than we now have, i.e., the perspective which God now has and which we will partially share when God's glory is revealed, that God's judgment in all these matters is just.

## CRITIQUE OF LUTHER'S POSITION

My tone in summarizing Luther's position has thus far been basically positive. But this has been due to my appreciation for his clarity in stating what the traditional doctrine of God implies about God's causation of *(prima facie)* evil, including sin. Of course, this clarity is not due solely to greater intellectual acumen and/or honesty, but at least partly to the fact, pointed out previously, that Luther perceived his primary theological concern to be supported more than undercut by the clear statement that God alone has the power to effect anything. But clarity of statement, all other things being equal, is a good, regardless of the contributing factors.

However, not all other things are equal. Adequacy is generally a higher good than consistency. And Augustine and Aquinas, in insisting upon the reality of free choice, however inconsistent with their basic theistic premises, were being more adequate to human experience in general and Christian faith and experience in particular than was Luther with his more consistent position. And in thereby insisting, however inconsistently in regard to the essential core of their theism, that God is not the direct cause of sin, Augustine and Thomas Aquinas were being truer to the basic substantive tenet of Christian faith, that God is love, than was Luther, who had to ask us to believe in the goodness of a God who condemns most persons to eternal punishment for sins that God directly and unequivocally causes them to commit. And Luther is somewhat inconsistent insofar as he suggests that this appearance of injustice on God's part is necessary if we are to have real faith, since Luther elsewhere makes clear that the issue of whether or not we have faith is eternally and unilaterally settled by God.

There are other problems to raise with Luther's solution. First, there is the problem of necessitarianism raised in the chapters on Thomas Aquinas and Spinoza. In his mockery of the distinction between the necessity of consequence and the necessity of the thing consequent, Luther assumes that it makes sense to say, "*If* God wills. . . ." But does it? As Luther himself pointed out, if God's nature is eternal and immutable, so is God's will. But the eternal and the necessary are equatable. Accordingly, whatever God wills must be willed necessarily. Hence, God could not have chosen not to create, or to have created another world. So the "free will" which Luther denies to creatures must, as Spinoza says, also be denied to God.

Furthermore, Luther says we need no one to tell us that the world is not God. However, I believe that Spinoza is not only right (on the basis of traditional premises) in saying that the world could not have been otherwise; he is also right in concluding from these premises that it cannot be other than God. If the world is as strictly necessary (and not only necessary by supposition) as God, then the divine and the nondivine among actual things cannot be distinguished as the necessary and the contingent. Furthermore, Luther denies, consistently enough, all power to the world, lodging all power in God. But upon what basis other than (at least partially) autonomous power can one actuality be distinguished from another? So, if what is called "world" is as necessary in all its details as what is called "God," and if the apparent individuals in this "world" have no power to act, there seems to be no sufficient basis to avoid following Spinoza in calling the whole thing "God."

This problem of ontology and semantics aside, there is another problem with Luther's solution. He asks us to have faith in a supernatural solution. But he does not ask for completely blind faith. He offers the "parallel case" based on the "three lights" to show that it is not unreasonable to believe that God is just, although we cannot understand this justice even in the gospel light of grace. He says that, since the light of grace clears up the problem that was insoluble by the light of nature—i.e., why the good suffer and the wicked prosper—it is reasonable to suppose the light of glory will clear up the problem insoluble by the light of grace, i.e., why God saves some and damns others when all are guilty of sin and the sin itself was necessary. But this solution is problematic. For if we cannot now see how this second problem can possibly be solved, then even the first problem has not been solved for us. In fact, one can well claim that it has been aggravated. Not all the "wicked" prosper in this life; many if not most of them have a relatively unpleasant existence. (Those who hold that "virtue is its own reward," and that virtue is necessary for an intrinsically rewarding life, would hold it to be axiomatic that the wicked would not be happy.) If we are then told that they will suffer eternally for their wickedness, even though this wickedness was necessitated in them by God, then there is no compensation for these persons offered by the doctrine of the future life, but only an apparent compounding of unjust suffering. When this problem is added to the other problems that have been raised against the theodicies based upon supernatural rewards and punishments (e.g., the disproportion between the crime and the punishment), one must conclude that Luther's attempt to make the fideistic supernaturalistic solution somewhat "reasonable" by means of the "parallel case" fails.

It is the traditional doctrine of omnipotence which necessitates a supernaturalist theodicy. There are several reasons for being far more dubious of this doctrine of omnipotence today than there were in medieval and Reformation times. To discuss most of these in the context of a criticism of the theodicy of Luther would be somewhat anachronistic, as they presuppose a cultural context quite different from his. (For example, a comparatively small percentage of people in "Christendom" today would accept the basic premise of Luther's theodicy, viz., that "this life is nothing more than a precursor . . . of the life that is to come.") Accordingly, most of these reasons for rejecting the traditional doctrine of omnipotence will not be discussed until Part III. But there are a couple of points that can appropriately be discussed at this time, since they could have been recognized by Christian theologians in medieval and Reformation times.

One has already been parenthetically mentioned in passing. This is the fact that Luther, who was quite critical of "natural theology" in some respects, still retained a doctrine of God that was not sufficiently reformed by the implications of the basic formal point of Christian faith, that God was supremely revealed in Jesus. Luther's doctrine of the two wills of God, the revealed and the hidden, not only separates God's loving mercy from God's power, but makes the latter more ultimate. God's hidden will is said to be "God Himself"; and this hidden divine Majesty is said to be inscrutable—except that we know it absolutely controls all things. Accordingly, Luther is in effect saying that the essence of deity is power—coercive, deterministic, monopolistic power. And Luther himself recognizes that there is nothing particularly Christian about this idea of God, as he sees it as expressed by "heathen poets" and in the common proverbs of humanity. The Christian idea that God is merciful love, rather than being used by Luther to reform the whole idea of deity, and especially the idea of divine power, is simply added on as a secondary characteristic. Any doubt as to which of the two "wills" of God is supreme is removed by Luther's own statement that God hidden in majesty is not bound by the revealed word, and is removed further by the fact that, wherever there is tension between the two wills (as on the question as to whether God wills all persons to be saved), it is the hidden will that determines the actual situation. It is Luther's assumption of this unreformed idea of divine omnipotence that necessitates the supernaturalistic solution, a solution that can be regarded as raising at least as many problems as it solves.

Another critical point to raise about Luther's supernaturalistic solution to the problem of evil is that it provides no solution at all to the problem of animal pain. As we saw, Luther quotes approvingly the proverb that God did not make heaven for geese. So how does one understand that an omnipotent and perfectly good creator and provider would permit, indeed cause, so much apparently unnecessary and unuseful pain among subhuman sentient beings? One possible solution to this problem, the Cartesian one of denying sentience to all subhuman beings, was probably almost as unconvincing in previous centuries as it is in post-Darwinian times. Another possible anthropocentric solution, that all animal pain is justified by its instrumental value to humans, is extremely dubious. It would take only one case of unnecessary, unuseful suffering to nullify it. Luther's own answer would doubtless be that we cannot expect to find a solution, but that we should have faith that the light of glory will provide one. This would certainly take faith, insofar as it is difficult to imagine what the justification could be; but one must admit that there *might* be one. This answer would force into the foreground one of the basic issues that is raised by Luther's theodicy in general, viz., does an acceptable theodicy need to provide a merely *possible* answer, or does it need to provide a *probable* answer? This issue will be discussed in relation to the theodicy of Leibniz.

In summary: Luther does not provide us with an acceptable theodicy for today. But his admirable clarity does help us to see more clearly what traditional theism entails about the relation between God and evil. And he helps us to see more clearly than most others what options we have if we are not to give up belief in a deity relevant to the faiths based upon the Biblical tradition: either give up the traditional notion of omnipotence, or take God's goodness on blind faith.

# 10
# Calvin: Omnipotence Without Obfuscation

ALTHOUGH an analysis of John Calvin's position on God and evil will be somewhat repetitious of the chapters on Augustine, Aquinas, and Luther, especially the latter, it will be helpful for seeing even better the implications of traditional theism. Like Luther, Calvin spells out these implications with little of the obfuscation present in the writings of many other theologians because of their introduction of subtle and illegitimate distinctions. And Calvin spells out these implications in more detail than Luther. Furthermore, much of the reaction against the God of traditional theism in modern thought has the God of Calvinism explicitly in mind, so it will be helpful in understanding this rejection to see what Calvin himself said.

In his discussion of God's omnipotence, providence, and predestination, Calvin makes it as clear as our previous three theologians that he would not reject either premise 2 or premise 3 of the formal statement of the problem of evil. He rejects ideas of divine omnipotence that regard it as a mere general impulse to the order of nature, or as an *ability* to do all things which sometimes sits idle. Rather, he says God is called omnipotent because "he so regulates all things that nothing takes place without his deliberation" (I. xvi. 3).[1] Coming close to saying explicitly that God's omnipotence means a monopoly on power, Calvin says that an inanimate object "does not exercise its own power except in so far as it is directed by God's ever-present hand," and that these objects are "nothing but instruments to which God continually imparts as much effectiveness as he wills" (I. xvi. 2). And he says that no creatures have any intrinsic power to harm us (I. xvi. 3). Nor is it simply the inanimate objects that are totally controlled by God, "but also the plans and intentions of men" (I. xvi. 8). There are not a multiplicity of self-moving movers in Calvin's universe; rather, God "is the beginning and cause of all motion" *(ibid.).* There are not a plurality of decision-makers: anytime one asks why something occurs, "we must always at last return to the sole decision of God's will" (III. xxiii. 4). In short, the "omnipotence of God" means that "he regulates all things according to his secret plan, which depends solely upon itself" (III. xxiii. 7).

According to Calvin's doctrine of providence, therefore, there is no chance in the universe. And this covers not just the general course of things but also the particular details (I. xvi. 1, 2). The Scriptures show that "not one drop of rain falls without God's sure command," and that "not even a tiny and insignificant sparrow falls to the ground without the Father's will." God determines it "when a branch breaking off from a tree kills a passing traveler." Also, "no wind ever arises or increases except by God's express command" (I. xvi. 5, 6, 7). Some mothers' breasts are fuller than others because God wills to feed some babies more liberally (I. xvi. 3). It is because of God's special favor that some women are barren while others have offspring (I. xvi. 7).

This doctrine of providence means that it is erroneous to suggest that anything is moved contingently, or that man can turn himself "hither and thither by the free choice of his will." And it is wrong to suggest that human affairs are due partly to God's providence and partly to human free choice. We have no free choice. Calvin endorses Augustine's statement that it would be absurd to hold that anything has happened without God's ordaining it, since this would mean that it happened without a cause (I. xvi. 4, 6, 8).

This view implies that "every success is God's blessing, and calamity and adversity his curse" (I. xvi. 8). And everything that happens happens by necessity. Calvin does look more kindly than Luther upon the distinction between relative and absolute necessity, and that between necessity of consequent and necessity of consequence; for these distinctions stress that no event is necessary of its own nature. But Calvin does not equivocate on the point that "what God has determined must necessarily so take place" (I. xvi. 9).

True to his intention to assert without equivocation God's total control of the world, Calvin rejects the distinction between God's "willing" and "doing" on the one hand, and God's "permitting" on the other. He recognizes that the motive behind this distinction is the desire to protect God's justice, since it seems absurd to some "for man, who will soon be punished for his blindness, to be blinded by God's will and command." However, Calvin responds, the Scriptures testify "that men can accomplish nothing except by God's secret command." And, he continues:

> They babble and talk absurdly who, in place of God's Providence, substitute bare permission—as if God sat in a watchtower awaiting chance events, and his judgment thus depended upon human will. (I. xviii. 1)

The notorious implication of the rejection of this distinction is Calvin's doctrine of "double predestination." He considers it both ignorant and childish to try to protect God's justice by saying that God elects some to salvation without condemning others to damnation. "Those whom God passes over, he condemns; and this he does for no other reason than that he wills to exclude them from the inheritance which he predestines for his own children." Accordingly, "God does not permit but governs by his power." Although Paul softens the harshness of the clause about the "vessels of wrath" in Rom. 9:22, "it is utterly inconsistent to transfer the preparation for destruction to anything but God's secret plan" (III. xxiii. 1). The reason why some accept the gospel and others do not is completely God's eternal election (III. xxi. 1). The reason all do not repent is that God does not will the repentance of all (III. xxiv. 15). Calvin agrees with Augustine that the Scripture passage which says that God wills all persons to be saved means only that God has not closed the door to any class or type of people (III. xxiv. 16).

Calvin also rejects as absurd any attempt to protect God's justice by saying that predestination is based upon God's foreknowledge of sin and merits. Election is the cause of virtue, not vice versa (III. xxii. 1, 2). And Calvin rejects a "subtlety" of Thomas by which the latter tries to make foreknowledge of merit the cause of predestination not on God's side but on ours (III. xxii. 9). Calvin maintains that there is no cause outside God's will for hardening some and showing mercy to others (III. xxii. 11). This doctrine means that Calvin will not follow those who try to maintain that humans are responsible and therefore guilty for our sins by saying that God's foreknowledge does not prevent us from being accounted sinners since the evils which God foresees are ours, not God's. Calvin's response to these theologians' "quibbling" is that, since God

> forsees future events only by reason of the fact that he decreed that they take place, they vainly raise a quarrel over foreknowledge, when it is clear that all things take place rather by his determination and bidding. (III. xxiii. 6)

Calvin sees that the only difference between his views and those of medieval traditional theists which is relevant to the problem of evil is that he states more clearly what is implied by this theistic position. But if he rejects the distinction between divine permitting and causing, how can he possibly justify belief in God's goodness, in the light of the evil in this life and the eternal punishment of people in the future existence? The evils of this life he forthrightly says are all curses from God. This is to be believed whether they apparently come through a human or a nonhuman agent, since, as we saw earlier, neither one really has any inherent power to cause harm (I. xvi. 8; I. xvii. 8; cf. I. xvi. 3). And the suffering in the future life is, of course, justified as punishment for sin in this life. But by what right does God punish any of us, in this life or the next, if in fact our wicked intentions and deeds were willed and caused by God?

Calvin attempts to answer this by employing a distinction between God's "will" (or "hidden," or "secret," or "effective" will) and God's "precept" (or "commanding will"). Just as Luther said we are to live by the revealed will of God, even though it is sometimes in tension with God's hidden will, Calvin says we are to be guided by God's precepts as revealed in Scripture (I. xvii. 2–5). When we fail to do so, we are guilty and are justifiably punished. Since Calvin does not always use his terminology consistently, his argument for this is somewhat confusing. Against those who say that sinners are God's ministers, since they do the divine will, Calvin first denies that they serve God's will (I. xvii. 5). Here he means God's "commanding" will. But then he grants that murderers and other evil doers *are* instruments of divine providence *(ibid.).* Here, of course, he means God's "hidden" or "effective" will. But how can God will (with a hidden will) that which is sinful for us, such as murder? Here Calvin appeals to Augustine's statement that "there is a great difference between what is fitting for man to will and what is fitting for God." And he further agrees with Augustine that "in a wonderful and ineffable manner nothing is done without God's will, not even that which is against his will" (I. xviii. 3).[2]

Calvin says this distinction removes the chief objection against God's justice, i.e., that since God governs the plans and intentions of the wicked, "men are undeservedly damned if they carry out what God has decreed because they obey his will." The problem with this objection is said to be that it involves a confusion between God's "will" and "precept," whereas they are "utterly different" (I. xviii. 4). The principle we are told to hold is this: "While God accomplishes through the wicked what he has decreed by his secret judgment, they are not excusable, as if they had obeyed his precept which out of their own lust they deliberately break." Of course, Calvin has clearly stated that the men could not have done otherwise—the secret will of God necessitates all things. But he says that in condemning individuals for their sin—e.g., Judas for his betrayal—"God does not inquire into what men have been able to do . . . but what they have willed to do" (I. xviii. 4). In short, we are justifiably condemned for our sinful acts, and even our sinful will to commit these acts, even though we could not have willed other than we did.

Internal to this argument (that we are responsible for what we will, even though we could not will otherwise) is the distinction between primary and secondary causation. Calvin discusses this topic in the more colorful terms of "naked" and "clothed" providence. Naked providence would be God's effecting something without using secondary agencies, whereas God generally clothes this providence by using secondary instruments as means. On the basis of this distinction Calvin argues that the doctrine that God effects all things does not remove the necessity for prudence and sloth-avoiding activity, since these are instruments used by God (I. xvii. 4). God's activity does not mean that we do not act: "Man, while he is acted upon by God, yet at the same time himself acts" (I. xviii. 2). "Man falls according as God's providence ordains, but he falls by his own fault" (III. xxiii. 8). Accordingly, God's providence does not exculpate our wickedness (I. xvii. 5).

This line of argumentation is very weak. Calvin has emphatically denied that we have any power whatsoever to exert causation of our own, so not even the slightest degree of evil desire could be ours prior to God's causation upon us. And Calvin himself repeatedly says that we cannot desire and will other than we do, since God totally causes this desiring and willing, down to the tiniest detail. One must say that, although he is comparatively free from it, Calvin does engage in some obfuscation when he says that "man himself acts" even though the actions are totally caused by God. Had Calvin been even more consistent in his rejection of illegitimate distinctions, he would have also given up that between primary (or principal) and secondary causes, since he has openly stated that the so-called secondary causes really contribute nothing of their own to the effect. In fact, the term "cause" is used equivocally in this distinction (as Karl Barth recognizes), and hence meaninglessly. This will be argued further in the chapter on James Ross.

This line of argumentation is also weakened by Calvin himself, as he retracts the distinction between God's two wills. After having said that God openly forbids by his law that which he decrees by his secret plan, he says:

> Yet God's will is not therefore at war with itself, nor does it change, nor does it pretend not to will what he wills. But even though his will is one and simple in him, it appears manifold to us because, on account of our mental incapacity, we do not grasp how in divers ways it wills and does not will something to take place. (I. xviii. 3)

Upon reading that God's will is not in tension with itself, and yet that it does and does not will the same thing, one can only suspect that something other than "our mental incapacity" is causing problems here. Furthermore, since we learn that there are not really two "utterly different" wills in God, but only one will, and we know that this one will is the cause of all events, any plausibility there might have been to the idea that we sometimes act against the will of God is completely undercut.

And Calvin really knows this. His major defense of the goodness of God lies elsewhere. His defense is that God really needs no defense. Or, to put it more precisely, there need be no defense that we can understand.

There is a defense of sorts, and this is the one that we have found to be finally required by the previous traditional theists, i.e., that there is no genuine evil in the universe. Calvin repeats the theme that God uses evil to do good (I. xvii. 5). And he says that we should accept every adversity without anger or impatience, since we know that God has willed it, and "he wills nothing but what is just and expedient" (I. xvii. 8). Most explicitly, Calvin says that the final outcome will show "that God always has the best reason for his plan" (I. xvii. 1).

However, when we examine the possible reasons that Calvin suggests, questions arise. For these possible reasons are:

> either to instruct his own people in patience, or to correct their wicked affections and tame their lust, or to subjugate

> them to self-denial, or to arouse them from sluggishness; again, to bring low the proud, to shatter the cunning of the impious and to overthrow their devices. *(Ibid.)*

This sounds plausible until one recalls what Calvin had said about God's omnipotence and providence. Since every detail of the world, including the deepest recesses of the human spirit, are what they are because God so willed, one wonders why anyone needs lessons in patience and self-denial, and why anyone has problems with wicked affections, lust, sluggishness, pride, and cunning impiety. God could have prevented these problems in the first place. Or, if God thought it better for some reason to cause them so that they could be removed, it would seem better for God simply to remove them directly, with "naked providence," rather than to employ indirect means that cause suffering in people who could not have avoided having these problems. This especially seems the case since God's direct causation upon the human spirit will still be needed, since this is what will finally determine precisely how people respond to the adversities with which they are confronted.

Calvin anticipates this objection, and the one raised earlier about the justice of God's punishing people for "sins" which they could not avoid, by saying that there is in "the Father's secret plan a broader justice than simply punishing each one as he deserves" (I. xvii. 1). So here Calvin openly admits that God inflicts adversities on people which they do not "deserve." And, in regard to the doctrine of double predestination, he labels as "frivolous" the argument that "since God is Father of all, it is unjust for him to forsake any but those who by their own guilt previously have deserved this punishment" (III. xxiv. 17).

This notion of a "broader" or "higher" justice leads us toward Calvin's real answer. Many passages, in part because of their content and also in part because of Calvin's sometimes indelicate way of expressing himself, suggest that his only answer is that we puny creatures are perverse even to question whether God is really good. For example, Calvin notes that some have raised objections to his doctrine of God's incomprehensible providence:

> Today so many dogs assail this doctrine with their venomous bitings, or at least with barking: for they wish nothing to be lawful for God beyond what their own reason prescribes for themselves. (I. xvii. 2)

Arguing that this doctrine is not his own, but is based upon Scripture and thus God's authority, Calvin says of those who oppose his doctrine of providence:

> What will they gain by spitting at the sky? Indeed, an example of such petulance is not new, for in every age there have been impious and profane men, who have frothed and snarled against this portion of doctrine. But they shall surely feel to be true what the Spirit declared of old through David's mouth, that God may overcome when he is judged (Ps. 51:4). David indirectly reproves the madness of men in the very unbridled license with which, out of their own filthiness, they not only argue against God, but claim for themselves the power to condemn him. (I. xviii. 3)

Against these "venomous dogs," Calvin indicates that his position —that no theodicy is really needed—is simply an echo of Paul's: "And Paul does not, as do those I have spoken of, labor anxiously to make false excuses in God's defense: he only warns that it is unlawful for the clay to quarrel with its potter (Rom. 9:20)." (III. xxii. 1.) In response to the question: "Whence does it happen that Adam's fall irremediably involved so many peoples, together with their infant offspring, in eternal death unless because it so pleased God?" Calvin says: "The decree is dreadful indeed, I confess." Yet he says that here the tongues of God's self-proclaimed defenders must become mute (III. xxiii. 7). At the close of his discussion of election, with its doctrine of reprobation, Calvin says:

> Let this be our conclusion: to tremble with Paul at so deep a mystery; but if froward tongues clamor, not to be ashamed of this exclamation of his: "Who are you, O man, to argue with God?" For as Augustine truly contends, they who measure divine justice by the standard of human justice are acting perversely. (III. xxiv. 17)

However, there is more to Calvin's position than simply the naked assertion that it is perverse to question God's judgment. Implicit in the foregoing, and at the center of Calvin's position, is the doctrine that God's will is *by definition* right. For example, he says that by the name "God's will" is designated "the supreme rule of righteousness" (III. xxiii. 5). Further, he states that "God's will is so much the highest rule of righteousness that whatever he wills, by the very fact that he wills it, must be considered righteous." This is the main reason why it is perverse to go beyond the answer that things happen as they do because God so willed. "If you proceed further to ask why he so willed, you are seeking something greater and higher than God's will." This does not mean, Calvin insists, that his is a "lawless God who is a law unto himself." Rather, the will of God is "the highest rule of perfection, and even the law of all laws" (III. xxiii. 2). Hence, God's ordinance, which destines some to destruction, "has its own equity—unknown, indeed, to us, but very sure" (III. xxiii. 9). But we cannot comprehend this law which is higher than our own standard of justice, since it has not been revealed to us. Calvin is here, of course, referring to the distinction between the hidden and the revealed will of God. The latter provides our own standard of righteousness; but at the same time we must remember that there is a higher standard by which God actually determines all things. The depth of God's secret judgment is such that our minds would be swallowed up if we tried to penetrate it. Yet it is wrong to condemn God's judgments the moment we do not comprehend them (III. xxiii. 4).

Calvin says that it is this position which lies behind Paul's famous statement in Rom. 9:20–21. When Paul answers the question about God's righteousness in preparing some vessels for wrath with the question, "Who are you, O man, to argue with God?" and then gives the analogy of the potter and his clay, this is no subterfuge, and not simply a statement that "God has a power that cannot be prevented from doing whatever it pleases him to do." Rather, Paul's point is that "divine righteousness is higher than man's standard can measure, or than man's slender wit can comprehend" (III. xxiii. 4). And Calvin believes this to be a satisfactory answer to every facet of the problem of evil, including that of the decree he himself confesses to be dreadful. He says that the Lord does not "need any other defense than what he used through his Spirit, who spoke through Paul's mouth" (III. xxiii. 5).

How are we to evaluate Calvin's position as a possible response to the problem of evil? I believe there are two major objections to be raised. These objections are most appropriately raised in relation to Calvin, because of the clarity and character of his relevant statements. But they could have been raised in relation to Augustine, Thomas Aquinas, and Luther, and hence are intended to be valid in relation to their thought also.

The first objection has to do with a central inconsistency in Calvin's position. Generally an internal criticism points out an inconsistency between two or more statements, each of which is deemed necessary to the articulated position. And we have seen that there are some inconsistencies of this type in Calvin's writings. For example, he first denies and then grants that murderers are ministers of God's will; he says that God does and yet does not will two contrary things; and he often speaks as if we are causes of things even though he explicitly lodges all causality in God. However, we have seen that these contradictions constitute the small amount of obfuscation found in Calvin's writings, and that none of them is essential to his theodicy, which simply makes God's will right by definition.

But there is a slightly different type of inconsistency. This is inconsistency between an author's explicit statements, on the one hand, and basic presuppositions which all persons inevitably hold in practice even if they deny them verbally, on the other. It is these basic presuppositions which must be used as the ultimate check upon the tenability of any profferred system of thought. For if we cannot help believing them, it simply does not make sense to doubt their truth. Accordingly, any position that denies one or more of them, whether explicitly or only implicitly, must be considered in that respect false. For example, David Hume presupposed the validity of causation, in the sense of the real influence of one thing upon another (so that the latter event implies the former, even if the reverse—the deterministic thesis—is not true), even while denying it verbally. Hume recognized that he still believed in causality "in practice," i.e., in his daily life. Accordingly, he made the distinction between "theory" and "practice" into a dichotomy, so that he assumed things in practice which he denied in theory, and denied things in theory which he did not—and in fact recognized that he *could* not—deny in practice. But this dichotomy means a radical rejection of the law of noncontradiction, the basic law of reasonable thought. Two propositions, one of which contradicts the other, cannot both be true. And beliefs involve propositions, whether these beliefs be labeled "theoretical" or "practical." Accordingly, if a proposition involved in an author's explicit statements contradicts propositions involved in his or her implicit beliefs, that author is guilty of self-contradiction. And if at least one of the implicit beliefs involved is deemed to be one of those basic presuppositions which we all hold in practice, then the author's position must be regarded as false, insofar as it depends upon that verbal denial of one of our undeniable assumptions.

I find Calvin to be involved in this type of inconsistency. The basic presupposition in question is that of the human capacity or power for the type of free choice that makes us responsible for our actions and even intentions, in the sense of being blameworthy or praiseworthy. As we saw, Calvin explicitly rejects the idea that we have any power of free choice. He says that we have no power to do anything—God does everything. And Calvin, like Luther before him, can state this doctrine much more unambiguously than most previous theologians, since for him the advantages of believing it outweigh any disadvantages occasioned by the problem of evil (cf. III. xxi. 3). For, with the belief in God's providence, we are set free from every anxiety and fear. This belief frees us from the fear of other creatures "as if they had some intrinsic power to harm us" (I. xvi. 3). And this includes Satan, for he and his crew "are not only fettered, but also curbed and compelled to do service" (I. xvii. 11). Calvin summarizes the benefits that come from knowledge of divine providence: "Gratitude of mind for the favorable outcome of things, patience in adversity, and also incredible freedom from worry about the future all necessarily follow upon this knowledge" (I. xvii. 7).

It is in regard to the "patience in adversity" that the inconsistency in Calvin's thought is most clearly evident. In expanding upon this virtue, he says:

> If there is no more effective remedy for anger and impatience, he has surely benefited greatly who has so learned to meditate upon God's providence that he can always recall his mind to this point: the Lord has willed it; therefore it must be borne, not only because one may not contend against it, but also because he wills nothing but what is just and expedient. To sum this up: when we are unjustly wounded by men, let us overlook their wickedness (which would but worsen our pain and sharpen our minds to revenge), remember to mount up to God, and learn to believe for certain that whatever our enemy has wickedly committed against us was permitted and sent by God's just dispensation. (I. xvii. 8)

This is clearly what the practical implication of the doctrine of absolute divine providence should be. But when Calvin vilifies his opponents, referring to them as "venomous dogs" and the like, the fact that he shares our inescapable belief in human freedom shines through. Calvin quite often wraps himself in the Holy Scriptures, saying that those who reject his teaching are really rejecting God's teaching. For example, he says of those who reject his doctrine of providence:

> As if what we teach were a figment of our brain, and the Holy Spirit did not everywhere expressly declare the same thing and repeat it in innumerable forms of expression. But, because some shame restrains them from daring to vomit forth these blasphemies against heaven, they feign it is with us that they are contending, that they may rave more freely. (I. xvii. 2)

It is hard to believe that Calvin would have spoken in such tones had he *really* believed that his opponents were directed by God to argue against his teachings as much as Calvin himself was directed by God to teach these things. Furthermore, in maintaining that those who oppose his idea that God causes all things are blaspheming against the Holy Spirit, he is in effect saying that the Holy Spirit has caused these men to blaspheme against Itself. This tension is seen further in the fact that Calvin says we cannot speak except as God wills us to speak (I. xvi. 6), and yet he says that those who replace the doctrine of providence with that of permission "babble absurdly" (I. xviii. 1). Does this not mean that Calvin is implicitly criticizing God for having caused Thomas Aquinas to speak of permission? Furthermore, against those who are hesitant to teach the doctrine of predestination openly, Calvin replies that they arrogantly "accuse God indirectly of stupid thoughtlessness, as if he had not foreseen the peril that they feel they have wisely met" (III. xxi. 5). But Calvin's doctrine of providence entails that God causes all events as completely as God caused the writing of the Bible. Hence, when Calvin holds that the teachings of his opponents are wrong and perilous, is he not indirectly accusing God of inspiring false and harmful teaching?

The point of the preceding argument is that Calvin was not true to his own statement that belief in his doctrine of providence should lead the believer to be patient with his adversaries. Perhaps because he recognized this inconsistency, he tried to justify it. In the paragraph immediately following the one recommending that the believer overlook the wickedness of others since God is the true cause of their actions, he states that the believer should not overlook the secondary causes. And this entails that the believer should not excuse a crime on the pretext of divine providence, "but in this same evil deed he will clearly contemplate God's righteousness and man's wickedness, as each clearly shows itself" (I. xvii. 9).

Certainly between these two contradictory attitudes, of overlooking man's wickedness or clearly contemplating it, one must say that Calvin himself primarily exemplified the latter one, especially in relation to his doctrinal opponents. But the question here is not Calvin's character, but his consistency. And it is inconsistent to say that we should both overlook and contemplate a person's wickedness. And, as the quote above shows, this problem is related to the schema of primary and secondary causation, which we have discussed before and will again, and which, in any case, Calvin himself in effect rejects by clearly stating that the reason for all things must be traced to the sole decision of God's will, and that God is the sole cause of all things.

Calvin further shows his implicit belief in the power of humans to make genuinely free decisions (even in relation to God) insofar as he maintains the validity of exhortation. In describing the benefits of the belief in God's omnipotence, he says that this belief encourages creatures "to put themselves in obedience to him" (I. xvi. 3). But this is self-contradictory, for what the belief in omnipotence entails is precisely that we have no power to "put ourselves" in any state of our own choosing, but that God decides unilaterally whether we will be "obedient" or not. In facing explicitly the question that was to be much discussed in Calvinist controversies, the question whether belief in predestination would destroy zeal for an upright life, Calvin replies that the intent of Scripture is that this doctrine will teach us to tremble at God's judgment and esteem God's mercy. To those who say that this doctrine will lead men to follow their lusts, since by their own actions they cannot affect God's eternal decree, Calvin replies: "If election has as its goal holiness of life, it ought rather to arouse and goad us eagerly to set our mind upon it than to serve as a pretext for doing nothing" (III. xxiii. 12). But it is inconsistent with his explicit teachings for Calvin to suggest that we have the power to decide how we are to respond to the doctrine of predestination, for according to this doctrine itself it will only "goad" us and cause us to "tremble" if God has eternally decreed that we will respond in this manner.

Calvin's response to the objection that the doctrine of predestination makes all exhortation meaningless is that Paul taught this doctrine and yet engaged in exhortation. The implied argument here, of course, is that Paul was infallibly inspired by God, so that if his implicit and his explicit teachings were apparently inconsistent, the inconsistency must be only apparent. To a great extent any criticism of Calvin for accepting the validity of this argument must be anachronistic, since we look at Paul and the rest of the Biblical authors through the eyes of centuries of cultural change in general and Biblical criticism in particular that give us attitudes toward the Biblical writings which were not possible for a theologian in Calvin's time. However, according to Calvin's own doctrine, the teachings of those who find in Paul an inconsistency are totally caused by God just as was Paul's own teaching. Furthermore, Calvin feels quite free to explain away (e.g., as accommodation or metaphor) those parts of the Bible with which he disagrees, passages such as those which suggest that God changes, or that God does not totally determine all things (I. xvii. 12–13; III. xxiv. 16). Hence it is not entirely the case that Calvin simply submitted himself to the teaching of the Scriptures without employing his own judgments. To some extent he accepted the parts of the Bible he wanted to accept. In any case, the reference to Paul's inconsistency cannot sanction for us today the inconsistency of Calvin or anyone else who holds that God determines all things unilaterally and yet implies through exhortations that we have the power of free choice.

The second objection to raise in relation to Calvin's doctrine is this: I believe we must see Calvin's position as involving a rejection of a premise he would not explicitly reject. That is, as was the case of those before him, he means to be rejecting premise 7 of the eight-step argument, and hence to be denying that anything happens that is not for the best. This denial is entailed by the premises concerned with God's omnipotence and perfect goodness, since they imply that God wills the best and can unilaterally effect exactly what he wills. However, I can only regard Calvin's position as a rejection of premise 5, that a morally perfect being would *want* to prevent as much genuine evil as possible. And since I take this to be the definition of moral perfection, I see Calvin's position as rejecting premise 4, that a perfect reality is a morally perfect being. And since I believe that a perfect reality must be morally perfect, this means that I must finally regard Calvin as rejecting the first premise, i.e., that God is a perfect reality. For me, Calvin's God is not perfect, is not worthy of worship, and hence cannot be called "God."

The reasoning behind this evaluation is the following: Calvin says that God's will must be regarded as righteous, even when we cannot understand the rightness of its judgments, since it is by definition the norm of righteousness. He says that we cannot always understand the rightness of God's decisions since the divine will has willed not to reveal its judgments to us fully. God has willed only for us to know that, above the standards that are based upon God's revealed will, there is a higher standard, which is God's hidden and perfectly efficacious will. In other words, we must say that God is perfectly good while recognizing that this is not a goodness that we can understand. Of course,

Calvin says with Augustine and Luther that we will someday be able to see the rightness of all God's judgments.

But there are problems with this view. The first is that it involves equivocation in relation to the idea of "moral goodness." If we are *now* to call some being morally good *meaningfully,* that being must be morally good *according to the criteria of moral goodness which we now hold.* To say, as Calvin does (citing Augustine), that it is fitting for God to will things which it is unfitting for us to will, i.e., that it is moral for God to will and cause us to desire and do things which it is immoral for us to desire and will, is to admit that the idea of moral goodness is being used equivocally. And this means that the term is being used meaninglessly in application to God. Accordingly, in spite of the verbal appearances, moral perfection is not really being attributed to God at all.

Second, the God that Calvin portrays is one which we must consider morally evil by our criteria; and this is a judgment we cannot *hope* ever to reverse. Calvin states that this God is not unjust for punishing those who do not deserve punishment. And Calvin says that this God fails to give saving grace to the reprobate because God hates them—and the reason God hates them is that they do not have the Holy Spirit, since God unilaterally chose to withhold it from them (III. xxiv. 17). I can only state that if "I" were ever to be converted into a person who could consider such a being morally perfect, that future person would be morally perverted. I believe we ought to join with Ivan in *The Brothers Karamazov* and hope that, if we are offered a place in "highest harmony" which requires all the sufferings of this world, we will give back our ticket and refuse to participate. Insofar as one admits the possibility of a being who is omnipotent in the traditional sense (which I do not admit), so that this "God" might in the future change us into "persons" who would agree that there had been no genuine evil in the universe, I believe with Ivan that we must renounce this change in advance, just as a man anticipating senility might compose a last will and testament with instructions to the courts that even he himself could not later alter it.

In sum, there are three major reasons for concluding that Calvin's God, and hence the God of traditional theism, is not morally perfect: (1) the ascription of morality to this alleged deity is equivocal and hence meaningless; (2) the actions attributed to this God must be regarded as positively immoral; (3) as discussed in the chapter on Luther, this deity with its "eternal decision" cannot be considered a free being in any sense, and hence must in the final analysis be considered amoral.

# 11
# Leibniz: The Best of All Possible Worlds

THERE ARE several reasons for including a study of the theodicy of Gottfried Wilhelm Leibniz (1646–1716) in this volume, besides the fact that he is the only one of our authors to write a book entitled *Theodicy*.[1] First, he is famous (or notorious) for saying that ours is "the best of all possible worlds," which is an explicit denial that there is any genuine evil in the universe. He thus makes central and open the defense of God's goodness that is the final but generally submerged theodicy offered by previous traditional theists. Second, he connects the substantive problem of evil with the formal problem of faith and reason in an especially clear fashion; and his position on faith and reason is one that is echoed by many present-day writers. Hence, an examination of Leibniz gives us a particularly good opening for examining this issue more thoroughly than hitherto. Third, his discussion of the relationship between God and future contingencies makes especially clear a crucial presupposition about the nature of finite actualities held by all those who believe that God already (or eternally) knows (and perhaps causes) the details of that which is still future for us. Fourth, I believe that most commentators have misinterpreted Leibniz' position, insofar as they have thought it to be significantly different from that of other traditional theists, particularly in regard to the question of divine omnipotence.

I will begin with this question of the proper interpretation of Leibniz. The usual summary of Leibniz' position is something like the following: There exists an eternal realm of possibilities. These possibilities can be arranged in an infinite number of ways, thereby forming an infinite number of possible worlds. God's creation of this world involved a selection of one of these many possible worlds to be the actual world. Because God is perfectly good and wise, the one that God chose to actualize is the best of all of these possible worlds. If it is the best, why is there so much sin and suffering in it? Many things that are possible by themselves are incompatible—they are termed "incompossibles." The actualization of one excludes the actualization of the others. Because of this feature of possibilities, every possible world includes some evil. Hence even the best possible world includes evil. Accordingly, even though there is much sin and suffering in our world, there is less than there would be in any of the other possible worlds.

According to this interpretation of Leibniz (which is accurate, except for the last sentence), he would handle the problem of evil by denying that God could have created a world without sin and suffering in it. Although there is no realm of eternal "matter" which confronts God with necessities, God is constrained by the nature of the eternal truths which, as eternal, are beyond volition, even God's. For those who say that, by definition, an omnipotent being can do exactly what it wills, this amounts to a denial of God's omnipotence, since God is regarded as compelled by factors beyond the divine will to create a world with evil in it (at least if God decides to create a world at all). And for those who take omnipotence in this sense to be essential to the idea of God required by Christian faith, Leibniz' idea of God is a sub-Christian deviation from traditional Christian theism. This represents the interpretation and evaluation, for example, of John Hick.[2]

However, Leibniz does not differ from previous traditional theists in regard to God's power. Verbally he certainly affirms divine omnipotence in uncompromising terms. He says that power, like all other perfections of our souls, is in God in its entirety, that God possesses it in boundless measure.[3] God's power is said to be absolute and infinite (Pref. 22, 30; PD 69).[4] To say God is limited in power would be to deny that God is the greatest conceivable being, and hence the true God (FM 117. ii; 122. vi).[5] God is said to be master of all things; the consequent will of God is infallibly successful (FM 22, 80). Hence events declare what this will is (Pref. 6). The divine power would be limited if God lacked the ability to do the best possible, but God does not lack this ability (FM 117. ii). Finally, God's agency has no element of passivity or "suffering" in it (FM 32).

Of course, the critic could reply that this attribution of omnipotence is only verbal. It only indicates that Leibniz believes that there is no preexistent matter which partly resists God's will and/or that the free will of God's creatures cannot fail to serve God's consequent will. But, the critic could continue, Leibniz' restriction upon God's power lies elsewhere. It lies in the fact that, while God's antecedent will wants to actualize every good possibility, the realm of eternal possibilities imposes its "necessity" upon God (FM 20) so that the consequent will, even though it chooses the best of the lot (FM 22, 80), must settle for a world that contains much evil (FM 121. vi). And this means that Leibniz has denied to God the kind of omnipotence attributed by Augustine, Aquinas, and Calvin. This is Hick's view.

However, this account distorts Leibniz' position. On the one hand, Leibniz does not differ from most traditional theists in holding that God's power is limited to the possible. Hick admits that "for the Scholastics, God's creative activity was conditioned by the existence within the divine Mind of a fixed inventory of kinds of creatable things." But, he maintains, "they did not think of this ideal realm as involving conflict and contradiction, and accordingly they did not make use of the notion of compossibility."[6] But this is not true. They said (as Hick knows) that God could not do the contradictory, e.g., God could not make a round square. And when Leibniz speaks of the "eternal verities" that God cannot violate, he means precisely those truths whose opposites imply contradiction, "the truths whose necessity is logical, metaphysical or geometrical" (PD 2).

Furthermore, and more importantly, it is *not* the case that Leibniz says that there must be sin and suffering in this world because there is sin and suffering in any possible world. Leibniz distinguishes between three kinds of evil: metaphysical, moral, and physical. While physical evil is suffering, and moral evil is sin, metaphysical evil is imperfection due to limitation. Now, a creature is necessarily limited, else it would be God (FM 31). Accordingly, as has been suggested by others, it is doubtful that the characteristic of the world that Leibniz calls "metaphysical evil" should be called "evil" at all, since (as Luther saw in regard to the term "relative necessity") all that is indicated by saying that metaphysical evil necessarily infects creatures is that creatures are not God. Especially in a Christian framework, where the world is seen as a good creation rather than a fall from deity, it seems inappropriate to imply that creaturehood as such is evil.

In any case—and this is the point most commentators have missed—it is *only* this kind of evil, whether it properly be called evil or not, that Leibniz says is necessary in all possible worlds. He does not say that the fact of incompossibility necessitates that there be moral and physical evil in every possible world. In fact, he denies it. He only says that the *best* possible world contains sin and suffering.

For example, he says, in reply to those who suggest that the world should have been without sin and suffering, that such a world would not have been better than ours (FM 9–10). He does say that the source of evil lies in the limitations of the creature which are necessitated by the eternal verities; but in regard to physical and moral evil he does not say that the eternal verities make them necessary, but only possible (FM 20–21). Elsewhere Leibniz says that, had the happiness of rational creatures been the sole aim of God, "perhaps neither sin nor unhappiness would ever occur, even by concomitance. God would have chosen a sequence of possibilities where all these evils would be excluded" (FM 120. v). Further, Leibniz says that God "could do the good that we would desire," which is that all persons should be happy (FM 122. vii). He suggests that God could have made all rational creatures so that they would always have a good will, but that God did not do so because it would not have been "proper" (FM 120. v). The fact that the existence of sin in the world is not due to divine impotence is clearly indicated by Leibniz' statement that if God loved virtue and hated vice absolutely and unreservedly, "there would be no vice in the world" (FM 117. ii).

Accordingly, Leibniz rejects neither God's omnipotence nor the idea that deity is such that it could have, with respect to its power, created a world devoid of sin and suffering. However, Leibniz says that it is not only divine power that we must consider in asking what God could have done. We must also consider God's infinite wisdom and goodness. Having perfect wisdom, God knows which of the possible worlds is the best. And, having perfect goodness, God necessarily chooses to create the world which the divine wisdom knows to be best. It is this combination of wisdom and goodness that Leibniz has reference to in saying that sin and suffering were not entirely excluded from the nature of things by "reasons of the supreme order" (FM 123. viii). Leibniz stresses that the constraint upon God to create this particular world was moral, not metaphysical. That is, the reason it was impossible for God to choose another world was not that this would imply a contradiction, but only that it would not have been fitting for another world to be chosen, for it would have meant a violation of the combined dictate of God's wisdom and goodness to do the best (FM 174. 130. xv). It would not have been fitting, since the world God did choose is the best of all possible worlds. In other words, a world with sin and suffering in it is better, all things considered, than any of those possible worlds without these types of evil. If all three types of good are considered—i.e., moral, physical, and metaphysical—this is the best possible world. Hence, in my terms, Leibniz is affirming that, although God could have created a world without sin and suffering in it, God had to create a world with sin and suffering in order to create the one possible world without any genuine evil in it. And Leibniz in fact gives in this context the definition that I have used for genuine evil: "A lesser good is a kind of evil if it stands in the way of a greater good" (FM 8). This means that a world without sin and suffering would have been good, but less good than the best possible, and therefore evil by comparison.

Accordingly, Leibniz affirms the first six premises of the formal statement of the problem of evil. He clearly affirms premises 1 and 2: that God is perfect, and that God's perfection includes omnipotence. And he most explicitly affirms premise 3, as he says that God has the power to, and in fact does, effect a world devoid of all genuine evil, i.e., anything which stands in the way of there being a better totality. And God could have created a world devoid of all sin and suffering, as far as divine power alone is concerned. Leibniz affirms premises 4 and 5, precisely in saying that God willed a world with sin and suffering in it, since God's perfect wisdom knew that only such a world, i.e., *this* one, is the *best* one, and hence the one with no genuine evil.

Leibniz clearly does not reject statement number 6, i.e., the validity of using logic in theology. Accordingly, Leibniz denies only premise 7 of the argument, that there is genuine evil in the world.

But on what basis does he commend this position to us? Our world certainly *appears* to have much in it without which a world would be better. Pierre Bayle, whose writings occasioned Leibniz' book on theodicy, argued that faith in God's omnipotence and goodness had to be held in opposition to reason's conclusions about the world. And Bayle's position would not differ in essence from Calvin's, as Calvin said that reason alone would conclude either that there is no God or that God is not good. Leibniz, on the other hand, says that faith should never be contrary to reason. Faith is not held in spite of reason; rather, reason supports faith. Reason as well as faith is a gift of God, so that disagreement between them would mean God was contending against God. If the objections of reason against any article of faith are insoluble, then it must be decided that this alleged article is not revealed but false (PD 29, 39).

This seems a far cry from Calvin, for example, who constantly hammered away at human ignorance and chastized human perversity for daring to question the statements of Scripture. He said that we must believe the Scriptural assertions even when they go contrary to our reason, e.g., that we are justly punished for our sins even though we could not avoid sinning. However, Leibniz' difference from previous traditional theists on the issue of faith and reason is more verbal than real.

Leibniz can say that faith is not contradicted by reason, while Bayle said that it was, because Leibniz is using "reason" with a much narrower meaning. For him, "reason" in the true sense of the term refers to the conclusions derived from linking together, by the laws of Aristotelian logic, the eternal truths, i.e., those which are necessary because their opposites are impossible or imply contradictions (PD 2, 3, 23, 27, 63, 64, 65). It is only if articles of faith were in opposition to reason in *this* sense that faith could be said to be *contrary* to reason. It is only if alleged articles of faith are contradicted by reason in this sense, i.e., by strict, logical demonstrations, that they must be given up (PD 3).

But there is another, less strict sense of "reason." The arguments of reason in this looser sense are not conclusive, but only *probable.* For example, all arguments dealing with the positive laws of nature are of this kind, since these laws are not metaphysical, but are ones which God established by free choice; hence the laws of nature, unlike the eternal verities, can be dispensed with by God, i.e., by miracles (PD 2–4). God chose these laws for good reasons, but can dispense with them for superior reasons. The objections that reason in this sense raises against articles of faith are only probable, not conclusive. Hence they do not force us to give up the articles. For one thing, Leibniz stresses, we are not very good at dealing with probabilities (PD 28, 31). Also, the mysteries of faith are by definition against appearances, i.e., they go counter to what usually occurs, and are thus not *expected* to be probable when judged from the standpoint of reason alone (PD 3, 28, 32).

Leibniz does not believe that we should believe all the alleged "mysteries" of the various religions, of course, just because they cannot be conclusively disproved. Rather, one believes the Mysteries of the Christian religion because of the "motives of credibility" which it possesses, i.e., the proofs which establish the authority of its Holy Scriptures and show it to be true (PD 5, 29). But once one has believed in the Christian Mysteries by reason of these proofs, then all that is necessary to justify continued belief in any one of these Mysteries is that it be upheld against all objections. Again, this does not mean showing that it is probable, since mysteries are by definition improbable. Rather, it means only showing that it is not contrary to any of the necessary conclusions of reason. Against those who intend to reject a Mystery by drawing a universal truth from instances of frequent occurrence, Leibniz says: "he who upholds the Mystery may answer with the instance of a bare possibility" (PD 79).

Accordingly, Leibniz' "reasonable faith" is not much different in actuality from Calvin's insistence that we subject reason to faith, since most of what Calvin means by "reason" is excluded by Leibniz from the reason that can challenge alleged revealed truths. And Leibniz says that, once the authority of Holy Scripture has been justified before the tribunal of reason by the "motives of credibility," reason then "sacrifices thereto all its probabilities" (PD 29).

Leibniz' stance on the relation of faith and reason implies that, in regard to the problem of evil, we begin not with an estimation, based upon empirical observation and probabilistic reason, as to whether this is the best universe that could have been created. Rather, we begin with the idea of a creator God who is perfect in all attributes, hence perfect in power, wisdom, and goodness. We know the existence of this God through infallible proofs (PD 42, 44; FM 7). (These proofs evidently belong to the "motives of credibility" for the Christian religion.) On the basis of this knowledge of God, we know that this world is the best, since it is the world this God chose (FM 8, 10). Hence, Leibniz argues that we must conclude:

> that there must have been great or rather invincible reasons which prompted the divine Wisdom to the permission of the evil that surprises us, from the mere fact that this permission has occurred: for nothing can come from God that is not altogether consistent with goodness, justice, and holiness. In God this conclusion holds good: he did this, therefore he did it well. (PD 35)

Leibniz clearly differentiates himself from the equivocal use of terms that was criticized in the previous chapter. He says that the fact that we must judge people according to probabilities but do not do this in regard to God does not mean that "we have no notion of justice in general fit to be applied to God's justice also; nor is it that God's justice has other rules than the justice known of men. . . . Universal right is the same for God and for men" (PD 35). "His goodness and his justice as well as his wisdom differ from ours only because they are infinitely more perfect" (PD 4). Rather, the differences in judging are due to the fact that the situations are different. The infallible proofs establish that God's intentions are good, no matter what the appearances are, far beyond the degree to which a man's integrity might be established by character witnesses (PD 36–37). If all the facts of the universe were known, "the probabilities which appear to throw doubt upon the justice and the goodness of God . . . would vanish away" (PD 38). If we could understand the universal harmony we would see that the things we call imperfections are false appearances (PD 44). But we cannot in our present state know these facts or see the universal harmony; hence it is impossible and therefore unnecessary for us to offer a detailed defense of God against the objections based on probabilities. Rather, as stated above, all we need to do is to reject ordinary appearances by showing that there is nothing that excludes the possibility that a particular evil is necessary for what is best on the whole (FM 145). Furthermore, it is not even necessary to come up with particular reasons why God may have permitted the evil in question; general reasons suffice (PD 34).

Leibniz proceeds to suggest several such general reasons as to why ours might reasonably be considered the best of all possible worlds. Sometimes an evil is necessary for a good; the church has, for example, sung "O felix culpa" (FM 10). Sometimes a little evil makes a good more discernible and therefore greater (FM 12). Sometimes disorder in the part is order in the whole, and the latter is God's proper concern (FM 128. xiii). Against those who claim that the evils outnumber the goods in our world, Leibniz maintains the opposite. Good exceeds evil even in this life (FM 251; cf. FM 13). The best order requires all degrees of existence (FM 120. v). The fragility of human beings is a consequence of our being this type of creature, i.e., reasoning and clothed in flesh and bones; and if the world did not have this type of creature, there would be a gap in the order of the species (FM 14). The injustice due to the prosperity of the wicked and the misfortune of the good will be remedied by the future life (FM 16–17). But what of the doctrine that the number of those damned eternally will be incomparably greater than that of those saved? Would this not give evil (the physical evil of suffering) an advantage over good in eternity? Leibniz says that the doctrine itself is disputable (FM 133. xviii; cf. FM 95). But, even if it is assumed, it could be true that evil would be "almost as nothing in comparison with the good, when one contemplates the true vastness of the city of God." For, there are an infinite number of planets which have as much right as this one to have rational inhabitants. "It may be that all suns are peopled only by blessed creatures, and nothing constrains us to think that many are damned." Moreover, Leibniz adds:

> Since there is no reason for the belief that there are stars everywhere, is it not possible that there may be a great space beyond the region of the stars? Whether it be the Empyrean Heaven, or not, this immense space encircling all this region may in any case be filled with happiness and glory. (FM 19)

Leibniz concludes:

> Thus since the proportion of that part of the universe which we know is almost lost in nothingness compared with that which is unknown, and which we yet have cause to assume, and since all the evils that may be raised in objection before us are in this near nothingness, haply it may be that all evils are almost nothingness in comparison with the good things which are in the universe. (FM 19; cf. FM 133. xviii)

Leibniz has been criticized for giving here "a thoroughly implausible reply," since "the part of the universe we know best (which *ex hypothesi* has a surplus of evil) would lead us to think that it is more probable that the rest of the universe does not have an abundance of good."[7] But it must be remembered that Leibniz has not committed himself to giving plausible (in the sense of probable) replies to objections; he says it is sufficient that they be barely possible.

Leibniz then proceeds to answer the objection that God is not justified in punishing people, since they sin by necessity. He argues, in essence, that the proximate cause of moral evil, and consequently of physical evil (since physical evil is always the result of our own moral evil, or else it prepares us for greater happiness and hence is not really evil [FM 241]), is free will, while the remote cause is the creature's original imperfection in the eternal ideas (FM 288). Accordingly, Leibniz maintains, God is neither the remote nor the proximate cause of sin. He claims that God does not will moral evil at all, but only permits it (FM 23–35). I will not debate the validity of this distinction in this chapter. But in passing I will note that it is somewhat strange that Leibniz follows Augustine and Thomas in trying to maintain that God, while in some sense willing physical evil, does not will moral evil at all. It was understandable that Augustine and Thomas went to such lengths to try to maintain this, since for them sin was intrinsically the greatest evil. But for Leibniz physical evil or suffering seems to be the greatest (if not the only) intrinsic evil, while the terribleness of sin lies primarily (if not only) in its instrumental effects. For example, Leibniz says:

> Moral evil is an evil so great only because it is a source of physical evils, a source existing in one of the most powerful of creatures. . . . One single Caligula, one Nero, has caused more evil than an earthquake. (FM 26)

Accordingly, there seems to be no reason why Leibniz could not have openly admitted that God wills and causes moral evil as directly as physical evil, since it is equally a necessary part of the best of all possible worlds.

In any case, Leibniz then argues at length that divine foreknowledge of human actions does not take away their freedom (FM 36–67). I will also not debate this issue here. For the present train of thought, suffice it to say that Leibniz concludes that we have "a sufficient degree of freedom to render rewards and punishments just and reasonable" (FM 67). Although our actions are necessary, this does not remove all justification for merit and demerit. For, punishing a man can serve to correct him, and rewarding him can motivate him; punishment of one person can serve as an example to others; and the fear of punishment and the hope of rewards can motivate people to do good; finally, even where punishment serves none of these ends, as when the pains of the damned continue, it has a foundation in the fitness of things, and provides satisfaction to the mind that likes order (FM 67–73).

A doctrine which especially seems to raise serious objections to God's goodness is that of original sin. Leibniz differs here from the "very harsh" opinion of Augustine that "original sin of itself is sufficient to earn the flames of hell." He thinks Christian theologians should speak moderately on this issue and "surrender these souls to the judgment and the clemency of their Creator" (FM 92–93). Furthermore, Leibniz adds, we do not "know all the wonderful ways that God may choose to employ for the illumination of souls." Leibniz sides with those who say that God grants all people a sufficient grace for them to avoid sin; "for it seems hard to damn them eternally for having done that which they had no power to prevent themselves from doing" (FM 95). And, in regard to the injustice of multitudes of people dying without the knowledge of God and Jesus Christ that is necessary for salvation, Leibniz says that we may doubt the fact; i.e., it is possible that God gives this knowledge miraculously "to all those who do, humanly speaking, that which in them lies." Leibniz concludes:

> Thus there are countless paths open to God, giving him means to satisfy his justice and his goodness, and the only thing one may allege against this is that we know not what way he employs; which is far from being a valid objection. (FM 98)

Leibniz concludes this discussion of general reasons that can be given to defend the belief that God does all things well by reminding us that none of the ones he offered need be accepted:

> All these attempts to find reasons, where there is no need to adhere altogether to certain hypotheses, serve only to make clear to us that there are a thousand ways of justifying the conduct of God. (FM 106)

This is the case, to repeat, since all that is needed to justify God's conduct is to provide a barely possible reason for it, for this is sufficient to show that the critic's objection is not conclusive, not deduced logically from eternal verities. In other words, because there are conclusive reasons for believing in a creator God who is perfect in wisdom and goodness as well as power, it is proper to presume God innocent of all wrongdoing in the face of any *prima facie* evil arising from experience or some article of faith, not only if a reasonable doubt of God's guilt exists, but even if it is barely possible to doubt it.

Leibniz' position on faith and reason can therefore be termed "rationalistic fideism," or "rationalistic authoritarianism." Like most theologians, he does not claim that the Christian theistic picture of the universe is *in itself* more reasonable than other accounts, in the sense of being more probable in terms of the criteria of self-consistency, adequacy to all the facts of experience, and power to illuminate these facts. Rather, the Christian theistic account of reality can only be accepted over others on the basis of faith, faith in the authority of the teachings of the Bible (as interpreted by its proper interpreters). However, this is not a blind faith; for there are good reasons for accepting this authority. Included in these good reasons, most theologians including Leibniz have held, are rational proofs of the existence of God, a God with the same attributes as the God of the Bible (except for the additional characteristics known only by revelation, such as God's Trinitarian character). Hence, it is rational to accept the Christian theistic picture of the universe of faith, in spite of the fact that this picture contains features that in themselves seem improbable and some that even *seem* self-contradictory. "Thus," in Leibniz' words, "faith triumphs over false reasons by means of sound and superior reasons that have made us embrace it" (PD 42).

Now, it must be granted here that Leibniz' logic is valid. If we do indeed have infallible rational proofs that there is "a sole Principle of all things, entirely good and wise," then it follows that all apparent evils in the universe as we observe it are only apparent (PD 44). And if there are proofs that this sole Principle has revealed itself and especially its plans for the salvation of human beings in the Bible, then it follows that it is reasonable to take the clear teachings of the Bible as articles of faith, no matter how much some of them seem to run contrary to what we would expect a perfectly good, wise, and powerful being to do.

If Leibniz' argument is logically valid, the only remaining question is whether his argument is sound, i.e., whether all the premises are acceptable. I believe they are not. First, I cannot agree that there is or ever has been any good argument for the existence of the God of traditional theism, i.e., a being who is necessary in all respects and hence cannot be affected by anything, who knows the temporal sequence of events eternally, and who can (and does) unilaterally determine this sequence of events. For example, the cosmological argument from the contingency of worldly beings to a necessary being, which Thomas Aquinas uses, only proves that there must be some actual being which *exists* necessarily; it does not prove that this being must be a "necessary being" in the sense of one that is necessary in all respects, so that it cannot have contingent ("accidental") aspects in its full reality. Leibniz believes that one can prove that there is a being who is perfect in knowledge and power, and that from this one can conclude that God knows the future and determines it. But, while for me religious faith involves believing in a greatest conceivable being, and this means one who is perfect in knowledge and power, I deny that it follows that this being can know or determine the details of the future. I will develop this argument later.

The second reason for questioning Leibniz' premises is that very few philosophers and theologians today would maintain that there are *infallible* proofs for the existence of God, i.e., of a being sufficiently similar to the God of the Judeo-Christian tradition to be considered worthy of the name "God" by people standing in this tradition. Most of those who accept arguments for the existence of God would put them in the category of the probable. The third reason, closely related to the second, is that few would think there are arguments for the reality of a good and powerful deity that can be developed independently of the problem of evil. Rather, most would favor some type of "global argument," which maintains that a theistic account of things is the most probable account because it can be more self-consistent and more adequate to and illuminating of *all the facts* of experience than any nontheistic account. The fact of an abundance of *prima facie* evil would have to be one of the most important of these facts of experience to be accounted for and illuminated. In other words, the doctrine of God would be constructed with the problem of evil in mind and in such a way as to illumine the experience of evil, rather than being constructed on completely different grounds and then only secondarily confronted with the apparent facts of evil.

All three of these reasons for rejecting Leibniz' strategy of rationalistic fideism are important to stress, since several writers today are employing essentially the same strategy, e.g., M. B. Ahern, who will be briefly discussed in Chapter 17. And it is important to stress the reason why Leibniz along with all other traditional theists who have wanted to make faith reasonable have had to resort to this indirect route to reasonableness. They could not claim that the Christian theistic account of the world is *directly* reasonable, in the sense of being more self-consistent, and most adequate to and illuminating of the facts of experience, than any competing view. This is because the traditional doctrine of omnipotence, which entailed that whatever occurs is God's will, when combined with the manifold experienced and observed evils in the world (and perhaps also with the additional apparent injustices introduced by the traditional doctrines relating to eternal salvation and damnation) made it impossible to present as probable the view that our world owes its existence to a good and wise creator and provider. This traditional doctrine of omnipotence implied that there was no genuine evil, that this was the best of all possible worlds. Since this theodicy is so implausible in itself, it could only be defended indirectly.

Accordingly, the substantive issue of the nature of divine power and the formal point of the relation of faith and reason are inextricably connected. If a different way of relating faith and reason is thought to be necessary, then the nature of divine power must be reconceived. This is the chief constructive purpose of the present book.

I will conclude the examination of Leibniz by looking at his argument that God can know and decree the sequence of actual events in advance. My concern is less with the validity of Leibniz' argument that this can happen without the contingency of these events being undercut than with the presupposition it requires about the nature of "actual events." And I will argue that, if this presupposition is false, it destroys the grounds for accepting premise 3 of the formal statement of the problem of evil.

Leibniz believes that God must possess all perfections to the greatest conceivable extent (Pref.; FM 117. ii). No one who agrees with Anselm that God must be formally defined as "that greater than which nothing can be thought" will argue with this. And Leibniz concurs with other traditional theists that if deity's knowledge is perfect, it must know future events, for a being who knows the future is greater than one who does not; and that if divine power is perfect, it must be able to make events happen exactly as it wills. Leibniz then attempts to explain how there can still be contingency in worldly events in general and freedom in human events in particular.

It will be necessary here to expand the previous sketch of Leibniz' portrayal of the relation between God's causation and worldly events. In God's understanding subsist the eternal ideas of possible events; God did not make these, "since he is not the author of his own understanding" (FM 380). God antecedently wills all the good possibilities; for example, God wills all rational creatures to avoid sin and to be saved. But, because some of these good possibilities are incompatible, they cannot all be actual; hence God's antecedent will does not produce actualities. God's consequent will effects precisely what it wills, which is the best sequence of events as known by God's perfect wisdom (FM 22, 80). Now, God is not the cause of the sins of the rational creatures, since God did not make the preexistent forms of their lives. God's creation of our world was simply the divine decree that this one of the possible agglomeration and sequences of events would be actual (FM 8, 84). "This decree changes nothing in the constitution of things: God leaves them just as they were in the state of mere possibility" (FM 52). The only change effected by God's fiat is the change from possibility into actuality. The source of a man's sin lies in the man himself, i.e., "in the idea of him as still merely possible, before the decree of God which makes him to exist" (FM 121. vi). Although the man will certainly sin, he does so freely. For his soul "was determined from all eternity in its state of mere possibility to act freely, as it does, when it attains to existence" (FM 323). In other words, contained in the idea of a particular possible person is the idea of his or her doing such and such freely. God's decree simply determines that these possible events will be actual events, but otherwise changes nothing about them, and hence does not destroy their freedom.

Leibniz does not argue that God's decree that a particular sequence of events will occur is compatible with there being any uncertainty in regard to these events. In fact, he insists that every event will infallibly and certainly happen just as God decreed it. Leibniz does distinguish between certainty and necessity, especially absolute necessity. No events are absolutely necessary, for their nonexistence would not be self-contradictory. Since they are not (absolutely) necessary, they are contingent; and the actions of rational beings are free. Yet they are certain; the truth about them is determinate before their actual occurrence.

One of Leibniz' two arguments for the determinateness of all events, including "future contingencies," is based on what he calls the principle of *determinant reason,* which states that "nothing ever comes to pass without there being a cause or at least a reason determining it" (FM 44). This is what many have called the principle of "sufficient reason," and I will so name it for the sake of consistency with later discussions. Now, with his system of the preestablished harmony of monads which have no "windows" by which they might be influenced by other monads, Leibniz does not believe any physical causation occurs between worldly beings (FM 290). The sufficient reason of an event is a combination of God's decree, which gave it actual existence, and itself, i.e., its essence or ideal nature anterior to its actual existence (FM 288, 291, 300, 323). Accordingly, although Leibniz says that all substances are monads which have spontaneity, or self-determination (FM 288, 290, 400), they never do anything in a given moment other than what it was antecedently determined, by God and the ideal forms, that they would do. Human actions are free, and yet they too are certain, since there is always a prevailing reason that infallibly inclines the will to adopt the course that it adopts (FM 43, 45; FM 310).

Leibniz develops the foregoing position in the context of agreeing with those who believe that God's will predetermines all things. However, in reference to the dispute as to whether divine foreknowledge is contrary to freedom, he sides with those who answer in the negative. He develops his position by means of his second argument for the determinateness of future contingencies. This "first and greatest principle of the truths of reason" is the principle that *every assertion is either true or false* (FM 169). This is identical with the principle of contradiction, which states that "of two contradictory propositions the one is true, the other false" (FM 44). This principle means, Leibniz says, that every assertion about the future is *now* either true or false; hence, the truth about the future is already determinate. The extent to which Leibniz finds this self-evident is shown by his attitude toward the position of Epicurus, who agreed with Aristotle that contingent futurities are not determinate. In reference to Epicurus' statement that assertions about future contingencies are neither true nor false, Leibniz says: "After that, he needs no refutation" (FM 169).

On the basis of this principle, Leibniz says that God's foreknowledge of events does not undermine their freedom, since future events are fully determinate, because of the nature of truth (which cannot injure freedom) and, hence, independently of their being foreseen. The fact that they are foreseen cannot add any more determinateness to them. In other words, they can be foreseen because they are determinate; they are not determinate because they are foreseen (FM 36–38).

Leibniz' account of what is involved in God's creation of this world, and his two arguments for the determinateness of future events, all contain a dubious presupposition about the nature of finite actualities. This is the presupposition that *the sufficient cause of an actual event can exist totally outside of or prior to that event.*

The implication that Leibniz draws from the principle of determinate (or sufficient) reason brings out this assumption most clearly. The principle in itself only states that there is a sufficient reason for everything that happens. As such, it leaves open the question as to whether all of this sufficient reason is in the past or whether part of it is in the present. But Leibniz takes the principle to imply that it is totally in the past (God's "eternal" decree is always treated as something in the past), for if at least part of the sufficient cause of an event lay in the present event itself, then that event would not in *principle* be knowable in advance. And if it were a metaphysical principle that actual events are at least partially self-determining in this sense (and some metaphysicians think it is), then it would not follow that a being with perfect knowledge, i.e., the greatest conceivable or possible knowledge, would know future events. The greatest possible knowledge would know everything knowable; but future events would not in principle be knowable, at least not fully so. (If they are only partially self-determined, they would also be partially determined by prior causes, and hence would be partially knowable in advance by one who knew these prior causes.) That Leibniz does not accept this as a metaphysical principle about actual events is clear, for he states it as one of the basic principles of his system "that the present is big with the future," and he means by this that "he who sees all sees in that which is that which shall be" (FM 360). No clearer statement could be desired of the metaphysical principle that the sufficient cause of any actual event exists antecedently to that event. However, although Leibniz expressed it with special clarity, this principle was accepted by all previous traditional theists, for they all held that the whole sequence of temporal events must be known by a being with perfect knowledge. (Those who develop a hybrid free-will defense are only partial exceptions, as they accept this principle in regard to actual events as such, and reject it only in regard to a particular type of actual event.)

Likewise, Leibniz' formulation of the law of contradiction presupposes the idea that the sufficient cause of an event is antecedent to that event. The law of contradiction could be formulated as follows: "Every statement about determinate things must be either true or false." This would leave open the question as to which "things" are determinate. The only basis for formulating it as Leibniz does, so that it implies total determinism of the future by the present, is the deterministic thesis itself (which is precisely the presupposition being questioned); hence the argument is viciously circular. There is nothing inherently false about the position (of Aristotle and Epicurus) that all statements are either true, false, or still indeterminate, and that at least some statements about the future fall into this third class, since the thing itself to which the statement refers is not yet determined. Leibniz' statement that Epicurus' position on this issue needs no refutation is pure bias, and a bias that is out of harmony with our experience of ourselves as agents who exercise some self-determination moment by moment. Of course, Leibniz is conscious of this universal experience. He says that the fact that we are not *aware* of the determining causes of our choices does not mean that they do not exist (FM 50). This is true, of course; but the fact that we are not aware of them certainly does not prove that they do exist. And some other reason will have to be given for the belief that the future is determined by the present—i.e., a reason other than this belief itself differently worded and dubbed the "greatest principle of the truths of reason."

Furthermore, this same presupposition about actual events is presupposed by Leibniz' whole account of creation. He holds that God unilaterally causes to become actualized "the whole succession and the whole agglomeration" of events that God wills (consequently) to occur. This assumes that an actual event is not of (metaphysical) necessity a partially self-determining thing, so that whether or not the possible events that God deemed best and consequently willed actually occur or not would depend in part upon the events themselves. To put it otherwise: it is only if the sufficient cause of an actual event can lie totally outside itself, so that it can be totally determined by some being (or beings) beyond itself, that it is even possible for one being unilaterally to effect exactly the actual events it wills. (Leibniz says that the sufficient cause of an actual event is God plus the ideal form of the event, which is its "formal cause," but this does not alter the point that the actual event itself has no say in whether or how it occurs, and that God is the sole efficient cause of all things and hence can effect precisely that sequence of events which he wills.) If it were held to be a metaphysical truth that actual events are at least partially self-determining, it would be impossible in principle for one actual being completely to determine the state of another actual being, even if the first being were God, and hence possessed perfect power. For, as most theologians and philosophers have agreed, perfect power does not include the power to do the impossible. Accordingly, if Leibniz' metaphysical premise about the nature of actualities is false, then his conclusion, that God would not have perfect power without the power unilaterally to bring about the best of all possible worlds, is also false. A being could do this only if it had a monopoly on power; and this would be possible only if it were the only being, or if all other beings were totally powerless to determine their own states and/or the states of others.

Another way of raising the issue is to doubt that any of the Leibnizian possible worlds is really possible. In one sense we can meaningfully talk about various possible worlds, each of which consists of a "succession and agglomeration" of possible events. For example, we can imagine that event A would be followed by event B, and B by C; while at the same time event 1 was followed by event 2, and 2 by 3; while at the same time event I was followed by event II, and II by III, etc. We can meaningfully suppose that God might will these potential events to become actual ones. Furthermore, we can meaningfully suppose that deity might succeed in inducing them to occur exactly as it willed. What is doubtful is that we can meaningfully suppose that deity could *guarantee* that this succession and agglomeration would occur exactly as it willed, i.e., that God could *unilaterally* bring about these events. In other words, the element in the Leibnizian possible worlds that seems to make them impossible is the notion that any one succession and agglomeration of possible events could be legislated into actuality by some being, even the most powerful being possible. Leibniz claims that God's decree that a certain possible world will be the actual world does not change the beings in that world at all, e.g., it does not affect their freedom; it merely changes them from possibilities into actualities. But this "mere" change can be regarded as an absolute change, the most drastic kind possible. For it can be regarded as precisely the change from beings that are devoid of all power of self-determination (among other things) into beings that possess this power (among other things). And if the difference between possible and actual beings should be understood in this way, as I will later argue, then Leibniz' entire discussion about contingent but determinate future events is meaningless.

I suggested earlier that I reject the soundness of Leibniz' argument for the compatibility of divine foreknowledge and human freedom. This could be debated in the same way as it has been debated in previous chapters. Likewise I could dispute the validity of Leibniz' attempts to say that God does not will moral evil in any sense, and that God gives sufficient grace to all persons, even though some refuse it. For example, Leibniz' distinction between "permitting" and "causing" will not withstand criticism. However, it is not necessary to engage in this type of argumentation here. This is partly because essentially the same arguments would pertain that were offered in previous chapters. But it is also partly because, if the basic assumption about the nature of actual events lying behind the whole Leibnizian account of the God-world relation is false, then criticisms of details of the system are superfluous. I will argue more fully later that this basic assumption, which was briefly discussed critically above, should be considered false.

# 12

# Barth:

# Much Ado About Nothingness

KARL BARTH, who at least for the most part reaffirmed traditional theism, is not only the most prolific theologian of the twentieth century; he is also generally regarded as the most influential, and many would rate him as the most acute intellectually. He also has written at great length on the problem of evil. Accordingly, it is virtually mandatory to include an examination of his thought in a critique of theodicies formulated within the context of traditional theism.

Furthermore, since one point at which Barth was critical of traditional theologies was their attempt to formulate Christian theology partly on the basis of "natural reason" and therefore only partly on the basis of the Biblical revelation, a study of Barth's thought provides an optimal occasion for continuing the reflection upon the relation between the substantive problems involving God, power, and evil, and the formal problems of faith and reason. I have already argued, especially in the chapter on Leibniz, that it is precisely the problem of evil that has prevented traditional theology from being able to present an account of reality that could commend itself on the basis of self-consistency, adequacy to the facts of experience, and illuminating power. Barth explicitly recognized this fact and chose faithfulness to what he considered the inescapable testimony of the Scriptures over the demand for logical self-consistency. An examination of his position should help others decide whether this is a viable possibility for them.

The central and most novel feature of Barth's theodicy is his doctrine of nothingness *(das Nichtige).* My examination of Barth's thought will be divided into two parts. In the first part I will discuss the relation between the creator and the creature in abstraction from the doctrine of nothingness. I will show that Barth explicitly affirms the perfection of the creation, and hence rejects premise 7, as long as nothingness is not brought into view. However, I will also show that Barth has problems, by his own admission as well as in fact, in presenting a view of reality that is both self-consistent and adequate to the Christian faith, even without the added problems introduced by his peculiar doctrine of nothingness. In the second part I will discuss this doctrine of nothingness, in terms of which Barth tries to say that there is, or at least has been, genuine evil in the world. I will argue that this doctrine adds to the lack of self-consistency in Barth's position, again by his own admission as well as in fact. Furthermore, I will question whether this doctrine, in spite of its apparent novelty and radicality and the great amount of space devoted to it, really makes Barth's position essentially different from that of previous traditional theists.

## THE CREATOR AND THE CREATURE

In contexts in which the problem of nothingness is not explicitly in view, Barth leaves no doubt that his affirmation of God's omnipotence is unconditional. He says that God would not be God if there were some place at which God's action were restricted (133).[1] No other will can be done but God's (19). A being would not be God if its will were not executed (114 f.). In harmony with the traditional doctrine of simplicity, Barth maintains that God's knowledge is God's will and work, that God's foreknowledge is God's omnipotence (114, 119–130). Belief in providence is belief in "God as the One who works all in all" (19). With this faith "there is no cause for anxiety lest something great or small should drop out of His will and work or be able to disrupt it" (34). And Barth applies this doctrine to faith itself, saying that a person has no option as to whether to believe in divine providence, but is elected to believe, and that this belief is forced upon him or her from without (17).

Barth says that this faith in God's all-determining providence is not an idea derived from observation and reason that provides a common meeting ground between Christian faith and other ideas about the relation between "God" and the "world" (27). Rather, the activity of God is known first through a revelation; in this particular event it is seen that this God is at work in the creation as a whole (141 f.). Accordingly, while Barth says God is known first through the history of salvation as made known to us by the Biblical report, he says there is no difference in regard to God's rule between salvation history and world history. So, while it is true that it is God "Himself who does what Moses and David do," it is equally true that "it is He who does what heaven and earth and the sun and rain and lightning and thunder do" (132 f.). It is God's will that is accomplished "in the slightest movement of a leaf in the wind" (133).

In brief, Barth does not mitigate the traditional doctrine of omnipotence one iota. In fact, although he believes that previous theists erred in making God's glory consist in the bare fact of divine power, whereas Barth wishes to stress that the God being discussed in Christian theology is the Father of Jesus Christ and therefore a God whose power works entirely for God's loving purpose (31), Barth nevertheless states: "The operation of this God is as sovereign as Calvinist teaching describes it. In the strictest sense it is predestinating" (131).

If this be the case, can there be creaturely freedom? Barth believes there can. He believes Christian faith requires belief in an actual world distinct from the creator. And he holds that for creatures to be actual they must have their own potency and activity (92, 96 f.). Pantheism, which is inimical to Christian faith, can only be avoided if the controlled and the controller each has its own life in face of the other (27). Accordingly, Barth maintains that God, in giving autonomous reality to humans and in fact to all creatures, gives them the freedom of individual action (87). And he affirms that evil can occur because the creatures can misuse this freedom which is entailed by their distinctness from their creator (III/1, 109).

But how is this creaturely freedom conceivable in the light of what has been said about divine omnipotence? Here Barth endorses the traditional doctrine of primary and secondary causation. He says that there is nothing wrong in employing the Aristotelian terminology of "causation," and that the Thomist experiment did not turn out badly (99, 100, 107). Furthermore, he says that this traditional presentation of the relation between divine and creaturely activity is formally correct, even normative (100). According to this view, God as the primary cause is the source of all other causes; and these secondary causes are not partly but absolutely conditioned by God, and in fact not merely conditioned but posited (99). The creatures have their own causation, their own independent activity. However, this does not mean that God's control is not total. It simply means that, although God does all things, God does them by means of the creature. "The fact that He controls it means that He is the Lord of the creature even while it has its own activity. He controls its independent activity as such" (165). God's causation consists "in the fact that He bends their activity to the execution of His own will" (105). Their activity is subordinate even in its autonomy (106). God controls the creature in such a way that "all the activity of the creature is His [God's] own activity" (105). God effects both the fact that each event happens and the way it happens, even to the most intimate depths (132). Because God's causation totally governs the other causes and their causation, God is the one true cause (99, 105). The secondary causes have only a limited share in the full force of the concept "cause" (99). In fact, "cause" is not a genus of which the divine and creaturely causes are species (102). Furthermore, since secondary causes are grounded wholly from outside, while the divine cause is self-positing, there is no analogy between the two causes (103).

The question to raise about this is whether it makes any sense. Does it make sense to use the same term "cause" for God and the creature when there is no analogy between them, so that the term appears to be used equivocally? Does it make sense to ascribe "causation" to creatures when their activity is totally governed by God? And is it not self-contradictory to speak of an "autonomy" that is totally controlled by another being? And if so, has not Barth by his own criteria denied in effect that God has created an *actual* world, one that is distinct from God in reality and not only in appearance?

Barth admits that it is not easy to understand the relation between the activity of the creator and that of the creature. He admits the tendency of his own tradition, the Reformed, to lean toward monism and fatalism. And he explicitly raises the question as to whether there is not an absolute contradiction between the freedom of God and the freedom of the creature (133, 188).

He seems to give four answers to the question of intelligibility that is involved. The first is the traditional answer that the notion of two agents makes sense if they belong to completely different orders (133; this is an idea that will be examined in detail in Chapter 14). He here endorses the analogy of writing, in which the action is done "wholly by the hand and wholly by the pen." This comparison is said to be good in that it teaches us that as "the hand guides and the pen is guided, so the divine activity overrules in its conjunction with the creaturely and on the part of the creaturely there can only be submission" (134). However, Barth has defined God's ruling activity in such a way that whether or not a creature "submits" to God's rule would be determined by God; the creature cannot even "concur" with God's activity (115). Furthermore, Barth elsewhere rejects the idea that creatures are mere "instruments" (145), which the analogy of the hand and the pen suggests.

Although Barth does not dispute the formal accuracy of the traditional ways of understanding the relation between the creator and the creatures, as the endorsement of the hand-pen analogy shows, he believes that putting all or even the primary stress upon purely formal concepts is the cause of the resistance to the idea of divine providence on the grounds that it destroys creaturely individuality and free activity. Barth says: "It is only empty concepts of God and His Will and work which will give rise to perverted notions of this type. They are excluded by concepts which are filled out with a Christian meaning." (118.) The Christian understanding of the *modus* of the divine activity is that God works always and everywhere as Word and Spirit, for this is the way God worked in the incarnation, the central event in the history of divine self-revelation, and God works always and everywhere as there revealed. By the divine Word, God works objectively, confronting the creature with a command; by the divine Spirit, God works subjectively in the creature, effecting the response (141–143). With this idea of God's activity, Barth says the supremacy of God's action does not prejudice "the autonomy, the freedom, the responsibility, the individual being and life and activity of the creature, or the genuineness of its own activity, but confirms and indeed establishes them." As a basis for this claim, Barth says: "The One who rules by His Word and Spirit recognizes the creature which He rules as a true other, just as He Himself as a Ruler of this type remains a true Other" (144). Barth's meaning seems to be that one who addresses another with a word is obviously respecting the otherness of the other. However, it is difficult to see how this is maintained when Barth goes on to say that God also *effects* the response of the other. How am I really other from God if, when I apparently act, it is really God who is acting?

Barth's answer to this type of question is given in the form of an answer to the question of how the demand that we willingly accept God's unconditioned rule is meaningful, since the doctrine of God's omnipotence seems to mean that the creature only appears to act but in fact is only acted upon (113). Barth's answer is:

> As believers in the Word of God and witnesses to the work of the Spirit we certainly lose any desire to discuss whether in face of the unconditional supremacy of God there can be such a thing as a human willingness to believe. (118)

This seems to be an example of the answer Barth often gives to the question of possibility—we as Christians know it is possible because we know it is actual. The problem with this type of answer is that it is question-begging. And this is not only the case in regard to a question raised from outside the circle of Christian faith, which Barth does not intend theology to answer. It also begs the question as to whether the *specific form* of Christian faith espoused by Barth, and particularly its idea of the creator-creature relation, belongs to the essence of Christian faith itself.

This answer, that we know that it is possible because we know it is actual, is Barth's third answer to the question of the compatibility of creaturely autonomy and individuality with omnipotent providence. A second form of this answer is that we know the two are compatible because they coexist in the Biblical record, and supremely in the incarnation. Barth says: "The preceding of the Creator and the following of the creature would be inconceivable . . . were it not that at this point [the incarnation] . . . they are seen in action" (94). In reference to doubt as to whether God's absolute control of the world is compatible with the reality and freedom of the creatures, he says: "When we turn . . . to the history of the covenant and salvation as attested in the Bible, we have to do with a totality of creaturely being and activity co-ordinated by God in face of which no such doubt can ever arise" (189 f.). Barth admits that the coexistence and cooperation of the divine and human subjects is "quite inconceivable" (106). And he says that the Bible gives no help on the "technical problem" as to *how* it can be that the creatures never do anything other than what God ordains for them, and yet that they are not like chessmen, but are beings whose activity has its own meaning and determination, and upon whom everything depends (189). Barth's point is that the mere fact that the Biblical record indicates *that* both things are true is sufficient.

There are at least three problems with such an answer. First, it is not clear that the Biblical witness is as unambiguous about God's total control of all events as Barth's argument requires. Second, even if it were, it would not settle the question for those people (both Christian and non-Christian) who cannot grant to the Biblical witness the kind of authority Barth believes it must have for the Christian. Third, if there is no way of conceiving the possibility of that which is verbally affirmed, it is difficult to see how a genuine affirmation, as opposed to a meaningless set of words, is stated at all.

Barth's fourth answer is different in kind from the other three. They were attempts to solve (or circumvent) intellectual problems. But Barth believes that the basic obstacle to the acceptance of the proposition in question, i.e., that the freedom of creaturely activity is not jeopardized by God's irresistible lordship, is "spiritual" rather than intellectual (146). And he says that the theological arguments for this proposition will acquire force only to the extent that this spiritual problem is solved (147 f.). This spiritual problem is "the fear-complex which suggests that God is a kind of stranger or alien or even enemy to the creature," so that it would be better for the creature to be independent in relation to God. Solving this problem involves perceiving this truth:

> God is the Father—not the father of a father-complex but the Father of Jesus Christ and therefore our beloved Father. It is thus the better for the creature the more fully it stands under the lordship of God, and the worse for it the more that reservations and restrictions are placed upon this lordship. . . . It is good for the *causa secunda* simply to be a *causa secunda* and no more. (146 f.)

Barth says further that the "creature cannot ask for itself anything better than to be ruled absolutely by the divine activity of grace" (149). This is, of course, not an argument for creaturely freedom vis-à-vis God, but only for the preferability of the lack of freedom in relation to a *good* God. And Barth says that the needed perception is not one that will come through argumentation, but only through prayer and fasting (147 f.). Hence there is no new argument here to which a response is needed.

Accordingly, Barth's answer to the conceivability of the coexistence of omnipotent providence with creaturely individuality and freedom is essentially that, although it is inconceivable, the Christian should accept it because he or she knows it to be a fact in his or her own life as well as in the Biblical record, and that once God's omnicausality is understood in a Christian sense there is no reason to resist the idea of God's irresistible rule. Although Barth says that our idea of the mode of God's activity should be based upon concepts derived from God's central self-revealing act rather than from "natural theology," the resulting idea of God's activity does not differ formally from that of theists who employed natural theology. Barth says that God "reveals himself as the one beside whom there is no other being or operation" (143). Hence, although God is said to work by addressing us and asking for a response, God is also said to determine the response, so that God is still the sole determiner of all events.

What is to be said of evil, then, if God is the sole ruler of all things, so that the divine will is *already* "done on earth as it is in heaven" (93)? Barth has two answers to this, depending upon whether nothingness is included in the discussion. When it is left aside (as it is in this first part of the chapter), Barth's answer is that there simply is no evil. The creation is perfect in its individual details and in its totality (III/1, 372). Barth says that Leibniz' thesis is very close to the Christian position, and Barth in fact endorses the statement that this is the "best of all possible worlds" (III/1, 385, 388, 404). Most of the things that most people think of as evils are grouped together by Barth under the "negative" or "shadow" side of creation. God is said to be the creator and Lord of this side no less than of the positive side of the world. (Barth at one place even includes death, demons, and human sin in this shadow side in which God's will is fully done [18–20], although this seems inconsistent with later statements.) This shadow side is a part of the creation's goodness (298). Creation is right as it is. Its apparent imperfection is integral to its perfection (III/1, 404).

Hence, Barth can say that it was the greatness of the eighteenth-century optimism that it declared the imperfection of creation to be illusory (III/1, 408). The basic difference between this optimism and the Christian position is that Christian faith puts the cheerful view of the world on a surer basis (364). Rather than relying upon dubious speculation, the Christian knows on the basis of God's incarnational self-revelation in Jesus Christ that the creation is good in its negative as well as its positive side (296, 303; III/1, 370). "In the knowledge of Jesus Christ we must abandon the obvious prejudice against the negative aspect of creation and confess that God has planned and made all things well, even on the negative side" (301). The basis for saying that this is the best of all possible worlds is that it is the arena, instrument, and object of God's action (III/1, 382, 385).

In what sense is this world perfect? Its perfection consists in its serviceability to God, for the rule of omnipotent grace through the lordship of Jesus Christ to accomplish God's own glory and the glorification of the creature (42, 168; III/1, 370). At this point, Barth joins with other traditional theists in appealing to ignorance, saying that what this serviceability consists of is known only to God, since we do not know the totality of God's rule. This perspective is said to answer all complaints against the supposed imperfection of the world (42 f.). It is true, Barth says, that the positive and negative aspects of existence are apportioned to creatures "in most unequal measure, their lots being assigned by a justice which is curious or very much concealed." But we should not doubt that there is a hidden justice which apportions these things. Barth's attitude is perhaps best revealed by the following statement:

> How surprised we shall be, and how ashamed of so much improper and unnecessary disquiet and discontent, once we are brought to realize that all creation both as light and shadow . . . was laid on Jesus Christ as the creation of God, and that even. . . . while we were shaking our heads that things were not very different, it sang praise of God just as it was, and was therefore right and perfect. (297)

Barth states many times that the perfect goodness of the world is knowledge that is given to us through revelation, and that we therefore need not form our own opinion about the world's goodness (III/1, 370, 380). We take on faith the truth that the world is created and ruled by an all-good and all-powerful God and is thereby itself good. And this does not only mean that this truth is not knowable to us apart from revelation (it is clear that Barth rejects "natural theology" in this sense). It also means that, even on the basis of revelation, it is still *inconceivable* to us how the history of the world can really be the history of God's glory. This truth cannot be seen by us even with the eyes of faith; it will be hidden until the consummation (16, 19 f., 296). In other words, the Christian theologian does not try to commend Christian faith by showing that it provides the starting point for the most self-consistent, adequate, and illuminating view of reality. That is, the theologian does not attempt to construct a "Christian philosophy" or "Christian natural theology" of the God-world relation that is superior to other philosophies in terms of the formal criteria for judging the excellence of philosophical positions. Rather, Barth says that faith is axiomatic knowledge, not a hypothesis. And faith is held on the basis of a "nevertheless" (16 f.). Faith is held *in spite of* the appearances, and not because it provides the starting point for a hypothesis by which the appearances can be comprehended more satisfactorily than by other available hypotheses. Furthermore, Barth differs from Leibniz in not even maintaining that it is necessary to show how this might *conceivably* be the best of all possible worlds. For Barth, it is sufficient that God's self-revelation (as Barth understands it) declares this to be so.

As we have seen in previous chapters, the traditional doctrine of omnipotence finally requires, if logical consistency is to be maintained, that the reality of genuine evil be denied if God's goodness is to be maintained. Barth differs from all the previous traditional theists save Leibniz only in the clarity with which he states this position (when the doctrine of nothingness is not in view). On this basis, Barth can confidently reject any suggestion which sees God's "sovereignty and omnipotence as limited, His activity as conditioned, concurred in or partly conditioned by the creature" (119). Barth regards the "line of retreat" which makes "of the God who is all in all a God who is only much in much" (119) a "form of unbelief, and perhaps the worst form of all," since if we subject ourselves to the will of God on this presupposition, it would not be subjection at all, and hence not Christian faith (115). The extent to which Barth thinks this "line of retreat" is neither necessary nor possible for Christian faith is shown by his statement that "the dreaded conclusion that. . . . God can and must be thought of as the author of evil can be avoided by other means than by the partial—and this means the total—repudiation of its decisive content, i.e., that the sceptre and dominion are in the hands of God" (121). The "other means" is of course the affirmation that the world is perfect, so that there is no genuine evil of which God could be the author.

However, there is another strand of Barth's thought, the strand which contains the doctrine of nothingness, which seems to say that there is power in reality other than God's by which the creatures go against God's will and thereby cause genuine evil. I now turn to this doctrine.

## NOTHINGNESS AS A THIRD FACTOR

One indication that not quite everything is right in the world was reflected in the quotation four paragraphs above, in which Barth says that discontent with the world is improper. This seems to mean, paradoxically, that failure to appreciate the perfection of the world destroys this perfection. This improper discontent seems to be something not willed by God. And Barth says elsewhere that it is not God's fault if we do not feel at home in the world (48). But, in the light of all that has been said above about God's total determination of events, down to their most intimate depths, one wonders whose fault it is. Barth has described the relationship between the creator and the creature in such a way that it would be impossible for the creature to do anything contrary to the will of God. It is at this point that Barth introduces nothingness into his theology as a third factor alongside the creator and the creatures.

Barth emphasizes repeatedly that nothingness is not to be included in the shadow side of creation. The shadow side of the creaturely existence belongs to the essence of creaturely nature, but nothingness does not (296, 350). It is a "left" which is not balanced by a "right." It is an absolute alien, opposed to all the elements of creation, negative as well as positive (302). To confuse the two is a great error; in fact it is triumph of nothingness. This is so not only because this confusion entails a slander on creation and thereby a wrongful indictment of its creator but also because it leads to a subtle concealment of the evil which is nothingness, as it becomes incorporated into one's philosophical outlook and finally justified as an essential, innocuous, and even salutary aspect of creation (299 f.). Barth thereby makes clear that, while he treated much of the *prima facie* evil of the world as only apparently evil, he does not mean to do this with nothingness. Nothingness is to be regarded as genuine evil. In fact, Barth gives a definition of real or genuine evil very close to the one employed in this book. After speaking of "real evil," he says that "real" means "in opposition to the totality of God's creation." Since Barth has described this creation as perfect and as the best of all possible worlds, that which exists in opposition to it would be that which prevents this greatest possible good from being realized.

But what is this nothingness? And in what sense does it "exist" as a third factor alongside God and God's creation? Formally, nothingness is that which God has negated or rejected, that which God does not will. Barth defines it as "the possibility which God in his eternal decree rejected and therefore did not and does not will" (74). Although it is described in the singular there, Barth elsewhere suggests its multiple nature, as he describes it as "the possibility, which God in His creative decision has ignored and despised, like a human builder when he chooses one specific work and rejects and ignores another, or it may be many others, leaving them unexecuted" (III/1, 108). The multiple nature of nothingness is further suggested by a Leibnizian-sounding passage in which Barth says that this which God did not elect and will "comprises the infinite range of all the possibilities which He passed over and with good reason did not actualize" (77).

However, when Barth moves beyond this purely formal definition to describe the content of nothingness, it is narrowed down to one idea. He lists the forms of nothingness as real sin, real death, the real evil of suffering, the devil, and hell (74, 300, 310). Sin is said to be the most important form (305). But suffering is said to be as inconsistent with creaturely existence as is sin (310). What all the forms of nothingness have in common is this: antithesis to the grace of God. "What confronts Him in us and all creation, what is alien and opposed to His gracious will—that and that alone is true nothingness, sin, evil, death in their true form as that which is bad" (331 f.). This must be regarded as the essence of evil, since for Barth the grace of God, as the basis and norm of all being, is the criterion of all good. Therefore the negation of God's grace is that which is intrinsically evil (354). Hence, while Barth thinks that much of that which most people consider evil should be regarded by the Christian as only the shadow side of a perfect world and hence only apparently evil, he says that the Christian should affirm the reality of genuine evil. "And this is evil in the Christian sense, namely, what is alien and adverse to grace, and therefore without it" (353).

This nothingness is a reality. But it is a reality *sui generis* (352). Only God and the creatures *properly* are. Nothingness has nothing in common with them. "In a third way of its own nothingness 'is' " (349). It has "the being of non-being, the existence of that which does not exist" (77). This is why Barth calls it nothingness *(das Nichtige).* It is real in an absurd way (III/1, 108). In fact, Barth states that it "is" only "as inherent contradiction, as impossible possibility" (351).

This description of the way in which nothingness exists answers the next question, which is: How can it exist? The answer is: It cannot. Only that which God wills can possibly exist. And nothingness is by definition that which God does not will. Hence it cannot exist. And yet it does. Hence, it exists as an impossible possibility.

If the critic says that this line of thought destroys whatever internal consistency there was to Barth's theology, Barth will not only agree, but will do so gladly. It is widely known that Barth rejected the idea of "systematic theology." But it is not always fully appreciated what this rejection means, nor what its principal basis is. It means not only rejecting the ideal of beginning with one central idea and working out all the other doctrines in relation to it. It also means rejecting the ideal of internal consistency among the various doctrines. And the problem of evil is the principal basis for this rejection.

Barth announces clearly that one should not expect systematic consistency in his discussion of God, the creatures, and nothingness. He says that all theology is necessarily "broken," that "it can progress only in isolated thoughts and statements directed from different angles to the one object." And he says that this applies to his previous discussion of the relationship between the creator and the creature which was carried out largely in abstraction from the problem of nothingness, and which he had described as being "in some measure intelligible and clear" (293, 290 f.). (Hence Barth evidently agrees with the assessment that this discussion was not *fully* intelligible.) But he says that it is in relation to nothingness that we have "an extraordinarily clear demonstration of the necessary brokenness of all theological thought and utterance" (293). If we had failed to see it elsewhere, "here at last we must surely see and acknowledge that our knowledge is piece-work." The reason for this "brokenness" is here and therefore in general "the existence, presence, and operation of nothingness." For, theology is supposed to be "the subjective reproduction of objective reality." But objectively the relationship between creator and creature is not a system, for "it is always disrupted by this alien element" (294).

In other words, Barth says that adequacy to the facts of existence takes priority over consistency. And because existence involves inconsistency, since something exists that cannot possibly exist, theology must likewise be inconsistent. Barth does say that we must proceed with "rigorous logic and objectivity." But he quickly makes clear that objectivity sometimes requires logical consistency to be sacrificed, as he adds: "The meaning of objectivity is that we must be prepared simply and without diminution to accept and take into account, each in its own place and manner, all the conflicting claims." And the first of these he names is "the claim that God's holiness and omnipotence should be equally respected" (295).

The source of the conflict is, of course, that one cannot attribute evil to God without violating the divine holiness, while one cannot join "with Pelagians old and new in ascribing evil solely to the creature, thus putting evil more or less outwith the providence and lordship of God and becoming guilty in consequence of an overt or covert denial of the omnipotence and omnicausality of God" (292). But since there is genuine evil, one must posit something at work which can be explained neither from the side of the creator nor from the side of the creature, and which is thereby inexplicable and "outside the sphere of systematisation" (292, 354). And this means that contradictory statements are made. For example, Barth says that humans had no capacity to sin, so "when man sinned he performed the impossible" (356). Since the impossible by definition is that which cannot be performed, this is as fully inconsistent as could be desired by one who believes "Consistency is the hobgoblin of little minds" (Emerson said, "a *foolish* consistency"). And, after having described God as the "sole ruler" of all creaturely occurrence, Barth now says that this third factor also affects and determines creaturely activity (290, 291). Furthermore, after saying that "it is absolutely the will of God alone which is executed in all creaturely activity and creaturely occurrence," and praising the Reformed theologians for carrying this doctrine to its logical conclusion (115), he now says that God is utterly not the creator of nothingness, that this challenger to God "was obviously nothing that He Himself had chosen, willed or done" (353, 304).

From this point of view, one would have to conclude that Barth's response to the problem of evil involves a denial of the validity of logic when discussing the relation between God and the world, and hence a rejection of statement number 6 of the formal statement of the problem of theodicy. And in fact, Barth rejects the "abstract" statement of the problem with its alternatives of denying either God's omnipotence or goodness if genuine evil is affirmed. He says that acceptance of these alternatives leads to "academic discussions" which are "of doubtful value for theology and the Church" (365 f.). And he questions whether there is any need to unify God's holiness and omnipotence in the face of nothingness (294). Of course, this rejection of logical consistency in theology is the price that must be paid if one is, with previous traditional theists, to hold to premises 2 and 3 on God's omnipotence and premises 4 and 5 on God's goodness, while refusing to follow them in the denial of premise 7, i.e., that there is genuine evil. Barth believes this price is not too high. But those who do find it too high, and yet cannot follow the previous tradition in denying the existence of genuine evil, should be prodded by Barth's extreme position into reexamining the premises that lead to this forced option of denying either logic or evil. Since I believe both premises 4 and 5 are required by any idea of deity compatible with Christian faith, I am proposing in this book that we reexamine either premise 2 or premise 3.

With this point made, this critique of Barth's position could have been concluded. However, there is more to Barth's treatment of the problem of evil than what is sketched above. There is a strand in his thought which, if developed explicitly and consistently, would involve a rejection of premise 3 instead of statement number 6. That is, it provides a way of reconciling the apparent inconsistency involved in saying that God's will is always effective, that God does not will nothingness, and yet that nothingness effectively exists.

In Barth's exegesis of the account of creation in Gen., ch. 1, he rejects the view that chaos, which he equates with nothingness, is a preexistent reality confronting God with its own independent reality and power, as in Plato's theory (III/1, 100, 103). And yet Barth says that chaos or nothingness is inimical to God, and in fact is in opposition primarily to God (290, 302–304). Accordingly, in his doctrine of creation Barth needs to say that God's will and act is somehow the basis for that which is hostile to God, and this without suggesting that God lacks wisdom or power. When explicitly introducing the concept of nothingness, Barth says "the whole doctrine of providence must be investigated afresh," since "the simple recognition that God is Lord over all must obviously be applied to this third factor as well" (289, 292). For even though it is an alien factor, "it cannot be envisaged and apprehended as outside the jurisdiction of the fatherly rule of God" (365). Barth's solution involves the notion of God's "alien work" *(opus alienum)* and the correlative notion of the divine "non-willing."

Barth holds on the one hand, that in order to take nothingness with proper seriousness, it must be seen as something that God does not will, and as in opposition to deity itself. However, in order to avoid any "Manichaean" limitation on God's omnipotence, he says that nothingness is absolutely subordinate to God, with no power over against God, and that it therefore provides no competition to God, no limitation upon God's sole rule (76, 77, 158, 331 f., 358). While it may appear to be a second God, it in reality constitutes no autonomous sphere, and has no power except what is allowed and given to it by God (76 f., 351, 358). It would not even have its negative actuality without God's creative act (74).

The question arises, now, as to why God gives to nothingness this negative actuality and power by which it is able to seduce the creatures and thereby partly to determine their actuality. Some of Barth's statements suggest, without quite affirming it definitely, that God could not help it. As we have seen, nothingness is defined as that which God does not will. But Barth suggests a distinction between God's positive and negative wills. The existence of nothingness is said not to be willed in the same way as the existence of the creature (353), which leaves the possibility open that it is willed in some other way. More clearly, Barth says that chaos does not belong to the *positive* content of God's will (III/1, 149), which suggests that it belongs to its negative content. And Barth explicitly says that God's negative willing, or "non-willing," is the ground of the existence of nothingness (353). The rejecting activity based on this non-willing is said to be God's alien work, the work of God's "left hand." Nothingness exists only "on the left hand of God as the object of his *opus alienum*" (361).

This much is clear. But the question not clearly answered by Barth is whether God could have created an actual world without giving nothingness its negative type of existence and thereby making it a third factor in reality alongside God and the creatures. The passages relevant to this question suggest a negative answer, i.e., that God's creation of an actual world entailed the necessity of nothingness. In the first place, Barth believes that God's proper work of saying Yes to the creature which God wills implies the alien work of saying No to that which God does not will. Barth says: "As He affirms and elects and works His *opus proprium,* the work of His grace, God is always active in his *opus alienum* as well" (353). And Barth speaks of "the inevitable divine negation and rejection" (361), and the inevitable would seem to be the necessary. He does say that "there is nothing to make God's activity on the left hand as necessary and perpetual as His activity on the right." But what he denies here is not the necessity of the alien work, but only its perpetuity, for he assigns to it a "transient necessity" (361).

In the second place, besides affirming the necessity of this alien work, Barth affirms that it must have an object which really exists. For example, he says of nothingness:

> Yet because it is on the left hand of God, it really "is" in this paradoxical manner. Even on his left hand the activity of God is not in vain. . . . His rejection, opposition, negation and dismissal are powerful and effective like all His works. . . . That which God renounces and abandons in virtue of His decision is not merely nothing. (351 f.)

And even more explicitly, he continues:

> For not only what God wills, but what He does not will, is potent, and *must* have a real correspondence. What really corresponds to that which God does not will is nothingness. (352; italics added)

Accordingly, Barth seems to say that not only does God necessarily engage in non-willing, although only temporarily, but this transient non-willing necessarily has an object, and this object is that which has been described as nothingness. If this is Barth's position (or at least one of his positions), it would imply Barth's rejection of premise 3 of the formal statement of the problem of evil. Barth would be saying in effect that although God is omnipotent, in the sense of possessing the greatest power a being could conceivably possess, God could nevertheless not create an actual world without nothingness and therefore genuine evil being present in it. It may be helpful to set forth the implicit syllogistic argument for the contrary of premise 3 (notwithstanding the fact that Barth would undoubtedly consider it hopelessly abstract):

A. Bringing about an actual world necessarily involves willing the actual existence of one set of possibilities and not willing the other possibilities.
B. An omnipotent being could not bring about an actual world without rejecting that which it does not will.
C. That which an omnipotent being does not will and hence rejects is nothingness.
D. Nothingness necessarily is genuinely evil, or produces genuine evil, in an actual world.
E. Therefore, an omnipotent being could not bring about an actual world without any genuine evil.

This doctrine of an effective negative will or non-willing in God reconciles most of the apparent inconsistencies in Barth's statements regarding the relation between God and nothingness. It explains that nothingness can be subordinate to and totally dependent upon God, i.e., upon God's non-willing and alien work, and yet how it can be in opposition to God, i.e., to God's positive will and proper work. It reconciles the existence of that which God does not will with the statement that only the will of God is executed, since it allows the idea of the "will of God" to be enlarged to include the negative will of God. And the idea of God's negative will and *opus alienum* explains how nothingness can be the object of God's providence in a "highly peculiar" manner (289). It accounts even for Barth's insistence that God is not the creator of nothingness. For he aligns God's creative activity terminologically with God's positive will and *opus proprium,* while aligning God's negative will and *opus alienum* with God's "rejecting" activity. Hence he can say that nothingness is due to God only in that God rejects it.

However, this position, if it is what Barth meant to say, albeit not loudly, involves a rather strange notion of omnipotence. The idea that God's power, since it is different from ours in being omnipotent, also differs from ours in that it necessarily gives some kind of actuality to that which is not willed, is quite paradoxical.[2] It seems more a form of impotence than of desirable power. It implies that deity, with its allegedly perfect power, is burdened with a fate that does not afflict us with our inferior power. Like Midas, who could not touch things without their turning to gold, God is cursed with the fate of not being able to reject the actual existence of something without thereby giving it a kind of actuality.[3] Accordingly, some readers may prefer to see Barth as rejecting premise 2 rather than simply premise 3.

Furthermore, even though this doctrine of God's negative will and work overcomes many apparent contradictions, it is hard to see how the terminological distinction between "creating" and "rejecting" really absolves Barth of the charge, in his own words, of "speaking, with Manichaeans, Priscillianists and similar early heretics, of a *causalitas mali in Deo* and thus violating the holiness of God" (292). For, whether one says that nothingness was "created" or "rejected," it is still God's activity that *caused* it.[4] This raises the question of whether Barth's position might be regarded as involving a rejection of one of the premises dealing with God's "holiness" or moral perfection. This does not seem to be the case. God's moral perfection (premise 4) is not rejected by the idea that deity necessarily rejects those possibilities which it does not will, since this is tautologous. And premise 5 says a morally perfect being would *want* to bring about an actual world without any genuine evil. This is not rejected by Barth's position as interpreted above, since it maintains *not* that God did not *want* to create an actual world without nothingness included as a factor, but that this inclusion was a necessity. Hence, insofar as one is not inclined simply to accept Barth's own suggestion that he has no consistent position by which the holiness and omnipotence of God can be reconciled with the reality of nothingness, he seems best understood as denying premise 3.

However, there is still more to Barth's position. Fortunately, this final aspect is stated clearly, so sketching it will not require the type of questionable interpretation involved in the above discussion of God's non-willing. And it is not in tension with, but complementary to, this interpretation. However, it is in possible tension with the earlier discussion of Barth's apparent acceptance of premise 7. And it raises another question of inconsistency.

Discussion of this last aspect of Barth's theodicy can be introduced by considering Barth's reasons for making an absolute distinction between the shadow side of creation, which is at most only apparently evil, and nothingness, which is really evil. A formal reason that could be given is that the proper exegesis of the first chapter of the book of Genesis requires this distinction. However, most Biblical scholars and theologians would agree with John Hick that Barth's claim to find his view of evil "in Genesis 1 is a quite patent imposing of his own speculations upon the text."[5]

One substantive reason which Barth gives for the distinction is that, if the distinction is not made, "we can never achieve the seriousness which is required in face of true nothingness" (299 f.). For, we will tend to rationalize all of it as an essential part of the good creation and hence as ultimately harmless, even good (300). He says we should instead fear and loathe the nothingness, and this we cannot do if we see it finally as being God's intention and act (301). We must see it as something that is hostile to deity itself, which God takes seriously, since it can have no reality for us if we are convinced that it has none for God (329, 349). Barth says that it is untenable from a Christian standpoint to regard nothingness as a mere semblance (353).

A second substantive reason for making the distinction, and thereby affirming the reality of genuine evil, is closely related to the first. If there were no genuine evil, then this would make nonsense of the centrality given to the reconciling activity of Jesus Christ in the Biblical witness. For there would be nothing to reconcile (318). The significance of the incarnation would be reduced to the sole function of revealing the goodness of God's creation on its negative as well as its positive side, whereas the Biblical witness makes clear that God became a creature also for the purpose of defeating a real enemy (303 f.).

But it is hard to see that the way in which Barth develops the doctrine of reconciliation through Jesus Christ is consistent with the previous point about the need for seriousness. Not only does he say that nothingness is really no problem for God, and that God can easily master it (77, 359); he also holds that God has *already* defeated nothingness in Jesus Christ. For example, in opposition to Judaism, Barth says that the only basis for confidence that God will do right is the knowledge that God has already done it (28). And at one point he says that there is a "grain of truth" in the view, which he here calls an erroneous view, that God has already done away with nothingness, so that for God it is not only nothingness, but simply nothing, and hence nothing that can still oppose, offend, or concern God. "But," Barth says, "we must not pursue this thought to its logical end" (356). However, for those who think that thoughts should be followed to their logical conclusions, it would seem that this grain of truth, which is elsewhere more than a grain, undercuts any basis for regarding nothingness with seriousness.

Furthermore, Barth concludes his discussion of nothingness with an explicit affirmation that it no longer really exists. As we saw earlier, Barth says that the divine *opus alienum,* unlike the *opus proprium,* is only a transient activity. It comes to an end when its object is eliminated, which is what occurred in Jesus Christ.

> This divine *opus alienum,* the whole activity of God on the left hand, was fulfilled and accomplished once and for all, and therefore deprived of its object, when it took place in all its dreadful fulness in the death of Jesus Christ. (362)

Accordingly, that which God negates no longer exists.

> Nothingness is deprived of even the transient, temporary impermanent being it had. Even the truth of falsehood, the power of impotence, the sense of non-sense and the possibility of the impossible which it is accorded on the left hand of God are withdrawn from it in the victory of God on the right. Even the permission by which it existed there is revoked. (362 f.)

The relationship between the creator and the creature is said to have been absolutely set free from nothingness in Jesus Christ, so that it is "no longer involved in the relationship as a third factor" (363).

But if all of this is true, how can we continue to fear nothingness? Barth himself even says that "in the light of Jesus Christ there is no sense in which . . . it is still to be feared" (363). Barth tries to reconcile the tension between this and his previous statements by saying:

> And strangely enough, the dreadful is feared only when it is realized that God has denied and deprived nothingness of perpetuity and therefore it is no longer to be feared. (366)

But this is quite unconvincing, especially in view of the fact that Barth had said that we cannot take it seriously if we are convinced that it has no reality for God.

Since nothingness was destroyed in the mighty act of salvation accomplished in Jesus Christ, it no longer exists, but only seems to because of our blinded eyes (363). This blindness will continue until the final revelation of its destruction. Until then it will only be a dangerous semblance (367). But why does it even have this semblance of validity?

> Nothingness can have even its semblance of validity only under the decree of God. What it now is and does, it can be and do only in the hand of God. . . . God still permits His kingdom not to be seen by us, and to that extent He still permits us to be a prey to nothingness. (367)

But why does God permit this? Because, Barth says:

> He thinks it good that we should exist "as if" He had not yet mastered it for us—and at this point we may rightly say "as if." (368)

Its apparent existence now serves as an instrument for God. God uses it to remind us what our enemy used to be, so that "at the sight of him we can never cease to flee to the One who alone has conquered him" (368).

Accordingly, Barth's doctrine is that there is *now* no genuine evil in the world. All apparent evil either belongs to the shadow side of creation, and is instrumentally good because it is necessary for this to be the best of all possible worlds, or else it is only the semblance of nothingness, and is instrumentally good because it serves God's purpose by promoting the highest good for the rational creatures, that they exist by relying on God alone.

It would seem, then, that Barth's position can best be seen as an interesting combination of rejecting both premise 3 and premise 7. In regard to the present, Barth joins with other traditional theists in rejecting premise 7 and hence the reality of any genuine evil. Since the defeat of nothingness in Jesus Christ, all, not merely some, of the *prima facie* evil in the world is only apparently evil. But prior to this defeat, some of the apparent evil was genuine, and this is evidently because God could not create an actual world, at least one with rational creatures, without that which was rejected by God existing temporarily as a third factor disturbing the relationship between the creator and the creatures. Hence, in regard to the world prior to the defeat of the power of nothingness, Barth seems to differ from other traditional theists by rejecting premise 3.

However, one final question can be asked about Barth's position: Is it *now* good that nothingness once existed? If the answer is Yes, this would mean that nothingness never was genuinely evil. For, if the world is finally better than it would have otherwise been because nothingness once existed and was then defeated, then nothingness cannot be judged in the final analysis as having been genuinely evil.

There are some suggestions of this view in Barth's position. For one thing, although Barth's entire position is built around a temporal distinction, i.e., before and after the incarnation, and he says that theology must be a report about history rather than a system, it must be remembered that Barth accepts the traditional doctrine of God. This makes it impossible to carry through the temporalistic perspective consistently. For example, in his exegesis of Gen., ch. 1, we find that already in the creation of the world, chaos was forced to serve God's purposes (III/1, 135). Also, the resolution achieved in Jesus Christ is an eternal resolution; Barth says that God has borne our cause against chaos from all eternity (III/1, 381). For another thing, in giving the reasons why the Christian should regard this as the best of all possible worlds, Barth includes the fact that it is the arena of the "divine contesting and overcoming of its imperfection" (III/1, 385). Since chaos or nothingness (as opposed to the shadow side of creation) is that which God contests and overcomes, the "imperfection" referred to in this statement must be nothingness. And since this "imperfection" is really part of that which makes this the best of all possible worlds, it cannot be considered genuinely evil.

Accordingly, it may be that in spite of the apparent novelty introduced into his position by his doctrine of nothingness, Barth's position is essentially no different from that of the traditional theists who have said more or less clearly that there is no genuine evil in the world.

One might think that this interpretation would completely nullify the previous interpretation, in which it was suggested that God could not choose to actualize a set of possibilities without the resulting creatures being menaced by the possibilities which God negated. That is, one might think that, if this final interpretation is accepted, Barth would have to be read as implying that God had freely decided to allow nothingness temporarily to menace his creation, even though an actual world without the presence of nothingness as a third factor could have been created. However, another conclusion is possible. Since the nature of God is necessary, God's creative activity would presumably bestow effective, if negative, actuality upon that which is rejected in relation to any actual world that God might create. So, if Barth should be read as finally denying that nothingness is genuinely evil, this does not necessarily imply that God chose to allow nothingness to exist as a third factor because a world in which it never existed at all would be less good than a world in which it temporarily existed and was then defeated. Rather, a world temporarily threatened by the power of nothingness could be the best of all possible worlds since a world not thus threatened would not be a possible world. Accordingly, one could hold that a world temporarily menaced by nothingness is the best of all possible worlds without holding that God allowed this temporary imperfection for reasons hidden in the inscrutable divine will. Rather, one could hold that this temporary imperfection is necessary because of the nature of God's power, that it cannot negate without giving negative actuality to that which it negates.

This would make Barth's position different from that of the previous traditional theists in this respect, that the apparent evil in the world would be due, not to an inscrutable, hidden, divine will, but to a necessity inherent in the divine nature. And Barth does explicitly reject the idea that the "divine rule on the left hand" is "to be regarded as the true way of the Creator over and with His creature" (35). There is no doubt in Barth that God's rule on the right, God's *opus proprium,* has the upper hand. Accordingly, there is less basis for doubting whether Barth's God should be considered morally good by our standards (the only standards we have) than was the case with previous theists, particularly Calvin. (This is especially the case in the light of the strong suggestion of universal salvation in Barth's theology.)

But, whereas there is little basis for thinking that Barth has implicitly rejected either premise 4 or premise 5, we have seen that it is difficult to decide exactly how his position should be understood. One strand of his thought suggests the rejection of premise 3, and therefore, many would think, of premise 2, since the implied notion of "omnipotence" suggests a type of impotence. Another strand suggests the rejection of premise 7. And yet another suggests the rejection of statement number 6, and hence of the need for logical consistency. (This latter rejection is consistent, of course, with the fact that it is difficult to decide what Barth's true position is.)

From my perspective, the basic reason for Barth's peculiar doctrine of nothingness and the related paradoxes and inconsistencies is that, although he dares to reject premise 3 of the argument, he rejects it on the basis of the nature of omnipotent non-willing, rather than on the basis of the nature of the creature. He followed the tradition in the absolute rejection of the idea that a creature, by virtue of being actual, might necessarily have inherent power. "Inherent" here need not mean self-derived, but only that, if a particular creature is actual, it necessarily has some power to determine its own state of being, even in relation to God, so that in principle it could not be totally determined by some being or beings other than itself, including God. This idea has always been rejected by traditional theists because it would stand in contradiction to the doctrine of God's impassibility and omnicausality. And this traditional doctrine of God has always stood in a relation of mutual reinforcement with the belief that Pelagianism and the related danger of self-righteousness must be avoided at all costs (what these costs are has been the focus of these chapters). This was seen in Augustine, whose favorite Scripture passage was, "What have you that you did not receive?" The connection is also seen in Barth, as he stated that Pelagians, in ascribing evil solely to the creature, are guilty of "an overt or covert denial of the omnipotence and omnicausality of God" (292). Because of the relation of mutual reinforcement, an attempt to solve the problem of evil by challenging premise 3 on the grounds suggested above will involve a criticism not only of the traditional doctrine of God but also of the traditional idea of humanity's basic problem.

And is it not time to ask whether every idea that could conceivably be labeled "Pelagian" should automatically be dismissed, without consideration as to whether its advantages might not outweigh its suspected disadvantages? And should pride, in the sense of self-righteousness, be considered as the worst of all possible sins? Should not pride be understood more in Reinhold Niebuhr's sense, as the tendency, on the part of individuals and groups, to value themselves more highly than they ought, and to feel, think, and act as if they were the center of the universe, as if everything else could be treated only as means for their ends? If the basic problem of humanity were understood as pride in *this* sense, so that the opposite would be a life lived in harmony with the rest of creation on the basis of a proper evaluation of one's own importance, the denial of human freedom vis-à-vis God would not be relevant to the transition from a state of sin to a state of salvation. Hence, the statement of the relationship between the creator and the creature would not have to be stated in such a way as to lead to the labyrinth of difficulties in relation to evil that we have seen in theists from Augustine to Barth.

# 13
# John Hick: All's Well That Ends Well

JOHN HICK, in *Evil and the God of Love,*[1] develops a form of what can be called the "hybrid free-will defense" of God's goodness. It is similar to the traditional free-will defense in that the traditional doctrine of omnipotence is retained. That is, God is still held to be the actual or potential controller of all things; there could be an actual world whose events were unilaterally determined by God. However, in the hybrid free-will defense it is held that God has voluntarily relinquished actual control of all things; deity has limited itself by creating beings with genuine freedom even vis-à-vis itself. The question of this chapter is whether Hick has shown that this position allows for an acceptable defense of a God who *could* unilaterally determine all things.

## THE IRENAEAN THEODICY

Hick's book is structured in terms of a comparison between what he calls the Augustinian and Irenaean theodicies. He sees some points of agreement and some of disagreement, and advocates the Irenaean position on the points of disagreement. However, some of these supposed differences tend to disappear under examination. I will discuss most of the points of agreement and alleged disagreement as a way of summarizing Hick's position. The first three relate to the doctrine of omnipotence.

1. Hick criticizes the Augustinian theodicy for trying to relieve God

of responsibility for evil. This is said to be misguided, since on the basis of Christian monotheism there can be no other being or principle as ultimate as God to which evil could be attributed (235, 258, 262). However, Hick sees that the traditional doctrine of predestination finally does admit God's omni-responsibility for all apparent evil; hence the only difference between the Augustinian view and the Irenaean (i.e., Hick's own) view is that the latter states God's responsibility for evil more openly (234, 264 f.).

2. Hick appears at times to be critical of the notion that evil is nonbeing (185 f., 200, 262). But the issue is really only the basis upon which the assertion is made. It should not be made as an empirical statement, as it sometimes seems to be in the Augustinian tradition; rather, it can only be made as a metaphysical statement based upon theological doctrines of God and creation (60–64, 185–188). As such, the privative definition of evil must be accepted. This definition

> represents the only possible account of the ontological status of evil in a universe that is the creation of an omnipotent and good God. From this standpoint evil cannot be an ultimate constituent of reality, for the sole ultimate reality is the infinitely good Creator. (186)

3. Hick says the two views agree that there are logical limitations upon divine omnipotence, and that these constitute no real restriction on God's power. "For the inability to do the self-contradictory does not reflect an impotence in the agent but a logical incoherence in the task proposed" (265, cf. 301).

The first three points show that Hick follows Augustine and the other traditional theists we have examined in saying that God can unilaterally bring about any state of affairs that is not self-contradictory. The next three points deal with the kind of world that such a being, who is also good, must be thought to have created.

4. Hick agrees that the world must be perfect. However, he takes issue with the Augustinian notion of the nature of this perfection, which he regards as somewhat "impersonal" (160, 199, 204). This notion is based upon seeing being as intrinsically good, and seeing each species of being as contributing something unique to the whole, so that variety as such is good (173, 176–178). This view of perfection is basically aesthetic (204). Humanity was created to fill in one of the niches in the chain of being (200). The other forms of being are good independently of their instrumental value for humans (173, 266). The Irenaean view propounded by Hick also sees this as the best of all

possible worlds. But the goodness of things is understood not philosophically, in terms of intrinsic goodness, but theologically, in terms of God's valuation of them (176–178). Hence the world must be seen as the best possible in terms of its suitability for achieving God's purposes (173, 202). Through the incarnation (the basis for Christian knowledge of God's nature and purpose) we learn that God's purpose is to create beings who will freely enter into personal relationships with God and develop moral qualities of life (201 f., 289–295). Accordingly, the subhuman world must be evaluated in terms of its goodness for this purpose (202). In other words, the criteria to use are ethical, not aesthetic (204).

Hick qualifies the difference between the two views somewhat. He says that the Irenaean position is not concerned to deny the positive divine valuation of the world in itself, and that the subhuman world may have further significance for God than simply as an environment for human life. He admits there is a danger of anthropocentrism in Irenaean and Protestant thought and this way of thinking probably should be willing to learn from Augustinian and Catholic thought (203, 266, 295 f., 353). However, he maintains that our affirmation of the world's goodness must be based not upon philosophical ideas about its intrinsic goodness but solely upon the fact that God created, wills, and values it, and that we know nothing about the value it has for him beyond its value for achieving God's purposes for the personal creatures (266, 353). Hence, Christian theodicy must treat the rest of the universe as if it were created solely as a fitting environment for human beings.

5. Besides contrasting the aesthetic view of perfection with the ethical, Hick contrasts it with the eschatological. The Augustinian tradition attributes to the world a perfection consisting in a balanced harmony of values, while the Irenaean theodicy sees its perfection in the fact that it is a process leading to an infinite good end which will justify all that has occurred on the way (264). Whereas Augustine said, "To thee there is no such thing as evil," the Irenaean repeats the eschatological insight of Mother Julian of Norwich: "Sin must needs be, but all shall be well. All shall be well; and all manner of thing shall be well" (264).[2]

6. However, this purported difference between eschatological and noneschatological notions of perfection is overcome by the next point, which is that both views agree upon the theme of "O felix culpa." This is the statement that makes of the fall of humanity an instrumental good, saying: "O fortunate crime, which merited such and so great a redeemer." Hick thinks that neither Augustine nor Aquinas allowed

this insight to affect their theodicies as a whole, as it does those of the Irenaean type (265). But this seems to me to be at most a matter of explicitness. As we have seen in most of the previous chapters, the evils of this life were finally justified in terms of their reference to a future life. In any case, Hick points to "the recognition in both kinds of theodicy that the final end-product of the human story will justify the evil within that story" (265).

7. The nature of the eschatological goal that justifies the evils of the world is said to be another major point of difference between the two views. The Augustinian view believes in an eternal hell as well as a heaven, and hence believes that some persons will never be redeemed, whereas the Irenaean view holds to the ultimate salvation of all persons. The Augustinian view denies that all of God's children are loved, and is a relapse into the idea of a God of an in-group (131); it is another example of the failure to think of God in fully personal and agapeistic terms (132). The doctrine of an eternal misery would be the largest part of the problem of evil, and in fact would make the vindication of God's goodness impossible (377, 263). However, while Hick has pointed to a genuine difference of opinion here, it is hard to see that he is justified in calling it a difference between Augustinian and Irenaean theodicies. There is nothing in the Augustinian position as he describes it that necessitates a doctrine of eternal hell, and nothing in the so-called Irenaean position that excludes it. And in fact it is said to be the Irenaean thinkers "since Schleiermacher" who have been inclined to reject the doctrine (263). Also, Hick places Barth in the Augustinian camp, and most have believed that his position implies universal salvation. In any case, the important things are that Hick believes a doctrine of an afterlife is essential, since God's purposes for human life so often fail in this life (252–255, 372); and that Hick believes the doctrines of God's love and his sovereignty imply that all persons will be eventually saved.

8. The final point is the one that really states the principal difference between the two views. The Augustinian view sees humanity as created in a state of perfection from which it fell, and hence puts great stress upon the fall and our responsibility for it (even though it is finally regarded as a "fortunate fall" predestined by God). The Irenaean view sees humans as imperfect not because we fell from perfection, but because we have not yet attained it (319). Humanity was created imperfect with an eye toward its eventual perfection. We were created in the "image of God," which is our character as free, intelligent, responsible beings, with the purpose that we eventually attain to the "likeness of

God," which will be "a quality of personal existence which reflects finitely the life of the Creator Himself" (217 f.). The process involves a development of moral attitudes toward fellow human beings and fiduciary attitudes (love, trust, obedience) toward God. It is in terms of the necessities for this process of development that Hick constructs his theodicy.

## ANALYSIS

Having sketched the main themes of Hick's theodicy, I will proceed to analyze it in terms of the categories employed in previous chapters. In the first place, it is clear that Hick does not reject premise 1, that God is perfect (35). Nor does he reject premise 2, the statement of God's omnipotence. He says that Christian monotheism excludes as Manichaean any form of ultimate dualism, such as the "external" dualism of Plato and J. S. Mill, in which there is some actuality not created by God that limits the divine sovereignty. This absolute monotheism is based on revealed theology, and is "not negotiable" (32–35). Hick also rejects as a form of Manichaeanism any view that says that evil in the world is necessary because of logical or metaphysical necessities (157, 170, 172, 197). God is the sole creator of all things visible and invisible (35).

Hick also affirms premise 3, at least in regard to natural and moral evil. He says that "Leibniz's doctrine of a realm of eternal possibilities, which does not permit there to be a world free from evil, is sub-Christian in the restriction that it sets upon the divine sovereignty" (171 f.). He indicates that any view which says God is unable to prevent evil would imply that God's power is finite (31 f.). In regard to suffering, Hick says that "God, being omnipotent, could . . . directly intervene in the workings of nature to prevent any occasion of suffering" (360); and that "omnipotence could presumably have created instead a different kind of world in which pain-producing situations would be systematically prevented by special adjustments to the course of nature" (341). And in regard to sin, he says that instead of having made persons, who by definition have the freedom to choose wrongly, "God could instead have created some other kind of being, with no freedom of choice and therefore no possibility of making wrong choices" (302). Accordingly, Hick says that God could have created a world that would be actual, and in fact like ours in many respects, and would have much value (370), but that there would be no sin or suffering in it. The question is then, of course, why God did not do this.

The answer clearly cannot be in terms of a rejection of premise 4. Hick bases his affirmation of universal salvation on "the supreme insight and faith of New Testament monotheism, that God loves all His children with an infinite and irrevocable love" (131). And he criticizes the denial by some Thomists that this is the best of all possible worlds as impugning God's perfect goodness (153, 168, 172 f.).

Hick, at least at first glance, does not follow the previous traditional theists (with the possible exception of Barth) in denying premise 7, the existence of genuine evil. He insists that sin and suffering are to be regarded as "genuinely *evil* and utterly inimical to God's will and purpose" (21 f.). Events such as Auschwitz show the demonic nature of evil, "evil which is utterly gratuitous," and "evil in so far as it is purely and unambiguously evil" (324, 325). Hick even affirms the existence of what I have called genuine evil. After describing evils such as Auschwitz as "horrors which will disfigure the universe to the end of time," he says: "It would have been better—much much better—if they had never happened" (397). And he explicitly rejects the view that evil is "*really* good but only *seems* from our finite human point of view to be bad." Finally, he admirably states the basic reason we should reject any speculative theory that makes evil seem good: "For it is an inevitable deliverance of our moral consciousness, of which nothing must be allowed to rob us, that evil in all its forms is to be abhorred and resisted and feared" (398 f.).

There is little if any tendency in Hick to favor the rejection of the need for logical consistency in theodicy.[3] And he explicitly rejects the view that the problem of evil is a purely practical problem so that the intellectual problem can (and perhaps should) be ignored (6–11). Accordingly, Hick does not try to avoid the problem by denying statement number 6.

This analysis leaves us with three possibilities: I have suggested that he perhaps affirms premise 7 only at first glance; premise 5 has not yet been examined; and I have suggested that there may be a sense in which he denies premise 3, since I limited his affirmation of it only to moral and physical evil. I will explore these three options in reverse order.

## THE HYBRID FREE-WILL DEFENSE

The definition of genuine evil I am employing in this study is a *comparative* notion, since it includes anything without which the world would have been a better place, all things considered. This would include any sin or suffering (*prima facie* evil) that is thought not to have been logically necessary for some compensating good. Hence, some *prima facie* evil might be thought to be only apparently evil, since its instrumental goodness would be thought to have neutralized its intrinsic evil when considered in a more inclusive context. However, this reversal of judgment can also work the other way. Things which are not *prima facie* evil might be considered evil when considered in a more inclusive context, since their actualization might be thought to have prevented the actualization of other possibilities that would have made the world a better place. Accordingly, while any sin or suffering that is considered genuine evil is considered so on the basis of a comparison with what might have been, and hence is "comparative evil," there could also be some comparative evil that does not involve sin or suffering. This latter can be called "strictly comparative evil."

In terms of an understanding of genuine evil that could include strictly comparative evil as well as sin and suffering, Hick's position can be understood to involve a rejection of premise 3.

The simplest way for Hick to have developed such a position would have been as follows: Persons are essentially free, self-directing beings who as such cannot be compelled to act rightly. The highest good is achieved when persons freely develop the habit of acting rightly. A world with such persons is more valuable than any world without them. Hence a world without persons will necessarily be less valuable than a world with persons might have been. Accordingly, there could not be a world without persons that is also without genuine evil, for it would at least contain strictly comparative evil. Therefore, for God to create a world devoid of genuine evil, it would have to be a world with persons. However, since God cannot guarantee that the persons will be moral, there may be some genuine evil also in this world, i.e., genuine moral evil. Hence, whether God creates a world with persons or without them, he cannot create a world guaranteed to be without genuine evil.

That this is Hick's position is suggested by some of his statements. For example, he says: "Personal life is essentially free and self-directing. It *cannot* be perfected by divine fiat, but only through the uncompelled responses and willing co-operation of human individuals" (291, italics added). On this basis he says that, while the first stage of creation, that up to the creation of humanity, must be considered as "easy for divine omnipotence," the second stage "cannot be formed by omnipotent power as such" (291). And he describes as "clearly sound" the argument that "the idea of the creation of personal beings who are not free to choose wrongly as well as to choose rightly is self-contradictory and therefore does not fall within the scope of the divine omnipotence" (302). And after saying that "God could instead have created some other kind of being, with no freedom of choice and therefore no possibility of making wrong choices," he indicates that such beings would not be as valuable as genuinely free ones who have the possibility of sinning (302 n. 2). Furthermore, that the best kind of world includes these kinds of beings is indicated by Hick's value judgment that "one who has attained to goodness by meeting and eventually mastering temptations, and thus by rightly making responsible choices in concrete situations, is good in a richer and more valuable sense than would be one created *ab initio* in a state either of innocence or of virtue" (292). And on this basis God's decision to create such a world can be justified, for "it is an ethically reasonable judgment . . . that human goodness slowly built up through personal histories of moral effort has a value in the eyes of the Creator which justifies even the long travail of the soul-making process" (292).

In terms of the distinctions introduced above, this would mean that God was justified in creating a world in which genuine moral evil would be possible, since this risk was necessary in order to avoid a world with genuine evil of the strictly comparative variety.

However, Hick's view is not this simple. For he does not believe the above argument is quite sound. He agrees with those, e.g., Antony Flew and J. L. Mackie, who say that freedom is compatible with character-determinism, which holds that we act freely if we are free from external constraints, even though we are caused to act as we do by our character or nature. Accordingly, an omnipotent creator could have initially given us a nature out of which we would always freely act rightly (304). Hick agrees with Mackie's three-step argument: (1) Since it is logically possible that one person on one occasion should freely choose the good, it is also logically possible that *all* persons should *always* do so. (2) Granted this, it is also logically possible that all persons should be *so constituted* that they always freely choose the good (this is based on the compatibility of freedom and character-determinism); and this can include the idea of their always resisting real temptations. (3) Granted this, it is also logically possible for God to *make* them so, so that they would be "*guaranteed in advance* always freely to act rightly." Hick agrees with Mackie's argument for this third point (to which I will return later): "If their being of this sort is logically possible, then God's making them of this sort is logically possible" (307).

This means that Hick does not agree that the existence of beings who freely do right requires the risk that they may also do wrong. And he explicitly says this:

> It would . . . seem that an omnipotent deity, creating *ex nihilo,* and determining solely by His own sovereign will both the nature of the beings whom He creates and the character of the environment in which He places them, could if He wished produce perfect persons who, while free to sin and even perhaps tempted to sin, remain for ever sinless. (303)

This negates all those passages which suggest that the achievement of God's purposes requires the possibility of sin since it requires going through a learning process, and one in which there is real temptation (e.g., 291, 344). According to Hick, we could be free, and go through a slow learning process, complete with real temptations, without the real possibility of sinning. (However, the phrase "free to sin" in the above quotation is illegitimate, since the natures of the persons would be such that they would be *guaranteed* not to sin.)

Accordingly, Hick undercuts the possible argument that God is justified in creating a world in which genuine moral evil is possible, since this possibility for evil is necessary to have a world in which there are beings who freely act rightly. How then is a free-will defense possible? At this point Hick distinguishes between two aspects of God's purpose.

> According to Christianity, the divine purpose for men is not only that they shall freely act rightly towards one another but that they shall also freely enter into a filial personal relationship with God Himself. There is, in other words, a religious as well as an ethical dimension to this purpose. (308)

In regard to the religious dimension, Hick believes that the free-will defense *is* sound. He argues that Mackie's argument ("If their being of this sort is logically possible, then God's making them of this sort is logically possible") is sound only "so long as we think of God's purpose for man . . . exclusively in terms of man's performance in relation to his fellows" (310). Hick believes it is not sound in regard to our relation to God, i.e., that "it would not be logically possible for God so to make men that they could be guaranteed freely to respond to Himself in genuine trust and love" (310).

Hick's argument for this is based on an analogy with a hypnotist and a patient. If the hypnotist gives the patient a posthypnotic suggestion to perform a particular act, that act is free in relation to the world since it is "not externally compelled but flows from the character of the agent." However, *in relation to the hypnotist* the patient is not free but is a mere puppet. Hence, if the posthypnotic suggestion would be that the patient love and trust the hypnotist, these attitudes would be "inauthentic," for the hypnotist would know that they had not arisen as an uncompelled response to the hypnotist's personal qualities (309). By analogy, if God so formed our nature that our responses were predetermined, we could be free in relation to fellow creatures, but not in relation to God. "He alone would know that our actions and attitudes, whilst flowing from our own nature, have in fact been determined by His initial fashioning of that nature and its environment" (310).

> Just as the patient's trust in, and devotion to, the hypnotist would lack for the latter the value of a freely given trust and devotion, so our human worship and obedience to God would lack for Him the value of a freely offered worship and obedience. We should, in relation to God, be mere puppets, precluded from entering into any truly personal relationship with Him. (310)

Hick says there might be great value in a universe where beings are divinely caused to respond to God with love and trust, but that such a universe would be inferior in value to ours (310).

Hick sees that this position requires a stronger conception of freedom vis-à-vis God than simply being free of external restraints while being determined by one's nature or character. He endorses the idea of freedom as limited creativity, according to which the action "is largely but not fully prefigured in the previous state of the agent," since the character itself is partially reformed in the moment of decision (312).[4]

Consistent with this stronger conception of freedom, Hick speaks of God's voluntary self-limitation in relation to free creatures (38). He says that "the thoughts and actions of free beings are in principle unknowable until they occur" (379). Since God cannot know that which is in principle unknowable, this would seem to mean that God's self-limitation involved surrender of omniscience in regard to the future. And Hick says that it would be a logical contradiction for it to be *predetermined* that the creatures endowed with free will would finally come to love and obey God (379; cf. 304, 312). Further, he says that, whereas the distinction between divine willing and permitting is not valid in relation to the physical universe, it is valid in relation to free beings (109 f.). This seems to imply that God voluntarily relinquishes the total determination of all events.

On the basis of this idea of the God-human relation required for the best possible world, it would seem that Hick's position can be described in these terms: Although dangerous freedom is not necessary for us to be moral, it is necessary if we are to be religious, and this higher purpose justifies God's giving us the leeway either to be self-centered and thereby immoral in relation to other people, or else to overcome this self-centeredness by freely coming to faith in God. Accordingly, Hick's position would seem to be that God would want to bring about an actual world without any sin and the resultant suffering in it (so that premise 5 is affirmed), but that the best kind of world requires that there be the *possibility* of moral evil. Hick's position, thus understood, could be formalized as follows (the idea of "free obedience to God" will be used in place of "authentic fiduciary attitudes," since the former is the element of the latter that is crucial in regard to evil):

A. An actual world that is less valuable than it could have been is thereby an actual world with genuine (strictly comparative) evil. (Definition)
B. An actual world forever without beings it could have contained that would have made it more valuable would thereby be an actual world with genuine evil. (Restatement of A)
C. There can be an actual world with persons who freely obey God. (Fact)
D. Persons who freely obey God are beings who would make any actual world with them more valuable than it or any other world would be without them. (Fact)
E. An actual world forever without persons who freely obey God would thereby be an actual world with genuine evil. (B-D)
F. An actual world forever without persons who freely obey God and also without genuine evil would be impossible. (Restatement of E)
G. An omnipotent being could not do the impossible. (By definition)
H. An omnipotent being could not bring about an actual world forever without persons who freely obey God and also without genuine evil. (F, G)
I. An actual world without persons would necessarily be a world without persons who freely obey God. (By definition)

J. An omnipotent being could not bring about an actual world forever *without* persons and also without genuine evil. (H, I)
K. Beings who are essentially partially free could not possibly be guaranteed by some other being to obey that being. (By definition)
L. Persons are essentially partially free beings. (By definition)
M. An omnipotent being could not guarantee (infallibly bring it about) that persons will obey that being. (G, K, L)
N. God is an omnipotent being, and the only one. (By definition)
O. Persons who do not obey God thereby cause genuine (moral) evil in the world that contains them. (By definition)
P. A world with persons could not possibly be guaranteed to be a world without any genuine (moral) evil. (M-O)
Q. An omnipotent being could not bring about a world *with* persons and also guaranteed to be without genuine (moral) evil. (G, P)
R. An omnipotent being could not bring about an actual world guaranteed to be without any genuine evil. (J, Q) (Explanation: The world would either have strictly comparative evil, or it could not be guaranteed against moral evil.)

I believe that this argument summarizes an essential aspect of Hick's position. And this means that, although he has criticized others for saying that God could not create a world without evil because of certain logical or metaphysical necessities (31 f., 171 f.), he himself is in effect saying this, since he says that it is logically impossible for the best possible world to be guaranteed against evil. If this were the whole of Hick's position, he would not be relieving God of the *ultimate* responsibility for (moral) evil (which he says theodicy should not attempt [258]), for he would be saying that God has willed and created a situation in which moral evil is possible. However, Hick could plausibly justify God's goodness, since he would be affirming premise 5, that God would like to have brought about a world devoid of genuine evil. The reason God did not do so is that the persons who were created with real freedom in relation to God used that freedom to sin. In other words, God is not indictable for not having brought about a world devoid of moral evil, since God could not have done so *unilaterally,* if the world is to contain beings with the type of freedom necessary for the best kind of world. (Hick says that if we attribute this "higher aim" to God, we must declare self-contradictory the idea of God's so creating persons that they will inevitably respond positively to God [310 f.].) If this kind of world is to be free of genuine evil, it will be partially up to the persons themselves. Hence, God would be justified, since God would have brought about the only kind of world in which there was at least the chance of avoiding genuine evil.

## OBJECTIONS TO THE HYBRID FREE-WILL DEFENSE

The hybrid free-will defense is a possible position. And, although it does not represent Hick's full position, all the ideas in it (except the affirmation of premise 5) are included in his full position. Accordingly, we can examine some objections to this version of the hybrid free-will defense before looking at the final element in Hick's position.

1. As I stated earlier, this is termed a "hybrid" free-will defense. On the one hand, it differs from the traditional free-will defense by rejecting the idea that creatures can be called free (at least in relation to God), even though their actions are totally determined by God; on the other hand, it agrees with the traditional theology in maintaining that God *could* have created an actual world in which the actions of all the creatures would be totally controlled by God. In other words, this view maintains that there is nothing inherently self-contradictory in the idea of God's totally controlling the actions of actual beings, but that God voluntarily relinquishes this control in regard to at least some of the actual creatures in order to make possible the achievement of greater values, ones that are sufficiently great to justify the risk of evil entailed by giving up total control of the creation. This position implies that God could at any time resume total control of those beings who had been endowed with autonomy, and that God could do this without destroying their *actuality.* Hence, God could prevent any and all sins and hence also all the suffering caused by those sins. For example, Hitler could have been converted; or his subordinates could have been caused to defy his orders. Furthermore, God could prevent all suffering in sentient beings caused by nonpersonal agents, and this whether or not these agents possess some autonomy vis-à-vis God. If they do, God could cancel out their freedom in the same way as with persons; and if they do not (as Hick assumes), then God could interrupt the laws by which they normally operate. For example, a bullet fired toward the heart of a person "too young to die" could be deflected or turned into rubber; the venom of a rattlesnake about to bite a virtuous person could be neutralized; the growth of cancerous cells could be retarded in cases where an early death would be particularly tragic.

The basic question this raises for any form of the hybrid free-will defense is this: If God could have created a world somewhat like ours but prevented all or at least some of its evils by suspending its freedom and/or its laws, why did God not do this? This basic question can take many forms. One is: If God could have created a world with beings in it who could enjoy all the types of values that we enjoy, including the value of thinking themselves genuinely free, and who would differ from us only in that they would not really have the freedom to sin, why did God not do this? Hick's reply to this has already been indicated: genuine persons (with genuine freedom vis-à-vis God) are sufficiently more valuable than pseudo persons to justify the evils brought about by genuine persons. He says:

> There might, indeed, be very great value in a universe of created beings who respond to God in a freely given love and trust and worship which He has Himself caused to occur by his initial formation of their nature. (310)

(The phrase "freely given love" is in contradiction with the rest of the sentence, given Hick's definition.) But, Hick says:

> Such a universe could be only a poor second-best to one in which created beings, whose responses to Himself God has not thus "fixed" in advance, come freely to love, trust and worship Him. (310)

Hick at times bases this value judgment on the same *a priori* argument as did Leibniz: If God chose it, it must be the best, since God is perfectly good and powerful. For example, Hick says that "since evil exists, and since God is sovereign, it must be that God has permitted it for some good reason" (182). And after saying that God could have created a world without genuine persons, Hick states: "But in fact He has chosen to create persons, and we can only accept this decision basic to our existence and treat it as a premise of our thinking" (302). This argument by itself, of course, would presuppose what needs to be shown, and would not even give a possible way of conceiving how God's choice might be a good one. But at other times Hick indicates that the greater value of genuine freedom is a judgment we can make from our own experience. For example, he quotes T. H. Huxley's statement:

> I protest that if some great power would agree to make me always think what is true and do what is right, on condition of being turned into a sort of clock. . . . I should instantly close with the offer.[5]

Hick says that few people would, after reflecting on the matter, be willing to agree with Huxley (302 n. 2). Also, Hick's conclusion that a sinless but unfree universe would be a poor second-best is based upon "human analogies" such as that of the hypnotist and the patient (310).

The success of Hick's theodicy depends, then, upon the number of people who would agree with him rather than Huxley. A good many people would certainly side with Huxley (insofar as his universe is thought to be a possible one). For example, Barth explicitly says that freedom in relation to God (who is a good God) would not be desirable. And Luther and Calvin both extolled the advantages of believing that all is controlled by God. Accordingly, Hick's theodicy rests upon a value judgment that many would find questionable at best. It is certainly not self-evident that the additional value that would accrue to God by God's knowing that the creatures' fiduciary attitudes were authentic, rather than spurious, is sufficient to justify all the evils that would have been avoided had God been willing to forgo this additional value.

A second form of the basic argument against the hybrid free-will defense is this: If God could have created an actual world in which all human pain and suffering were prevented (341, 360), why did God not do so? The reason why God did not eliminate all human pain is that a "soft, unchallenging world would be inhabited by a soft, unchallenged race of men" (343). The Christian claim is that God created the world as a place for soul-making, not as a hedonistic paradise for a maximum amount of pleasure (344). And if all forms of suffering were excluded, then there would be no point to moral values. "To act wrongly means, basically, to harm someone." But if there were no suffering, if would be impossible to harm anyone; likewise, it would be impossible to benefit anyone. Accordingly, since they would have no function, qualities such as self-sacrifice, care for others, devotion to the public good, courage, and the capacity to love would never be developed (360 f.). In other words, it is precisely the features of the world that present us with challenges, uncertainties, and dangers that "underlie the emergence of virtually the whole range of the more valuable human characteristics" (362 f.).

If one agrees with Hick that God should not have prevented *all* moral evil and *all* pain and suffering, there is still a third form of the basic question to raise about the hybrid free-will defense: Why does God not prevent the worst of the moral and natural evils? Granting that a world with real persons is better than one without, why does not

God suspend the freedom of these beings from time to time? For example, God could have, in a second, unilaterally converted Hitler from his hatred for Jews. True, in that moment Hitler would not have been a "person," since his freedom would have been temporarily suspended. But he would have been a person before and after that one second, and the loss of one second of personhood would be a small price to pay if the atrocities of World War II could have been avoided. Even if one were to maintain that Hitler would not have been a genuine person after the conversion, since the rest of his life would have been based upon a forced conversion, still the loss of Hitler's personhood would have been a small price to pay to have prevented all the suffering caused by the fully personal Hitler.

Hick's argument against the idea that God should interfere occasionally to prevent the worst moral evils is that the notion of "worst" or "exceptional" evil is a relative term. If God had prevented the evils that we now classify as the worst, then the ones that are now second-worst would be the worst, and we would complain that God should have interfered to prevent them, and so on. "There would be nowhere to stop, short of a divinely arranged paradise" (363). And such a paradise would not be the best kind of world for soul-making; for if we knew in advance that no serious threat to humanity would arise, the struggles that bring out the highest moral qualities would become unreal (364 f.).

There is an initial plausibility to Hick's slippery-slope argument. However, it suggests a lack in divine wisdom. For we as human parents are able to decide rather well where the proper balance is between overprotecting our children so that they fail to develop on the one hand, and exposing them to so much danger that they will probably perish before they have a chance to develop, on the other. Surely God, if perfectly wise, could find some place to strike a balance between the present world, which is somewhat too dangerous for most of God's children, and a world in which moral qualities would not develop at all. In fact, one might suspect that a world in which evil was somewhat less victorious than in our present one would evoke *more* moral qualities, since many people in the present world give up on the battle for goodness because it often seems so hopeless.

I have thus far considered Hick's reply to the moral evil (i.e., that which is caused by moral agents) which seems excessive or dysteleological (i.e., not productive of good). He takes more seriously the apparently excessive suffering that belongs to the category of "natural evil," which for Hick means suffering due to nonhuman causes (19).

He gives as examples gigantic famines from which millions perish, volcanic eruptions burying whole cities, earthquakes killing thousands of terrified people, and diseases such as cancer and cerebral meningitis. These more extreme and crushing evils, which seem to be distributed in random and meaningless ways, often crush the character rather than ennobling it (365–367, 369). He says we cannot know why God does not prevent this excessive evil. It is a mystery. And yet, the great value of this suffering may lie precisely in its mysteriousness and irrationality. For it is precisely this utterly destructive evil which falls upon other people with haphazardness and inequity, especially in dramatic forms such as earthquakes, that evokes sympathy, compassion, and self-giving love, which are among the highest values of personal life (370 f.). As for those who are crushed physically or morally by these excessive evils, Hick says that the future good in the life beyond death is sufficiently great to make up for all the evils encountered on the way (376, 377).

I personally find Hick's suggested justification of excessive evils appalling, and cannot accept the goodness of the God he is attempting to defend. However, there is no way his position can be refuted by argumentation, for what is involved are differing value judgments. I can only repeat Hick's own statement made in reference to the idea of an eternal hell, which he finds appalling: "A theology cannot go unchallenged when it is repugnant to the moral sense that has been formed by the religious realities upon which this theology itself professes to be based" (98). I believe on this basis that a God who would permit or cause such excessive evil for the reasons Hick suggests should be rebelled against as fully as the God portrayed in Camus's *The Plague.* I find this especially self-evident in light of the third objection, below. In any case, the above discussion indicates the basic difficulty faced by any form of free-will defense which holds that the capacity for self-determination is voluntarily bestowed upon creatures by God, so that God could have created actual beings, even ones quite like us, without this capacity.

2. However, there are further problems with Hick's particular version of the hybrid free-will defense. One is caused by the apparent existence of animal pain. Hick (rightly, I believe) makes no attempt to deny its real existence. He says that it is probable that some animal consciousness differs only in degree from human consciousness (346). And he even attributes some form of psychic distress to animals, such as loneliness, fear, jealousy, and bereavement (347). How is the existence of this suffering to be justified?

Hick says that the real question is not so much why subhuman creatures suffer, but why they exist at all (350). As we have seen, he rejects any "principle of plenitude" argument which suggests that every species of being has its unique form of intrinsic value, so that the greater the variety of species, the more value in the totality (350). Theodicy must justify the existence of the nonhuman species solely in terms of their instrumental value for humanity (204). Hick offers this justification: For humanity to have cognitive freedom in relation to God it may be necessary for it to be embedded in a larger stream of organic life. This sets persons in a situation in which awareness of God is not forced upon them. Given this "epistemic distance," they can come freely to God. The existence of animal life is thus justified by the contribution it makes to our epistemic distance from our creator (317, 351 f.).

One question to raise about this answer is whether it is credible. If a history of the planet earth were to be written comparable in length to Barth's twelve-volume *Church Dogmatics,* with each page covering half a million years, Homo sapiens would show up somewhere on the last page of the last volume. Is it any longer credible to suggest that the rest of the universe was created for the sake of human beings, as Hick does (173, 263)? In any case, the view would be somewhat incompatible with God's wisdom and omnipotence.

Hick says that his justification for animal existence is "in terms of a vast complex evolutionary development, with its own inner contingencies, which has produced man and which links him with the natural world" (353). But why have this complex evolutionary process in the first place? If God creates *ex nihilo,* rather than out of some primordial stuff which can be only gradually ordered, why did God take so long to get to the main act? If a natural world is needed in which humanity can be embedded, humanity and the rest of nature could have been produced simultaneously and instantaneously. And God could have created in such a way that it would appear that humanity had emerged out of a long evolutionary process, if this belief has some value. And of course some theologians have suggested that God did precisely that. But Hick surely would not join their camp. But if not, he has not explained why the evolutionary process was used by an omnipotent and omniscient deity if the only value we can attribute to the rest of the world is its instrumental value in giving us epistemic distance from God.

Furthermore, Hick says that "the justification of animal pain is identical with the justification of animal existence" (352). But this does not seem to follow. Why should the animals not exist without pain and suffering? Hick says that the power of the omnipotent creator is, by definition, not limited. Hence,

> it cannot be said that He *must* or that He *can only* create a world in which life devours life and in which creatures are wounded, maimed, starved, frozen, diseased, and hunted to their death.(110)

But this is what Hick himself seems to do when he says that, insofar as animals feel pain, "this occurs within the general system whereby organic life is able to survive" (348). And Hick also seems to violate his own dictum when he says that, in a world devoid of pain and the threat of extinction, "the evolutionary process would scarcely have progressed beyond its earliest stages, and the world would probably still be inhabited mainly by jellyfish" (342).

In a statement (from 353) quoted above, Hick spoke of the "inner contingencies" of the evolutionary development. This suggests that much of its suffering was not directly intended by God, but happened because of the inherent freedom of the emerging creatures. However, God's self-limitation is only in relation to persons. In regard to the rest of the universe, Hick says there is no distinction between God's permitting and willing (190 f.). Accordingly, there can be no suggestion that the suffering of animals is somehow beyond God's control and will. Hence, we need an answer as to why God would will a world in which there would be so much unnecessary animal pain.

This is especially the case since Hick does not believe there will be any heaven for animals to compensate for their sufferings. This disbelief is understandable enough. But it forces upon the reader the question as to whether Hick's God is perfectly good even by Hick's criteria. Hick rejects Cartesian dualism and holds that animal consciousness is different only *in degree* from human consciousness. And yet he holds that God's attitude toward animals, even the highest vertebrates, is totally different *in kind* from his attitude toward humans. God loves human beings and values them for themselves, but values other animals (as far as we know) only because of their usefulness for furthering God's goal with humans (200, 202–204, 263). Does this not mean another form of tribalism, in which God is the "Lord of a chosen in-group whom He loves," against which Hick rightly protested in rejecting the heaven-hell dichotomy? Does not this anthropocentrism reduce God's love "to the proportions of our own partisan human attitudes" (131)?

3. There is another problem with Hick's particular form of the hybrid free-will defense. His argument in brief is as follows: Whereas God could have guaranteed that persons would be moral in relation to each other, divine power could not guarantee that they would enter into an authentic fiduciary relationship with the divine person. The epistemic distance they must have in order for them freely to come to God entails that they may become self-centered rather than God-centered. And from the sin of self-centeredness flows moral evil, "man's inhumanity to man" (298–300, 359). The connection between the two is indicated in this statement: "Man must be free—free to center his life upon himself and *so* to bring suffering upon both himself and others" (359; italics added).

However, Hick never shows why the kind of freedom that he says is needed in order to develop authentic fiduciary attitudes toward God entails the necessity for moral evil in the sense of acting wrongly toward other human beings. Hick has said:

> The divine purpose for men is not only that they shall freely act rightly towards one another but that they shall also freely enter into a filial personal relationship with God Himself. (308)

Hick fails to explain why the requirements for the latter (religious) dimension of this purpose necessitate the breakdown of the former (ethical) dimension of the purpose. Hick has said that God could have determined our nature in such a way that we would *always act rightly* in relation to other human beings. On this assumption, God could have done this and still have left us free in regard to whether we would come to acknowledge God's existence and be willing to enter into a personal relationship with God. Whereas it is natural for theologians to think as Hick does, that a lack of faith in a God who loves all humanity (or creation) will leave one in self-centeredness, which will lead to acting unjustly toward one's fellow creatures, there is no necessary causal connection involved. That is, fully ethical attitudes and actions toward one's fellow creatures do not necessarily lead to, or presuppose, faith in God. Hick's argument for the necessity of the possibility of moral evil is therefore unsound. In summary: Hick tends to use the word "sin" ambiguously to refer either to moral evil or to lack of authentic fiduciary attitudes toward God. But he does not show how the conditions for sin in the latter sense entail that sin in the former sense also needs to be possible.

4. There is still another problem revolving around Hick's distinction

between the two dimensions of the divine purpose. Given the argument he accepts for the compatibility of freedom with divine determinism in regard to humanity's moral relationships, he provides no valid argument for considering them incompatible in regard to humanity's religious relationship. As pointed out earlier, in regard to the relationships of human beings toward each other, he accepts Mackie's argument: "If their being of this sort is logically possible, then God's making them of this sort is logically possible" (307). The argument that Hick accepts as sound can be more fully explicated as follows:

A. An omnipotent being can infallibly bring about any being that is logically possible.

B. A being that is free and yet is so constituted that it always chooses the good is logically possible.

C. Hence, an omnipotent being can infallibly bring about a being that is free and yet so constituted that it always chooses the good.

But Hick denies that it is "logically possible for God so to make men that they will freely respond to Himself in love and trust and faith" (308). The argument which he thereby implicitly rejects could be explicated as follows:

D. An omnipotent being can infallibly bring about any being that is logically possible.

E. A being that is free and yet is so constituted that it freely responds to God in love, trust, and faith is logically possible.

F. Hence, an omnipotent being can infallibly bring about a being that is free and yet so constituted that it responds to God in love, trust, and faith.

On what basis can Hick reject F? The form of the argument is the same as the previous one, which he said was valid. Accordingly he must either change his mind about this validity, or reject one of the premises. D is the same as A, which he says is true. Hence he would have to reject E. But is this not a description of the condition he thinks will characterize the saints in heaven? (Also, Hick would possibly say that Jesus exemplified this state.) Hence it is logically possible. Accordingly, Hick's rejection of this latter argument, given his acceptance of the former one, appears to be purely *ad hoc.* Hick's reluctance to accept F would be due to the fact that the "omnipotent being" and "God" are one and the same being. For example, he states as a principle: "It is logically impossible for God to obtain your love-unforced-by-anything-outside-you and yet himself force it" (309). And I agree with this, of course. But the point is that Hick has no basis for rejecting F, given his acceptance of the previous argument. The fact that the same being is involved in both premises under different names is irrelevant. If the premises are true, and the argument valid, then the conclusion cannot be rejected.

The reasoning behind Hick's distinction between the two cases is patently unsound. It will be recalled that he employed the analogy of the hypnotist and the patient. He says the patient, given the posthypnotic suggestion to act in a certain way, will be free in relation to other people, but unfree in relation to the hypnotist. Why so? Because the hypnotist alone will *know* that the patient is acting on the basis of psychological manipulation. But surely Hick is here confusing noetic and ontic issues. If the patient is acting under psychological manipulation, he or she is really unfree in all relations with other persons, whether aware of it or not. For example, suppose that Smith is the patient, and Jones is a fellow employee whom he does not like. On Monday morning the hypnotist gives Smith the posthypnotic suggestion that he will like Jones. For the remainder of the day, Smith likes Jones and manifests this feeling, and they patch up their differences and become friends. However, on Tuesday the hypnotist tells Jones what happened. This will surely change Jones's evaluation of the events; Hick is clearly right on this point. But it will not change the nature of the events in regard to their freedom. It will not be the case that Smith was acting freely in relation to Jones up until the moment that the hypnotist let Jones in on the truth. Accordingly, Hick's argument that the conditions for religious freedom differ from those for moral freedom is unsound. For he rests it entirely on the fact that God alone would *know* it if our actions were determined by our natures. But this is irrelevant. If our attitudes and actions are thus determined, then, depending upon how the word "free" is being defined, we are either free in relation to every other being, including God, or we are unfree in relation to every other being, including God. Hence, if Hick wants to maintain the soundness of Mackie's argument, then he has no basis for a hybrid free-will defense. He would have no basis for rejecting the traditional free-will defense, which accepted the compatibility of human freedom and responsibility with God's total determination of all our actions, attitudes, and feelings. This would bring us again to the schema of primary and secondary causation.

## AMBIVALENCE ON GOD'S SELF-LIMITATION

And in fact, there is another strain in Hick's thought in which he seems to come close to the more traditional position. He calls "promising" (why I do not know) the view of Charles Werner that, although God cannot foresee the actions of free beings who have not yet been created, once these free beings have been created God can see "their contingent future actions in His own eternal present" (185). And Hick is possibly indicating his own position in representing Werner's view as follows:

> Having once created them God does not go back upon His own creative act; He respects His creatures' freedom and responsibility even when He now sees that they are going to misuse it. (185)

Furthermore, although Hick has spoken of persons as having the capacity for choice that is in principle unpredictable and unknowable until it occurs (304, 312, 379), he elsewhere says that God must have foreseen that the free creatures would fall, and that God knew from the first the course his creation would take (197, 234). And Hick seems to endorse the traditional view that Christ's death was divinely foreseen (391). Also, in discussing demonic evil, which "seems to have got out of hand and to have broken loose from God's control," Hick says:

> It cannot be unforseen by the Creator or beyond his control. We must not suppose that God intended evil as a small domestic animal, and was then taken aback to find it growing into a great ravening beast! The creator to whom this could happen is not God. (325)

This clearly undercuts the suggestion that, in creating free beings, God had effected a self-limitation in regard to foreknowledge. This passage also suggests that God is still controlling all things. This is stated even more clearly in a passage in which Hick explains the sense in which God is responsible for evil:

> One whose action, A, is the primary and necessary precondition for a certain occurrence, O, all other direct conditions for O being contingent upon A, may be said to be responsible for O, if he performs A in awareness of its relation to O and if he is also aware that, given A, the subordinate conditions will be fulfilled. (326)

And Hick says that if the agent involved is God, one cannot speak of the *risk* of a disastrous outcome, since God cannot be in ignorance as to whether the event will actually occur. Although Hick does not say that God is the "sufficient condition" of evil, this seems to be implied, as he says:

> His decision to create the existing universe was the primary and necessary precondition for the occurrence of evil, all other conditions being contingent upon this, and He took His decision in awareness of *all* that would flow from it. (326; italics added)

Furthermore, in one place Hick apparently endorses Schleiermacher's rejection of the distinction between divine causing and permitting, by which Christian thought has tried to shelter itself from the logic of monotheism, which implies that God is ultimately responsible for the existence of sinful creatures and the evils which they cause and suffer (234). Here Hick does not even allow that the distinction is valid in relation to free personal beings, as he does elsewhere (109 f.).

Consistent with this line of thought, Hick appears to affirm the traditional view of primary and secondary causation. He says that the identity of divine permitting and causing does not deny our blameworthiness for our own sins, for "our individual human responsibilities hold good on a different plane from that of the ultimate divine responsibility, in such a way that the one does not lessen the other" (234). In this and the other places in which he discusses this idea of the "two levels" of responsibility, Hick does not make clear exactly how he understands it (cf. 326 f., 396). But he makes no criticism of Schleiermacher's view (236 f.), which is essentially the same as that of Augustine, Aquinas, and Calvin.

But if Hick is retaining the idea that God controls all events, even those of free beings, then God would be *directly* responsible for all evil. And this is what Hick seems to maintain. Up to this point I had been treating Hick's thought as if he had said that God was responsible for the situation in which moral evil is possible, but that God did not will or cause the sin itself. However, Hick says that in the situation created for man, "it is not only *possible* for him to center his life upon himself rather than upon God, but . . . it is virtually *inevitable* that he will do so" (359; italics added). Although Hick generally speaks of the "virtual inevitability" of sin (229, 320–322, 327, 389), he sometimes speaks of it as simply "inevitable" (262, 264), and even as "necessary" (343).

This idea of inevitability or necessity is in accord with the theme which Hick says should be one of the cornerstones, even the heart, of Christian theodicy—the "O felix culpa" (182, 400). He refers to this as a "bold and exciting suggestion" and "a religiously and morally profound conception, whose daring matches the depth of the problem and which must surely constitute one of the few authentic flashes of light that we possess upon the mystery of evil" (116). Hence, Hick's enthusiasm for the idea cannot be doubted.

What is questionable is the necessity in his thought of the idea that God willed not only the possibility of sin, but its actuality. He says it must be the case "that sin plus redemption is of more value in the sight of God than an innocence that permits neither sin nor redemption" (182). But this statement leaves out a third possibility, that humanity might have had the possibility of sinning without actually doing so. Why would God not have hoped for this situation, even though it could not have been guaranteed, rather than one in which humanity actually sinned? According to Hick's analysis of the conditions for "authentic fiduciary attitudes," which God desires from us above all, all that is needed is a genuine freedom vis-à-vis God, a freedom that gives the possibility of rejecting God and thereby the possibility of accepting God freely. How can that line of thought be connected with this other line according to which evil itself (not merely its possibility) was allowed (or caused) by God so that God could "bring out of it an even greater good than would have been possible if evil had never existed" (182)?

Hick attempts to connect these two strands of thought, saying: "The paradox of creaturely freedom is that only those who are initially against Him can of their own free volition choose to be for Him. Man can be truly *for* God only if he is morally independent of Him, and he can be thus independent only by being first *against* Him!" (323.) Why this is the case is not clear. He does elsewhere seem to give a reason, saying that "God is so overwhelmingly great that the children in His heavenly family must be prodigal children who have voluntarily come to their father from a far country" (359). The idea of the "far country" is a reference to the need for "epistemic distance." But Hick does not explain why those in the far country must actually be *prodigal.* Hence, I cannot see that Hick successfully connects his argument for the necessity of freedom vis-à-vis God to the idea that actual sin is a fortunate fact.

Furthermore, the possibility of "epistemic distance" from a God who is "so overwhelmingly great" is questionable. Hick asks: "How can a finite creature, dependent upon the infinite Creator for its very existence and for every power and quality of its being, possess any significant autonomy in relation to that Creator?" After making the suggestion that distance is needed for autonomy, he then asks a second question: "How can anything be set at a distance from One who is infinite and omnipresent" (317)? He answers that spatial distance is impossible—epistemic distance is what is needed. This means that God would be hidden, so that his reality would "not be borne in upon men in the coercive way in which their natural environment forces itself upon their attention" (317). He then concludes that this "will secure for man the only kind of freedom that is possible for him in relation to God, namely cognitive freedom, carrying with it the momentous possibility of being either aware or unaware of his Maker" (317). But this is problematic. If it is the case, as indicated in Hick's first question, that a finite creature is dependent upon God for "every power and quality of its being," how can it be free even in regard to whether it is aware of God? If it does not know God, this must be because deity has hidden itself from it, not giving it the quality of God-consciousness. Hence, if the human creature begins its life not knowing God, which Hick says is inevitable, this does not mean that the creature is cognitively free. To the contrary. It is cognitively unfree, since this ignorance was determined by God.

The point of this criticism is to reinforce the fact that Hick oscillates between two points of view. On the one hand, he seems to think that the reality of genuinely free persons involves a limitation on God's prescience and control, and that no "Manichaean dualism" is suggested as long as this limitation is not based on any metaphysical necessity but is due to a voluntary self-limitation. In harmony with these ideas, Hick says that it is not logically but only morally certain that all persons will eventually be won to God. "There would be a logical contradiction in its being, in the strict sense, *predetermined* that creatures endowed with free will shall come to love and obey God." Accordingly, it is logically possible that some, or even all, persons will in their freedom eternally reject God (379). We can only have a practical, moral certainty of universal salvation (379 f.). But, on the other hand, Hick often writes as if God's foreknowledge and control of all events are not limited by the presence of persons in the world.

## THE DENIAL OF GENUINE EVIL

Finally, Hick's view that God ordains the actuality of sin, rather than simply its possibility, means that he must finally be seen, along with the previous traditional theists, as denying the reality of genuine evil. If he had held the former position, that God only wills a situation in which evil is possible, and that the creatures are really free to cause evil which God did not desire, and perhaps even more than God had expected, then the reality of genuine evil could be affirmed. For it could be maintained that while the freedom to cause evil is good, the actual exercise of this freedom has resulted in events not necessitated by this freedom, and without which the world would have been a better place, all things considered. However, once it is said that God wills the actual moral evil, that God foresaw it all and this because it all flowed from the divine decision, and that it can all be accounted for in terms of the principle of "O felix culpa"—then it seems impossible to hold that any of the apparent evil is genuine.

Hick does try valiantly. As we saw earlier, he speaks of that which is "purely and unambiguously evil, genuinely evil and utterly inimical to God's will." He says that some evils will "disfigure the universe to the end of time," and that "it would have been better—much much better —if they had never happened." However, Hick also suggests that the fall of God's free creatures cannot "constitute a permanent stain upon His universe" (184). And we have already seen Hick's affirmation that God permitted moral evil in order to "bring out of it an even greater good than would have been possible if evil had never existed" (182). How then can it have been better if evil had never happened? How could it even be better if some of the worst evils, such as Auschwitz, had never happened, in the light of Hick's affirmation that these do not represent evil out of control, or even evil become greater than God had expected? And, as we saw, Hick even brings "dysteleological" evil within the framework of those things that contribute to soul-making, thereby finally seeing them as teleologically (i.e., instrumentally) good.

Hick admits that the most difficult problem of theodicy is to reconcile "a serious facing of evil *as evil*" with an acknowledgment of the "ultimate omni-responsibility of God," i.e., to reconcile the view that moral evil is a "virtually inevitable outcome of God's own creative work" and yet "truly at enmity with Him" (325, 388 f.). But both views are in the Bible, and hence they must be reconciled (389). In his attempt to reconcile these two points of view, Hick distinguishes between two perspectives from which evil is viewed.

> Experienced from within the stresses of human existence, evil is a sheerly malevolent reality, hostile alike to God and His creation. . . . Seen, on the other hand, in the perspective of a living faith in the reality of the great, ongoing, divine pur-

> pose which enfolds all time and all history, evil has no status in virtue of which it might threaten even God Himself. (395)

However, this distinction does not save the genuineness of evil, for *prima facie* evil which only seems evil when viewed from a limited perspective is precisely the definition of "only apparent evil."

However, Hick's more fundamental distinction is between a "present interim dualism" and an "unqualifiedly monotheistic faith" within which it is set (22). But this distinction also fails to save the genuineness of evil. Hick says that "what now threatens us as final evil will prove to have been interim evil out of which good will in the end have been brought" (400). But what does this mean other than that its ultimate instrumental value outweighs any present intrinsic or instrumental evil in it? Hick says that "the Kingdom of God will be an infinite, because eternal, good, *outweighing* all temporal and therefore finite evils" (386; italics added). He says that sin and suffering "really are evil and will remain so *until* they have been forced to serve God's creative purpose" (400; italics added). But this clearly means that, from the final and ultimate perspective, they are not evil. And Hick explicitly says that in relation to the fulfillment of God's purpose "nothing will finally have been sheerly and irredeemably evil. For everything will receive a new meaning in the light of the end to which it leads" (399). While evil is really evil from the point of view of our present experience, from the point of view of that future completion it will not have been merely evil, for it will have been used in the creation of infinite good (400). All of this is, of course, Hick's explication of the theme, "O fortunate crime, which merited such and so great a redeemer" (400), and of the "mystery that was revealed" to Mother Julian of Norwich: "Sin must needs be, but all shall be well. All shall be well; and all manner of thing shall be well" (264, 325). Hick's apparent attempt to reject premise 5 finally means the rejection of premise 7.

## REVISING THE DOCTRINE OF GOD: THE REJECTED POSSIBILITY

I have suggested that part of the problems in Hick's theodicy would be present in any hybrid free-will defense, and that these problems arise from the view that God *could* totally control an actual world, and that the problems would be avoided if one would maintain that any actual world will, by metaphysical necessity, be composed of beings with some power of self-determination, even vis-à-vis God, so that it is logically impossible for God unilaterally to prevent all evil. And Hick himself says that such a view "is capable of being expanded into a comprehensive and consistent position, and one that has the great merit that it solves the problem of evil" (35). The obvious question, of course, is why Hick does not adopt such a position. Hick's answer is that from the point of view of Christian theology, such a position "is unacceptable for the simple but sufficient reason that it contradicts the Christian conception of God" (35).

Hick seems to give three distinguishable reasons why such a view is unacceptable. First, he believes that the rejection of such a position (which he calls "dualism") is "a corollary of revealed theology" (35). Now he quite often refers to "revealed truth," the "Biblical revelation," the "Christian revelation," and "revealed theology" (122, 129 f., 149, 185, 211, 255 f.). However, he does not make clear the criteria for deciding what is to be counted as revealed truth. It certainly is not everything in the Bible, or even in the New Testament, since he excludes Paul's teachings about the origin of sin (211). Sometimes the teaching of Jesus seems to be definitive; but Hick rejects the doctrine of hell, which Jesus did evidently teach. Hick does suggest that this "cannot safely be affirmed," and that the textual evidence must be interpreted in the light of "Jesus' teaching as a whole," at the heart of which is said to be the sovereign divine love (382). But this removes any unambiguous basis for deciding precisely what "the revelation" is. The lack of any basis for speaking of "revealed theology" is further suggested by Hick's statement that faith is an "uncompelled interpretative activity" (317), and that it arises from religious experience (281). This would seem to indicate that a human theology is not something revealed, but is a human and therefore fallible interpretation of experience. I am sure Hick agrees with this. But what basis does he have, then, for speaking as if there has been some revelation of the nature of God's providence that is so unambiguous that it puts the validity of traditional theism beyond discussion (as he implies by saying it is "not negotiable")?

What is the basis, then, for saying that a view of creation something like Plato's is excluded by "revealed theology"? Who mediated a revelation of the falseness of the metaphysical claim that actuality qua actuality has some power of self-determination and hence cannot in principle be totally controlled by some other being or beings? It may be replied that this idea is excluded by the doctrine of creation *ex nihilo.*

But this is doubtful. And, in any case, one can ask why this should be considered a revealed doctrine. Even Barth admits this doctrine is not taught in Genesis. Hick speaks of God as the "sole creator of heaven and earth and of all things visible and invisible" (35), thereby alluding to the Nicene Creed. But is it a revealed truth that God created the "invisible" things such as logical and metaphysical principles? As we have seen, Hick does not evidently think God could violate logical principles, so he evidently does not think of those as dependent upon God's will. However, at times he seems to think it is leaning toward a pessimistic Manichaean dualism to speak of eternal logical necessities (170–173). And the statement that "God has determined in His absolute freedom all the conditions of creaturely existence" (325 f.) seems to exclude the possibility that some of the conditions of creaturely existence are *metaphysical* in nature and hence beyond choice. Further, Hick explicitly rejects the idea that evil can be explained by "metaphysical necessity" (197). Is there anything in Jesus' teaching as a whole, even if this could be accurately summarized and also simply taken as revelation, that provides a basis for decisions on such subtle matters? That question is, of course, meant to be rhetorical.

A second objection that Hick makes to the view in question is that "natural theology" says that it is "metaphysically unsatisfying" (35). Hick's claim is based on the assumption that a God who is not "the creator of everything other than Himself" would not be "an eternal self-existent Being." Hence, one would have to ask who created God (36). But Hick fails to show the connection between these two ideas; and in fact there is none. There is nothing in the idea that God has always existed and is self-existent which implies that God has created strictly everything other than himself. The argument in Hick's mind is evidently the following: (1) A deity who has not created everything other than himself is a "finite God." (2) A "finite God" must be finite in every respect. (3) Hence such a God would not be self-existent. This is an unsound argument, since the second premise is not true. (Part III will present a doctrine according to which God is finite in some respects and infinite in others.) It is an example of the careless reasoning that is commonplace when traditional theists consider any doctrine of God which can *prima facie* be considered "finitism."

Hick's third reason for rejecting the view of God in question is that Christianity is a "religion that understands and worships God as that than which nothing more perfect can be conceived" (35). And he quotes approvingly F. H. Bradley's remark that "it is an illusion to suppose that imperfection, once admitted into the Deity, can be stopped precisely at that convenient limit which happens to suit our ideas" (36).[6] Hick has here, of course, assumed what needs to be shown, i.e., that his doctrine of God is the "greatest conceivable," and that any doctrine which he would call "finitism" would necessarily imply "imperfection" in God. I too accept the Anselmian formal definition of deity—premise 1 of the formal statement of the problem of evil is based upon it. And I will argue in Part III on the basis of this definition that the doctrine of God which Hick and the other traditional theists hold is not the greatest conceivable, because it is not genuinely conceivable at all.

# 14
# James Ross: All the World's a Stage

IN THE PREFACE of his book *Philosophical Theology,*[1] which he describes as "the beginnings of an analytic reconstruction of scholastic natural theology," James F. Ross announces his intention to give sympathetic attention to three scholastic doctrines:

> (a) that one can establish the existence of a being which could (and perhaps does) have the attributes orthodox Christians attribute to God;
> (b) that it is consistent and intelligible to conceive of God's power as limited only to the logically possible;
> (c) that there is no theoretical conflict between the universal causality and the absolute entitative and moral perfection of God, on the one hand, and the admitted reality of the evils of the world and the premised freedom of man, on the other. (vii)

In this critique only the latter two doctrines will be examined directly. However, the first is relevant in that it emphasizes Ross's concern, which is not with an examination of various possible conceptions of "God," but with a defense of God as defined by "orthodox Christianity" (46). His commitment to this task is relevant to the third doctrine, for he says the problem of understanding how God's power and goodness are related cannot be solved by "attributing to God a defect or deficiency in power or in anything else. Orthodoxy entirely excludes such concessions" (46). As he states in the second doctrine, Ross maintains that God can do anything that is logically possible. I will suggest that the basic formal problem in Ross's position is that he does not sufficiently consider the power that it is logically possible for God to have in relation to an actual world.

The critique of Ross's position is central to my critique of traditional theism for two reasons. First, Ross makes explicit and central in his theodicy an idea that was presupposed by most of the previous traditional theists, the idea that the distinction between primary and secondary causation makes creaturely freedom compatible with divine sufficient causation. Second, Ross's argument for the intelligibility of this idea raises explicitly a question that is implicitly raised by previous traditional theists, the question as to whether the world is actual or merely a stage play in the divine mind.

As indicated above, Ross does not try to resolve any problems by modifying traditional theism's doctrine of God's power. If anything, he brings out more explicitly than most the implications of the traditional doctrine of omnipotence. He defines it as entailing that whether or not a certain contingent state of affairs occurs is logically equivalent to whether or not God chooses for it to occur. "Whatever He chooses is *in fact* the case and vice versa"; also "whatever He might have chosen *must* have been the case"; furthermore, "nothing could have been the case had God not willed it" (211).

Ross holds that for God to choose *x* provides logically or causally sufficient conditions for *x* to occur. This raises the obvious objection that divine governance and free will seem to be in conflict. How can Jones freely murder Smith if God's choice is the sufficient cause of this act? And if no one acts freely, there is no such thing as moral evil. This is one of the problems Ross believes he can solve.

Closely related to this problem is that of the affirmation of the divine goodness in the light of the evil of the world. One way out, as we have seen repeatedly, has been to deny, implicitly or explicitly, the full reality of evil. But Ross says that any interpretation of God's relation to the world which conflicts with the supposition that moral and physical evil are real is "obviously false" as well as being contrary to Christian doctrine (253). Some might claim that these evils are not genuinely evil from the ultimate point of view, since they or at least the conditions for their possibility are necessary for a greater good that would be impossible without them. But Ross dismisses all such views. The evils of pain, ugliness, and sin in our world could have been avoided by God absolutely. "Whatever end was to be attained in this creation could have been attained in some other in which these evils are not present" (237). "God could have avoided all moral evil through grace without interfering with the natural behavior of things" (245). There is no reason to think that "God could not have created only persons who would act right throughout their lives" (238). In short, this is not the best of all possible worlds, not only because (as we have seen that Journet says) there is no such world (237, 286), but also because God could have created a much better world. And God could have done it without any cost or moral fault (264). Hence, Ross explicitly affirms premises 3 and 7. This raises the obvious question as to why God then did *not* create a better world. Does this not count against God's moral goodness? Ross also believes he can refute this objection, that he can show that "there cannot be acceptable grounds for the disbelief in the moral perfection of God . . . on the basis of the evil in the world" (249 f.).

Ross's argument to reconcile both human freedom and the divine goodness with the divine omnipotence revolves around the notion of "metaphysical dependence," which involves the notion of "different levels of reality." Because of the importance of these notions to Ross's argument, I will quote his definition in full:

> *b* is of a lower level of reality than *a*, if and only if *b* belongs by essence to a class of things *B* such that no member of that class could exist unless: (1) some member (or members) *a* of the class *A* exists; (2) produces the existing members *b* of class *B;* (3) maintains a conserving relation to those members *(b)* throughout their existence; and (4) no member of class *B* has any property whatever that is not bestowed upon it by *a* or by some member of *A* or some member of some class of things to which the members of *A* stand in relations (1), (2), and (3). (254)

*Metaphysical dependence* is "the relation a thing of a lower level of reality has to the particular thing of higher level which produced it, conserved it, and determined its properties" (254). The creature-creator relationship as defined by orthodox Christianity exemplifies the criteria of metaphysical dependence.

Ross believes that these notions help make explicit what is involved in the idea of *two levels of causality,* which was presupposed in scholastic theology: "God is said to be the sufficient cause of whatever is done by His creatures; but in some other sense, the creature-cause is also said to be the sufficient cause of what is done" (250).

This doctrine of the difference between *metaphysical causality* and *natural causality* is said to be necessary in regard to freedom. For if God's causality were on the same level as natural causality, then the fact that God is a sufficient cause of human acts would destroy their freedom and responsibility (266); but God must cause our sinful actions in such a way that we do what we ought not to do with full responsibility (253).

In order for us to have some idea how this can be, there must be a known case of metaphysical dependence. This is supplied, Ross says, by the dependence of a fictional character upon its author. Every detail of a character's activity is determined by the author, and yet this does not mean that the character does not act freely. Shakespeare's choice was the sufficient cause of Othello's murdering Desdemona; but this does not mitigate Othello's freedom and hence his responsibility for the act. Since there are two types of causality involved, total determination (on the level of metaphysical causality) does not eliminate freedom (on the level of natural causality).

This is of utmost importance for the problem of divine predestination and human freedom, Ross believes, for it provides a refutation of the principle that is needed to argue their incompatibility, i.e., that "if *x* acts freely, *x* is not metaphysically dependent upon something else." If that principle were true, Ross says,

> it would be impossible to create a character which is free since all characters are dependent in this way. But we know this is false; from that we know the falsity of the premise that nothing which is metaphysically dependent is free. (258)

(The "facile amendment" [258n] that the principle is true when limited to *real* beings will be discussed below.)

Ross also believes the notion of metaphysical dependence can be used to resolve the alleged conflict between this omnipotent God's goodness and the reality of physical and moral evil. Regarding physical evil, Ross believes that theism entails the following premise:

> God, Who is of higher level than His creatures, could have precluded all the sufferings in His creatures, without performing an act of lower moral value than He has performed. (263)

But to *blame* God for not doing so, Ross says, requires the following premise:

> $R_1$: Any being that could avoid or preclude the sufferings of others without performing an act of lower moral value than it would otherwise perform ought to do so. (263)

But this principle would commit us to the following one:

> $R_2$: Any being that could (without performing, etc.) preclude the sufferings of other beings on a lower level of reality, or in beings which are metaphysically dependent upon it, ought to do so. (263)

But $R_2$ is false, Ross claims, for "we know it is false that Shakespeare ought to have prevented the wounding of Paris"; and "a person who deliberately imagines a suffering lion . . . is committing no moral crime" (264). Hence, the principles that are necessary to indict God on the basis of physical evil are said to be false.

What about moral evil? Is God not imperfect for causing morally evil beings, since morally perfect persons could have been created without the loss of any important values? The "most likely principle" (266) for this argument, Ross says, would be the following:

> $R_3$: When a being of higher level is sufficient cause for the free evil action of a being of a lower level, the higher being is morally defective and ought not to have done so. (265)

But, Ross says, "this principle is demonstrably false" (265). If God were responsible for our sins, then we would not be responsible and hence we would not have sinned. One ends with the paradox that "God is morally defective for creating a world with moral evil in it only if He did not do so" (265).

Hence, Ross's solution to the problem of evil appears to involve a denial of premise 5. My criticism will center around two major points: (1) Insofar as the relationship of an imaginary being to its thinker is put in the same class as the world's relationship to God, the implications in regard to the reality of the world are unacceptable, and no real solution is given to the problems. (2) Insofar as these relationships are *not* regarded as similar in essential aspects, the causal terms involved are used equivocally; hence the apparent assertions employing them are without meaning, and can thus provide no solution.

Ross defines "metaphysical dependence" in such a way that it applies to the relation of a thought to the thinker, a dream to the dreamer, an imaginary being to the mind, a fictional character to the author, as well as of the world to God (255 f.). But if these relations all belong to the same class, does this not imply that the world, when considered with respect to its relation to God, has only the status of being an idea in the divine mind? Ross is concerned with defending the position of Christian orthodoxy; but does it express the *intention* of orthodoxy to suggest that the world has no more reality in relation to God than an idea in a mind? It is noteworthy that Ross, in explicating his two types of causality, does not hesitate to compare them to Berkeley's two types, so that *metaphysical* causality is compared to the relation between minds and ideas, and *natural* causality is compared to that between ideas (260).

Insofar as there is no essential difference between the thought-thinker relation and the creature-creator relation—and all of Ross's arguments for human freedom and the divine goodness based on known cases of metaphysical dependence make sense only if there is no *essential* difference—the reality of human freedom and hence of moral evil is not theoretically established. In what sense does a fictional character have freedom? Certainly there is a sense in which we can discuss the extent of Othello's freedom, but we are aware that we are discussing how free he *would* have been *if* he had been an actual, as opposed to a fictional, person. In regard to Othello's freedom in relation to Shakespeare we realize that he had none, and this is what is relevant to the subject at hand. Given Shakespeare's decision that Othello was to kill Desdemona, Othello could "do" no other. Likewise, given God's decision that Jones is to kill Smith, Jones can do no other. The example from literature in no way shows that metaphysical causality, as defined by Ross, is consistent with real freedom. If God be the sufficient cause of our acts, then we do not really act freely.

Of course, the term "freedom" has been defined in various ways. As is implied in the previous paragraph, a human decision is free in the sense that is required for responsibility only if a different decision could have been made at that point in space and time, with all the antecedent conditions exactly as they were. When discussing God's freedom, Ross seems to accept as a general principle that "its being logically possible that one should have done other than as one did" is a logically necessary condition of "having done freely what one did" (280). But according to Ross's own formulation of God's causality, for God to will that Jones stab Smith *logically entails* that Jones is going to stab Smith. Hence, it is logically impossible that Jones should have done other than as he did. Hence, Jones did not act freely.

Ross says that Jones murders Smith freely even though God causes him to do it, since God makes him murder *at* will, not *against* his will (212). Ross believes this makes the act a moral evil, since such an act must be done by an intellectual being "in the absence of conditions defeating his voluntariety of action" (252). But this move depends on an artificial distinction between willing and acting, so that "stabbing" is said to be an action, but "deciding to stab" is not. The important question is whether Jones could have done other than will to kill Smith. Not at all, given God's effective decision. And it would be irrelevant to say that Jones could have done otherwise, *if* God had willed otherwise. For the issue is whether men can be said to have any freedom, *given* God's universal determining will.

Since Ross has not shown that persons are free in the sense required for moral responsibility if they are related to God as he says, his entire discussion of moral evil is baseless. His procedure, as we saw, is to have principle $R_3$ be the center of his opponent's argument. He then shows that this principle leads to paradoxes which constitute a *reductio ad absurdum* of the view that God is morally imperfect for causing people to sin. But principle $R_3$ is by no means one that an opponent of traditional theism would use, for it is precisely the meaningfulness of this principle that is denied. It is simply inconsistent to speak of one being as the *sufficient* cause for "the free evil action" of another being. Despite Ross's efforts, nothing has been said that makes that into an intelligible idea.

The real objection to traditional theism in regard to sin is not that God is guilty for having caused sin, but that real sin (defined as a transgression of God's will) is impossible. Hence traditional theism is self-contradictory in that it speaks both of God's omnipotence and of human sin. Ross's attempt at a *reductio ad absurdum* is therefore misplaced. The question of God's culpability in regard to sin comes up only in regard to the doctrine that God damns to punishment persons whom God caused to sin. The principle in question is that "a being which makes entities that will be damned for their sins is morally imperfect" (267). Ross responds to this objection brusquely, saying that a perfect being can create beings who are *justly* damned. However, Ross has failed to show that people have freedom in any sense that makes meaningful the idea of their being "justly damned." Ross's rhetorical questions ("Why should a man not be damned for his sins? Why shouldn't Macbeth have been damned for his murders?") show that Ross is here still thinking of persons as having the same freedom in relation to God that a dramatic character has in relation to the playwright, i.e., none at all.

Ross's attempt to reconcile the divine goodness with the reality of *physical* evil is no more successful. As we saw, his refutation of the general validity of principle $R_2$ revolved around the fact that it is not evil for an author to have a fictional character suffer, or for a person to imagine a lion suffering. But imaginary beings do not *really* suffer any more than they really have freedom. Hence, he has not shown that $R_2$ is meaningful, so $R_1$ remains valid.

Also, insofar as Ross sees God's relation to the suffering in our world as being essentially the same as a person's relation to the "suffering" of imagined beings, he is suggesting (against his own explicit statements, to be sure) that our suffering is not really real from the divine viewpoint, so that it would not be genuinely evil. And if he is to have any argument at all, he *has* to be regarding these relations as essentially the same, for two relations that were essentially different could not be classified as the same type of relations, i.e., those of "metaphysical dependence." Only if these relations are regarded as essentially the same do the examples based on thinkers and thoughts have any relevance to the question of the relation of God and the world.

However, Ross is aware that the reader will insist that there is an essential difference between real and imaginary beings, and that the principles discussed thus far apply only to *real* beings (Ross says "real" where I would say "actual"). That is, one might insist that in the premise, "If *x* acts freely, *x* is not metaphysically dependent upon something else," *x* stands for a *real* being. Then the moral principle must be rendered as follows:

> P: Any being which could, without cost or moral defect, preclude or avoid the evil acts and sufferings of other real beings and fails to do so is morally imperfect. (264)

Ross regards this restriction of the principles to real beings as exemplifying the "fallacy of facile amendment" (264); and he sees no reason why there should be this restriction, except as an attempted *ad hoc* escape from his argument (269). It is hard to believe that Ross really thinks the distinction between actual and merely ideal existence to be as trivial as this response suggests. In any case, his treatment of this issue is somewhat confusing. At one place it appears that he himself is going to insist on an essential difference in the types of relations involved. That is, he says that he is *not* drawing an analogy between the relation of imaginary beings to their authors and that of the world to God, or arguing by analogy. And yet in the same paragraph he says that the moral principles ($R_1$, $R_2$, $R_3$) which could be used to indict God for divinely caused evil are "clearly false because the author-character and dreamer-dream cases are counter examples which fulfill the conditions of the dependence relation" (269). That argument surely presupposes an analogy, at the very least, between these relations and the God-world relation. And Ross himself says that these relationships are "parallel" (266), and he speaks of the "inductive evidence there is from the analogy with literature" which "supports the claim that premise $R_2$ is false" (264 f.). The oscillation throughout the entire discussion, which is exemplified in this paragraph, will be discussed a little later.

Ross's central response is to allow the "facile" restriction and then to accuse its defender of begging the question. In regard to the issue of freedom he says:

> It is generally conceded that the only possible case (granting the consistency of the proposition, "God exists") of the metaphysical causation of the attributes of real beings is the case of God's causality. (258)

Now this statement stands in considerable tension with the preceding line of argumentation. As mentioned above, Ross's whole argument thus far depends on there being no essential difference between the God-world relation and the thinker-thought relation. They must both be examples of the relation of "metaphysical dependence." But now Ross casually implies that there *is* an essential difference, since there is a difference involved between real (or actual) and possible beings. If that is not an essential difference, what could be? Furthermore, although Ross repeatedly claims that one would have to engage in question-begging to reject his position, it is clearly he who begs the question. For what is at issue is whether "the metaphysical causation of the attributes of real beings" is a "possible case." Far from being "generally conceded," that is precisely what is disputed. For, entailed in the idea of "real (i.e., actual) being," I would claim, is the element of power. And if the beings of the world are metaphysically dependent (as defined by Ross) upon God, then they have no power of their own. If they have no power, then they have no actuality.

The question-begging of Ross's position becomes especially clear when he speaks of the metaphysically dependent beings as having freedom. If God is the sufficient cause of Jones's action, it is simply inconsistent to say that Jones acted freely (if "freely" is so defined as to entail responsibility). How does Ross reply to this charge? By saying that it begs the question, since "it has never been supported by a deduction of the claimed inconsistency" (259). But surely no elaborate deduction is called for—it is simply a question of *definition:* If a real being acts freely, then its action is not totally determined by something else. Ross replies to this, amazingly enough, by referring back to his previous examples of the compatibility of freedom and determination in regard to the acts of *imaginary* beings (259). The circularity involved in this is clearly question-begging. For the issue at hand is precisely whether, if the beings of the world are *real,* there is any basis for an analogy between their relation to God and an imaginary being's relation to its thinker. One cannot legitimately employ examples involving imaginary beings to refute the contention that certain principles are true when restricted to real beings!

Ross goes on to say that his opponent has no *inductive* evidence for the claimed incompatibility between divine predestination and human freedom (253). But the subject of inductive evidence is totally irrelevant when the question is one of logical consistency. Of course, any determination of logical consistency or inconsistency depends on an unequivocal use of the key terms involved. And, indeed, any apparent plausibility that Ross's whole argument has rests finally upon an equivocal use of words.

This can be seen best if we look first at his attempt to resolve the problem of evil where the moral principles involved are understood as referring only to real beings. As we saw, the basic principle would be the following:

> P: Any being which could, without cost or moral defect, preclude or avoid the evil acts and sufferings of other real beings and fails to do so is morally imperfect. (264)

But, Ross says, P does not entail the needed principle, which is as follows:

> R′: Any real being which could, without cost or moral defect, avoid or preclude the evil acts and suffering of real beings which are metaphysically dependent upon it and fails to do so is morally imperfect. (269)

Again, Ross sees this as question-begging, for God is the only being to which the principle could possibly apply, since God is the only being upon which other real beings are metaphysically dependent. Hence, R′ cannot be used as a premise from which to deduce God's moral imperfection.

In reply, it must again be said that it is Ross who begs the question by assuming the meaningfulness of R′, which is simply a limitation of $R_2$ to real beings. But far from wanting to limit $R_2$ to real beings, as Ross assumes, the critic of traditional theism denies precisely that $R_2$ can be applied to real beings at all. Especially do I deny that one can meaningfully speak of "evil acts" of "real beings which are metaphysically dependent." As Ross himself insists, for a person to perform an evil act he or she must act freely; but, as was argued above, to say that a person is the cause of his or her act and yet that it is totally caused by another being is self-contradictory.

It is self-contradictory, that is, if the term "cause" is used with any consistency of meaning. But it is not thus used by Ross, and hence his whole argument finally hinges upon an equivocation. He claims that the generally valid principle that there can be only one sufficient cause for an event does not apply if one is speaking of different *kinds* of sufficient causes (262). And he explicitly says that the term "causation is an equivocal term when beings are of different levels of reality" (265). Generally this would mean that the term is used in two *completely* different senses, although one might speak thus and mean that the two uses are partly the same and partly different, and hence "analogical." But the former interpretation must be placed on Ross's words. For he says that principle P is confirmed by our moral experience, but that P does not entail R′:

> For to say R′ follows from P is to equivocate upon the term "cause" which is involved in "preclude" and "avoid." There are at least *two kinds* of precluding or avoiding. Our evidence for P is based upon experiences which involve natural causality. How can we, without further reason, swing to a principle involving metaphysical causality, especially when cases (now conceded for the argument) were given in which the stronger rule, $R_2$, did not hold—that is, in which the dependent beings were not restricted to real beings? (269 f.)

Again Ross accuses his opponent of the fault (here, equivocation) of which he himself is guilty. For he is the one who has insisted that there are "two kinds" of causality (cf. also 250, 253, 262). But if we are to have *any* notion as to what "metaphysical causality" is, there must be *some* similarity between it and the natural causality we understand from direct experience. And if there is a similarity between God's causation and natural causation, then there is no reason to say that R′ (if it could otherwise be interpreted meaningfully) does not follow from P.

Hence, Ross is faced with the following dilemma: If the causal terms in R′ are used meaningfully, R′ is as true as P. If they are not used meaningfully, then R′ offers no escape from P. The only other possible reaction to R′, that it is totally inconsistent, also leaves us back with P, and hence with the original argument against God's goodness. Again, Ross's mention in the above quotation of the cases in which the moral principle did not hold is irrelevant, since those were all cases involving the thinking of imaginary beings, and the issue Ross is supposed to be considering is whether the moral principles in question are valid when limited to actual beings. (Ross is evidently misled into mentioning these examples where they are out of place by his tendency to think of $R_2$, the formulation of the moral principle which is not restricted to real beings, as a "stronger rule.")

I believe it is now clear that Ross fails to give a sound argument for the compatibility of God's omnipotence either with the reality of human freedom or with the divine goodness (granting the reality of genuine evil). His argument is vitiated by question-begging, circularity, and most importantly, equivocation. The fact of his equivocal use of causal terms is made even clearer by his statements as to the conditions presupposed in moral evil. Unlike some philosophers (e.g., Antony Flew, Wallace Matson), he does not believe that it is consistent to say that a person's act is free, so that the person is responsible for it, if the natural causes operating on the person totally determine that act. "Ordinarily, if *A causes B* to do *x,* this exonerates *B* from having sinned" (265). It is because of this that God's causality must be said to be on a "different level" than natural causality; there must be "logically diverse kinds" of causality (250, 253). There can be only one sufficient cause of any event, unless there is a difference "in the kind of sufficiency in question" (262). What can this finally mean, other than that Ross is using causal terms equivocally? For, given what "sufficient cause" normally means, his statement can only be interpreted thus: There can be only one sufficient cause of any event, unless the term "cause" when applied to God has no relation at all to its meaning when applied to finite beings.

What Ross does, then, is to oscillate between two ways of thinking of divine and human causation. At times he thinks of God's causation in a meaningful way, a way having a basis in our experience. That is, God's causality is thought of as essentially the same as our causation of our own imaginary creatures. When Ross is thinking along these lines he can speak of God's omnipotence in a meaningful way. Real meaning is given to the idea of God's causality, when it is defined as implying that, if God wills *x,* then *x* will occur; for we all know that we can cause our imaginary beings to "do" as we wish.

Of course, this intelligibility comes at a high price; for it entails that there is no human freedom and hence no moral evil. For, if God's causation is like that between a mind and its ideas, then our causation is like that between ideas, i.e., it is no causation at all. (Although we may speak carelessly at times of one idea as causing another idea, we know upon reflection that there must always be an agent involved who has actual, as opposed to merely ideal, existence.) And this intelligibility entails finally that there is no actual world. For if the relation of the world to God is essentially the same as the relation of a play to its author, then from the divine viewpoint—which must be regarded as the ultimate standard of truth—the world has no actual existence. The world is God's "play," as some Oriental thought has held.

Accordingly, Ross in effect denies what he insisted he would not, i.e., the reality of evil. For if the world is not actual, there can be no actual sin or suffering in it. So, Ross has not denied premise 5, as he claims, since he is not really talking about an actual world. As with previous traditional theists, the apparent denial of premise 5 is really a denial of premise 7.

At other times Ross thinks of us as actual beings, and hence of our exerting real causality. But in thus applying causal terms meaningfully to us, he must apply them to God without meaning. He says that the sufficiency of God's choice to effect contingent states of affairs requires that "the type of influence God exerts must be quite different from that with which we are acquainted in ordinary life" (271n). Rather, it must be *wholly* different. Insofar as Ross admits that the God-world relation is really unlike the author-character relation, he destroys the only analogical basis he has for giving us any insight into how there can be *two* "sufficient causes" for an act.

As we have seen in previous chapters, all traditional theists who have maintained the reality of human freedom (and Luther is the only one examined above who forthrightly denied it) have presupposed, more or less explicitly, that the primary-secondary schema of divine and creaturely causation made sense, so that one could meaningfully attribute causation to the creatures even though God's causation was thought of as sufficient for the production of all events. This analysis of Ross's thought suggests that the only way that the notion of two sufficient causes for one event can make sense is if the world is thought of as non-actual in relation to God, as a mere idea in God's mind. Accordingly, Ross has not more than verbally affirmed premise 3, since he is only verbally speaking about an actual world. And I would say that this is not unique to Ross, it is only clearer in him. All traditional theists have in effect denied the actuality of the world by implicitly or explicitly lodging all causality in God, and thereby at most attributing power and hence actuality only verbally to the world.

I have examined the essential substantive elements of Ross's treatment of the correlative problems of freedom and evil. But there is one further element that bears criticism. This is a formal point, concerned with the procedure of "natural" or "philosophical" theology.

As we saw earlier, Ross defines his task in terms of the concept of God held by "orthodox Christians." Some might criticize him in terms of some other idea of what natural or philosophical theology is or ought to be, such as that it should be more neutral, or that *it* should decide which is the best concept of God. There is, however, no one right description of the task of "natural" or "philosophical" theology; any number of projects could legitimately be so entitled.

But it is one thing to defend the existence of God as conceived by the tradition of orthodox Christian theology, and to say in regard to such problems as that of predestination that "no answer will be considered correct which does not accord with the other and more definitely settled elements of the [orthodox] concept of God" (48). It is quite another thing to appeal to this tradition itself as evidence for the consistency and meaningfulness of this orthodox doctrine of God. The appeal to tradition for this purpose may be permissible within Christian theology proper, according to some conceptions of this enterprise (such as Karl Barth's), but it is out of place in natural theology altogether.

And yet Ross, in regard to a definition of the relation of God's omniscience to states of affairs, says it is "a conceptual relation for whose consistency there is at least a millennium of support" (214). In regard to the idea of two levels of causality, he points out more than once that his view is similar to that of the traditional metaphysicians and theologians (213, 262n). This may be interesting historically, but is irrelevant philosophically, especially at a time when it is precisely the intelligibility of the traditional views that is at issue. And he even says that "quite adequate evidence for the sufficiency of God's choice to effect contingent states of affairs is provided in Christian teaching" (271n). But this is perhaps the aspect of the traditional views that is today most widely held to be inconsistent by critics, Christian and non-Christian alike. No matter how "long" the "theological tradition of orthodox Christianity" is, and how "profound and authoritative" one holds it to be (52), an appeal to it is irrelevant in deciding whether one of its assertions is self-consistent.

Ross's attempt to rescue creaturely freedom and divine goodness in the face of divine omnipotence is ingenious but patently unsuccessful. The basic problem lies in Ross's failure to apply his analytical ingenuity soon enough. That is, he simply assumes the meaningfulness of the traditional doctrine of perfect power and then tries to reconcile it with other beliefs, rather than beginning with an analysis of the meaningfulness of this doctrine itself. And this forces him to accept an idea of actual beings that has been accepted implicitly by all traditional theists, i.e., that they are not essentially different from merely possible or ideal beings. Prior to Ross, this was seen most clearly in Leibniz. The virtue of Ross is that, with his analogies (and his virtual equation of worldly beings with Berkeley's "ideas") he makes this nondifference explicit.

If the problem of evil is to be solved in the context of a position that is both meaningful and compatible with Christian faith, the reconstruction of "natural" or "philosophical" theology must be more thoroughgoing than Ross's. Primarily what is called for is a more thoroughgoing analysis of what it is *possible* for a being with perfect power to do. Ross stresses that such a being cannot do that which is *logically* impossible. But he, like most others who have written on this problem, abstracts the discussion of *logical* possibility from any analysis of *metaphysical* possibility. I do not see how this abstraction can be legitimately made. For, if the conclusion of a syllogism is to be used to decide what an omnipotent being could do in relation to other actual beings, it must be decided whether the ideas about the nature of "actual beings" contained explicitly or implicitly in the premises of the syllogism are true. And this question about the nature of actuality qua actuality is a metaphysical question, probably the central metaphysical question. Ross's failure to incorporate this type of analysis into his argument is shown by his assumption that there is no essential difference between actual and merely ideal or imaginary beings, so that the former could be as totally controlled as the latter.

Part III of the present book will contain an analysis of the meaning of "actuality" and of what "perfect power" can mean in a world with a plurality of actual beings. It will be argued that premise 3 of the problem of evil can be rejected without accepting Barth's strange notion of omnipotence, Brightman's suggestion that God has an internal problem (see Chapter 16), or Hick's idea of a voluntary divine self-limitation, and yet without, in Ross's words, "attributing to God a defect or deficiency in power."

# 15

# Fackenheim and Brunner: Omnipotence Over Logic

THE DISCUSSION thus far has focused upon the possibility of rejecting one or more of the following premises: 2, 3, 4, 5, or 7. But allusion has also been made to the possibility of rejecting statement number 6, i.e., of rejecting the validity of following the normal rules of logic when discussing the relation between God and evil. Some form of this move characterizes a considerable number of contemporary writings on the problem of evil.[1] In this chapter, I will discuss two of the better-known theologians whose positions can best be thus characterized. I will suggest that it is the impossibility of finding an adequate theoretical solution which lies behind the suggestion that no theoretical solution is needed, and that it is the retention of the idea of divine omnipotence which in turn lies behind this impossibility.

## EMIL FACKENHEIM

Emil Fackenheim, contemporary Jewish theologian and philosopher of religion, has confronted the problem of evil especially as it has been raised for Jews by the Nazi holocaust. His writing on the subject is in part a response to the writings of Richard Rubenstein. The latter has asserted that "after Auschwitz" no Jew can believe in God as the omnipotent author of history.[2] To believe in such a God means that one must accept Hitler's actions as God's will, and the SS as God's instruments, and this idea is simply too obscene.[3] Rubenstein sees that Jews and Christians have agreed that God is omnipotently active in history, so that events express the divine will, and that the logical implications of this idea combined with that of God's beneficence lead to the justification of the holocaust.[4] Rubenstein's response is to give up the idea of divine providence in history altogether, and to affirm the God of nature, or the gods of the earth.[5] He realizes that this means giving up all metahistorical meaning and saying that the cosmos is ultimately unfeeling and meaningless. But he believes that a meaningless cosmos is better than one with a horrible meaning.[6] Rubenstein gives no sign of having considered the other alternative, that of retaining divine providence in history without the traditional doctrine of omnipotence that required equating historical events with God's will.

Fackenheim cannot accept Rubenstein's solution. He sees that giving up the God of history would mean the end of Judaism. And this would mean handing Hitler a posthumous victory (*QPF* 20).[7] But Fackenheim agrees with Rubenstein that it would be blasphemous to try to find religious meaning in Auschwitz (*QPF* 18). And he rejects the view that all persons are God's instruments; sin is not an instrument of God (*GPH* 18, 26, 73).[8] Nor can all sufferings be understood as just punishment for sins (*GPH* 73). In other words, Fackenheim agrees with Rubenstein that premise 7 must be affirmed, that there is genuine evil in the world. And he rejects the idea that all evil is willed by God; hence he affirms premise 5.

The view that not all human events are willed by God entails the affirmation of real human freedom vis-à-vis God. Fackenheim rejects all views of God as "sole power" that do not allow room for human freedom and evil (*GPH* 19). Vital religion requires the notion of human freedom; if Fate controlled man's inner attitude, there could be no such thing as conversion, whereas this is the whole point of religious wisdom (*QPF* 197).

However, Fackenheim does affirm that God is the "sole power" (*GPH* 13 f.). Any view that limits the divine power is "paganism," for if God were not the sole power, God would be finite (*QPF* 16 f.; *GPH* 19). This means that both doctrines must be affirmed:

> Is it not equally absurd to solve the religious problem of human freedom and divine omnipotence by denying the reality of either the one or the other, when it seems that every vital religion requires both? . . . Within traditions such as Judaism and Christianity, every genuine prayer affirms divine omnipotence. And every such prayer affirms human freedom. (*QPF* 199, 201)

Accordingly, Fackenheim rules out rejection of either premise 2 or premise 3. He also rules out rejection of 4, 5, 7, and, of course, 1. This leaves only statement number 6, and this in fact is what he rejects, i.e., the validity of logic in relation to this question. He rejects the idea that religious faith is to be judged by the standard of "objective rationality" (*QPF* 200). Rather, he says, religious discourse has its own logic (*QPF* 201 ff.). Elsewhere, instead of "religious discourse" in general he speaks of "Midrash" as having a logic of its own, by which it can hold fast to contradictory affirmations in stories, parables, and metaphors (*QPF* 16 f.). In any case it is clear that Fackenheim "resolves" the problem of evil by denying the validity of logic in this realm, as he rejects the validity of the law of noncontradiction.

Fackenheim's attempted justification for rejecting the laws of reason in the area of religion involves a *non sequitur.* For he goes from the fact that religious faith lacks "objective, rational proof" to the conclusion that religious belief need not be judged by the standard of objective rationality, which means for him that the theologian can eschew ordinary logic. But the fact that there is no rational proof for the truth of a position does not imply that the truth of that position cannot be falsified by its failure to conform to the standards of rationality. In fact, it is becoming increasingly accepted that this is the relation between rational proof and philosophical positions in general (and assertions about the relation between God and humans are philosophical assertions, whatever else they may be as well). That is, reason alone cannot prove the truth of any philosophical position. The most it can do is to show whether the position is possibly true, by examining whether it does or does not violate the requirement of logical consistency. Hence, to assert that religious belief cannot be proved by objective, rational means does not differentiate it from any philosophical belief, and hence does not move it outside the circle of beliefs which must be tested by the general requirements for responsible beliefs, the minimum one of which is logical consistency.

As stated before, I do hold that adequacy to the facts of experience is a higher virtue than logical consistency. And since I believe that genuine evil in the world is one of the most indubitable facts, and in fact find with Rubenstein and Fackenheim the attempt to deny it obscene, I prefer Fackenheim's eschewal of logic to the denial of genuine evil. And I believe he is right in holding that the whole of Biblical religion is undercut if the reality of human freedom and of real evil is finally denied by carrying out the logic of the idea of divine omnipotence as the sole power. Nevertheless, although the denial of logical consistency is better than the denial of evil, it is still a drastic step, and one which should be avoided if at all possible. And, of course, it is possible by following Rubenstein in the rejection of divine providence altogether, or by following Albert Camus in the complete acceptance of atheism. And, if forced to choose between accepting one of these two resolutions, on the one hand, or rejecting the validity of logic in religious discourse, on the other, I would have to follow either Rubenstein or Camus.

Fackenheim no more than Rubenstein appears to have given serious consideration to the other alternative, that of maintaining belief in divine providence in history, but holding that this providence is not all-determining. Fackenheim for the most part dismisses all views which deny that God is the sole power as "paganism," and as unsatisfactory for "vital religion." Insofar as he does consider the idea of "limiting" divine power, to make room for human freedom, he assumes that this would mean removing divine power from history altogether. And, since human power over nature continues to advance, this would seem to mean the exclusion of divine power from nature as well. God would be a mere ideal, therefore not God at all (*QPF* 198 f.). Hence, Fackenheim manifests that same all-or-nothing attitude in regard to divine power that Rubenstein does. The Western theistic tradition in general has been so successful in inculcating this attitude, with its insistence that "God" simply means "the power to control everything," that the view that God influences all events, while determining none of them, is generally not even considered. And this remains largely true even today, although such thinkers as Charles Hartshorne have been articulating and defending this latter view for decades. Further examples of the unreasoned dismissal of this view will be given in Chapter 17. The purpose of the present chapter is to emphasize that the rejection of such a view, along with the admirable refusal to deny the reality of genuine evil, requires either the denial of a providential deity or the denial of the validity of the basic principles of rationality in religious matters.

## EMIL BRUNNER

A further example is provided by the Christian theologian Emil Brunner. Brunner begins his discussion of the problem of evil by saying that no one can ignore the question as to how God, if responsible for the things that happen in this world, can be both almighty and a God of love (148).[9] And, after saying that nothing that happens to people of faith personally can make them doubt God, he adds:

> But what about the things that happen to others? And how can we combine the thought of the love and the righteousness of God in face of the mass of innocent and unjust suffering with that of an all-inclusive Divine Providence? This problem, that of the theodicy, cannot be separated from that of Providence; we must put it to ourselves. (159)

Furthermore, having evidently affirmed that innocent and unjust suffering (and hence genuine evil) occurs, and that we must raise the question of theodicy, particularly in regard to the sufferings of other people, he says: "No one can preserve his Christian faith in God without having found an answer to this question. . . . To find no answer here is to have to confess loss of faith" (178). This seems to suggest what I argued above in relation to Fackenheim, that reasoning can in principle invalidate religious faith.

What, then, is Brunner's answer? At first he seems to reject premise 3. For he says that if the doctrine of omnipotence were to become that of God's sole power and activity, the distinction between God and the world would be lost, and pantheism would be virtually adopted (149). He insists that creaturely independence is needed (150). He criticizes the doctrine of omnipotence held by Zwingli, Calvin, and the young Luther as being the product of speculation or "natural theology" rather than the Biblical revelation (174). Furthermore, he says:

> The God of revelation is indeed not the *potestas absoluta* of speculation, but the God who limits Himself, in order to create room for the creature. . . . The two ideas, Creation and self-limitation, are correlative. (172)

And he adds that the idea of *potestas absoluta* or of omnicausality has been given up when one talks of creation (173). Furthermore, Brunner rejects altogether the application of the notion of causality to God: "There is causality between created objects, but there is none between the Creator and the Creation" (153). The causal idea "belongs to the sphere of 'things' " (154).

Brunner seems to be saying that God is omnipotent in the traditional sense, but only prior to creation; the act of creation implies a self-limitation on God's power, since the creatures by definition must have their own power and activity. This would seem to imply the rejection of premise 3, since if creatures by definition have their own power and activity, even vis-à-vis God, then God could not create a world and guarantee it to be free from evil.

However, in other passages he suggests that his answer is a modification of this view, making his position closer to that of John Hick. In places he seems to affirm the above view, that creatures in general must have power and independence in relation to God, while affirming that this independence has "real religious significance only in view of human freedom" (173). But elsewhere he seems to posit a free-unfree dualism between humans and the rest of the creatures. For example, he distinguishes between divine "preservation," which is related to natural existence as such, and divine "government," which is related to history, and says that the problem of government is different from that of preservation "only where man comes upon the scene" (176). More explicitly, he says:

> God has not only created the creatures who are not free, who cannot do anything other than obey His will; but He has also created creatures who have a free will, who *can* become disobedient, who can decide against His will. (181)

In the light of his earlier criterion for avoiding pantheism, it is hard to see how the position enunciated in this passage differs from that of the personal idealists, according to which nothing other than persons are distinct from God. But, in any case, Brunner evidently means to affirm the freedom of at least the human creatures. That this is so is suggested further by his statement that "whatever may be said about Providence, one thing is certain—that this original relation of the revelation which contains God's 'call' to man, and responsibility, may not and cannot be questioned" (173). This seems to be an affirmation, parallel to Fackenheim's, that no doctrine of omnipotence can be allowed to contradict the freedom vis-à-vis God that is implied throughout the Biblical tradition, especially in the idea that God calls us and that we are responsible for our response. Furthermore, that Brunner has rejected the traditional position that all events in the world are finally caused by God, albeit perhaps by God's "left hand," is further suggested by his rejection of double predestination (181). Finally, if Brunner affirms that some events are really not totally caused by the all-good God, one would expect him to affirm the reality of genuine evil; and Brunner does explicitly reject all attempts to explain the reality of evil away by seeing all apparent evil as means for a higher good (179).

Hence, there is much evidence that Brunner's position involves a rejection of premise 3, at least if the world that is created contained human-like beings. The theodicy implicit in this position would be similar to Hick's: God could indeed create a world in which the creatures had no power to disobey God and hence to cause evil, but God has chosen, for the sake of higher values, to create a world with personal beings in it, beings with the power to violate God's will. Carried out consistently, this hybrid free-will defense would argue that God cannot prevent the evils that these persons cause, at least not without violating their freedom and hence destroying their status as persons.

However, Brunner does not develop this position consistently. For, despite all that has been said, he still holds to the traditional doctrine of omnipotence. Although he rejects applying the term "causality" to God, he does hold that God "influences" creatures (154). And, more than that:

> Everything that happens has its final ground in God: All that happens is connected with the divine Purpose; all is ordered in accordance with, and in subordination to, the divine plan, and the final divine purpose. (155)

Furthermore, he, like Hick, lumps those "modern thinkers who abandon the idea of divine Omnipotence" together with Manichaeans as "dualists." And he clearly indicates his opinion of any such dualism:

> A God who looks on impotently while the devil, or the evil in man, devastates His Creation, who is indeed innocent of all this evil and suffering, but also unable to do anything to prevent it, is certainly not the God of the Biblical revelation, of the Christian Faith. (180)

The reason we cannot say that God cannot prevent evil, Brunner says, is the message of the cross. The cross is the supreme product of human malice and yet it is God's sovereign act for our redemption (177, 180 f., 182). While Judas and Pilate are enemies of God, they are nevertheless God's instruments; God has such power over evil as to be able to make it an instrument (182).

Accordingly, even though Brunner claims, like Barth and Hick, to base his view of divine power on the New Testament revelation rather than upon natural theology, and even though Brunner (unlike Barth) uses words such as "ground" and "order" rather than "causality" and especially "omnicausality" to describe the divine influence, the doctrine of omnipotence does not finally differ from that of other traditional theists: God has the power to control all events, even in a world with persons.

Accordingly, Brunner's solution cannot be understood as a rejection of premise 3. The next possibility is suggested by Brunner's endorsement of Luther's distinction between the "real" and "alien" work of God. He says this distinction is inevitable for anyone who sees both sides of the truth about the cross, i.e., that it is our salvation, and yet the result of human malice and blindness. Reminiscent of earlier discussions of God's two wills, he says:

> God does not will both in the same way, although it is certain that for the sake of the one, which He really wills, He wills the other which He does not really will. (180 f.)

This must be used to interpret the earlier discussion of human beings as having the freedom to decide contrary to the divine will. This passage shows that they decide contrary to the will of God only in one sense (what Luther called the revealed will), while they actually decide in conformity with the will of God in another sense (the hidden will). This, together with the previous discussion of God's omnipotence, seems to imply a rejection of premise 5, that God would want to bring about a world without evil. Further evidence of this rejection of premise 5, which involves an assertion of what a morally perfect God would want to do, is Brunner's statement that it is arrogant to say that God ought to allow himself to be measured by our standard of justice. Like Calvin before him, Brunner says of God: "As Creator He is absolute Lord, who is not bound to give any account of Himself to His Creation. . . . He is not tied to our standards of justice" (184 f.).

We have seen in previous authors that an apparent rejection of premise 5 really involved a rejection of premise 7. And there are passages in Brunner which suggest this denial of any genuine evil. On the one hand, he seems to take back his earlier affirmation of innocent, unjust suffering, as he says that the New Testament discloses the presence in us of a guilt for which no suffering would be too great a punishment. On the other hand, we learn from the cross that suffering is a means of discipline, and the way to eternal life, as suffering purifies us, thus preparing us for a life without suffering (182–183). And, for those outside the circle of faith, the fact that they cannot solve the problem of theodicy is said to be part of their punishment for sin! (183.) These statements, together with the previous ones implying that human malice is in one sense willed by God and used as an instrument to effect the divine purposes, suggest that nothing really happens without which the world would be a better place.

However, this denial of genuine evil no more represents Brunner's dominant position than do the other theoretical solutions he suggests. Besides his explicit rejection of rational theories which purport to explain evil away, he means to reject rational or theoretical solutions altogether (180, 182). He says that the problem of theodicy is theoretically insoluble (184), that all theoretical solutions are "false" and "sham" (184). And, consistently with this position, he says that the "glimpse into the mystery of the divine government of the world" which we get from seeing the cross as that which God does not will, yet as the divine instrument, cannot be generalized to explain world history in theological terms (182). This evidently means that we cannot say in general that God's enemies are instruments of God's "alien" work.

The only solution to the problem, Brunner says, is an "existential" or "practical" one (182). Since the contradiction between the creature and the creator generating the problem is a reality, it cannot be eliminated by thought, but only by another reality (184). "The real solution to the problem of theodicy is redemption" (183).

However, the solution Brunner speaks of seems to be a purely personal, individual solution. It does not help with the problem he himself had singled out as raising the problem of evil in the most acute form, the unjust suffering of others. His answer to this seems to be provided by the following statement:

> The theodicy problem finally proves to be a form of unbelief, insofar, that is, as the question is raised from a point outside one's own responsibility, according to the connexion between the will of God and the evil in the world. (183)

Brunner here seems to be saying that we should not ask the question about the righteousness of the Almighty God in relation to the calamities that befall others. We can only deal with evil as it affects us personally. To reflect upon that which befalls others is to take up the attitude of the spectator, and theoretically to objectify and therefore falsify the problem (184 f.). "Only the man who yields to the temptation to abandon [the] attitude of faith, and to usurp the place of the judge, is confronted by the theodicy problem; and then it is insoluble" (184). Hence, whereas Brunner earlier said that we cannot preserve our faith without finding a solution to the problem of theodicy—and whereas he singled out the unjust sufferings of others as the major issue—he now says that if we have faith we will not raise the question. And if we do raise it, we cannot solve it.

Brunner does not reject the validity of logic in relation to the problem of evil as explicitly as does Fackenheim. But his position finally amounts to this, since he says that the problem is insoluble, and yet he does not reject belief in a loving God. And Brunner is forced into this choice for the same reasons as was Fackenheim. That is, he not only agrees that one cannot deny the divine governance of the world within the context of the Biblical doctrine of God (177), but he also finally holds, after considerable hesitation, that this governance must be total control. Then he also insists that this control cannot be such as to negate human freedom and hence responsibility, since this is also essential to the Biblical perspective. And his conclusion is the same as Fackenheim's: That we must hold the independence of creaturely, or at least human, activity while we also affirm omnipotent divine activity, even though we cannot understand how these two activities are interwoven (154). Brunner adds that this mystery is somewhat parallel to our inability to understand how the human spirit and brain are related (154).

It seems evident that it is this inability to solve the problem within the context of divine omnipotence that leads Brunner to adopt the position, however inconsistently, that no theoretical solution, but only an "existential" one, should be expected, and finally that the theoretical problem should not be raised by a believer in the first place. This same shift occurred in Brunner's Christology, which also involves, of course, the question of the relation between divine and human activity. In his first book on the subject, although denying in some passages that one should do so, Brunner proffered a theory as to how God was related to the man Jesus.[10] But in his later discussion of Christology, after it was apparent that his earlier position was untenable (it was widely and rightly criticized as monophysite), he consistently maintained that theology should not attempt to answer the question as to how God was present in Jesus without destroying his full humanity.[11] This parallel case, the admission of the impossibility of understanding the interweaving of divine omnipotence and creaturely freedom in general, and the fact that Brunner does in fact give many "theoretical" responses to the problem of evil (while saying they are not complete solutions), together suggests that it is the impossibility of resolving the problem, rather than any totally "practical" or "existential" nature of the problem, that leads Brunner to suggest that no theoretical solution is needed for it, and to imply thereby that the conclusion of a sound argument can be ignored.

I agree with Brunner and Fackenheim that one cannot talk about "God" in our context, decisively molded as it is by the Biblical tradition, without affirming God's providential activity in the world, and also the reality of human freedom and of genuine evil. But I also maintain that, while the problem of evil is obviously a practical or existential problem, it also has a definite theoretical dimension to it, and that it is irresponsible of the theologian to try to deny this theoretical dimension, or the legitimacy of someone with "faith" raising questions about it, and to offer a totally practical solution to the theoretical side of the problem, and thereby to assert or imply that the believer can and even should hold beliefs in the face of admittedly sound arguments which contradict these beliefs. It seems evident that the only way for theology to meet its responsibility to help people reconcile their beliefs based upon revelation with the "facts which everyone can see," as Brunner says should be done (151), is to develop or adopt an understanding of divine providential influence which is not total determination. And this means going beyond the issue of semantics. Brunner does not talk about divine "causality," since he understands this word as referring to the influence exerted by one "object" or "thing" on another; and yet his understanding of God's power is as fully deterministic as those who have more explicitly derived their understanding of divine influence by analogy from the causal impact of one object or thing, such as a stick or a stone, upon another. Of course, the problem is not the use of analogy as such, since some analogue taken from our direct experience must be used if talk about divine influence is to be meaningful. The problem is what is used as the analogue. The Biblical understanding of both God and the human person as subjects of experience suggests that the relations of influence between persons would provide a suitable starting point. While Brunner in fact claims that this is the basis of his theological program, the causal relation between subjects is never one of complete determination, but always one of persuasion, where the influenced subject necessarily makes a partially free response. Hence there is no experiential basis for speaking of the influence exerted by the divine subject on creaturely subjects as if it involved complete control. This issue will be discussed more fully in Part III.

# 16

# Personal Idealism:

## God Makes a Sensational Impression Upon Us—More Unorthodox Conclusions from Orthodox Premises

PERSONAL IDEALISM is the doctrine that nothing exists except minds (or spirits, or persons) and their ideas. The founder of this doctrine in modern Western philosophy was Bishop George Berkeley (1685–1753). In the first section I will examine Berkeley's ideas. In the following sections I will look at the views of some of his intellectual descendants.

### BISHOP BERKELEY: THE SUPERFLUITY OF NATURE

The idealistic thesis as formulated by Berkeley is that there are no *actual* entities other than conscious, intelligent minds, so that "nature" is not composed of actualities but only of ideas. My main contention in this section is that, although the primary argument for the idealistic thesis is not based upon the traditional doctrine of God (but upon the incoherence of and problems resulting from the notion of "matter"), the proponents of this thesis have rightly seen that it is compatible with the traditional doctrine of God, and that it could be derived therefrom.

It is not necessary here to review in detail Berkeley's arguments for the idealistic thesis; a brief sketch will suffice. Berkeley's major purpose is to show that there is no reason to believe in "matter," or "corporeal substance," in the sense of unperceiving substance. His principal contention is that the very notion of unperceiving substance is self-contradictory, so that such things cannot possibly exist. But he argues further that, even if such things could be believed in without contradiction, there would be no reason to affirm them.

His most famous (though generally underestimated) argument is that "to exist" or "to be" can only mean "to perceive" or "to be perceived." A perceiving thing is a mind, spirit, or soul. A perceived thing is an idea. And an idea can exist only in a mind. Hence, nothing exists besides minds and their ideas. And, since Berkeley assumes (without argument, so far as I know) that what we call "nature" is not composed of perceiving things (e.g., Leibnizian monads), this means that natural things have no existence independently of the minds that perceive them, but are simply ideas in those minds. Although he sometimes speaks of animals as perceiving (*D* 25, 29, 31),[1] and he refers to the possibility of other intelligent beings besides humans (*D* 101; cf. *PC* 443, 723),[2] the only perceiving things he usually has in view are God and human souls. In any case, the only "substances" are God and the finite spirits. There are no material substances. All of nature, including the human body, is constituted by ideas, ideas which God causes us to perceive.

Berkeley has various arguments for his position, besides the above argument based on the meaning of "existence." He says that with our senses we perceive nothing but our own ideas or sensations, and hence from our senses have no basis for thinking there is any external "matter" which is the source of these ideas. Berkeley does not reject the notion of causation, and the principle that every effect must have a cause. Hence he holds that those ideas which manifestly are not of our own making (i.e., which are not produced by memory and/or imagination) must have a cause external to us (*P* 26).[3] This cause must be another spirit. For one thing, the ideas could not come from an unperceiving thing, since ideas by definition can exist only in minds (*D* 87; *P* 91). And an idea cannot "copy" or "represent" that which is not an idea, since an idea can only be like an idea (*P* 8, 90). Also, we have no understanding of how "matter" could influence spirit (*P* 50). Furthermore, spirits are the only things we can meaningfully talk about as exerting activity, as being efficient causes; we have no notion of action distinct from volition (*D* 80, 87; *P* 28, 61, 102, 105; LJ 1).[4]

Here we see that by "spirit" Berkeley means more than a thing that simply perceives; it is a thing that also wills. The active side is as essential as the passive, receptive side. "As it [the spirit] perceives ideas it is called the *understanding,* and as it produces or otherwise operates about them it is called the *will*" (*P* 27). Since Berkeley defines an "idea" as something totally inert, and says that something inert cannot represent something active, he denies that we have any idea, properly speaking, of a spirit. But he says that we do have a *notion* of it, in that we know, from reflection upon our own spirit, what we mean by the word.

From the above arguments, Berkeley concludes that all sensible things (e.g., rivers, trees, books) either do not exist when no created spirit is perceiving them, or else they are constantly perceived by an Eternal Spirit. Since the former is incredible, the latter must be the case. Berkeley considers it one of the chief virtues of the idealistic thesis that it provides such an easy proof for the existence of God. And Berkeley assigns to the God thus proved all the traditional attributes. God is said to be impassible, immutably omniscient, purely active, omnipotent, cause of all things, and infinite in wisdom and goodness as well as power. (*D* 59, 71, 88, 100–103; *P* 30, 57, 72.)

Berkeley says that the thesis that God does all "natural" things directly by implanting ideas in our minds is compatible with traditional Christian teaching about God and the world. In fact, he believes it is more compatible than the view that there are, besides created spirits, also unperceiving material substances. The view that nature is a being distinct from God was produced by heathens who did not know of the omnipotence and infinite perfections of God (*P* 150). In the Bible, God is understood as the sole and immediate author of those effects which some heathens and philosophers ascribe to nature or matter or some other unthinkable principle (*D* 83).

Of course, as we have seen in previous chapters, traditional theists have held that, while God *could* produce all effects directly without using natural or secondary causes, God has chosen generally to use such causes. Berkeley argues against this view. In the first place, people use tools and instruments to make up for their deficiency in power, so it does not honor God's power to say that he uses instruments (LJ 3). God is an omnipotent spirit, on whose will all things absolutely depend, and as such, God has no need of instruments (*D* 63). Accordingly, to affirm that God nevertheless employs them is to suggest that God has created a world that is totally superfluous. Why would one suppose that God would use such a roundabout method to achieve that which all admit could have been done in a more direct way? (*D* 57, 63; *P* 61.) Furthermore, no one can understand how material substances, if such could exist, could be employed as causes, since no one can understand how body could act upon spirit, or even how a material thing could exert efficacy at all (*P* 19, 61; *D* 107). Malebranche recognized this difficulty, and said that matter was not the cause of ideas in our minds but only the occasion for God to impress these sensations upon our minds. But this is explicitly to admit that matter is superfluous (*P* 53). In either case the materialist position is precarious, "since it is to suppose, without any reason at all, that God has created innumerable beings that are entirely useless, and serve to no manner of purpose" (*P* 19).

Berkeley argues that his view is consistent with the Biblical doctrine of creation. The creation of nature occurred when God caused created spirits to begin perceiving it (*D* 99–101). The Biblical assertion that natural things were created prior to humans can be reconciled with this view of creation by holding that there were nonhuman intelligent beings created prior to the creation of human beings (*D* 101; *PC* 443, 723). (It should be remarked that Berkeley's answer, if forced, is self-consistent. But those who today reduce nature to sense-data, yet cannot follow Berkeley in the appeal to the existence of angels or other nonearthly perceivers, have considerable difficulty in affirming the view that things existed prior to the evolution of beings with sense-organs.) Furthermore, Berkeley seems to believe his view of nature is more compatible than the materialistic view with the notion of creation out of nothing. For he regards the difficulty of conceiving the creation of matter out of nothing as one of the causes of atheism (*P* 92), while he regards his own view as something we can conceive on the basis of experience, since we all have the experience of creating ideas through our power of imagination (*PC* 830).

It seems to me that Berkeley's arguments from traditional theistic premises are well taken. If God is omnipotent in the sense of being able unilaterally to bring about any logically possible state of affairs simply by willing it, it is superfluous to employ instruments. The (Thomistic) argument based upon the value judgment that it is more fitting for God to use instruments which have been given power can easily be questioned, as we have seen. Furthermore, traditional theism did not really attribute power to secondary causes, but only did so verbally. And, if the only experientially based and hence meaningful notion we have of a "substance" or an "actuality" involves the exercise of power, then the traditional position was not meaningfully ascribing actuality to natural things. The only difference between that position and Berkeley's is verbal (as Ross's position makes clear).

Berkeley could have supported his position even further by reference to the traditional doctrine that God's perception of the world is creative rather than passive. This doctrine entails that the world does not exist prior to and hence independently of God's knowledge of it, but that this divine knowing creates it. It is difficult to see anything more than a verbal difference between this and Berkeley's view that the world, insofar as it exists independently of the perception of finite spirits, exists only in the mind of God. Berkeley does hold that deity is purely active, with no passivity involved in its perception. He suggests that no Christian should be shocked by the doctrine that "the real tree, existing without his mind, is truly known and comprehended by (that is, *exists in*) the infinite mind of God" (*D* 81). And he says that no one with "notions of the Deity suitable to the Holy Scriptures" should maintain that sensible things have "an *absolute* existence, distinct from being perceived by God, and exterior to all minds" (*D* 82). But he does not (to my knowledge) explicitly connect his idealistic thesis with the doctrine that the divine knowing is creative rather than receptive. Perhaps it simply did not occur to Berkeley. Or perhaps he saw that an explicit use of this doctrine would have caused problems in regard to the reality of finite spirits, an issue to which I will return. In any case, this aspect of the orthodox doctrine of God as well as the more direct meaning of omnipotence suggests that nature should be thought of as a set of ideas directly implanted upon our minds by God. Within the context of traditional theism it is superfluous and even of doubtful meaning to suggest that there are some beings which serve as mediators of the providence of God.

Berkeley claims to be able to answer all objections to his views, or rather, all that apply uniquely to his views. It is now time to see what objections can be raised to the idealistic thesis on the basis of the world's evil.

As we have seen, Berkeley holds that God is infinite both in goodness and power. He shows no inclination to differ with traditional theism in regard to these attributes. But how can God's goodness be affirmed? Is God not responsible for all murder, rape, adultery, etc.? Berkeley demurs, pointing out that sin does not consist in outer actions, but consists in the internal deviation of the will from the laws of reason and religion (*D* 83; LJ 4). Hence, sin is to be imputed to the finite spirits. Letting this answer stand momentarily, it still seems that Berkeley's position raises insuperable problems. Even though the sin itself may lie in the internal state of mind, i.e., in the intention to commit murder or rape, nevertheless the *effects* of the intention are experienced by the victim only because God impresses these effects upon the victim's mind. As Berkeley explicitly states, that the motion of the limbs of one person's body "should be attended by, or excite any idea in the mind of another, depends wholly on the will of the Creator" (*P* 147). Although Berkeley does not discuss the subject in these terms, it seems that his view here would be like that of Malebranche. That is, upon the occasion of Jones's willing to stab Smith, God would, after the appropriate interval of time, induce the appropriate pain in Smith (remembering, of course, that God does all of this nontemporally). Accordingly, even if Jones can be said freely to will to inflict pain on Smith, he cannot actually inflict any pain upon him; only God can do this. Hitler and his henchmen could, for all their evil intentions, not cause a single Jew to suffer and die. An American president and his military organization could not cause a single Japanese to suffer from an atomic bomb. Hence, all pain and suffering purportedly due to human agency is really due to divine agency. Furthermore, all apparent evil which is not related to human agency is even more clearly due totally to God. In this category would be hurricanes, tornadoes, earthquakes, most famines and droughts, and many fires and floods.

Berkeley's response to the problem of evil is quite brief. The argument to which he gives the most attention involves the idea that much of what we label "evil" is due to the fact that God causes sensations in us in a regular manner, which we call the laws of nature. This regularity, the laws of which we can learn from experience, is necessary for us to develop foresight in ordering our lives. That is, we learn that such and such means will produce such and such ends (*P* 31, 65). And we know that, from such and such visual sensations, such and such tactile sensations will follow if we proceed in such and such a direction (*P* 42–44, 65). Berkeley believes that this consideration alone outbalances all the "inconveniences" which arise from the laws of nature (*P* 151). He also repeats very briefly the aesthetic argument, saying that the blemishes and defects of nature "make an agreeable sort of variety, and augment the beauty of the rest of creation" (*P* 152). And in regard to the pain and uneasiness resulting from the general laws of nature, Berkeley says that if we

> enlarge our view . . . we shall be forced to acknowledge that those particular things which, considered in themselves, appear to be evil, have the nature of good, when considered as linked with the whole system of beings. (*P* 153)

Hence Berkeley's response to the problem of evil, at least in relation to everything except evil volitions, is to deny the reality of genuine evil.

But Berkeley's main defense of his idealistic system in the face of the problem of evil is that he need not give a defense. For he is concerned only with those objections which apply uniquely to his position. Problems which are equally difficult upon the assumption of material substances pose no objections to his thesis. And he says that this is true of the problem of evil.

> The imputation . . . upon the sanctity of God is equal, whether we suppose our sensations to be produced immediately by God, or by the mediation of instruments and subordinate causes, all which are his creatures, and moved by his laws. This theological consideration, therefore, may be waived, as leading besides the question; for such I hold are points to be which bear equally hard on both sides of it. (LJ 4)

On this score Berkeley is surely correct. As long as deity is defined as omnipotent in the traditional sense, God is equally responsible for all murders, rapes, and earthquakes, whether one says that God works by means of secondary causes or that all such phenomena are directly implanted upon our experience by God. Substantively there is no difference, in regard to natural evil, between Berkeley's view and that of other traditional theists. The only difference is the explicitness with which Berkeley denies all actuality and efficacy to natural beings, so that it is unambiguously clear that all effects which appear to be due to natural causes must be attributed directly and totally to God. In this way personal idealism, insofar as it is consistent with traditional theism and could even be deduced therefrom, helps us see more clearly what is entailed by it, and how severe its problem of evil is.

Thus far I have focused attention on apparent natural evil, all of which Berkeley attributes to God, but denies that it is genuinely evil. But, as was briefly mentioned, Berkeley believes that sin, or moral evil, is not attributable to God. And he evidently believes, therefore, that it is genuinely evil.

But is his belief that sin can be attributed to finite spirits consistent with his retention of traditional theism? As we have seen, other traditional theists finally had to maintain that God controlled human actions, including the most interior decisions of the human spirit, as fully as all other happenings.

Berkeley certainly assumes and asserts genuine human freedom. Whereas he believes that we are completely passive in our perception of ideas (which are totally the product of God's will), he does not believe that our passions, imagination, and volitions are totally determined by these ideas which we receive from without (*P* 144; *D* 59). He says that God is not to be considered the author of our opinions (*D* 91). He even attributes to us some power to produce motion, i.e., to move our own bodily limbs (*D* 84; *P* 147; *PC* 548)—although this can finally mean only that, upon the occasion of our willing to move our limbs, God causes us and others to perceive ideas of these limbs as moving. Further, Berkeley derives his notion of God by heightening the powers of the soul (*D* 78), especially the power of creating ideas, and he shows no inclination to precede Ross in basing his notions of God's powers experientially upon those of the soul only to end up by denying all power to the soul.

However, Berkeley never (to my knowledge) explains how the freedom of self-determination which he attributes to the soul is compatible with God's attributes. If God is immutably omniscient, and "knew all things from eternity" (*D* 102), this must include all human volitions. It is probably true that in making such statements Berkeley had in mind all sensible objects (cf. *D* 100). But it is impossible to understand how God could know all of these from eternity without also knowing all human volitions, in view of the correspondence between the two. For example, God's knowing eternally that I am now seeing a typewriter, paper, and the above words before me requires that God knew that I would decide to type today, and in fact that my parents and grandparents would make the decisions that led to (i.e., were the occasion for) my even existing. Also, since God is purely active and cannot be affected by anything, it is impossible that we can make decisions not foreknown by God. Furthermore, Berkeley says God is the cause of all things, and that we are absolutely dependent upon God (*D* 103; *P* 155). Here again Berkeley perhaps had in mind only all our sensations. But, by the same argument as above, God must also cause all our volitions, or we would be likely to will things that would not correspond with the sensations God has eternally willed to affect us.

Accordingly, as long as the doctrine of God as immutably omniscient and omnipotent is retained, the same arguments that can be used to argue from the nature of God to the thesis that natural beings must exist only as ideas in the divine mind can be used to argue against the actuality of created souls as well. In other words, personal idealism provides no stable halfway house; consistency demands either changing the doctrine of God or advancing to the position implicitly taken by Ross and explicitly by Spinoza (insofar as Spinoza should be interpreted as a pantheist rather than an atheist).

Berkeley's version of personal idealism contained several tensions. One is the tension just mentioned between God's traditional attributes and the freedom of the human spirit which is required if sin is not to be attributed to God. Another is the tension between God's perfect goodness and the magnitude of natural evils, a tension that was increased in obviousness if not substantively by the denial of subpersonal actualities. In the next two sections I will briefly examine the treatment of these two difficulties within the later tradition of personal idealism.

## ABSOLUTISTIC PERSONALISM AND MYSTERIOUS INTELLIGIBILITY

Some modern personal idealists have retained the main points of Berkeley's views outlined above. For example, Borden Parker Bowne and his disciple Albert C. Knudson both maintain that all natural events directly express God's will. And they maintain that God's creation of free spirits does not necessarily mean a limitation of God's knowledge, i.e., of the future. The maintenance of the former doctrine leads them to admit that the problem of natural evil cannot be solved theoretically, and to urge that a practical solution is all that is necessary as well as possible.[5] They do suggest that some light can be thrown on the problem by realizing that pleasure is not the highest value, that sin is a worse evil than pain, and that all the world is designed to build virtuous character.[6] However, there are evils that we cannot understand even when judging the world in terms of its purpose of character-building. Here all we can do is admit our ignorance, while not doubting that there is a solution known to God alone.[7] Knudson likes Lotze's statement:

> Where there appears to be an irreconcilable contradiction between the omnipotence and the goodness of God, there our finite wisdom has come to the end of its tether, and we do not understand the solution which yet we believe in.[8]

And, rather than accept a solution involving a limitation of omnipotence, Knudson says:

> The very essence of faith is trust both in the power and goodness of God in spite of appearance to the contrary. The fact of suffering may baffle us if we hold to the divine omnipotence, but better a baffled faith than no faith at all.[9]

This treatment of the problem of natural evil stands in considerable tension with Bowne's assertion of the complete intelligibility of the universe,[10] as well as with Knudson's rejection of a dualism between faith and reason, and his claim that a personalistic philosophy provides the basis for a rational justification of religious faith.[11]

Their treatment of the relation between divine omniscience and human freedom also involves problems of intelligibility. They say that human freedom cannot be regarded simply as psychological freedom (absence of complete determination from *external* sources), but must be interpreted as involving real or metaphysical freedom, the freedom of self-control or self-determination. Yet Bowne holds that God foreknows our free acts, either because time is merely ideal, and hence not real for God, or because God has means of knowing that are inscrutable to us.[12] Although evidently somewhat more disturbed by the apparent contradiction, Knudson says that we cannot definitely affirm the incompatibility of divine foreknowledge and human freedom, and this for the same two reasons given by Bowne for affirming their compatibility.[13] However, Knudson admits that we cannot understand how this foreknowledge of a contingent future is possible.[14] Since two of the central problems of intelligibility in traditional Christian faith involve the compatibility of natural evil with omnipotence and goodness, and of freedom and hence moral evil with immutable omniscience and omnipotence, and Bowne and Knudson have not even shown how this dual compatibility is conceivable, they have not really provided a rational justification of faith. The most they can legitimately claim in this area is, with Berkeley, that the problem of evil is no more difficult for them than it is for those traditional theists who affirm the substantiality of matter. But, as we have seen, this means the difficulty is considerable.

Personal idealists are split between "absolutists" and "finitists." Fortunately there are definitions of these terms accepted by members of both camps. An absolutist holds that God is not limited by anything ultimately independent of the divine rational will; any limitations are either due to beings which God freely creates, and hence are self-limitations, or else they are aspects of God's own nature (e.g., love and rationality) which have God's self-approval. A finitist holds that there are conditions independent of God's will which oppose this will. Plato was a finitist, holding that God faced a "necessity outside of him." A finitistic personal idealist would have to hold that any limiting conditions are within God's own nature.

Berkeley, Bowne, and Knudson are all absolutists. L. Harold DeWolf is also an absolutist. But he differs from his predecessors in regard to divine omniscience and omnipotence. He says that, since deity has given human beings some freedom of choice, it has thereby limited its own power and its knowledge of the future.[15] This position is possible within an absolutist understanding of God, DeWolf maintains, since the limitation is voluntarily self-imposed by God, and represents no necessity independent of God's own will.[16] DeWolf does not (to my knowledge) discuss the possible problems associated with the concept of self-limitation. For example, was God at one time immutable, eternal, and impassible, later becoming mutable, temporal, and passible? If so, would this involve a change in essential attributes? And if so, is this meaningful? Or has God eternally created "persons" so that there has always been a divine self-limitation? DeWolf does say that "it is reasonable to believe that human souls are not the only persons God has created,"[17] and he says there are various degrees of complexity and value in the one metaphysical kind of being, i.e., souls.[18] He further indicates that human characteristics may be shared with other creatures on earth or other orders of being.[19] But he does not (again, to my knowledge) discuss the issue as to whether there have always been created beings with freedom, and hence whether God's self-limitation is eternal. But, in any case, his unambiguous statement that God's power, including the power to know the future, is limited by the presence of creatures with freedom removes part of the problem of intelligibility involved in the earlier position of personal idealism.

However, the problem of natural evil remains unchanged. DeWolf holds the idealistic view that nature is an effect going forth from God into human experience, and that every sense perception is a direct effect of divine activity.[20] And he points out, as did previous personalists, that there is no practical difference between this and the more traditional view of a nature which God created *ex nihilo* and then sustained:

> So long as He is regarded as the one unconditioned Creator, cause or ground of all being, every experience we have of the material world results from His activity.[21]

Since DeWolf makes no modification of this traditional view, he correctly says that "the greatest theoretical difficulty confronting the Christian faith is the problem of evil."[22] He makes some of the same suggestions as Bowne and Knudson, saying it is our hedonism that has made finitistic solutions attractive, but that the problem of pleasure and pain is really of minor importance in relation to that of righteousness and sin, and that the world is designed not for pleasure but for the "training of immortal souls for heroic faith and love."[23] He suggests that the natural evil with which the world is scarred (e.g., earthquakes) is somehow connected with human sin,[24] but he does not explain what this connection might be. He stresses that much of our suffering is inflicted by the sins of other humans—murder, war, starvation, disease, venereal disease due to sexual immorality, and "floods and droughts which follow the recklessly greedy exploitation of forest lands."[25] However, DeWolf does not face squarely the fact that all the effects resulting from human intentions follow only because God cooperates with these intentions. As E. S. Brightman, while he still held the absolutist position, candidly said:

> Storm and calm, disease and health, are alike the literal will of God. . . . Let us not blink the fact that if God be immanent in all nature, every motion of the murderer's hand, and of his weapon, and all its deadly effect, down to the subtlest tremor of the most minute electron, was all the deed of God's will.[26]

DeWolf's final solution is essentially the same as that of Bowne and Knudson: Although we cannot fully understand how this can be so, it is in principle intelligible that apparent evils are good in God's infinite perspective, and as absolutists we believe "that even the worst pains we suffer have some good reason in relation to the ultimate purpose of God," so that all natural evils are means by which God's will is being done.[27]

## E. S. BRIGHTMAN: GOD'S INTERNAL PROBLEM

Edgar Sheffield Brightman stands firmly within the tradition of personal idealism. He says that the rule of parsimony supports the rejection of all nonexperiential entities, and that it is superfluous to suppose that the physical universe exists other than ideally in God (*POR* 323, 332).[28] Even the human nervous system exists as an emanation of God's energizing in our consciousness, so that the interaction of mind and body is really an interaction between the divine and human minds (*POR* 214, 369).

But, unlike the previous personalists, Brightman has a finitistic rather than an absolutistic doctrine of God. Like DeWolf, he holds that God's creation of persons entails a limitation upon God's power to control the world, and a limitation upon God's knowledge of the future (*POR* 260, 331; *PG* 101, 124, 132; *FG* 182).[29] He totally rejects the idea that God might be nontemporal, saying that "an experience which is at no time and contains no temporal sequence is a round triangle" (*PR* 324; cf. *PG* 129, 133).[30] And this means a rejection of the doctrine of impassibility, since God is affected by the free choices of other personalities (*POR* 366). But the results of this creation of persons would by itself not mean a rejection of omnipotence, since the creation is a free choice of God's will, so that the resulting limitations are self-imposed.

Brightman became a finitist because he did not believe that the limits imposed upon God by free persons, plus those "limitations" which most theists have admitted, such as the laws of logic, are sufficient to account for the evil in the world (*POR* 260 f., 303; *FG* 13). For one thing, if God were omnipotent, he could have created free persons who would freely avoid sin (*FG* 173). But much more central in Brightman's thought is the problem of natural evil. Although for a while he accepted the position of Bowne, Knudson, and DeWolf, he soon rejected the idea that we could, on the basis of ignorance, assume that all *prima facie* natural evil is only apparent (*POR* 242, 245, 269 f., 309 f.). The position that everything which seems evil to us must really be good, in the ultimate perspective, leads to a complete relativism regarding good and evil (*POR* 269 f.; *PAR* 96).[31] And, more importantly, that position is unfair to our experience. There clearly seems to be "surd evil," a surplus of evil beyond that which can be rationalized (*POR* 277, 278 f.; *FG* 172). "There seems to be evil in the universe so cruel, so irrational, so unjust that it could not be the work of a good God" (*POR* 318).

Brightman believes that the only way to save the goodness of the divine will is to hold that deity's power to effect its will is limited, that God faces conditions which the divine will neither created nor approves (*POR* 282; *PAR* 85 f.). This is the defining essence of finitism, and aligns Brightman with Plato. However, for Brightman the limiting conditions for natural evil cannot exist in natural substances external to God, since there are none. The problem has to be in deity itself. In the first book in which he enunciated this position, Brightman described this internal problem in this way:

> There is with him [God], in addition to his reason and his active creative will, a passive element which enters into every one of his conscious states, as sensation, instinct, and impulse enter into ours, and constitutes a problem for Him. This element we call the Given. The evils of life and the delays in the attainment of value, in so far as they come from God and

> not from human freedom, are thus due to his nature, yet not wholly to his deliberate choice. (*PG* 113)

As Brightman points out, there is nothing new in saying that there is a Given for God's will (*FG* 187). Most theists have held that God cannot violate the laws of rationality. Hence, rather than speaking simply of the Given, he comes to distinguish the nonrational from the rational Given. The rational Given is comprised of logical, ethical, aesthetic, and religious norms (*PR* 57 f.). God's will approves of these, so they do not constitute finitude. The nonrational Given is constituted by sense qualities, the forms of space and time, emotions, disorderly impulses and desires, experiences such as pleasures and pains, and "whatever in God is the source of surd evil" (*PR* 58; *POR* 337). Part of this nonrational Given in God's nature is opposed by God's will; this is the novel element in Brightman's theory.

This nonrational Given provides an instrument for the expression of God's purposes, but also an obstacle to them. God's power is finite; God's control of the Given is not complete determination (*POR* 319, 327, 338). On this basis, and only on this basis, can Brightman maintain the idealistic thesis that God alone is the source of nature, and yet hold that God's will is totally good. Brightman also uses the nonrational Given to explain the existence of moral evil (a fact often overlooked by commentators):

> There must be something in "the nature of things" to render impossible the creation of a race of free beings who would never sin, even though they were free to do so. If it were possible, God would have created them. The impossibility must lie in the very nature of God. (*FG* 173)

He explains elsewhere that when God created humanity God had

> to create as a will limited both by reason and by nonrational content. Thus when man is created there enter into his being the same constituents that obtain in God and in all his deeds (*POR* 333)

Hence, Brightman uses the theory of the nonrational Given in God to reconcile both the presence of moral evil and surd natural evil in the world with the perfect goodness of God's will.

Of course, God is responsible for the evil committed and suffered by persons in the sense that God chose to create a world with persons in it. And a critic might assert that God, foreseeing the types of evil that would not be preventable, should have abstained from creating such a world. Brightman answers this charge as follows:

> One may suppose that there lay before God only two alternatives: that of creating other persons whose existence must contain many irrational evils and that of not creating at all. The latter would forfeit all the values of a social universe, and all the possibilities of human existence. . . . One may well think that a good God would be willing to endure all the added suffering that would be entailed, and to help humanity to endure and control it, rather than to have a universe without human values. Who would deem this choice wrong? (*POR* 333 f.)

This answer seems completely sound to me. It reflects the understanding that God's goodness should be understood primarily positively as the will to create value, rather than primarily negatively, as the will to prevent evil.

How should Brightman's position be understood in terms of the formal statement of the problem of evil? Which premise is rejected? We have seen that he does not reject premise 7, as his term "surd evil" is close in meaning to my term "genuine evil." He does not reject statement number 6, i.e., the validity of logic. And the whole point of his doctrine is to save premises 4 and 5. Regarding premise 5, one might suggest that God could bring about an actual world without persons, and thereby have an actual world devoid of evil. For some personal idealists, this would be impossible, since human (and superhuman) persons are the only actualities there are. But Brightman holds that there are subhuman perceivers. He thinks it probable that all living beings are "selves," meaning that they have at least a simple consciousness. And he even thinks of the higher mammals as "elementary persons," with "person" being defined as a self that is potentially self-conscious and rational (*POR* 350). On this basis Brightman overcomes the anthropocentrism of most personal idealists, as he suggests that God has brought forth many ranges of valuable existence (*FG* 190). However, it does not follow from this that there could be an actual world without evil. For Brightman believes that there would be natural evil in any possible creation (*POR* 334), and hence even in a world with only subpersonal selves; therefore, avoiding the creation of persons would not prevent natural evil. Furthermore, as we saw in the quotation above, he evidently thinks that a world without the values of personal existence would be so poor in values that the existence of such a world in place of our world would, in my terms, constitute a genuine evil. Hence, God's free decision to create a world with persons in it does not negate premise 5, that God as a morally perfect being would *want* to bring about an actual world without any genuine evil.

This brings us to the premises dealing with omnipotence. As we have seen, Brightman affirms premise 3, that an omnipotent being could unilaterally create a world without genuine evil. It is precisely because our world has genuine evil, both natural and moral, that Brightman says God is not omnipotent. And Brightman does not reject premise 2, that a perfect reality would be omnipotent. He seems to agree that the absolutist idea of God "is the ideal of the best and greatest that man can think, and includes perfection of power and knowledge, as well as perfection of goodness" (*POR* 306).

Brightman's position, then, can best be understood as a rejection of premise 1, that God is a perfect reality. This denial is made explicitly and repeatedly. For example, he thinks the absolutist idea "overemphasizes the perfection of God" as well as falsely declaring the creation to share in this perfection (*POR* 282 f.). And he directly says that God's power is not perfect (*POR* 324 f., 326; *PG* 137).

But if Brightman denies God's perfection, and if we can only worship perfection, how can we worship Brightman's God? This question is usually posed on the basis of the problem in God's nature that accounts for evil. Brightman's answer in effect is that the object of worship is not God as such, but God's will, which is infinitely good. But, besides the internal problem in God's nature, there is the additional fact that God is not perfect in power. Brightman's statement about God's worshipfulness in view of this limitation is:

> There is nothing worthy of worship in power as such; only the power of the good is adorable, and it is adorable because it is good rather than because it is power. . . . The object of religious worship is a perfect ideal rather than a perfect power. (*POR* 319, 325)

Furthermore, Brightman rightly suggests that our ideas as to what is worshipful are greatly historically conditioned, which means that we could change our minds (*POR* 308, 324–326).

However, although I am advocating belief in a God who is finite in terms of Brightman's definition, I must agree with those critics who argue that Brightman has solved the problem of evil only by means of a God that is not worthy of worship. If we can only worship a perfect reality, and a perfect reality is the greatest possible, and this can not be less than the greatest conceivable, then Brightman's God is not worthy of worship. Brightman makes no claim that God as conceived by him is the greatest conceivable being. In fact, he rather clearly indicates that the God who in fact must be thought to exist is imperfect in comparison with another idea of God that can be conceived. This is suggested by passages such as the following: "It is not a question of the kind of God we should like to have. It is a question of the kind of God required by the facts." (*FG* 137 f.) And the "facts" Brightman has in mind are thought to be contingent features of our particular world, not conditions thought to obtain necessarily in any possible world (*POR* 311). This indicates that Brightman believes there could be a possible world (or worlds) whose facts would not require postulating that its creator has a nonrational Given which rendered its power finite. Furthermore, passages referred to above clearly show that Brightman thinks that God's power is less than perfect. And he makes no attempt to argue that a God with irrational desires and impulses which can be overcome only with difficulty and then only partly by the divine will is the greatest conceivable being. Hence, Brightman's own statements show his God to be not worthy of worship.

To some extent Brightman's acquiescence in the idea that his deity is imperfect is unnecessary. He accepts the equation of possibility and conceivability (*POR* 320). And he rejects the idea that a personal God could be nontemporal on the grounds that a nontemporal experience, like a round triangle, is a contradiction and hence impossible. Why does he not say the same thing in regard to the traditional doctrine of omnipotence? If it is inconceivable, then it provides no standard by which divine power that is conceivable can be called imperfect. Brightman could at least say this in regard to God's inability to prevent *moral* evil. He could argue that the idea that one being could unilaterally determine the actions of another being with self-determination, even if the former is called the "creator" of the second, is self-contradictory. Hence there is no basis for looking for a reason why God did not create free beings who would never sin.

Of course, for Brightman to claim that a God who cannot prevent all *natural* evil is the greatest conceivable reality would require a substantive change in his position. But not as great a change as might be thought. Brightman rejects the limitation of actuality to God and humans. He says, "We have no means of knowing how far below man . . . the ranges of conscious life in the universe may extend" (*FG* 190), and that "there is good reason to believe that every living being experiences itself as a self" (*POR* 350). If every cell is a self, then a good portion of our earth need not be thought of as mere ideas emanating from God's mind, but can be assigned its own actuality. Brightman evidently did not attribute any power of self-determination to subpersonal selves (*PG* 124; *POR* 352), but he offers no rationale for this, and indicates no way of justifying any absolute line—in fact his talk of other higher mammals as "elementary persons" suggests a continuum rather than any absolute dualism between those selves with and those without some power of self-determination vis-à-vis God. If this continuum were made an explicit doctrine, and if it were added that actuality as such must have some power of self-determination, the basis would be laid for showing how all pain and suffering apparently caused by living beings could really be attributed to them, and that the possibility of such evils is necessary in any actual world. The further step required for making the decisions of living beings the causes of suffering in other sentient beings (and not simply the occasions for God to inflict this suffering) is to say that the "material body" of the living being is simply the outer objective aspect of the living being which is, in itself, an experiencing subject. The tiger as perceived through our senses is a blurred simplification of the outer aspects of those billions of cells which constitute the tiger's body, and which to a great extent carry out the directives of the dominant subject in the total organism, the tiger's psyche. On this basis one could retain the central Berkeleian insight, that to be actual is to be an experiencing agent, without having to look for a flaw in God to explain why tiger bodies often rip human bodies to shreds (and why human bodies often needlessly kill tigers and other animals).

The final step that would be needed to handle all natural evil on this basis would be to attribute some sort of perception or experience to all natural unities. This would mean a doctrine of "panpsychism," or, as I prefer, "panexperientialism." Whereas Berkeley apparently did not consider this option, the later personalists have rejected it. However, their reasons seem far from convincing. Mainly they rely upon the general feeling that such a position seems implausible, and contrary to common sense. I will limit myself here to two comments. First, it is somewhat strange for those who tell us that all natural objects are simply ideas implanted in our minds by God to argue against another possible position on the grounds that it diverges from common sense. Second, since Brightman accepts the idea of subpersonal experiences, and to some extent endorses the idea of a continuum, it would also seem more plausible to extend the continuum all the way down, rather than drawing some arbitrary line between life and nonlife. Where would the line be drawn, e.g., above or below the virus? And is it not strange to think of the cell as having its own actuality, while the molecules, atoms, and subatomic entities are thought of as mere ideas implanted upon the experience of the cell and/or the human scientist?

In any case, the panexperientialist position would obviate the necessity for speaking of any internal flaw in God's nature that is a problem for the divine will. All worldly beings would be active experiences, or aggregates of such, and as such would in principle not be totally controllable by God. Since this situation would characterize any possible world, God's power would not be imperfect in the sense of less than the power of some conceivable creator. And the cosmic drag would not be in God's nature; deity would thereby not be split within itself, having a perfect will fighting an imperfect nature. There still might be tension in God's experience, in the following sense: Through love for the creatures God would empathize with each of their individual desires for fulfillment. Many of these desires would not be compatible with each other and with the good of the whole. Accordingly, God's will and resulting influence would run counter to many things which God in one sense desired. (This could be called a tension between God's "antecedent" and "consequent" wills; this distinction would be intelligible in this case, since temporality would be affirmed of God's experience, and other actualities would be attributed power to affect God's experience.) But this type of tension should not be seen as reflecting any imperfection in God's nature, since empathetic love for others should (at least by a Christian) be regarded as a perfection, not a flaw.

In closing, it should be noted that this doctrine would overcome what has been seen by many as the major incoherence in Brightman's doctrine. He suggests that we understand the various elements in the divine experience in analogy with our own experience. Accordingly, in speaking of the nonrational Given as a passive, unwilled element in God's experience, he compares it to human sense experience. However, he has to say that "the content of the Given is analogous to sensation without its having an analogous cause."[32] The reply has been made, with justification, that this lack of an analogous cause undercuts the analogy altogether.[33] If Brightman had moved to the panexperientialist position, this inconsistency would be overcome. For there would always be—Brightman has already affirmed that creation is eternal (*PG* 123; *POR* 329)—genuine actualities whose decisions would affect God, supplying a given or passive element in the divine experience.

But, whatever the problems in Brightman's own views, he must be admired for honestly facing the problem of evil. Personal idealism as a whole shows that, if nature is to be given no autonomy in relation to God, it is superfluous even to posit nature's actual existence. And when nature is made merely ideal, the fact becomes more dramatically evident that traditional theists must attribute all natural evils directly to God. This forces one either to deny that any natural evil is genuinely evil or else to locate the source of this evil in God. Since the former alternative is really implausible, and leads to all sorts of problems, the latter alternative is inevitable. Brightman's position represents an honest admission of this. That God has an internal problem is the unorthodox conclusion that has been lurking for centuries in the closets of classical theism, hidden behind illicit distinctions, such as those between God's "antecedent" and "consequent" wills, or God's "hidden" and "revealed" wills. And, of course, since traditional theists have not even given persons any autonomy vis-à-vis God, and since they have regarded moral evil as more difficult to justify than natural, the same conclusion must follow, and even, *a fortiori,* in relation to moral evil.

# PART III

## *A Nontraditional Theodicy*

## 17

# Worshipfulness and the Omnipotence Fallacy

PART I of this book focused on some of the sources for the traditional Christian theodicies. The intention was to show that there were notions in the Greek and Jewish backgrounds which were ignored or rejected by traditional theists, and that a quite different theodicy could have been constructed out of the same backgrounds. Part II looked at various forms of the traditional theodicy. The defining essence of this traditional position is the idea that God is the actual or potential controller of all events. The primary purpose of that part of the book was negative: to stress by various examples the difficulties entailed by this view of God as controller. However, interspersed with this negative argument were several positive suggestions for a reconstructed, nontraditional theodicy. The primary purpose of this third part of the book is to explicate and defend such a theodicy on the basis of ideas of God and the world suggested by the process philosophers Alfred North Whitehead and Charles Hartshorne. This theodicy will include those other ideas in the Greek and Hebrew sources which were rejected by traditional theodicies.

The present chapter defends the notion of God advocated here against charges that it does not describe a reality which is perfect and hence worthy of worship. The main point is that, if the world is understood as *actual,* the traditional idea of what is entailed by "omnipotence" involves a fallacy, and hence cannot be used as a standard by which to consider imperfect the power of God as conceived in a nontraditional way. Chapter 18 will explain Whitehead's particular way of understanding God's power in the world, and why it by necessity cannot be all-controlling. A major point of these chapters is the rejection of premise 3 of the formal statement of the problem of evil. That is, I deny that a being with perfect power could unilaterally bring about an actual world devoid of genuine evil. But it is still possible to wonder, granted that there must be *some* genuine evil, whether our world had to contain the possibility of the *horrendous* amount and types of evil that have occurred on our planet. Chapter 18 will also attempt to face this question.

I now turn to the topic of the present chapter. The basic question is: Given the difficulties in the traditional theodicy, why not reject the traditional doctrine of omnipotence, i.e., either premise 2 or premise 3? One reason seems to be that a lack of precision in regard to the meaning of "evil" tends to obscure the fact that a problem of logical inconsistency is involved in the statement of the problem. Writers such as J. L. Mackie, H. J. McCloskey, and H. D. Aiken have said that there *is* a logical contradiction involved in the set of propositions asserting the existence of an omnipotent and morally perfect God, on the one hand, and evil, on the other.[1] But opponents such as Nelson Pike, M. B. Ahern, Alvin Plantinga, and Keith Yandell have argued that there is no such contradiction involved, since one of the required premises, viz., "a good thing always eliminates evil as far as it can" (Mackie's wording of my premise 5), is not true. The basic reason for this controversy is that few of the writers have stated carefully what they mean (formally) by "evil." Like Edward Madden, Peter Hare, and Nelson Pike, they prefer the "common-sensical extension of evil" to "confusing philosophical criteria."[2] This lack of careful definition on both sides has led to false charges of naïveté.

But careful reading of the authors shows that those who claim that there is a logical inconsistency involved are thinking of "evil" as "genuine evil," while those who see no logical inconsistency are thinking in terms of *prima facie* evil which is, or at least may be, only apparently evil. For example, what McCloskey has in mind, in claiming that a logical inconsistency is involved, is not simply *prima facie* evil, but "unnecessary" or "superfluous" evil.[3] Plantinga normally argues that no logical inconsistency is involved. His reason is that all of the *(prima facie)* evil may be justified. But he agrees that if any "unjustified" evil occurs, "it follows that there is no omnipotent, omniscient, wholly good being."[4] Roderick Chisholm's term for genuine evil is "indefeasible evil."[5] Using "pointless evil" as a synonym for this, Terence Penelhum says:

> It is logically inconsistent for a theist to admit the existence of pointless evil. . . . If such evils seem to exist in fact, then the problem of evil presents itself to the theist as the logical difficulty it has traditionally been thought to be.[6]

Edward Madden and Peter Hare repeatedly say it is "foolish" to formulate the problem of evil as a formal inconsistency, since "some evil obviously serves good ends which could not otherwise be achieved."[7] Hence they are speaking of *prima facie* evil, recognizing that some of it can be considered only apparent evil. But they clearly believe there would be a formal inconsistency involved in traditional theism if the existence of "gratuitous evil" (their term for genuine evil) were admitted.[8]

J. L. Mackie, who argues that a logical inconsistency is involved in the traditional position, lists among the "adequate solutions" the position of Alexander Pope, "that disorder is harmony not understood, and that partial evil is universal good."[9] In other words, he recognizes that the inconsistency can be overcome by saying that all *prima facie* evil is only apparently evil. Plantinga, Pike, and Ahern do not really rebut Mackie's view that genuine evil is incompatible with benevolent omnipotence, but simply affirm a modern version of Pope's view, saying that it is possible that all *prima facie* evils such as "instances of suffering" (Pike) are only apparently evil, so that there is no genuine evil.

In other words, the dispute as to whether a logical inconsistency is involved in the problem of evil is a purely verbal one. Both sides agree that there is no inconsistency if the reality of genuine evil is not affirmed; and both sides agree that there is an inconsistency if the reality of genuine evil is affirmed.

The issue then becomes whether the reality of such evil should be affirmed. That is, should we affirm that some things happen which really do not "turn out for the best"? Do events occur without which the universe would have been a better place, all things considered? On this question the lines are drawn, but not between those who affirm the reality of genuine evil and those who deny it, and not even between those who say it probably exists and those who say it probably does not. Rather, the issue revolves around the relation between "faith" and "reason," especially reason in the sense of estimations of what is probably true.

John Wisdom says that it is "probable that some of the evils in [the world] are not logically necessary to a compensating good."[10] Austin Farrer says that, although evil is a possible occasion for good, good breeds more good than any evil can, and evil tends to breed other evils. Furthermore, the use of evil for good does not sterilize it—it continues to breed evil. And the compensating factor fixed upon by apologists is not necessarily the dominant effect. Farrer concludes that it is "probably wrong" to say that things are "all for the best."[11]

Those who do not affirm the reality of genuine evil do not reject the view that reasoning on the basis of experience would lead one to affirm the probability that genuine evil exists. They only maintain that it is *possible* that justifying reasons for all *prima facie* evils exist, so that none of them would be genuine. That is, the critics of theism cannot *prove* that any genuine evil exists. For example, M. B. Ahern says that to know that there is some unjustified evil, "it would be necessary to have an exhaustive knowledge of possible good and its logical connection, if any, with actual evil. We lack this knowledge."[12] Ahern concludes that the existence of any evil, regardless of kind, degree, and number of instances, cannot be shown to be incompatible with the existence of a good and omnipotent God.

Furthermore, defenders of this view claim that they do not need to show how the *prima facie* evils could be justified. For example, in order to claim that the theist must show what the justifying reasons are, says Keith Yandell, one would need to affirm this principle: "If a case of innocent suffering were explainable compatible with [the proposition that an all-knowing, all-powerful, all-good God exists], we would have discovered the reason for this suffering." But, he says, this principle is not true, for "the plans of Providence, if such there be, are no doubt immensely complex."[13] Ahern says that if there are solutions, "there is no reason to suppose they should be available to us."[14] Plantinga says that "to rebut the charge of contradiction the theist need not hold that the hypothesis in question is probable or even true."[15]

Accordingly, we see that those who honor logical consistency (unlike Brunner and Fackenheim), but refuse to give up traditional theism by rejecting either premise 2 or premise 3, do so in terms of a position on the relation of faith and reason reminiscent of that of Leibniz. These contemporary theists maintain that one's faith position on the existence and nature of deity need not be altered by any reasoning concerning the problem of evil, so long as it can be shown that no outright inconsistency is present in the believer's theistic position. And the believer can show this simply by suggesting possible hypotheses which remove the alleged inconsistency, even if these hypotheses are not considered probable, or even more simply by pointing out that there may be considerations which remove the apparent inconsistency, even though we have no idea what those considerations are.

Of course, as we saw, Leibniz' fideism was itself based upon reason. He believed that there were proofs, based upon necessary truths, for the existence of God as traditionally understood. And he believed that there were sufficient reasons for accepting the authority of the Christian Scriptures, which testify to the existence of God. In other words, the existence of the traditional God seemed so well attested when considered in abstraction from the problem of evil that the contrary evidence presented by the presence of *prima facie* evil was not sufficient basis for rejecting or reforming the traditional idea of God.

Contemporary defenders of the Leibnizian position on faith and reason also assume that the existence of God (as traditionally conceived) is somehow so securely established prior to the confrontation with the problem of evil that this confrontation cannot force a rejection or reformulation. For example, Nelson Pike's complacent statement that the problem of evil should be regarded by the theist as "a noncrucial perplexity of minor importance"[16] presupposes that believers, including theologians, take God's existence, goodness, and omnipotence as axiomatic, i.e., as beyond question.[17] Ahern's position presupposes that there are arguments independent of the problem of evil by which God's existence can be proved.[18]

This attitude was probably still largely justified in Leibniz' time. That is, faith in God was probably axiomatic for most Westerners, and most of those who thought about such things believed that there were direct proofs for God's existence and/or indirect proofs by means of establishing the veracity of the Scriptures. Accordingly, it was appropriate to begin with God's existence as firmly established and then to approach the problem of evil only secondarily. In this context it was reasonable to admit that the appearances run counter to the hypothesis of an all-good God who is in complete control of all events, and yet to treat this potential disconfirmation as a noncrucial perplexity.

However, I would strongly maintain that this context no longer obtains. A progressively lower percentage of people who reflect about these matters can take faith as axiomatic in the sense of holding certain doctrines as being beyond refutation by experience and argument. And two centuries of Biblical criticism have undermined for an increasing percentage of people the possibility of affirming ideas solely on the authority of the Bible. Also, most of those who have considered the question of "proofs for the existence of God" have decided that they do not provide proofs in the strict sense; they at most suggest the probability of a divine reality. Furthermore, many follow Kant in the opinion that the arguments, while they may support the existence of some kind of deity, do not support the existence of a God as traditionally conceived.

In this context, simply showing the bare possibility that God's existence might not be contradicted by the world's evil does not do much toward solving the problem of evil. In our situation, the theologian needs a "global argument," the purpose of which is to show that a theistic interpretation can illuminate the totality of our experience, including the experience of evil, better than nontheistic interpretations.[19] And, as George Mavrodes has said, "the proof that the existence of evil is logically compatible with some other fundamental theistic doctrines provides in itself only a bare minimum of the desired illumination."[20]

Thus far I have suggested two closely related reasons why many of the participants in the recent discussion of the problem of evil reject neither premise 2 nor premise 3. First, because of the ambiguity of the word "evil" when it is not carefully defined, many believe that logical inconsistency can be avoided without rejecting either of these premises. By thinking in terms of *prima facie* evil which might be only apparent evil, they believe they can reject the premise stating that a good God would want to prevent all evil. Second, they fail to place the problem of evil in its context of contemporary experience, in which the reality of genuine evil is overwhelmingly more evident to most people than the reality of anything nameable as "God." Hence, they fail to see that any "solution" with any possible relevance to contemporary experience will have to be one that not only maintains logical consistency but also holds that genuine evil occurs.

However, there is another reason why many theologians and philosophers of religion think it necessary for the theist, especially the Christian theist, to retain both premise 2 and premise 3. Both affirmations are thought to be required if God is to be worthy of worship. For example, C. A. Campbell says that

> the religious attitudes of worship and adoration are difficult to sustain in conjunction with an explicit recognition that the Being to whom they are directed is defective or imperfect in any way whatever. And we can hardly pretend to ourselves that limitation of power is not an imperfection.

He further asserts that

> religious peace of mind is just not possible, at any rate at a reflective level, once the infinitude of God has been compromised, and forces independent of God and either actually or potentially hostile to Him have been admitted.[21]

Ahern says that a being of limited power would not be a fitting object of worship, "which supposes that a greater being is inconceivable," and that if God lacks the power to prevent evil, unrestricted obedience would not be justified.[22] In an article devoted to a disproof of God's existence, J. N. Findlay refers to the consensus that it is "wholly anomalous to worship anything limited in any thinkable manner" and says that this leads us "to demand that our religious object . . . shouldn't stand surrounded by a world of *alien* objects, which . . . set limits to its influence."[23] G. E. Hughes believes that Findlay "has a much better idea than [other atheists] have of what is involved in theism," so that the theist cannot rebut his argument "with the remark, 'But that is not at all the kind of being in whose existence I believe.' "[24] Roland Puccetti also agrees that Findlay has stated what is required if God is to be an "adequate object of religious attitudes."[25] On this basis he mockingly describes William James's view of God as "a sort of well-intentioned Zeus doing his best to help us in the common struggle against evil and adversity." Puccetti portrays a God who cannot save one from a raging flood, or quite pull off a threat to end the world, and then comments that such a deity "could hardly provoke the unstinted adoration and fearsome awe appropriate to total religious commitment. To address [this deity] as 'My Lord and God' must strike the reflective theist as sheer idolatry."[26] In reply to Mill's position that the idea of omnipotence comes from our wishes, Puccetti says that it comes instead from the "demands" of "reflective theism."[27]

Sometimes the notion of worship is not explicitly mentioned, but it is clear that this notion is closely related to the terms used, e.g., "theism," "Christian monotheism," "Christian faith," "religious beliefs," etc. For example, H. J. McCloskey says that a simple way to solve the problem of evil is to adopt a "weakened form of theism" by asserting that "God is not powerful enough to make a world that does not contain evil." But, he says, "such solutions ignore the real inspiration of religious beliefs."[28] Mackie says that to modify the traditional view of omnipotence "would seriously affect the essential core of the theistic position."[29] John Hick says: "To solve the problem of evil by means of the theory . . . of a finite deity who does the best he can with a material, intractable and co-eternal with himself, is to have abandoned the basic premise of Hebrew-Christian monotheism; for the theory amounts to rejecting belief in the infinity and sovereignty of God."[30] Any such view which would deny the infinite power of God would be Manichaean and therefore sub-Christian.[31]

This dominant attitude, as reflected by theists and anti-theists alike, is summed up by Terence Penelhum in a passage that connects Christian faith with the "demands of religious worship":

> From time to time thinkers suggest that there is a God who is all-good but not all-powerful, or who is all-powerful but not all-good. Such suggestions clearly avoid the problem of evil; but we are merely bored by them. The alternatives are always tacitly restricted to two—either there is a God who is all-powerful and all-good, or there is no God at all. Christianity may not have convinced everybody, but it has certainly made us all very finicky. For . . . the only God in whose existence we can evince interest is one whom it would be proper to worship. And worship in the Western world does not mean the appeasing of an angry God or the encouragement of a weak one. It necessarily includes submission and moral reverence.[32]

I believe there are three major reasons for this consensus in regard to omnipotence. These are: (1) cultural conditioning; (2) polemical motives; and (3) a fallacious argument, which I call the "omnipotence fallacy." I will discuss them in this order.

1. The cultural conditioning is pointed to by Terence Penelhum. Many people simply cannot take seriously a view of God that would modify the traditional assumptions about omnipotence, even if such a view could solve the problem of evil. Although most of the above writers would agree that a worshipful being must be perfect only in the sense of being the "greatest conceivable" (cf. statements by Findlay and Ahern), they do not carefully consider the arguments of the so-called "finitists" that only their revised view of God, not the traditional one, really meets this criterion. Rather, they are so "bored" with the "finite" God that they curtly dismiss it with mockery and name-calling.

But this form of argument is only based on what many people in the Western world have in fact come to regard as worshipful, under the influence of a particular tradition, not what they *ought* to regard as worshipful. And it can be countered at this level. For example, the following passage from Alfred North Whitehead is directly relevant to most of the above comments:

> The churches . . . have put forward aspects of religion which are expressed in terms . . . suited to the emotional reactions of bygone times. . . . What I mean . . . is that religious appeal is directed partly to excite that instinctive fear of the wrath of . . . an all powerful arbitrary tyrant behind the unknown forces of nature. This appeal to the ready instinct of brute fear is losing its force.[33]

Charles Hartshorne's position is that all direct power is persuasion, and that this is the form of power deity has. But against pacifists, who suppose this is the only kind of power that need be considered, he argues that "brute power," though an indirect type of causality, "is none the less practically efficacious, for good or ill, and has to be reckoned with." But, he adds, "the one thing we need not and ought not to do is . . . to worship it."[34] Against the argument based on cultural conditioning, Paul Kuntz cites passages from people such as Whitehead, Hartshorne, William James, and F. S. C. Schiller, and concludes:

> It can be shown that there are indeed many varieties of religious experience. If the argument is in part *ad hominem,* what God must be like to satisfy religious need, at least there is evidence that not all feel they must have a God defined as absolute in all respects.[35]

2. The second reason for insisting that theism cannot reject either premise 2 or premise 3 seems to be, frankly, the desire on the part of some anti-theists to have a vulnerable opponent. Traditional theists have long sneered at doctrines that involve a redefinition of divine power, and many anti-theists have been more than happy to join this sneer campaign.[36] For example, Antony Flew says that the minimal definition of Christian theism includes the ideas that God is an "infinitely powerful Creator" and that creatures can disobey their Creator's will.[37] That God is omnipotent Creator "precisely means that absolutely nothing happens save by his consenting ontological support. Everything means everything; and that includes every human thought, every human action, and every human choice." Flew can then easily show that this is inconsistent with the possibility of creaturely sin.[38] All other views of God he classifies as "the more way-out, off-beat, in-

dividualistic interpretations."[39] Specifically, a doctrine that would suggest that God is limited by powers beyond himself would abandon "an essential doctrine of Christian monotheism"; it would be Manichaeanism, not "true theism," and could be dismissed with the rebuke, "Your God is too small."[40]

Roland Puccetti, after insisting that the traditional notion of omnipotence belongs to the very "concept of God," concludes that what the argument from evil "really does, when properly formulated, is not to show that God lacks unlimited power, knowledge, or goodness; these qualities God *must* possess if he is to be an 'adequate object of religious attitudes'; rather, it shows that God *cannot exist,*" for it shows that "the concept of God is self-contradictory."[41] As does Flew's, Puccetti's argument involves a theological "Catch-22": Anyone not holding an incoherent concept is not really "reflective," while all "reflective theists hold an absurd or impossible concept of God."[42]

Against those who would argue that moral evil is compatible with the existence of an omnipotent God, since it is inconsistent to speak of God's *causing* us to do good *freely,* Dewey Hoitenga replies that traditional theists such as Augustine and Calvin have not thought it was inconsistent. Furthermore, allowing any iota of independence to the human will would conflict with the "universal" theistic attribution of all good to God, and would set a limit to God's control over the world, which would "conflict with the theist's belief in providence."[43] Holding to the compatibility of human freedom and divine determinism requires, of course, a "mysterious kind of 'higher causality.'" But there is no reason for theists to shrink from this, since Pike, Hick, and Plantinga affirm a similarly mysterious kind of "higher goodness" that includes not preventing evil.[44] (Had these men defined evil carefully, Hoitenga would have had no grounds for this charge, since none of them think God's goodness is compatible with the nondesire to prevent *genuine* evil.) Hoitenga concludes that theism is essentially "a faith *lacking* understanding," that "what really goes on in theistic apologetics . . . is that each and every proposition is *retained,* but what is *given up* is the intelligibility of its terms."[45]

This is, of course, an outrageous argument. Every assertion by theists that some traditional assumption is unintelligible is countered by a reply from Hoitenga to this effect: You must believe it is intelligible —Augustine thought so! Then after disallowing all attempts at increased intelligibility, he concludes that theism is unintelligible. His article, one hopes, was written with tongue in cheek; but in any case it could well serve as a parody of many of the so-called "philosophical scrutinies" of theism. In most cases the strategy is not as obvious, but it is essentially the same. Theists, to be worthy of the name, are required to hold a position that could not possibly be rationally defended. It is difficult in many cases to avoid the conclusion that the concern of anti-theists here is primarily for an opponent that is easily vanquished. Since it is a recognized philosophical principle that one should consider the strongest rather than the weakest forms of a position one rejects, there is no need to argue against this second "reason" for rejecting premise 2 or premise 3. It is sufficient to note that it probably does play a role in the debates.

3. Having considered two forms of prejudice against a position which would reject premise 2 or premise 3, we shall now consider the arguments which, usually implicitly, lie behind the view that premises 2 and 3 must both be affirmed. The argument for the retention of premise 2 can be formulated as follows:

A. A perfect reality must exemplify all admirable attributes in the greatest possible manner.
B. For our thought the "greatest possible" is to be defined in terms of the "greatest conceivable."
C. Power is an admirable attribute.
D. A being that is omnipotent is conceivable.
E. Therefore a being that is omnipotent is possible. (B, D)
F. Therefore a perfect reality must be an omnipotent being. (A, C, E)

Aside from the fact that it would take more steps to move logically from the idea of a "perfect reality" to the statement that such a reality is a "being" (steps indicating, for example, that only "a being" can exercise power), this argument seems valid. As for its soundness, which requires acceptable premises, premise D is the only one which I might regard as unacceptable. This would depend completely on the meaning of the term "omnipotent being." If this term is taken simply as a synonym for "a being with perfect power," then the statement is acceptable. For I take "perfect" to be synonymous with "greatest conceivable" and hence with "greatest possible." Accordingly, the statement only asserts that it is possible for a being to have the greatest power that it is possible for a being to have. Hence it is tautologous. And in this case the conclusion states only that a perfect reality must have the greatest power that it is possible for a being to have. This leaves entirely open the question of the extent and nature of the power that it is possible for a being to have. It allows this to be decided on the basis of what is genuinely, i.e., consistently, conceivable. With this definition, the statement that a perfect reality, and hence God, is an omnipotent being does not in itself entail premise 3, that an omnipotent being could unilaterally bring about an actual world without any genuine evil. But if "omnipotent being" is taken to entail this premise, then I would reject premise D of the above argument, and hence premise 2 of the original argument. Accordingly, the crucial question is that of the basis for affirming premise 3. There is an argument for it, usually implicit, yet sometimes expressed. But the argument is fallacious.

Most authors agree that omnipotence should not be defined as the power simply to do anything that happens to be *verbalizable.* For example, after stating that "there are no limits to what an omnipotent thing can do," Mackie notes that most theists have excluded the logically impossible, and says that this qualification "does not reject anything that is essential to theism."[46] And most would agree with Thomas Aquinas that it is more accurate to say that the logically impossible cannot be done than to say that God cannot do it, as if this were some limitation on divine power.[47]

So far so good. But the actual definitions of omnipotence are quite ambiguous. For example, Ahern gives the following definition: "The power to bring about what is logically possible for a being of unlimited power to bring about."[48] Presumably no one would disagree with this definition, at least if "unlimited" were equated with "greatest possible." But most authors, including Ahern himself, actually assume the following definition: "The power unilaterally to effect any state of affairs, if that state of affairs is intrinsically possible." Hence God could not effect a world with round squares in it, since such a world is intrinsically impossible; but God could unilaterally effect a world devoid of evil, since such a world is intrinsically possible.

But these two definitions of omnipotence are not identical. In the first, the idea of "what is logically possible" is applied not simply to a state of affairs in itself, but to what God could *bring about.* It does not necessarily follow from this definition that, simply because a state of affairs (SA) is intrinsically possible, a being with perfect power could unilaterally bring about SA. In other words, "SA is logically possible" is not identical with "It is logically possible that something distinct from SA could unilaterally and therefore infallibly bring about SA." And it is this latter premise that is needed to show an inconsistency between "A good omnipotent being exists" and "Genuine evil exists." If premise 3 were stated simply as "An omnipotent being could prevent all evil," and this were taken to mean only that "It might be able to, if it is lucky, but then again it might fail," the argument from evil will not get off the ground. It is only if God is an omnipotent being, and as such *could guarantee* the absence of genuine evil in an actual world, that the presence of genuine evil is contradictory to the existence and/or the goodness of God.

It is this distinction which is overlooked in the supporting argument for premise 3. Here is Plantinga's version:

> An omnipotent being . . . can perform (roughly) any logically consistent action; hence either it is a logically necessary truth that evil exists or else God is able to eliminate any case of evil whatever. No reputable theologian, so far as I know, has held that the proposition *There is evil* is logically necessary; accordingly, I shall assume henceforth that God can eliminate every case of evil whatever.[49]

The point to note is that in the first part of Plantinga's first sentence the statement is about an *action* that is logically consistent. But then the focus changes to whether or not a certain *state of affairs* is logically consistent. That is, Plantinga's point is that, since the existence of evil is not logically necessary, a state of affairs devoid of evil is a state of affairs that is intrinsically possible. But his conclusion again concerns the logical consistency of a certain action, i.e., God's *elimination* of evil. He evidently does not notice this oscillation, which invalidates the argument.

Premise 3 of our formal statement of the problem of evil speaks in terms of an actual world devoid of evil. Plantinga, in his statement, does not explicitly say that *a world* without evil is possible, although I think this is what he means. But, in any case, Ahern, in his statement, in which the same oscillation between an action and a state of affairs is evident, does explicitly mention a world. After giving the definition of omnipotence cited above, he says: "It is conceivable that a world without evil should exist. . . . Hence an omnipotent being could prevent all evil."[50] The first sentence concerns a state of affairs that is conceivable, hence logically consistent, intrinsically possible. But the second statement states that a certain *action* is possible, i.e., the *prevention* of all evil.

The statements by Plantinga and Ahern are examples of what I term the "omnipotence fallacy." The nature of the fallacy can be made clear by formalizing the argument as follows:

P. An omnipotent being can unilaterally bring about any state of affairs that it is logically possible for a being unilaterally to bring about.

R. An actual world (i.e., one with a multiplicity of actual beings) devoid of genuine evil is a logically possible state of affairs.

S. Therefore an omnipotent being could unilaterally bring about an actual world devoid of genuine evil.

The argument is not formally valid, since the oscillation between a logically possible action (P, S) and a logically possible state of affairs (R) makes this a form of the four-term fallacy. Another premise is needed to connect the two issues. Accordingly, the argument would need to be expanded by the insertion of premise Q:

P. An omnipotent being can unilaterally bring about any state of affairs that it is logically possible for a being unilaterally to bring about.

Q. If a state of affairs among a multiplicity of actual beings is logically possible, it is logically possible for one being unilaterally to bring about that state of affairs.

R. An actual world (i.e., one with a multiplicity of actual beings) devoid of genuine evil is a logically possible state of affairs.

S. Therefore an omnipotent being can unilaterally bring about an actual world devoid of evil. (P, Q, R)

The addition of premise Q makes the argument formally valid. But is it sound? Specifically, is Q acceptable? It *has* been accepted by all traditional theists (although some have excluded states of affairs among some actual beings, such as human beings, from its scope—see pages 271–272, below). Of course, this acceptance has been for the most part implicit, as Q has rarely if ever been explicitly formulated, since the clear distinction between logically possible things or states of affairs and logically possible actions is rarely made. But, once the distinction is clearly made so that the issue is brought into focus, what justification is there for accepting Q? That is, on what basis can one move from the assertion that a state of affairs among a multiplicity of actual beings is intrinsically possible to the assertion that some one being could unilaterally effect this state of affairs? For example, J. L. Mackie makes this move quickly in a discussion of free but sinless beings, as he says: "If their being of this sort is logically possible, then God's making them of this sort is logically possible."[51] The key premise needed to support Q would be the following:

X. It is possible for one actual being's condition to be completely determined by a being or beings other than itself.

If X is accepted, nothing stands in the way of the acceptance of Q. And if Q is accepted, then S follows (assuming R),[52] and we are returned to the center of the problem of evil. But should X be accepted?

Premise X, which speaks of *actual* beings, begins: "It is possible . . ." But what kind of possibility is at issue? This is not an issue that can be settled by logic alone. Rather, this is a *metaphysical* issue. In fact, this is what many would consider the metaphysical issue par excellence, the difference between actuality and the other types of "being," such as possibility. (Even if one proclaims their nondifference, this is a metaphysical claim.) And yet much and perhaps a majority of the recent discussion of the problem of evil has been carried on as if the issues could be adjudicated apart from any metaphysical commitments. It is the implicit acceptance of this metaphysical premise without any explicit recognition and hence justification of this metaphysical claim that lies behind the omnipotence fallacy. The problem is the assumption that the meaning of perfect power or omnipotence can be settled apart from a metaphysical discussion of the nature of the "beings" upon whom this perfect power is to be exercised. This leads writers into arguments that are formally invalid because devoid of necessary premises.

Haig Khatchadourian has spoken of the "crying need for an adequate delimitation of the concept of perfection, of perfect goodness, perfect power, and so on," and has rightly said that "without this, little headway can be made."[53] What is striking in the recent discussion of the problem of evil is the small amount of attention devoted to the delimitation of the concept of perfect power, compared with the amount devoted to that of perfect goodness. Delimitation of the concept of perfect power requires a discussion of the nature of "world." For the power involved in the problem of evil is a relational concept. It is God's power in relation to something distinct from God, i.e., the world (insofar as monism, acosmism, or absolute idealism is not accepted). Put otherwise, to exert power is always to exert power over something (even if that something is oneself). Hence, before drawing implications as to what a being with perfect power could do, the nature of the things upon which power is to be exerted must be considered. If the "things" are thought to be beings constituting a world distinct from God, then the nature of such a world must be examined. For a number of reasons (e.g., the influence still exerted by traditional ideas about omnipotence, and the recent neglect of metaphysics in favor of logic and "ordinary language"), the metaphysical question of the nature of a "world" is overlooked in most recent discussions of God and evil. The result is that writers assume that the meaning of omnipotence is easily established. For example, Penelhum asserts that the meaning of omnipotence is "fairly clear."[54] Ahern says that principles about power (in contrast to principles about goodness) "can be dealt with quickly," and that "it is easy to supply analytically true principles about power." Such a principle is Hume's: "A being willing to prevent evil but not able is impotent."[55] But "impotent" compared with what? Ahern means, of course, impotent compared with a being exemplifying the traditional notion of omnipotence. His argument for the conceivability of this traditional idea is based on the omnipotence fallacy: "Since it is logically possible for there to be no evil, the general problem cannot be solved by claiming that although God is omnipotent, He cannot prevent evil." But since this argument as it stands is not valid, the traditional idea may be inconceivable, and hence would provide no standard by which to call the God of another view "impotent."

The above discussion has been almost purely formal, with only a hint as to the substantive or metaphysical issue at stake. I will now focus directly upon this metaphysical issue, indicating thereby my reason for rejecting premise X which is that it is possible for one actual being's condition to be completely determined by a being or beings other than itself. And this should make clearer the reason why the above discussion of unexamined premises, as abstract as it is, is so important.

I will begin negatively. For premise X to be accepted, actual (in distinction from imaginary or ideal) entities would have to be totally determinable, in all respects, by some being or beings other than themselves. In other words, they would be totally devoid of all power—power to determine themselves, even partially, and power to determine others, even partially. (Power to influence others presupposes the power of self-determination. If an entity contributes nothing to itself, but is a mere product of other powers, it cannot meaningfully be said to have any power to influence others.)[56]

Now, it has been increasingly accepted, since Berkeley, that the meaningful use of terms requires an experiential grounding for those terms. What reality could one point to that would supply an experiential basis for the meaning of "a powerless actuality"? This thing would have to be directly experienced, and directly *experienced as being devoid of power.* I do not experience anything meeting these criteria which I would term an actuality. Many might debate whether or not we experience anything as having power. That is the question as to whether we experience casual efficacy, or only infer it (or, as a third possibility, only apply it as one of the necessary conditions of experience). But the issue at hand is whether we experience anything that we might term an actual thing as being devoid of power. I say that we do not. The idea that there are some actualities devoid of power is a pure inference. Even those, such as Spinoza, who deny that we ourselves have any power of self-determination admit that we *seem* to have such power. The conclusion that we in reality do not is based upon argumentation, not direct experience. Spinoza at least drew the proper conclusion, i.e., if we are totally devoid of power, we are not actualities. But those who talk of actualities that are totally devoid of power do so without any experiential grounding for the meaning of the concept.

To illustrate by contrast: one who speaks of actualities as having power has an experiential grounding. My present experience is an actuality. In fact, as many philosophers have pointed out, it is one thing I am certain actually exists, so it would be somewhat strange to deny actual existence to it (in comparison perhaps with some other supposedly "more actual" things). And I have direct experience of my experience itself as having some power to determine itself, i.e., to determine precisely how it will respond to all the influences upon it. Accordingly, this provides me with an experiential basis for speaking meaningfully of an *actual* entity which I can then transfer by analogy to other things. That is, whether or not I *experience* other things as having power, I can *meaningfully say* that at least some of them have power, since the meaningfulness of "powerful actuality" is grounded in my immediate experience. A critic might consider this analogical transference questionable. But what is often overlooked is that, if this affirmation is questionable, the *denial* that other things considered actual are to be understood by analogy from one's own experience is *doubly* questionable. For I at least know that it is possible for an actuality to have power, since each moment of my experience is an example of such an entity. But the person who assumes the existence of powerless actualities does not even have any direct knowledge that such entities are possible. On this point Berkeley is absolutely right. Talk of powerless actualities is finally meaningless, since it cannot be given any experiential basis. Accordingly, premise X should be rejected not simply as false, but as meaningless. And this means, then, that there is no acceptable premise behind premise Q (see page 264). So, the argument which I have termed the omnipotence fallacy is fallacious not only because it involves jumping to conclusions with insufficient premises but also because the central additional premise that would be needed is itself unacceptable.

I will try to make the central point still clearer by discussing what the term "perfect power" or "omnipotence" can mean if it is a metaphysical truth that actual entities as such have some power, and that any actual world would have to contain actual entities.

First, I take it for granted that most will agree that only individual actual beings can have or exert power. Power is not exerted by mere possibilities, nor by abstractions such as "being itself" (or "energy" or "creativity"), nor by mere aggregates of individuals. Accordingly, if we are speaking of a reality with perfect power, we are necessarily speaking of an individual actual being. "Perfect power," then, must be defined as the greatest power it is conceivable (possible) for a being to have. (In the remainder of this chapter "a being" will be used to mean "an individual actual being" unless otherwise indicated.) Presumably no one would dispute this formal definition. It is simply a version of Anselm's equation of perfection with the greatest conceivable. The dispute arises only when one begins to indicate answers to the questions as to how much power and/or what kind of power it is conceivable for a being to have.

The traditional theodicy has said in effect—although often denying it verbally—that one being could simply have all the power. That is implied if one accepts premise Q, and hence X behind it, since if one holds that *B*'s condition can be totally determined by *A,* this implies that *B* really has no power in relation to *A.* And if *B* represents the totality of the world, and *A* represents God, this means that God has all the power, while the world has none.

However, if there is an actual world, and an actual world by metaphysical necessity contains a multiplicity of beings with power, then it is impossible for any one being to have a monopoly on power. Hence, the greatest conceivable power a being can have cannot be equated with all the power. Charles Hartshorne has stated these ideas clearly in an article on "Omnipotence." He says that omnipotence

> is sometimes viewed as a monopolistic concentration of power—the wielding, by one agent, of all the power there is or could be. This implies that all other beings are powerless. But if "being is power" (Plato), then power over being is power over power, and the ideal or perfect agent will enjoy the *optimal concentration of efficacy which is compatible with there being other efficacious agents.*[57]

Such a view greatly alters the problem of evil. Even a being with perfect power cannot unilaterally bring about that which it is impossible for one being unilaterally to effect. And it is impossible for one being unilaterally to effect the best possible state of affairs among other beings. In other words, one being cannot guarantee that the other beings will avoid all genuine evil. The possibility of genuine evil is necessary.

The distinction between saying that genuine evil is necessary (which I see no reason for saying, since it is always possible that the best set of possibilities in any situation will be actualized) and saying that the *possibility* of genuine evil is necessary is often overlooked. For example, we saw above that Plantinga moved quickly from the assertion that evil is not necessary to the assertion that an omnipotent being could preclude the possibility of evil. He apparently neglected the middle position, which is that the possibility of evil is necessary, which would imply that no being, not even one with perfect power, could preclude its actualization.

Nelson Pike points out that one way to deny a contradiction between God and evil is to say that "evil is logically necessary" in any world.[58] But Pike passes over this suggestion quickly, moving on to the possibility that all *prima facie* evil might be only apparent. He evidently agrees with others that a world without evil is logically possible. But he and many others fail to see that one does not need to affirm that "evil is logically necessary in any world" in order to avoid the conclusion that an omnipotent being could unilaterally prevent all evil in a world. All that is needed is the position that "it is logically necessary that the *possibility* for evil will exist in any world."

This position follows from the meaning of "world" as containing self-determining beings, since it is not logically possible for one being completely to determine the activity of another entity that by definition has activity that is underived from any other being. Again, it may be that an omnipotent being might be successful in preventing all genuine evil in such a world (just as a father *might* be successful for fifteen years in preventing any fights between his children). But the omnipotent being cannot be the *sufficient* cause of that state of affairs, and hence cannot guarantee it; whether or not it occurs will be partly due to the worldly entities themselves. Hence, the actual presence of genuine evil in the world is no disproof of the existence of an omnipotent being who wants to prevent all genuine evil.

This view can be called "C omnipotence." The C stands for both "coherent" and "creationistic." It is the only view that is coherent if one is talking about the power a being with the greatest conceivable amount of power could have over a *created,* i.e., an actual, world. If the world is an actual creation, and not simply a complex idea in the divine mind, or simply aspects or "modes" of God, then all-powerful *cannot* mean having *all* the power. And if there are many centers of power, then no state of affairs in which these entities are involved can be completely determined by any one of them. The logic of C omnipotence would then involve the *denial* of the principle that God can unilaterally effect any state of affairs that is in itself intrinsically possible. Although an actual world without genuine evil is possible, it is impossible for an omnipotent being to guarantee such a world.

That God really have *all* the power is the requirement set by writers such as Flew, Hick, Campbell, Puccetti, and Findlay for "true theism," "Christian monotheism," or "an adequate religious object." They require that there be no genuine powers besides God, no powers that could have the slightest degree of independent activity in terms of which they could be hostile to deity, limit its influence, and thwart its will. With this requirement, monotheism becomes monism, or acosmism—one is saying in effect (if to be actual is to have power) that creatures can only worship God if they, the creatures, do not actually exist.

"I omnipotence" can be used to refer to the traditional doctrine that an omnipotent being can unilaterally effect any state of affairs, if that state of affairs is intrinsically possible. The I can stand for either "incoherent" or "idealistic," since such a definition is incoherent if it refers to an omnipotent being's dealings with an actual world. It is only intelligible if worldly entities are defined as being completely determinable by another being. And the only experience we have of such complete determination is our experience of controlling ideal beings, i.e., beings existing in our minds. Hence, this view is in effect the idealistic doctrine that worldly beings are simply ideas in the divine mind. This idealism could not, of course, exclude finite persons from this status. The idealism would have to be absolute: all worldly beings, including so-called finite selves, would have to be mere ideas in God's mind, as James Ross's analogies imply.

The fact that one cannot discuss what an omnipotent being can do apart from a consideration of the nature of those unto whom it is done has not been totally overlooked in recent discussions. In response to Mackie's statement of the omnipotence fallacy ("If their being of this sort is logically possible, then God's making them of this sort is logically possible"), S. A. Grave has replied:

> There is, by definition, the definition a consistent theism has to give, no logical impossibility in a man's freely choosing the

> good on every occasion. There is, by definition, a logical impossibility in God's making him freely choose the good on any occasion.[59]

Plantinga also indicates the fallacy by pointing out the ambiguity in Mackie's statement that "God can create free men such that they always do what is right." This is consistent, Plantinga says, if it means, "God created men and these free men always do what is right." But if it means, "God creates free men and brings it about that they always freely do what is right," it is inconsistent; for if God *brings about* their right actions, they do not do the actions *freely*. Hence, only the first interpretation is meaningful, and it cannot be used to deduce from the existence of (genuine) moral evil the nonexistence of benevolent omnipotence, since "whether the free men created by God would always do what is right would presumably be up to them."[60]

The arguments of Grave and Plantinga point, I believe, in the right direction. However, both men seem to apply the above reasoning only to human beings. They apparently believe that an actual world devoid of beings with some power of self-determination would be possible. That Grave assumes this is shown by his suggestion that we have freedom in order that our actions might have "real merit."[61] And Plantinga's affirmation of the logic of I omnipotence was quoted earlier. But let us assume that it is a metaphysical truth that any actual world would contain self-determining entities. Then, even if such a world could possibly be free from genuine evil, it would not be true that God could unilaterally prevent all evil in it. Whether the worldly entities would always avoid evil would finally, in Plantinga's words, "be up to them."

Plantinga evidently affirms the logic of I omnipotence in general, and applies the doctrine of C omnipotence only in relation to human beings. Extending the doctrine of C omnipotence to *any* world has important advantages. I have mentioned them before, but will review them briefly here. The main point is that, if this doctrine is applicable only to human beings, and hence is only a contingent matter, the "free-will defense" runs into serious difficulties. First, God could, on this hypothesis, occasionally violate human freedom for the sake of an overriding good, or to prevent a particularly horrible evil. Of course, in those moments, the apparent human beings would not really be humans, if "humans" are by definition free. But this would be a small price to pay if some of the world's worst evils could be averted.[62]

Second, the anti-theist can quite plausibly suggest that a world of happy beings who are just like us, except that they are predetermined always to do right, would be preferable to a world such as ours with genuine free will but also with all its correlative evils.[63] To reply that the "real merit," or "authentic fiduciary attitudes" which the endowment of freedom makes possible must, in God's eyes, be worth all the evil, only again throws into question God's moral goodness. If most of the values of human existence could be actualized by beings who only apparently had freedom, the benefits of genuine freedom would seem to be outweighed by its risks.

Third, making C omnipotence a contingent matter, and limiting its scope to human existence, means that the problem of evil in the subhuman world must be treated in terms of some other principle, and none of these has proved satisfactory. Of course, one *can* extend the free-will defense to the subhuman realm, without positing any inherent power of self-determination to its entities, by pointing to the irrefutable possibility that all evils in this realm are due to Satan and his cohorts.[64] But such a suggestion only returns us to the previous point about the general illumination that theism needs to provide to render itself plausible in our day.

I will conclude this chapter with a brief discussion of the worshipfulness of a God who has C omnipotence, and not simply as a voluntary self-limitation. A doctrine that denies I omnipotence has been called a "weakened form of theism." But surely making a doctrine coherent is not to weaken it. Some will speak of the view advocated here as a doctrine of "finite God." And certainly this God is finite in some sense. God is not literally "the infinite." For if the world is actual, then God cannot be all of the actual, and have all the power. But the expression "finite God" is generally used to suggest that such a God is imperfect because finite in comparison with some other conceivable notion. But the position affirmed here is that the supposedly greater concept is only verbalizable, not coherently conceivable. As an impossibility, the other "God" cannot serve as a standard by which to judge the God of a coherent doctrine imperfect.

It will be said by some that if God cannot unilaterally bring about any intrinsically possible state of affairs, then "God's power is limited." But it is one thing to say that *God* is limited, i.e., limited by the decisions of other actualities. It is something else to say God's *power* is limited, for this language suggests that it is limited in comparison with that of some greater conceivable creator. For example, M. B. Ahern was cited earlier as saying that a being of limited power would not be a fitting object of worship, since worship "supposes that a greater being is inconceivable." And C. A. Campbell was quoted as stating that we cannot worship a being who is recognized as imperfect in any way, and that limitation of power is an imperfection. One can agree with these authors that a being who has less than the greatest conceivable power would not be worshipful, without further agreeing with them that a worshipful being must be able unilaterally to determine all things. Charles Hartshorne has again expressed the point clearly:

> It has become customary to say that we must limit divine power to save human freedom and to avoid making deity responsible for evil. But to speak of limiting a concept seems to imply that the concept, without the limitation, makes sense. The notion of a cosmic power that determines all decisions fails to make sense. For its decisions could refer to nothing except themselves. They could result in no world; for a world must consist of local agents making their own decisions. Instead of saying that God's power is limited, suggesting that it is less than some conceivable power, we should rather say: his power is absolutely maximal, the greatest possible, but even the greatest possible power is still one power among others, is not the only power. God can do everything that a God can do, everything that could be done by "a being with no possible superior."[65]

This issue is of utmost importance for the problem of theodicy. One has not really "justified the ways of God" if the justification involves the loss of God's perfection and hence deity. Since the basic meaning of "God" is rooted in the context of worship, and since we can only worship perfection, the resolution of the problem of evil is not really a theodicy if it suggests that God exemplifies admirable attributes in a less perfect manner than some other possible (conceivable) being. This is one problem with Brightman's solution, i.e., he suggests that the evil in the world forces us to believe that the deity which in fact exists is imperfect in comparison with some conceivable deity. If that is the case, then the God of our world would truly be called "finite."

But the doctrine being advocated here is intended as an affirmation of the first premise. God is a perfect reality, that greater than which nothing can be consistently thought. This is so, in spite of the fact that God cannot unilaterally prevent all evil in the world, because it is impossible in principle for one being completely to determine the dispositions of other actual beings. Since this cannot be done, it is no limitation on divine perfection that God cannot do it. Accordingly, there is nothing in this theodicy which undercuts God's perfection and hence worshipfulness. Of course, many may, because of cultural-psychological conditioning, find it difficult to worship God as here conceived. But, unless premise X and hence premise Q (see page 264) are accepted, the fact that God as here understood does not in fact inspire worship in someone does not indicate that this God is not *worthy* of worship. It only indicates that there is a gap in the person between notions (coherent or not) which in fact elicit religious emotions, due to past conditioning, and present notions of perfection, to which religious emotions in principle should be attached. According to Whitehead, a major element in the history of religion is the long time it takes for novel general ideas to be appropriated with emotional intensity and hence found interesting. This is due to "dominant interests which inhibit reaction to that type of generality."[66] This, of course, is a serious problem. But it is not a problem for philosophical theology as such to solve.

In the first part of the following chapter I will explicate Whitehead's view as to how divine causation is related to worldly activity. This should help make clearer, by concrete example, the basic formal point of the present chapter. It will indicate how, on the basis of Whitehead's metaphysical intuitions, it would be impossible in principle for a God unilaterally to determine any state of affairs in an actual world.

# 18
# A Process Theodicy

THE PREVIOUS chapter has dealt with the fundamental point of difference between "traditional" and "nontraditional" theodicies, as I am using the terms—i.e., in nontraditional theodicies God not only does not but also in principle *could* not completely control events in the world. (Hence, either premise 2 or premise 3 of the formal statement of the problem of evil is rejected.) There are several nontraditional theodicies extant today. In this concluding chapter, I will sketch the position that seems to me superior in terms of the criteria of consistency, adequacy to the facts, and illuminating power. This is a theodicy based on Whiteheadian-Hartshornean process philosophy. The resulting theodicy is in part simply a restatement of certain explicit themes in Whitehead's thought, in part an explication and application of certain notions that are only implicit therein, and in part a modification of Whitehead's position along lines suggested by Hartshorne—a modification that is regarded as making Whitehead's own position more self-consistent.

The "facts" to which a relevant theodicy in our context must be "adequate" include the value judgments regarding "perfection" and hence worshipfulness that have been formed in our tradition. Of course, as I have argued in the previous chapter, this does not mean that we need try to repeat every aspect of the transmitted *verbalizations* about deity. But it does mean that, in terms of those value judgments which we find inescapable, it must be possible to regard the proposed concept of deity as pointing to a reality greater than which no other reality is genuinely conceivable. In the previous chapter, I have already argued that a God not able unilaterally to prevent all evil is not *ipso facto* imperfect and hence unworthy of worship. The central task of the present chapter is to show that God as conceived by process thought in particular exemplifies perfect moral goodness by the criteria of moral goodness which we actually employ.

The strategy of the traditional theodicies was to say that God is responsible for evil but not indictable for it. They did this by maintaining that all evil is merely apparent, so that there is no genuine evil. Process theology also says that God is in an important sense responsible for much of the world's evil but not indictable for it. But it does this without denying the reality of genuine evil.

The general thesis of the process theodicy which follows is that the possibility of genuine evil is rooted in the metaphysical (i.e., necessary) characteristics of the world. In Whitehead's words: "The categories governing the determination of things are the reasons why there should be evil" (*PR* 341).[1] In the following sections, I will discuss the metaphysical categories that are most directly related to the necessity of the possibility of evil.

## UNIVERSAL CREATIVITY AND DIVINE PERSUASION

The first element in the process solution has already been suggested: God's power is persuasive, not controlling. Some traditional theodicies have indeed said that persuasion is the divine *modus operandi* (at least in relation to some of the creatures). But they have regarded the reason for this to be moral rather than metaphysical. That is, it is said to be *better* (so that certain desired ends can be attained) for God to exercise persuasive rather than controlling power. This *modus operandi* is thus said to result from a divine self-limitation. According to process thought, the reason is metaphysical, not moral. God does not refrain from controlling the creatures simply because it is better for God to use persuasion, but because it is necessarily the case that God cannot completely control the creatures.

The metaphysical category behind this necessity is the category of the ultimate, which involves "creativity," "many," and "one." "Creativity" (by which the many become one and are increased by one) is a universal feature of actuality. It is inherent in actuality (*AI* 230). This does not mean that creatures derive their creative power from themselves, or that they are not dependent upon God for their existence. But it does mean that to be an actuality is to exercise creativity, and that there is necessarily a realm of finite actualities with creativity of their own.

To say that an actuality has creativity is to say that it has power. The nature of this creative power is twofold—the power of self-creation and of other-creation. In the language of causation, it is the capacity to exercise final causation and efficient causation. To explain how these two dimensions of creativity are related and to prepare the way for other points, it is necessary briefly to explain Whitehead's unique understanding of what an "actual entity" is.

An actual entity is an "occasion of experience." In the first place, this means that, as for Berkeley and Leibniz, all actual entities experience; there is no dualism between experiencing and nonexperiencing actual entities. However, only genuine *individuals* are considered actual entities. As Leibniz held (unlike Berkeley), things such as sticks and stones, which rather obviously do not experience, are regarded as *aggregates* of actual entities.

In the second place, the idea that an actual entity is an *occasion* of experience means that the full-fledged individuals of the world are momentary events. Unlike Leibnizian "monads," which endure indefinitely through time, a Whiteheadian actual entity happens and then "perishes" in a sense, making room for succeeding events. Partly to indicate this event-character of actual entities, Whitehead calls them "actual occasions."

Each actual occasion exists in two modes, first one and then the other. An occasion comes into being as an experiencing subject. The data of its experience are provided by previous actual occasions. Its reception of these data is called its "feelings" or "positive prehensions" of those previous occasions. (There are also "negative prehensions," which are said to "exclude from feeling.") It becomes a unified subject by integrating these feelings. This process of integration into a concrete unity is called "concrescence" (*AI* 303).

When the process of concrescence is complete, so that the actual occasion has achieved a unified experience of all its data and its subjective reactions to them (each feeling has its "objective datum" and its "subjective form" of response to this datum), the occasion becomes an object of experience, i.e., an object for other subjects. Its subjectivity perishes, and it thereby acquires objectivity. It transmits some of its feelings to subsequent actual occasions. This process, in which data are passed from one occasion to another, is termed "transition" (*PR* 320, 322 f., 236).

These two processes, concrescence and transition, embody the two forms of creativity, the two types of power, inherent in each actual occasion. The process of concrescence embodies the occasion's power of self-determination, its power of final causation. Although the present occasion is largely determined by the power of the past upon it, it is never thus completely determined.

> However far the sphere of efficient causation be pushed in the determination of components of a concrescence . . . there always remains the final reaction of the self-creative unity of the universe. (*PR* 75)

This is an explication of the metaphysical category of "Freedom and Determination" (*PR* 41). It is because of their inherent power of self-determination that actual entities cannot be completely determined by others: "The freedom inherent in the universe is constituted by this element of self-causation" (*PR* 135).

The actual occasion then manifests its power of other-determination, its efficient causation, in the process of transition. This dimension of power is equally essential to the occasion's actuality:

> Its own constitution involves that its own activity in *self*-formation passes into its activity of *other*-formation. (*AI* 248)

> The world is self-creative; and the actual entity as self-creating creature passes into its immortal function of part-creator of the transcendent world. (*PR* 130)

> An actual entity arises from decisions *for* it, and by its very existence provides decisions *for* other actual entities which supersede it. (*PR* 68)

The main point to be stressed here is that the fact that our world is composed of actualities with this twofold type of power is not a contingent feature of our particular world. It exemplifies a *metaphysical* principle about reality: *any* world would necessarily contain actualities with this twofold creativity. After stating that the Category of the Ultimate includes "creativity," "many," and "one" as the three ultimate notions, Whitehead says:

> Creativity is the universal of universals characterizing ultimate matter of fact. It is that ultimate principle by which the many, which are the universe disjunctively, become the one actual occasion, which is the universe conjunctively. It lies in

> the nature of things that many enter into complex unity. . . . The ultimate metaphysical principle is the advance from disjunction to conjunction, creating a novel entity other than the entities given in disjunction. (*PR* 31, 32)

Referring elsewhere to this passage from the many in disjunction to the one in conjunction, he says:

> It is a metaphysical principle belonging to the nature of things, that there is nothing in the Universe other than instances of this passage and components of these instances. (*AI* 303)

Reference to creativity as the "ultimate metaphysical principle" which lies in "the nature of things" indicates that the fact that the world's actual entities have creative power is not a contingent feature of reality. It is beyond all volition, even God's. Whitehead makes this point as he rejects the notion that "the ultimate creativity of the universe is to be ascribed to God's volition" (*PR* 343 f.). Further, he says that we should not pay God the dubious "metaphysical compliment" of being "the foundation of the metaphysical situation with its ultimate activity" (*SMW* 258). And Whitehead makes the connection with the problem of evil, saying that if God is thus wrongly conceived,

> there can be no alternative except to discern in Him the origin of all evil as well as of all good. He is then the supreme author of the play, and to Him must therefore be ascribed its shortcomings as well as its success. (*SMW* 258)

Also, God's way of relating to the creatures is not due to a decision. Whereas Plato grounded these relationships upon the divine will, Whitehead says, "metaphysics requires that the relationships of God to the world should lie beyond the accidents of will, and that they be founded upon the necessities of the nature of the World" (*AI* 215). Furthermore, that there be an actual world of some sort or other is not a contingent matter. There would simply be no meaning to "God" apart from "creativity" and the worldly "creatures" (*PR* 344). The notion of creation out of absolute nothingness, so that creation would be "the beginning of matter of fact," is rejected in favor of the creation of order out of chaos (*PR* 146–147, 519).

Accordingly, it is impossible for God to have a monopoly on power. There must be an actual world; and every actual world will necessarily contain actualities with power—some power of self-determination, and some power to influence others. This twofold inherent power provides the twofold reason why God cannot unilaterally effect any state of affairs in the world that is intrinsically possible. God cannot totally determine the concrescence of any actual occasion: (1) since that occasion will necessarily be partly determined by previous actual occasions, which themselves could not have been totally determined by God; and (2) since the present occasion necessarily has some power to create itself, beyond all the influence of others, including God.

Whitehead explicitly says that actual occasions have the power of self-determination vis-à-vis God. After saying that every creature is *causa sui* since all creatures embody creativity, he says:

> All actual entities share with God this character of self-causation. For this reason every actual entity also shares with God the characteristics of transcending all other actual entities, including God. (*PR* 339)

Again, the connection with the problem of evil is explicitly made. The world must transcend God in the sense of having its own creativity by which it can refuse to conform to the divine input, since this input is good and yet there is evil in the world (*RM* 85). Evil arises from this capacity not to conform to the divine purpose: "So far as the conformity is incomplete, there is evil in the world" (*RM* 60).

In Whitehead's opinion, "one of the greatest intellectual discoveries in the history of religion" was Plato's suggestion "that the divine element in the world is to be conceived as a persuasive agency and not as a coercive agency" (*AI* 213). Whitehead provides a conceptuality for understanding God's *modus operandi* as persuasive. All pure possibilities, termed by Whitehead "eternal objects," are contained in the "primordial nature" of God. This primordial nature is an envisagement of these ideals or eternal objects, with the urge toward their actualization in the world (*PR* 47; *AI* 357). Each actual occasion begins by prehending God and therefore this divine urge for the realization of possibilities. Each occasion thereby receives from God an "ideal aim" or "initial aim." This is an initial persuasion toward that possibility for the occasion's existence which would be best for it, given its context (*RM* 152; *PR* 128). This aim is sometimes termed the "initial subjective aim," but it is not to be identified with the occasion's "subjective aim" itself. The "subjective aim" is the aim which the subject actually chooses, and hence that possibility which it in fact actualizes. It *may* be identical in content with the *initial* subjective aim, but it need not be. The initial aim is given by God; the subjective aim is chosen by the subject. The fact that the power of this divinely given initial aim is not coercive, so that divine determinism is avoided, is made clear in many passages:

> An originality in the temporal world is conditioned, though not determined, by an initial subjective aim supplied by the ground of all order and of all originality. (*PR* 164)

> Each temporal entity . . . derives from God its basic conceptual aim, relevant to its actual world, yet with indeterminations awaiting its own decisions. (*PR* 343)

> The initial stage of the aim is rooted in the nature of God, and its completion depends on the self-causation of the subject-superject. (*PR* 373)

> God . . . is that actual entity from which each temporal concrescence receives that initial aim from which its self-causation starts. The subject, thus constituted, is the autonomous master of its own concrescence into subject-superject. (*PR* 374)

Accordingly, the category of freedom and determinism, which is one implication of the category of the ultimate, holds good even in regard to the creatures' relation to God—the creatures have freedom even in relation to the determination received from God.

Hence, while Whitehead does not reject divine providence altogether in order to solve the problem of evil (as have thinkers such as Richard Rubenstein), he does consistently reject the traditional notion of "unqualified omnipotence," which is "accompanied by responsibility for every detail of every happening" (*AI* 217). And he grounds this rejection upon the metaphysical position that creative power is inherent throughout the realm of actuality. Hence, the fact that God's *modus operandi* is persuasive rather than coercive is not due to a decision on God's part which *could* be revoked from time to time.[2]

As suggested in Chapter 17, a process theodicy need not necessarily reject the application of the term "omnipotent" to God. This term can be taken simply as a synonym for "having perfect power," and this can be defined in terms of "C omnipotence" as opposed to "I omnipotence" (see pages 269–270). This is the approach I have taken. Hence, premise 2 of the problem of evil is allowed to stand, while premise 3 is rejected.

## THE TWO CRITERIA OF INTRINSIC GOOD AND THE TWO DIMENSIONS OF EVIL

The second step in this process solution to the problem of evil is to recognize that there are two dimensions of intrinsic evil, not only one. These two dimensions are the opposites of the two criteria of intrinsic good. That which is "intrinsically good" is that which is good in and for itself, apart from considerations as to its usefulness for other things. Experience is that which can be intrinsically good in this sense. Since, according to Whitehead, all actualities are experiences, the notion of intrinsic goodness is relevant to all actualities. And the same criteria of intrinsic goodness are relevant.

What are the criteria of intrinsic good? That is, what factor or factors in experience determine whether it is good in and for itself? According to Whitehead, experience is good in itself to the extent that it is characterized by beauty. Hence, the criteria are aesthetic criteria. They can be summed up under "harmony" and "intensity." That is, experience is good to the degree that it is both harmonious and intense.

The criteria of intrinsic evil are, accordingly, the opposites of these. The opposite of harmony is "disharmony" or "discord." This occurs when two or more elements of an experience clash, so that there is a feeling of mutual destructiveness (*AI* 329). "This is the feeling of evil in the most general sense, namely physical pain or mental evil, such as sorrow, horror, dislike" (*AI* 330).

The opposite of intensity can be called "triviality." In human terms we speak of this dimension in terms of boredom, lack of zest and excitement. The fact that intensity is at least as important as harmony is evidenced by the fact that we often risk great pain, both physical and psychic, for the sake of excitement. Of course, people differ in regard to the relative value which they place on each of these criteria, with some risking present harmony for increased intensity, while others forgo the possibility of greater intensity for the sake of preserving the harmony which has been achieved. But everyone wants both factors to some degree. A person may even prefer death to the continuation of experience in which either harmony or intensity is outweighed by its opposite.

Why is it that intensity and harmony are somewhat in tension, so that efforts to achieve one may endanger the other? It is because increased intensity requires increased complexity which can bring together a greater variety of detail into contrast. Bringing more details into experience may upset the harmony which had been achieved among the elements that had previously been combined. If harmony is to be achieved, it will have to be a more complex harmony. It is for this reason, for example, that some people at some stage in life refuse to entertain seriously any new thoughts; they fear that a harmony between these thoughts and others which they value will not be achievable, at least not without more effort than they want to expend. But it is also partly for this reason that we believe that continuing to learn is good. Continual learning provides the possibility for increasingly intense experiences, since it continually provides new elements to be integrated into an increasingly complex harmony.

There are two senses in which an experience can be "complex," and both of these contribute to intensity. First, there is complexity in the sheer amount and variety of elements which are integrated in an occasion of experience. Each experience begins by appropriating data from previous experiences. For example, an occasion of human experience receives influences from its own past experiences, from its body, and from God. The act by which an occasion of experience absorbs data from other experiences is called a "feeling" or a "positive prehension." The act of excluding data from feeling is called a "negative prehension." What is excluded are some of the feelings that were combined in the previous experiences.

All worldly occasions combine positive and negative prehensions in their reception of that which the past world has to offer. Hence, a worldly occasion will feel or positively prehend some of the available data, but will negatively prehend the rest, thereby excluding it from contributing positively to its own internal reality. However, worldly actual occasions differ in regard to the balance of positive and negative prehensions. Some occasions are more complex in the sense of being able to appropriate more of the available data.

To be able to appropriate data means to be able to bring it together into effective contrast. Some data which a more complex occasion could integrate into *contrasts* will constitute *incompatibilities* for a less complex occasion. Hence, the less complex occasion will negatively prehend feelings which a more complex occasion could have integrated into a more complex and thereby more intense harmony. Hence, the growth of complexity in this first sense means the growth in the intensity of experience.

The second sense of complexity is, paradoxically, the ability to simplify. It presupposes the previous sense of complexity. After receiving a great amount and variety of data the complex occasion is able to simplify this data and thereby achieve a greater intensity of experience. Conscious sense experience, in which myriads of feelings are transmuted into the appearance of a relatively few objects, is the most obvious example. It is because of this correlation between intensity and simplicity in this sense that the assertion that increased complexity is a condition for increased intensity seems counterintuitive at first. The reconciliation of the assertion and our intuition comes from seeing (1) that it is the most complex experiences which are able to effect this simplification; (2) that this simplified result presupposes the positive appropriation of a vast quantity and variety of data; and finally (3) that the intensity associated with this simplified result comes in part from the fact that it is held in contrast with the welter of feelings of which it is a simplification.

The fact that complexity is a condition for intensity will be central to the sketch of the evolutionary process in the next section. But at present an important distinction between triviality and discord must be mentioned. Discord is evil in an absolute or noncomparative sense. Since discord means some kind of suffering, it is evil in itself, apart from any comparison with that which might have been (*AI* 329–330). (Of course, we might think that the instrumental value of the suffering is great enough to make it better, in the long run, that the suffering occurred than had it not occurred; but we are here discussing *intrinsic* evil.) Triviality, however, is evil only by comparison, i.e., if an experience is more trivial than it need have been. A hog's experience is not evil simply because it is less intense than human experience. But human experience is evil if it degenerates to a porcine level; it is evil by comparison with what it could have been (*RM* 94).

This means that Whitehead rejects the notion of "metaphysical evil," the notion that finite experiences should be called "evil" simply because they are finite. Rather, the fact that the lower forms of actualities must exclude (through negative prehensions) much of the potentially available data in their environments "does not derogate from 'perfection.' There is then 'perfection' in its kind—that is to say, in its type of finiteness with such-and-such exclusions" (*AI* 329). Hence, trivial experience is not evil simply because it is trivial; it is evil only if it is more trivial than it had to be.

The recognition that there are two criteria of evil, discord and unnecessary triviality, complicates the attempt to rate experiences in terms of intrinsic goodness. One cannot simply say that an experience which is harmonious is *ipso facto* "better" than one which is more discordant. It is true that "the more discordant the feeling, the further the retreat from perfection" (*AI* 330). But it is also true that "Perfection at a low level ranks below Imperfection with higher aim" (*AI* 331, cf. 330). Accordingly, encouraging the emergence of forms of experience which will be more intense but also more discordant than present ones is not necessarily inconsistent with moral goodness.

A brief statement from Whitehead summarizes the two types of evil, discord (physical and mental) and unnecessary triviality: "Now evil is exhibited in physical suffering, mental suffering, and the loss of the higher experience in favor of the lower experience" (*RM* 92). The explicit recognition of these two forms of evil is of utmost importance for theodicy. Of these two forms, most discussions focus on discord or suffering, ignoring the fact that unnecessary triviality must also be overcome if the highest good is to be achieved.

## CREATION OUT OF CHAOS AND THE DIVINE PURPOSE

Recognizing that unnecessary triviality is an evil provides a basis for understanding the evolutionary development of our world as manifesting the creative purpose of a good God. The usual, simple statement of the problem of evil states as one of the premises: "If God is all-good, God would want to prevent all evil." The "evil" that is normally in mind is discord—pain and suffering. But if this were the only evil to be avoided, the easiest way to avoid evil would be to avoid creating a world altogether! One would at least expect a deity whose moral goodness was thus defined to refrain from bringing forth any creatures capable of any significant forms of suffering, i.e., living creatures.

Stating this implication openly helps us realize that there is more implied in our usual notion of a "morally good being" than simply the intention to avoid discord. Since moral goodness involves the intention to promote intrinsically rewarding experiences, it includes the intention to avoid the other type of evil, unnecessary triviality. With this second criterion in mind, we can understand our world as the (partially self-created) product of a morally perfect being.

It has already been pointed out that, according to process thought, there was no beginning of a realm of finite actualities. There has always been a plurality of actual occasions. But there is no reason to believe that the types of order exemplified in our world are eternal and hence necessary. In fact, there is good reason to think that these forms of order have evolved (except for those most general principles which seem metaphysical, since they are without conceivable alternative). Whitehead suggests that there is a series of cosmic epochs. Each such epoch is characterized by particular forms of order. These forms develop gradually, are sustained for a period, and then gradually dissolve (*PR* 142; *FR* 18–25). Out of the resulting chaos the order of another epoch gradually emerges. Hence the creation of our world is understandable as a process of bringing order out of a state of absolute or near chaos. The question is whether the two criteria of value provide a rationale for this creative process.

In a state of absolute chaos, there would be no "social" order among the myriad occasions. They would simply happen at random, without any of them being ordered even into the most elementary "societies." The simplest form of social order that actual occasions can exemplify is purely temporal or serial order. In such a society, there is only one member at a time. Each occasion in that society repeats the form (the complex eternal object) actualized by the previous members. Each occasion inherits from other past occasions too, of course, but the inheritance from the past members of its own society is dominant over the other lines of inheritance. Such a society is called an "enduring object," or an "enduring individual."[3] An electron provides an example; each electronic actual occasion largely repeats the form of the previous occasions in that serially ordered society. It is this constant repetition that constitutes the enduring individuality of the electron, its identity through time. Protons and neutrons provide other primitive examples. Subprotonic and subelectronic enduring individuals would provide even more primitive examples (*PR* 152).

A state of absolute chaos would be devoid of even these most primitive enduring individuals.[4] Such a chaotic state would have *some* intrinsic value, since it would contain actual occasions, and hence experiences. But the value enjoyed by those occasions of experience would be extremely trivial. "In proportion to the chaos there is triviality" (*PR* 169). The reason for this is that complexity of experience presupposes order in the environment. The character of an actual occasion is governed by the datum from which it arises. "There can be no transgression of the limitations of capacity inherent in the datum" (*PR* 168). The datum is a function of the environment. Hence, the environment determines what kinds of occasions of experience can arise. Complex occasions require an orderly environment. Hence, although it is harmonious intensity rather than "order" which is intrinsically good, God brings order out of chaos for the sake of increased intensity.

> The ultimate creative purpose [is] that each unification shall achieve some maximum depth of intensity of feeling, subject to the conditions of its concrescence. (*PR* 381)

> God's purpose in the creative advance is the evocation of intensities. The evocation of societies is purely subsidiary to this absolute end. (*PR* 161)

> What is inexorable in God, is valuation as an aim towards "order"; and "order" means "society" permissive of actualities with patterned intensity of feeling arising from adjusted contrasts. (*PR* 373 f.)

Whitehead understands the subjective aim of every actual occasion as twofold: it is an aim at intensity in the present, and also an aim to contribute intensity to the future (*PR* 41, 424). I suggest that this twofold aim also characterizes the divine aim in bringing forth each step in the evolutionary process. That is, each breakthrough makes possible a greater enjoyment of experience in the present. It also provides the necessary conditions for the emergence of a more complex form of actuality in the future, which will be capable of even greater intrinsic good.

The first stage of evolution out of chaos can be thus understood. The form which is repeated by each member of an enduring individual is a form of value experience. The fact that it is reiterated by each occasion contributes to the intensity felt by each occasion (*SMW* 137, 278; Imm. 688–690). This is the simplest exemplification of the principle that stability of order is necessary for importance of experience (*MT* 87). Hence, the development of enduring individuals is the first step in rescuing the finite realm from triviality (Imm. 693).

The subsequent stages can be understood as manifestations of the same twofold purpose. For example, the emergence of the atom out of enduring individuals at the level of protons and electrons can be understood as enabling a gain in intrinsic value, if only a slight one. The atom is not merely the sum of its subatomic parts, but is unified by a higher-level series of actual occasions which receive values from the subatomic occasions. These atomic occasions are able to harmonize a greater variety of the available data than are any of the subatomic occasions. Hence, a more intense harmony is possible.

The relationship between the molecule and its submolecular (i.e., atomic) parts can be understood in essentially the same way. Hence, atoms not only represented a gain in intrinsic value in themselves, but also were instrumentally valuable in making possible the emergence of molecules. Likewise, molecules can be understood as representing still another gain in intrinsic value and likewise as instrumentally valuable in the emergence of the living cell. They provide the more complex environment out of which the cell can emerge.

The cell likewise is not merely the sum of its (molecular) parts, but contains a higher-level series of actual occasions. These cellular occasions are the loci of the life of the cell; they are "living" occasions. In Whitehead's thought this is not an absolute difference in kind (more recent discoveries of macromolecules, which have some of the properties of "life," have supported this view); but it is an important difference.

> In a sense, the difference between a living organism and the inorganic environment is only a question of degree; but it is a difference of degree which makes all the difference—in effect, it is a difference of quality. (*PR* 271)

The difference in degree involves the significance of the "mental pole" in the occasions of experience. "Mentality" for Whitehead does not necessarily involve thought, or even consciousness. The physical pole of an occasion is that occasion's reception of data from other actualities. The mental pole is that occasion's self-determinative response to this received data. It "introduces the subject as a determinant of its own concrescence" (*PR* 380). Hence, to say that every occasion has mentality is simply to say that there is at least some iota of self-determination in each occasion. It is thus through the mental pole that some novelty might come into the world. However, in nonliving occasions, the origination of novelty in the occasion's exercise of final causation is negligible.

> In its lowest form, mental experience is canalized into slavish conformity. It is merely the appetition towards, or from, whatever in fact already is. . . . It is rather a capacity for mentality, than mentality itself. But it *is* mentality. . . . It is degraded to being merely one of the actors in the efficient causation. (*FR* 33 f.)

In living occasions, significant novelty is introduced by the mental pole.

> A single occasion is alive when the subjective aim which determines its process of concrescence has introduced a novelty of definiteness not to be found in the inherited data of its primary phase. (*PR* 159)

The importance of this characteristic of life lies in the fact that order is not the only necessary condition for significant intensity of experience. Novelty of reaction is also necessary. The cell is a complexly ordered organism. It is ordered in such a way that its nonliving societies (molecules) contribute a rich variety of data to the living occasions. However, if these cellular occasions could not introduce novelty, they would have to exclude most of the proferred feelings as incompatibilities, since a merely conformal response to the variety of feelings would produce incompatible subjective forms in the cellular occasions. But, by introducing novelty in their reactions to the data, they can achieve a higher synthesis which reconciles the inherited values (*PR* 155, 161 f., 334 f.). "Some negative prehensions are thus avoided, and higher contrasts are introduced into experience" (*PR* 162).

In other words, an individual occasion's intrinsic good, or beauty, is not produced solely by the environment, or solely by the individual. Both are factors:

> The Beauty realized in an occasion depends both on the objective content from which that occasion originates and also on the spontaneity of the occasion. (*AI* 328)

This means that both extremes are wrong: joy is not *entirely* an "inside job"; nor can happiness be *guaranteed* by improving the social order. This also means that God does not only seek order. The divine aim to maximize beauty also leads God to encourage the development of mentality or the power of self-determination in the world.

> God is the organ of novelty, aiming at intensification. (*PR* 104)

> God . . . is . . . the foundation of order, and . . . the goad towards novelty.[5] "Order" and "novelty" are but the instruments of his subjective aim which is the intensification of "formal immediacy." (*PR* 135)

Whitehead explicitly speaks of the development of the living cell as manifesting the divine purpose. In a section in which the cell (which is a complex "structured society") is the topic of discussion, he says:

> A structured society which is highly complex can be correspondingly favourable to intensity of satisfaction for certain sets of its component members. This intensity arises by reason of the ordered complexity of the contrasts which the society stages for these components. Thus the growth of a complex structured society exemplifies the general purpose pervading nature. (*PR* 152 f.)

However, besides the fact that cells represent a significant advance in intrinsic value (probably a more significant advance than any of the previous emergences), they also provide the necessary basis for an even greater advance beyond themselves. Cells themselves can form even more complex structured societies, i.e., multicellular animal bodies, especially those with central nervous systems, which set the stage for the appearance of the psyche, or soul.

The animal soul is not an ontologically unique kind of individual. It is simply a higher-level series of occasions of experience. Nevertheless, it is greatly different in degree, especially in the higher animals, and most especially in humans. Its emergence means a great increase in intrinsic value. There are several reasons for this great increase. First, the locus of the soul, at the apex of the central nervous system, means that the riches of feelings from the body pour into it. "The harmonized relations of the parts of the body constitute this wealth of inheritance into a harmony of contrasts, issuing into intensity of experience" (*PR* 166 f.). Hence the body provides data out of which a very complex experience can emerge. Second, the soul is an enduring individual. As such, it enjoys the intensity that comes from the repetition of those forms which constitute the character of that individual. Third, the soul is a particular type of enduring individual called a "living person." Since it is *living,* it enjoys that higher kind of value which comes through the introduction of novelty. Fourth, it can "canalize" and thereby intensify its novelty (*PR* 163). That is, that which is introduced as a novel element in one moment can be repeated in subsequent moments. The "form" which constitutes the identity of the soul through time can thereby be constantly enriched. "Thus life turns back into society: it binds originality within bounds, and gains the massiveness due to reiterated character" (*PR* 163). ("Massiveness" is Whitehead's term for variety held in effective contrast [*AI* 325].)

Although all four of these features contribute to the fact that the soul can enjoy such high forms of value, the very emergence of the soul

depends upon the complex organization of the body, w
a particularly intimate part of the environment for the so
fact that cells, which are of significant value in themselve
a soul illustrates in the highest manner known to us the s
evolutionary process to its main problem, which is "the development of enduring harmonies of enduring shapes of value, which merge into higher attainments of things beyond themselves" (*SMW* 137). This development can be seen as one more example of the twofold purpose of God's creative activity, to maximize intrinsic good in the present in such a way as to provide the foundations for greater good in the future.

The process of creation can thereby be understood in terms of Jesus' message of the Rule of God, according to which equal emphasis is put on the future and the present. Of course, Jesus was not thinking in terms of a gradual development. But in regard to the question of how the sacred reality's activity in our world is envisioned, there is a structural parallelism: God is active in the present, and for creatures to respond positively to this present activity brings immediate good; but this present activity also has an essential reference to the future, in which a greater good is intended.[6]

## METAPHYSICAL CORRELATIONS OF VALUE AND POWER

The first step in this process theodicy was the explanation as to why the power of God in the world is necessarily persuasive rather than controlling. The second step involved raising to explicit consciousness our at least implicit knowledge that intensity as well as harmony is required for the more valuable forms of experience, so that moral goodness will seek to overcome unnecessary triviality as well as discord. The third step is the explication of the correlations involving value and power that are implicit in the foregoing sketch of the evolutionary process by which the present state of our world was created out of a more chaotic state.

These correlations involve the following variables: (1) the capacity for intrinsic goodness; (2) the capacity for intrinsic evil; (3) freedom, or the power of self-determination; (4) the capacity for instrumental goodness, or the power to contribute to the intrinsic good of others; (5) the capacity for instrumental evil, or the power to be destructive of the potential intrinsic goodness of others. The correlations among these variables are positive—as one rises, the rest rise proportionately. They are also taken to be metaphysical, necessary. Whitehead does not explicitly include this set of correlations among his metaphysical principles; but its metaphysical status is implicit throughout his philosophy.

I will begin with the positive correlation between the capacity for intrinsic goodness, on the one hand, and freedom, or the power of self-determination, on the other. In the evolutionary process, the increase in the capacity for enjoying intrinsic goodness means the increase in the power to integrate harmoniously an ever-greater variety of data from the environment. But this power is one and the same thing as the power for self-determination. This is made especially clear by the fact that harmonious integration of disparate feelings requires the introduction of novelty by the integrating subject. The introduction of novelty is the sign of mentality, and mentality is nothing other than the subject's determination of its process of concrescence.

This provides the basis for a somewhat different answer than that which is found in most theodicies to the question, Why did God create free beings? Of course, in process thought *all* actualities have *some* freedom, so the question has to be modified to ask, Why did God bring forth creatures with high degrees of freedom? The answer is not primarily that freedom is worth all the evils which it can produce simply because it is so overwhelmingly valuable in itself, or because only those moral and religious acts and/or virtues which are genuinely free are valuable in the sight of God. Rather, the answer is that no significant degree of intrinsic value would be possible without a significant degree of freedom. If there is trivial freedom, there is trivial value.

The freedom that is involved in beings with consciousness and the capacity for rationality is the freedom to commit moral evil. An act is "morally evil" insofar as it involves the *intention* to be destructive of the potential intrinsic good of other actualities (unless this is necessarily part of a more inclusive intention to maximize intrinsic value in the world). In other words, a conscious event is not morally evil simply because it in fact turns out to be instrumentally evil; it must have intended this effect. Since moral evil is defined as the intention to actualize oneself in such a way as *not* to maximize the conditions for intrinsic good in the future, it can also be called "sin," since it involves a rejection of the divinely given ideal aim. But, whatever it be called, the main point here is that the freedom which is entailed by the capacity to enjoy human-level values is necessarily the freedom to *intend* to inflict injury upon others. The significance of this is increased, of course, by the fact that these beings also have a high degree of power to inflict evil upon others, which will be discussed below.

In recent discussions it is often asked why God did not create beings who were like us in every respect except that they would not really be free to sin—they would only think they were free. Being "like us in every respect" involves enjoying all the kinds of values that we can enjoy. (Since they would think they were free, they could even enjoy the smug satisfaction derived from complimenting themselves on their moral virtue.) The process answer to this question is that God could not create such beings. To enjoy the high-level values of which we are capable entails genuinely having a high-level power of self-determination, even vis-à-vis God. As stated in the previous chapter, God *might* have brought forth free saints. But God could not have unilaterally done this; if the creatures always avoided evil acts, this result would be partly "up to them." In Whiteheadian terms: if a creature always follows the ideal aim for it, this is due not only to the impetus received from the ideal aim itself, but also to the creature's free decision to actualize it.

Another correlation is between the capacity for intrinsic good and that for intrinsic evil. Here the "evil" that is in view is primarily discord. Greater intensity of experience, by which triviality is overcome, makes possible greater enjoyment. But it also makes possible greater suffering. "The more intense the discordant feeling, the further the retreat from perfection" (*AI* 330).

The feelings embodied in actual occasions as subjects are intrinsically valuable. As those occasions become objects for a subsequent subject, those embodied feelings become potential instrumental values for that subsequent subject. But if those potential values are to be appropriated, the subject in question must be complex enough to coordinate those values with the other ones being contributed by the environment. Insofar as this is done, variety and therefore intensity of experience is achieved. However, this is done

> at the cost of eliciting vivid experiences of effective tones, good and bad. It makes possible the height of Beauty and the height of Evil: because it saves both from a tame elimination of a tame scaling down. (*AI* 336)

In other words, while increased complexity overcomes triviality, the result may be anywhere on the scale between the height of beauty, which is intense harmony, and the evil of extreme discord. The same delicacy of perception that makes possible great intrinsic good also makes possible great pain (*RM* 93).

For example, much of the good in animal and specifically human life is derived from sharing sympathetically in the feelings of the body. This is unambiguously good, as long as the body is well-fed, exercised, and otherwise healthy. But when the body is hungry, thirsty, or racked with pain, the fact that the psyche incorporates the bodily feelings, with a large degree of conformation to those feelings, becomes a source of evil for it. Likewise, much of the good of the life of humans (and other higher mammals, to varying degrees) derives from sharing in the feelings of loved ones. This is a source of happiness as long as the loved ones are themselves happy and healthy. But when they die prematurely, or suffer prolonged and intense bodily and/or psychic agony, then genuine concern for them becomes a source of suffering—so much so that we are advised by some religious traditions not to form any bonds of affection that make our own happiness dependent upon the condition of others.

Furthermore, just as intrinsically good experience is due in part to the environment and in part to the way the subject actualizes itself, the same is true of intrinsically evil experiences. The same freedom which allows a person to synthesize the feelings contributed by the environment in an intrinsically rewarding way also allows the person to appropriate those same data in a discordant, even a self-destructive, manner. The freedom to enjoy a wide variety of bodily, moral, and religious values intensely is also the freedom to make ourselves miserable.

In other words, precisely the same conditions that allow us to enjoy those experiences which we value most highly and would not want to live without are the conditions that lead us to suffer so intensely. Cats enjoy experiences far beyond the reach of lowly amoebae; but amoebae are not susceptible to the variety and intensity of pain that can be undergone by cats. Human beings can enjoy riches of experience far beyond the wildest feline dreams; but cats have no inkling of the depths of suffering undergone by those fellow creatures who share their dwelling and give them milk—few cats commit suicide.

This is part of the process answer to why there is so much suffering in the world. The answer is not that all the suffering that has occurred and will occur in the world is necessary—there could have been much less, had the creatures actualized themselves differently. It is that the *possibility* of all this evil is necessary *if* there was to be the possibility of all the good that has occurred and may occur in the future. Hence, the question is whether the good that has been achieved and is achievable is worth the risk of all the evil that has occurred and may yet occur. I will return to this question below.

The next correlation to lift up is that between intrinsic good, on the one hand, and potential instrumental good, or the power to influence others for good, on the other. This correlation was implicit in the foregoing description of the evolutionary process. It is the reason why each new emergence is both an increase in the capacity for intrinsic goodness and the basis for further advance. Those actualities which are more complex and intense in themselves also have more to contribute to others. A weak individual exerts a weak influence and a strong one exerts a strong influence (*AI* 367). It is this necessary correlation (rather than the necessity for every niche in the chain of being to be filled) which is the reason for the step-by-step nature of the creative process.

For example, living cells could not have emerged directly out of an arrangement of enduring individuals as primitive as protons and electrons. Those lowly creatures cannot contribute the types of data necessary for the emergence and sustenance of living occasions of experience. The intermediate stages of atoms and molecules were needed. Likewise, an animal soul, even as simple as that of a chipmunk, could not emerge directly out of a complex combination of molecules. Molecules do not have the capacity to contribute the variety, type, and intensity of data necessary to provide an adequate basis for a soul.

Accordingly, even if one assumed anthropocentrically that humans were the only beings on this planet with any significant intrinsic value and hence any real value for God, one would not need to puzzle over the reason for God's use of the long, slow, often pain-filled evolutionary process to get to something like human beings. No route other than a step-by-step process was possible.

The importance for the problem of evil of the correlation between intrinsic value and instrumental power becomes more evident when we bring in the next variable, the capacity for instrumental evil, or the power to influence others for ill. An actual occasion, even if it is intrinsically good, can be either a creative or a destructive force in its impact upon others (*RM* 93).

> Each event infects the ages to come, for good or for evil, with its own individuality. . . . It bequeaths its character to the future, in the guise of an effective element forever adding to, or subtracting from, the richness of the world. For good or for evil. (*S* 47, 58 f.)

Hence, the development of high-grade actualities which can enjoy great intrinsic good necessarily means the development of effective entities which can wreak havoc.

As just indicated, an experience which is intrinsically good can be instrumentally bad. This is because its actual effects upon some subsequent experiences may, in combination with other feelings coming from the environment, produce discordant results. "The nature of evil is that the characters of things are mutually obstructive" (*PR* 517). However, intrinsically good experiences tend to be instrumentally good more regularly than do intrinsically evil experiences. Those experiences which are intrinsically evil tend to be also instrumentally evil. Of course, there are exceptions. Masochism and sadism are examples of deriving enjoyment from the intrinsically evil experiences of others (in masochism the "others" are one's bodily cells); but we regard these as perversions. Also, as we have seen, traditional theodicies have devoted much energy to pointing out the ways in which that which is intrinsically evil can be regarded as instrumentally good. But process thought supports the judgment of Austin Farrer, that "good breeds more good than any evil can," and that the "use of evil for good ends does not immediately sterilize it; it continues to breed after its own kind."[7]

This point adds to the awareness of the dangerousness of the freedom which God has evoked in the world. As stated above, the more freedom we have the greater capacity we have both to be hurt by the beings in our environment and also to create ourselves in intrinsically unsatisfying ways. The present point means that the suffering which we undergo because of one and/or the other of these reasons is not purely private; we inflict others with our misery to some degree. The recognition of psychosomatic illness is a recognition of the way in which the disharmony characterizing the human psyche affects its nearest neighbors. Also, we all know that people who do not enjoy life are generally not enjoyable to be around. And is the history recounted in history books in large part not the history of the misery which a few miserable human beings have inflicted upon many?

The key point regarding these correlations between intrinsic value and the power for self-determination and other-determination is that they are considered to be metaphysical correlations. As such, they have not been freely determined by God, but are correlations that would obtain in any possible world that God might create. Accordingly, the theodicist need not try to find reasons that would justify God's establishment of these correlations, or appeal to the inscrutable reason which God, being all-wise as well as all-good and all-powerful, *must* have had for establishing them. However, since traditional theism has thought the existence of such metaphysical correlations to be antithetical to theism, and also since certain passages in Whitehead could be taken to mean that he did not think such correlations to be beyond divine decision, this notion must be examined.

## THE NOTION OF METAPHYSICAL PRINCIPLES BEYOND DIVINE DECISION

The first point to note is that there is a positive correlation between the notion of creation out of chaos and the notion that there *are* metaphysical principles. Traditional theologians have been consistent in rejecting the idea of principles (other than perhaps logical ones) which God could not surmount, on the one hand, and in affirming creation out of nothing, on the other. These ideas go in pairs. Metaphysical principles are simply descriptions of the way actual entities become and interact. If there has always been a multiplicity of actual entities it makes sense to think in terms of a set of eternal and hence necessary principles which describe the way they interact. But if our world was created out of absolutely nothing, rather than being formed out of a chaos of interacting actualities, then it does not make sense to speak of metaphysical principles. The principles descriptive of the way things interact would come into being with those beings. And it would make sense to suppose that the creator could freely decide those principles. Accordingly, since Whiteheadian thought requires that there has always been a realm of finite actualities, it is consistent for a process theodicy to employ the notion of metaphysical principles of interaction which cannot be surmounted. They are in the nature of things.

A second issue is whether the notion of such principles is antithetical to theism. The notion that there are principles to which God must conform has seemed to many to throw God's deity into question. The issue has most commonly been discussed in terms of the principles of good, and has been posed in terms of a dilemma: Is the good good because of divine volition? Then the good is arbitrary. Is the good good independently of God's decision? Then there is a standard of value outside of God which is superior to God and hence by implication more divine than God. However, Charles Hartshorne has refused the dilemma, suggesting a third position:

> The ideal is not good because God arbitrarily wills it, nor are his acts good because they express goodness as something nondivine; they are good, as our acts . . . are good, because

> of an abstract ideal antecedent to each such act; however, this ideal is not antecedent to God but his eternal and unchangeable purpose. . . . We and God serve the same ideal; but in us it is our glimpse of God's essence. . . .[8]

Hartshorne does not limit this notion to the principle of the good, but applies it to all the metaphysical categories—they belong to the eternal essence of God: "God in his eternal aspects is . . . the categories in their pure or unqualified meaning."[9] Hence, "God is not 'subject' to the categories, as though they were something antecedent to his own individuality."[10]

In taking the position that the metaphysical categories are beyond all decision, even God's, I am accepting Hartshorne's revision of Whitehead's position. Whitehead suggested that the metaphysical principles were the result of a "primordial decision" by God. However, I believe that Hartshorne's position on this issue is really implicit in Whitehead's thought, and that accepting Hartshorne's position on this issue makes a Whiteheadian position more self-consistent. Although defending this statement requires entering into some rather technical issues, the point is sufficiently central to my thesis to warrant this technical excursion. The process theodicy which I am presenting here hinges upon the notion that there are metaphysical principles which are beyond even divine decision. It is important to show that this notion is not an *ad hoc* revision of Whiteheadian process thought designed to solve the problem of evil, but that it is implicit in the whole metaphysical position.

Whitehead's explicit position is that God's "primordial nature" is a "decision" (*PR* 73, 75) which, in ordering the eternal possibilities, establishes the metaphysical principles:

> This ideal realization of potentialities in a primordial actual entity constitutes the metaphysical stability whereby the actual process exemplifies general principles of metaphysics. (*PR* 64)

> His conceptual actuality at once exemplifies and establishes the categoreal conditions. (*PR* 522)

This position is not demanded by any principles in Whitehead's philosophy; and it is in tension with some of them.

First, it is problematic to think of God's "primordial nature" as a decision. Whitehead says of "decision" that it "constitutes the very meaning of actuality" (*PR* 68). It is true that Whitehead does sometimes speak as if the primordial nature of God were an actual entity. But it cannot be, since it is only one aspect of God. And, when focusing explicitly on the question, Whitehead says that "it is a mere factor in God, deficient in actuality" (*PR* 50; cf. 521, 532). Hence, the primordial nature of God, being an abstraction, cannot be or make a decision.

Second, the notion that the metaphysical principles are rooted in a "decision" is undercut by the distinction between cosmological generalities, which hold true only for a particular cosmic epoch, and metaphysical principles, which hold true in all cosmic epochs (*PR* 53, 133 f., 147, 441). In Whitehead's thought, the forerunner to the primordial nature of God was the "principle of limitation," which was introduced in *Science and the Modern World* (1926) to account for "those matter-of-fact determinations . . . which are inherent in the actual course of events, but which present themselves as *arbitrary* in respect to a more abstract possibility" (*SMW* 323; italics added). As examples of these arbitrary factors he lists "the three dimensions of space, and the four dimensions of the spatiotemporal continuum" *(ibid.).* These items are described in *Process and Reality* (1929) as "arbitrary, as it were 'given,' elements in the laws of nature" which "warn us that we are in a special cosmic epoch" (*PR* 139; cf. 140). As such they are distinguished from metaphysical principles. Now, metaphysical principles are called "necessary" (*PR* 4, 5), and are said to be "characteristics so general that we cannot conceive any alternatives" (*PR* 441). Since they are without conceivable alternative (Whitehead and Hartshorne agree on this formal definition), they are not "given" in the sense of being "arbitrary." Hence, in *Process and Reality,* after the distinction between arbitrary cosmological principles and necessary metaphysical principles has been made, Whitehead should no longer speak as if the latter required grounding in a decision. A "decision" by definition cuts off alternative possibilities and results in that which is "given" in distinction from that which is *not* "given" (*PR* 68 f.). Since the metaphysical principles have no conceivable alternatives, they are not "given," not "arbitrary," and hence should not be thought of as resulting from a volition.

There is a third basis in Whitehead's thought for rejecting his own explicit doctrine that the metaphysical principles result from the primordial nature understood as a primordial decision. Whitehead himself suggests that there are metaphysical truths presupposed by the primordial nature of God. He says that God's primordial nature "presupposes the *general* metaphysical character of creative advance, of which it is the primordial exemplification" (*PR* 522). But the metaphysical categories are simply explications of how this creative advance occurs. Hence, they must be equally presupposed by God's primordial nature. Or, better, as the second part of the quotation suggests, God's "primordial nature" could be thought of as the primordial exemplification of the eternal and hence necessary principles, as Hartshorne says. But, either way, the metaphysical principles would not result from a divine decision.

Hence, in spite of Whitehead's own statements, the acceptance of a Hartshornean position on this issue does not constitute an *ad hoc* revision of Whitehead's position to make it a more adequate basis for a theodicy. (Historically, Hartshorne's own "correction" of Whitehead on this point seems to have been made without reference to its benefits in regard to the problem of evil.)

## THE FURIES AND THE GOODNESS OF GOD

God is clearly responsible in one sense for all of the evil of discord in the world, even though God is not ever fully responsible for the details of the events that occur. In order that the perfect forms of experience might be achieved, God's persuasive activity has led the finite realm out of a state of trivial chaos, and discord has appeared as "the half-way house between perfection and triviality" (*AI* 355). And Whitehead does not underestimate the extent and depth of this evil. In discussing Plato's treatment in the *Symposium* of the urge toward ideal perfection, Whitehead comments: "It is obvious that he should have written a companion dialogue which might have been named The Furies, dwelling on the horrors lurking within imperfect realization" (*AI* 189).

God is not totally responsible for any of the horrors, of course, since all creatures have the power of self-determination and other-determination. But God is responsible in the sense of having urged the creation forward to those states in which discordant feelings could be felt with great intensity. The question is whether God is indictable. In other words, is the God of process theology morally perfect? There are three dimensions of this more general question that have been raised as objections against the moral goodness of God as conceived by Whiteheadian process thought: Is this God not morally deficient (1) since aesthetic considerations are primary in the goodness God seeks, (2) since evil is overcome by good in God's own experience, and (3) since this God, while lacking the power to prevent discord, has nevertheless led the creation to a stage where horrendous evils of this type can occur? I will deal with these three questions in order.

1. As the previous discussion has made clear, the criteria of intrinsic goodness are aesthetic criteria—harmony and intensity of experience. Does this fact make God's aim morally unapprovable? Some critics have claimed that it does. Stephen Ely concludes his critical interpretation with this judgment as to the meaning of Whitehead's view:

> All values are then fundamentally aesthetic. . . . God . . . is not concerned with our finite sufferings, difficulties, and triumphs —except as material for aesthetic delight. God, we must say definitely, is not primarily good. He does not will the good. He wills the beautiful.[11]

Similarly, Edward Madden and Peter Hare claim that Whitehead's God "sacrifices human feelings to aesthetic ends,"[12] and say that "a God who is willing to pay any amount in moral and physical evil to gain aesthetic value is unlovable."[13] Their conclusion is that, since this deity is concerned only for aesthetic value, it is "not all good as a theistic God should be."[14]

Common to these two criticisms is the assumption that aesthetic goodness is to be distinguished from both physical and moral goodness, i.e., that neither physical suffering nor moral evil detracts from aesthetic enjoyment. Both aspects of this assumption represent misinterpretations of what Whitehead means by "beauty" and "aesthetic" enjoyment.

The fact that "physical" goodness cannot be played off against aesthetic goodness is obvious from the above discussion. Aesthetic goodness requires harmony as well as intensity, and physical pain is a primary example of dis-harmony or discord. In discussing the Whiteheadian criteria of aesthetic value, Madden and Hare do not mention "harmony" but only "massiveness" and "intensity" of experience.[15] This oversight probably lies behind their assumption that pain is not only compatible with but contributes to God's aesthetic enjoyment.

It is also the case that moral goodness is not excluded from the type of beauty or aesthetic enjoyment which is the chief end of creation. When Whitehead makes this kind of statement, he is referring to "beauty" or "aesthetic experience" in a deeper sense than the simple sense in which these terms are often understood. By the "simple" sense I mean aesthetic experience as one dimension of human experience among others. That Whitehead does not mean that aesthetic experience in this simple sense is the aim of God is made clear in his discussion of "important" experience. After listing aesthetic enjoyment as one form of importance along with others—logical, moral, religious, and practical being the other forms—he says:

> Not one of these specializations exhausts the final unity of purpose in the world. The generic aim of process is the attainment of importance, in that species and to that extent which in that instance is possible. (*MT* 12)

He says that this generic aim is "at greatness of experience in the various dimensions belonging to it" (*MT* 14). However, he then uses aesthetic categories to explain what he means by "greatness of experience." It is that union of harmony, intensity, and vividness which involves the perfection of importance for that occasion (*MT* 14). This is aesthetic experience in the deeper sense. Likewise, Whitehead can use "beauty" in the simple sense, distinguishing it from truth and moral goodness, and accordingly concluding: "All three types of character partake in the highest ideal of satisfaction possible for actual realization" (*AI* 12 f.). But then he shifts to the use of "beauty" in the deeper sense, saying that the three together "can be termed that beauty which provides the final contentment for the Eros of the Universe" (*AI* 13). Elsewhere he says that rightness of conduct is one of the forms of beauty (*AI* 190). So the beauty which God seeks is not one which is indifferent to moral goodness, but one which includes it.[16]

2. The second charge that has been leveled against the moral approvability of Whitehead's God is based on some statements which say that worldly evil is transmuted into good when it is taken into God's experience. Two implications have been drawn. First, it is claimed that Whitehead's God selfishly overcomes evil with good only in the privacy of the divine experience and not in the world. Second, it is claimed that this means that the reality of genuine evil is ultimately denied, since the divine experience is the ultimate standard of truth and reality. The second implication is reflected in the comment by Madden and Hare that "what appears as gratuitous evil [their term for "genuine evil"] is really just the makings of aesthetic value in the Consequent Nature" of God.[17] Both implications are reflected in Ely's criticism:

> We can hardly suppose that many will take pleasure in the reflection that God enjoys himself by making mental additions to one's pain and grief and frustration. It is no help for

> present ills to know that God sees them in such a way that they are valuable for him. . . . The affirmation that what is evil for us is not evil for God does not help. For such an affirmation is merely a denial that we experience real evil.[18]

This interpretation results in part from the misunderstanding of the meaning of "aesthetic value" discussed above. But it also follows in part from taking some of Whitehead's statements about the "transformation" or "transmutation" of worldly occasions in God's experience (God's "consequent nature") out of the context of Whitehead's total position on this subject.

Whitehead does say that worldly events which are intrinsically evil are transformed or transmuted as they are received into the divine experience, and he even sees this as a generalization of "the aesthetic value of discords in art" (*PR* 531). But he does not mean this in such a way that the evil loses its character of evil so that the divine experience would be, as traditional theism said, "pure bliss." For example, he says that it is a profanation to ascribe mere happiness to God—the divine happiness is always conjoined with sympathy and tragedy (Imm. 698). The beauty of the divine experience is always "tragic beauty" (*AI* 381). Furthermore, Whitehead says:

> God has in his nature the knowledge of evil, of pain, and of degradation, but it is there as overcome with what is good. Every fact is what it is, a fact of pleasure, of joy, of pain, or of suffering. (*RM* 149)

This statement shows that for a fact of suffering to be "overcome with what is good" in God does not keep that fact from being "what it is, a fact . . . of suffering." By looking closely at Whitehead's meaning, one can see that no self-contradiction is involved.

Whitehead's meaning is that the evil is "overcome by good" in the sense that God, in responding to the evil facts in the world, provides ideal aims for the next state of the world designed to overcome the evil in the world. In *Religion in the Making,* in which the ideal aim is termed the "ideal consequent," Whitehead says:

> Each actual occasion gives to the creativity which flows from it a definite character in two ways. In one way, as a fact . . . it contributes a ground. . . . In another way, as transmuted in the nature of God, the ideal consequent as it stands in his vision is also added. (*RM* 151)

This passage shows that "transmuting" an occasion means providing an ideal aim for the next stage of the creative advance. Hence, for an evil fact to be overcome by good in God means for it to be transformed into an ideal aim which can serve to overcome evil in the world.

> Its very evil becomes a stepping stone in the all-embracing ideals of God. Every event on its finer side introduces God into the world. Through it his ideal vision is given a base in actual fact to which He provides the ideal consequent, as a factor saving the world from the self-destruction of evil. (*RM* 149)

Accordingly, it is a misinterpretation to say that evil is overcome only in and for the benefit of the consequent nature of God, and that evil is overcome in such a manner as to negate its genuineness. The falsity of this interpretation is shown most clearly by the following passage, in which Whitehead uses the term "kingdom of heaven" for God's consequent nature:

> The kingdom of heaven is not the isolation of good from evil. It is the overcoming of evil by good. This transmutation of evil into good enters into the actual world by reason of the inclusion of the nature of God, which includes the ideal vision of each actual evil so met with a novel consequent as to issue in the restoration of goodness. (*RM* 148 f.)

Part of the source of confusion in interpreting Whitehead on this issue arises from his doctrine that it is God's own experience which is finally most important, being "the final end of creation" (*PR* 530) and "the final Beauty with which the Universe achieves its justification" (*AI* 381). This could lead one to suppose that God's experience in itself is thought to be the only important experience, which would imply that it is only important that evil be overcome by God in the privacy of the divine experience.

However, there is no experience which is purely private; what is first experienced privately then becomes a public fact, conditioning the future world (*PR* 443 f.). Whitehead gives terminological application of this doctrine to God by speaking of God's "superjective nature" (*PR* 135). And he points out that the transformation of a worldly fact into a "perfected actuality" in the consequent nature does condition the future world.

> For the perfected actuality passes back into the temporal world, and qualifies this world so that each temporal actuality includes it as an immediate fact of relevant experience. For the kingdom of heaven is with us today. What is done in the world is transformed into a reality in heaven, and the reality in heaven passes back into the world. (*PR* 532)

Hence, there is no basis for a dichotomy between the overcoming of evil in God and in the world. In fact, since it is "overcome" in God's consequent nature in the sense that it is responded to with an ideal aim which aims at restoring goodness in the world, this "overcoming" in God is precisely for the sake of overcoming evil in the world.

The manner in which God seeks to overcome a chief source of evil in the world connects the present point with the previous one about the place of moral goodness in the highest forms of aesthetic experience. As stated earlier, a chief source of evil in the present state of the world is that those beings—ourselves—with the greatest destructive power also have the power deliberately to intend to be destructive of the potential intrinsic good of others. This capacity for moral evil is the chief source of the threat we pose for each other and the planet as a whole. Hence, one of the most relevant things God could be doing toward overcoming evil with good in the world would be to be seeking to overcome our proclivity for moral evil. Whitehead contends that God is doing just that.

For Whitehead, "the effect of the present on the future is the business of morals" (*AI* 346). More specifically, in a passage in which "importance" is used for beauty in the deeper sense, he says:

> Morality consists in the control of process so as to maximize importance. . . . Our action is moral if we have . . . safeguarded the importance of experience so far as it depends on that concrete instance in the world's history. (*MT* 13 f., 15)

In the words that we have been using, this means that morality involves actualizing oneself in the present so that one's potential instrumental value will be such as to maximize the opportunities for the intrinsic good of future experiences.

Further, Whitehead understands our prehension of God to be the source of our feeling that we should be moral.

> God, as conditioning the creativity with his harmony of apprehension, issues into the mental creature as moral judgment according to a perfection of ideals. (*RM* 114)

> There are experiences of ideals—of ideals entertained, of ideals aimed at, of ideals achieved, of ideals defaced. This is the experience of the deity of the universe. (*MT* 103)

> God is that function in the world by reason of which our purposes are directed to ends which in our own consciousness are impartial as to our own interests. . . . He is that element in virtue of which our purposes extend beyond values for ourselves to values for others. (*RM* 152)

Finally, Whitehead suggests that this functioning of God is not disconnected from God's functioning to lure us to achieve the greatest intrinsic good open to us; in fact, it is part of that functioning. This coalescence of the two divine aims for us—to actualize both aesthetic and moral goodness—is based upon the fact that the twofold aim of an occasion of experience—to achieve value in the immediate present and in the relevant future—is not as divided as it might appear at first (*PR* 41). The "relevant future" consists of those elements which are effectively "anticipated" by the decision of the present occasion, in the sense that the occasion considers the real potentiality for those elements to be derived from itself (*PR* 41). This anticipation of its own effects in the future is not divided from the aim to achieve intrinsic value, since this anticipation enters into the quality of the occasion's present value experience (*AI* 346). This means that the anticipation that our present decision will contribute to the good of others in the future contributes to our present enjoyment.

Of course, we all know that there can be a strong tension between these two aspects of our essential aim, the tension we normally describe as that between desire and duty. But there is the possibility that this tension can be overcome, Whitehead suggests:

> The antithesis between the general good and the individual interest can be abolished only when the individual is such that its interest is the general good, thus exemplifying the loss of the minor intensities in order to find them again with finer composition in a wider sweep of interest. (*PR* 23)

When this occurs, even though we have given up some of the "minor intensities," we will enjoy the "extreme ecstasy of Peace" (*AI* 372), which is the highest good. In other words, the highest aesthetic enjoyment open to human beings requires the incorporation of moral goodness.

God is luring us to realize this highest form of enjoyment.

> He is that element in virtue of which the attainment of such a value for others transforms itself into value for ourselves. (*RM* 152)

Hence, while moral good is not of the essence of intrinsic goodness (since there can be intrinsic goodness in those beings who are incapable of moral goodness or evil), or even of the intrinsic goodness of human life, it *is* of the essence of that type of intrinsic good which God seeks to promote in us; and this promotion involves God's enlistment of our deliberate support in the drive to overcome evil in the world by maximizing good. In Whitehead's words:

> The function of being a means is not disjoined from the function of being an end. The sense of worth beyond itself is immediately enjoyed as an overpowering element in the individual self-attainment. (*PR* 531)

This statement, which is more or less true of finite actualities, is ideally true for God. It is precisely because of this ideal harmony, between immediate enjoyment and aims for future welfare, that there is no tension between God's overcoming of evil in the divine consequent nature and in the world. The self-determining response by God (in distinction from God's purely receptive response to the values achieved in the previous moments of creation) which brings the greatest immediate enjoyment to God is the provision of ideal aims which will influence the future state of the world toward the greatest good open to it. This is why the provision of ideal aims for the future can be referred to as the overcoming of evil by good in God's own experience.

Incidentally, Whitehead points out that "in a purified religion . . . you study his [God's] goodness in order to be like him" (*RM* 40). To the extent that the tension between our interest and the general good is overcome, we imitate the goodness of God. God is perfectly good, not, as traditional theism said, because the divine activity in relation to the world is free from any self-interest, but because God's self-interest is not selfish interest but is an interest in the welfare of the world. There is no tension in God between desire and duty, since God, being completely receptive of all the joys and sufferings in creation, desires nothing other than the greatest possible joy for the entire creation. To the extent that the scope of our sympathy is enlarged, to that extent the scope of the interest behind our aims will be enlarged, and to that extent we will experience a resolution of the tension between desire and duty.

3. A third objection that could be raised against the moral goodness of Whitehead's God is this: Since God does not have controlling power, and therefore cannot prevent the occurrence of genuine evil, should not God have abstained from creating a world, at least one in which the more intense forms of evil are possible?[19] This question raises directly the issue as to whether God can be seen as responsible in an important sense for the suffering in the world without being morally indictable for it.

Although not totally responsible for any evil event, of course, God is responsible for all the suffering in the world in an important sense. If God had ceased stimulating novelty prior to the advent of life, there would be no pain in the world. If God had rested content with the state of creation prior to the emergence of animals with central nervous systems, the intensity of pain in the creation would have been low. Or if God had even ceased stimulating the development of mentality before the rise of rational creatures, the planet would have been spared its most intense horrors. Human beings have been the causes and the victims of the most horrible forms of evil experienced on our planet; and it is our species which threatens to bring all the life of the planet to a premature end.

Should God have avoided bringing order out of chaos, or at least avoided the higher forms of order, so that the higher forms of evil would not have been possible? An unambiguously positive answer would seem to assume that discord is the only type of evil to take into consideration. From that assumption it *would* follow that a being who is morally perfect (defined as one who wants to prevent all genuine evil) but lacks controlling power would refrain from creating a world. But if it is recognized that unnecessary triviality is also genuinely evil, then genuine evil cannot be avoided by leaving the world in chaos, or by calling off at some stage the quest for the higher perfections. In fact, to do so would be to *guarantee* the existence of genuine evil (since all experience which is more trivial than it need be is evil by comparison with what it could be). To stimulate more complex and thereby more intense forms of experience is to risk the possibility of more intense discord; but it is also to make possible the enjoyment of the more intense harmonies.

In this context, the question as to whether God is indictable is to be answered in terms of the question as to whether the positive values that are possible in our world are valuable enough to be worth the risk of the negative experiences which have occurred, and the even greater horrors which stand before us as real possibilities for the near future. Should God, for the sake of avoiding the possibility of persons such as Hitler, and horrors such as Auschwitz, have precluded the possibility of Jesus, Gautama, Socrates, Confucius, Moses Mendelssohn, El Greco, Michelangelo, Leonardo da Vinci, Florence Nightingale, Abraham Lincoln, Mahatma Gandhi, Chief Joseph, Chief Seattle, Alfred North Whitehead, John F. Kennedy, Oliver Wendell Holmes, Sojourner Truth, Helen Keller, Louis Armstrong, Albert Einstein, Dag Hammarskjöld, Reinhold Niebuhr, Carol Channing, Margaret Mead, and millions of other marvelous human beings, well known and not well known alike, who have lived on the face of this earth? In other words, should God, for the sake of avoiding "man's inhumanity to man," have avoided humanity (or some comparably complex species) altogether? Only those who could sincerely answer this question affirmatively could indict the God of process theology on the basis of the evil in the world.

Another point that is relevant to this third question is the fact that God responds to the world sympathetically. If God were an impassive absolute, then all the previous talk about the necessity of risk-taking in order to achieve higher values would mean that it is the creatures alone which suffer the consequences of God's decision to take risks. But in process thought, the quality of God's experience depends in part upon that of the creatures. As clarified above, worldly events of pain and sorrow are received into God just as they are. God suffers with our sufferings, as well as enjoying our enjoyments. Since the world always contains a mixture of good and evil, beauty and ugliness, the divine beauty is always tragic beauty. Accordingly, the risks which God asks the creation to take are also risks for God. Stimulating the world toward greater intensity means the risk that God too will experience more intense suffering.

Awareness of this aspect of God as envisioned by process thought not only removes the basis for that sense of moral outrage which would be directed toward an impassive spectator deity who took great risks with the creation. It also provides an additional basis, beyond that of our own immediate experience, for affirming that the risk was worth taking. That being who is the universal agent, goading the creation to overcome triviality in favor of the more intense harmonies, is also the universal recipient of the totality of good and evil that is actualized. In other words, the one being who is in position to know experientially the bitter as well as the sweet fruits of the risk of creation is the same being who has encouraged and continues to encourage this process of creative risk-taking.

Why, then, can we say that God is good in spite of all the evil within the divine creation? Because all individuals within the creation necessarily have power partially to determine themselves and others; because both intensity and harmony are necessary for intrinsic goodness, so seeking to increase intrinsic goodness means seeking to overcome triviality as well as avoiding discord; because the conditions for the possibilities of greater good are necessarily the conditions for the possibilities of greater suffering; because God does not promote any new level of intensity without being willing to suffer the possible consequences; because God constantly works to overcome the evil in the creation with good, and in human experience does this by simultaneously seeking to increase our enjoyment of life and to enlist our support in the effort to overcome evil by maximizing good.

# Appendix: Theodicy and Hope for a Future Life

Belief in a life beyond bodily death was an essential element, often the central element, in most of the theodicies examined in Part II of this book. This belief was central also to Plato, Plotinus, and the New Testament authors. It is obviously not central to the present process theodicy (as the relegation of its discussion to an appendix would by itself indicate).

The argument in Chapter 18, which stated that the human soul is not ontologically different from other enduring individuals, and that it was able to emerge only on the basis of a complex society of cells whose formation took billions of years, might suggest that life beyond bodily death would be rendered impossible by process thought. However, Whitehead himself does not draw this conclusion. He said that his own philosophy was "entirely neutral" on the issue, i.e., that it rendered survival of the soul neither necessary nor impossible (*RM* 107). He suggests that, on the basis of other prehensions, "the soul may be freed from its complete dependence upon the bodily organization" (*AI* 267). I have sought to explain elsewhere why the human soul, once it has developed, might be thought to be capable of survival apart from the human body, even though it could not have originally emerged apart from the type of organization exemplified in the human body.[1] I would add here that a future life in this sense would be in line with the general pattern of God's creative activity, according to which individuals at each stage are not only valuable in themselves, but are also preparations for forms of existence with greater value in the future. Also, insofar as much human life is characterized by more suffering than intrinsic good, the development of a postbodily psychic existence could be one more example of God's overcoming evil with good.

However, I do not believe that hope based on belief in a postbodily life should be central to a process theodicy, for a combination of reasons. First, I do not believe that such a hope is necessary to an affirmation of human life, and hence to a justification of God's goodness and wisdom in having brought us forth. Second, this belief cannot play the role it played in traditional theodicies, that of providing an existence in which God would unilaterally rectify all the injustices of the present life. For, even in a situation where our souls would no longer be influenced by our bodies, there would still be a multiplicity of influences upon each individual, and each individual would still have its capacity for self-determination, even vis-à-vis God. The same metaphysical principles which make evil possible now would still obtain then. Hence, if God's goodness and wisdom could not be defended in terms of our present existence, belief in a future life would not provide a sufficient basis for overcoming the weakness in the defense. Third, while there is nothing irrational in the belief in a postbodily life within the context of process thought, it is too uncertain to be made a central pillar in the construction of a theodicy. In short, belief in a life after death is not an essential element in a process theodicy because it is unnecessary and insufficient as well as too uncertain.

This is in line with the position taken in my previous book. There I indicated that I think the belief that we will have further occasions of experience beyond bodily death, along with the related belief in the resurrection of Jesus (in the straightforward sense that the postresurrection appearances were derivative from new occasions of experience of that enduring individual named Jesus of Nazareth who had suffered bodily death on a cross), should be regarded as an optional dimension of Christian faith.[2] As such, it cannot be essential to the defense of the goodness of the God of Christian faith.

As I have also said elsewhere, the fact that this belief is optional does not mean that whether or not it is held may not make a tremendous difference in the nature of a person's faith.[3] I personally believe that the inclusion of this belief can give one's faith additional dimensions of both vitality and peace, and that this belief also generally deepens one's sense of the importance of other human life and thereby one's concern for others, including the concern for human justice. Furthermore, hope that our present human life, besides having its present intrinsic value, is also in part a preparation for a higher form of existence in the future, can add a final ground for affirming this present life.

In summation: I do not find the possibility that human life in the future will become increasingly miserable, and even that it may come to a catastrophic, premature end, undermines belief in the goodness and wisdom of the Creative Power that brought it forth, even if this life is all there is. I do not consider faith that there actually will be a happy future for humanity in this world to be essential for theodicy. No matter how bad the future actually turns out to be, it will not cancel out the worthwhileness of the human goodness enjoyed during the previous thousands of years. Nor do I consider it essential, if a happy earthly future for humanity is not expected, to anticipate a transearthly existence. However, hope for a better future in one or the other of these forms does add enthusiasm to one's Yes-response to past and present human life and hence to its creator. Without making either of them essential to its theodicy, process thought provides support for both of these forms of hope.

# Notes

## Preface

1. John Hick, *Evil and the God of Love* (Harper & Row, Publishers, Inc., 1966), p. 36.

## Introduction

1. David R. Griffin, *A Process Christology* (The Westminster Press, 1973), pp. 138–140, 151–166.

## *Chapter* 1. The Biblical Tradition

1. For the most part I will simply cite the passages out of context, without considering them in light of modern principles of Biblical interpretation. In this chapter, I am primarily considering Biblical material insofar as it was used as a source for the traditional theodicy; and during the formative period of theodicy the Biblical texts that had direct implications for the subject were for the most part considered as a set of authoritative, divinely inspired statements that had to be brought together into a consistent position.

2. All Biblical quotations are from the Revised Standard Version.

## *Chapter* 2. Plato

1. All quotations from Plato are from Benjamin Jowett's translation.

## *Chapter* 4. Plotinus

1. All references to Plotinus' *Enneads* are to the translation by Stephen

MacKenna and B. S. Page. See Robert M. Hutchins (ed.), *Great Books of the Western World* (Encyclopaedia Britannica, Inc., 1952), Vol. 17.

2. Arthur O. Lovejoy, *The Great Chain of Being: A Study of the History of an Idea* (Harvard University Press, 1936; Harper & Row, Publishers, Inc., Harper Torchbooks), p. 61.

*Chapter* 6. AUGUSTINE: THE TRADITIONAL FREE-WILL DEFENSE

1. Below are given the works to which the symbols refer, along with the translations from which quotations are made:

| | |
|---|---|
| *C* | *The Confessions.* Tr. by Edward Bouverie Pusey. |
| *CG* | *The City of God.* Tr. by Marcus Dods. |
| *E* | *Enchiridion.* Tr. by J. F. Shaw |
| *FW* | *On Free Will.* Tr. by John H. S. Burleigh. |
| *GFW* | *Grace and Free Will.* Tr. by P. Holmes. |
| *NAG* | *Nature and Grace.* Tr. by P. Holmes. |
| *NOG* | *The Nature of the Good.* Tr. by John H. S. Burleigh. |
| *PS* | *On the Predestination of the Saints.* Tr. by R. E. Wallis. |
| *SL* | *On the Spirit and the Letter.* Tr. by P. Holmes. |
| *TR* | *Of True Religion.* Tr. by John H. S. Burleigh. |

*The Confessions* can be found in Robert M. Hutchins (ed.), *Great Books of the Western World* (Encyclopaedia Britannica, Inc., 1952), Vol. 18.

*The City of God, Enchiridion, Grace and Free Will, Nature and Grace, On the Predestination of the Saints,* and *On the Spirit and the Letter* are found in *Basic Writings of St. Augustine* (2 vols.), edited and with an introduction and notes by Whitney J. Oates (Random House, Inc., 1948).

*On Free Will, The Nature of the Good,* and *Of True Religion* are found in *Augustine: Earlier Writings,* Vol. VI of The Library of Christian Classics (The Westminster Press, 1953).

*Chapter* 7. THOMAS AQUINAS: DIVINE SIMPLICITY AND THEOLOGICAL COMPLEXITY

1. *ST* stands for *Summa Theologica.* Quotations are taken from the translation by the Fathers of the English Dominican Province as revised by Daniel J. Sullivan. (See Robert M. Hutchins [ed.], *Great Books of the Western World* (Encyclopaedia Britannica, Inc., 1952), Vols. 19 and 20. The Roman numeral in the citation indicates the part of the *Summa* referred to; the first Arabic number indicates the Question, while the second Arabic number indicates the article; "ans" indicates the main body of the article, which always begins with "I answer that . . . ;" and "ad" followed by a number indicates a reply to one of the objections. The initials *SCG* refer to the *Summa Contra Gentiles,* sometimes called *On the Truth of the Catholic Faith.* I have taken all quotations from the

translation by Vernon J. Bourke. In these references, the first Roman numeral indicates the book, while the second one (if there is a second one) indicates the part of that book; the first Arabic number indicates the chapter, and the second one the paragraph.

2. Carl Becker, *The Heavenly City of the Eighteenth-Century Philosophers* (Yale University Press, 1932), pp. 66 f.

3. Jacques Maritain, *God and the Permission of Evil,* tr. by Joseph W. Evans (Bruce Publishing Company, 1966). This book will be indicated in the text with the symbol *GPE.*

4. The symbol *STPE* stands for Jacques Maritain's *Saint Thomas and the Problem of Evil,* tr. by Mrs. Gordon Andison (Marquette University Press, 1942).

5. Charles Journet, *The Meaning of Evil,* tr. by Michael Barry (P. J. Kenedy & Sons, 1963). This book will be referred to in the text by the symbol *ME.*

*Chapter* 8. SPINOZA: EVERYTHING IS SIMPLY DIVINE—UNORTHODOX CONCLUSION FROM ORTHODOX PREMISES

1. Journet, *The Meaning of Evil,* p. 95.

2. All references to Spinoza are to his *Ethics.* The Roman numerals indicate the part in question. All quotations are from the translation by W. H. White, as revised by A. H. Stirling. See Robert M. Hutchins (ed.), *Great Books of the Western World* (Encyclopaedia Britannica, Inc., 1952), Vol. 31.

*Chapter* 9. LUTHER: THE EXPLICIT DENIAL OF CREATURELY FREEDOM

1. All quotations are taken from Martin Luther, *On the Bondage of the Will,* tr. by J. I. Packer and O. R. Johnston (Fleming H. Revell Company, 1957).

2. All references refer to the numbering of the Weimar edition of Luther's works, which is given both in the Packer and Johnston translation (from which my quotations are taken) and in the translation by Philip S. Watson and B. Drewery in Vol. XVII of The Library of Christian Classics, entitled *Luther and Erasmus: Free Will and Salvation* (The Westminster Press, 1969).

3. For example, John Dillenberger seems to suggest this view, as he says: "By 'the bondage of the will' Luther does not mean that man is incapable of making significant and meaningful decisions. . . . But he did mean that there is no act or capacity of will by which the self can successfully will itself into an adequate and proper relation to God." Dillenberger does point out that Luther developed his point "through his concept of the 'all-working' character of God and of the notion of predestination," and hence in deterministic categories. But Dillenberger then says that "it is as if the argument was that if God determines all things, no one has any ground for self-defense or merit" (*Martin Luther: Selections from His Writings,* ed. and with an introduction by John

Dillenberger; Doubleday & Company, Inc., Anchor Books, 1961, pp. xxvii–xxviii). However, it is not "as if" this were Luther's argument; this *is* his argument.

*Chapter* 10. CALVIN: OMNIPOTENCE WITHOUT OBFUSCATION

1. All references in the text are to Calvin's *Institutes of the Christian Religion,* ed. by John T. McNeill, tr. by Ford Lewis Battles, Vols. XX and XXI of The Library of Christian Classics (The Westminster Press, 1960).

2. Calvin is referring to Augustine's *Enchiridion,* XXVI, 100 f.

*Chapter* 11. LEIBNIZ: THE BEST OF ALL POSSIBLE WORLDS

1. All the references in this chapter are to Gottfried Wilhelm Leibniz, *Theodicy: Essays on the Goodness of God, the Freedom of Man, and the Origin of Evil,* tr. by E. M. Huggard from C. J. Gerhardt's edition of the *Collected Philosophical Works* (1875–1890) (Yale University Press, 1952). All the references except one can be found in Leibniz, *Theodicy* (Abridged), ed. and abridged and with an introduction by Diogenes Allen [tr. by E. M. Huggard] (The Bobbs-Merrill Company, Inc., 1966).

2. Hick, *Evil and the God of Love,* pp. 162, 171–172.

3. All references are to paragraphs. "Pref." stands for the Preface of the *Theodicy.* Unfortunately, the paragraphs in the Preface are not numbered; but, as the Preface is short, the correct paragraph can be easily located. (The correct paragraph can be found in Allen's abridged edition by noting that the first deletion omits four paragraphs, the second omits fourteen, the third omits one, and the fourth omits only the end of one and the beginning of another.)

4. PD refers to the "Preliminary Dissertation on the Conformity of Faith with Reason," which follows the Preface.

5. FM refers to "The Freedom of Man and the Origin of Evil," which follows PD.

6. Hick, *Evil and the God of Love,* p. 162.

7. Diogenes Allen, "Editor's Introduction," in Leibniz, *Theodicy* (Abridged), p. xi.

*Chapter* 12. BARTH: MUCH ADO ABOUT NOTHINGNESS

1. In this chapter, unless otherwise indicated, references are to Barth's *Church Dogmatics,* Vol. III/3, *The Doctrine of Creation,* tr. by G. W. Bromiley and R. J. Ehrlich (T. & T. Clark, 1960). In the occasional references to Vol. III/1 of the *Church Dogmatics* the volume number is given before the page number.

2. I believe John Hick is wrong in saying that Barth employs an anthropomorphic notion of divine choice, suggesting that God must choose between alternatives in a previously existing situation (Hick, *Evil and the God of Love,* pp. 142, 193). Rather, for Barth, nothingness does not exist indepen-

dently of God's choice, but is brought into being by this choice in its negative dimension. And, rather than saying that God's choosing is like ours, Barth says it is unlike ours in that its power is such that it must give some actuality to that which is rejected.

3. Hence, I believe Hick is wrong in saying that Barth has a notion of a "limited God" because his "God is limited by something that holds independently of Him," namely nothingness (*ibid.*, pp. 144 f.). But for Barth, nothingness is not independent of God, but arises from God's negative will. The only limit on God is God's too-potent power. Barth is as fully concerned to deny that any finite actuality exists independently of God's will as is Hick or any of the other traditional theists.

4. Hick rejects this interpretation, according to which nothingness arises from God's non-willing, because it offers "a merely verbal and apparent solution"; but he means by this that one can still ask whether the rise of nothingness is intended by God or arises from necessity (*ibid.*, p. 148). Again, Hick seems to have overlooked Barth's statements that it is a necessity, due to the nature of God's power. Hence, while I find the difference between "creating" and "rejecting" purely verbal, I do not think Barth's answer to the question of the origin of nothingness is purely verbal—although it *is* strange.

5. *Ibid.*, p. 149.

*Chapter* 13. JOHN HICK: ALL'S WELL THAT ENDS WELL

1. John Hick, *Evil and the God of Love* (Harper & Row, Publishers, Inc., 1966). All references in the text are to this book.

2. The quotation is from *The Revelations of Divine Love of Julian of Norwich*, tr. by James Walsh (London: Burns & Oates, 1961), ch. 27, p. 92.

3. The one explicit indication that Hick is willing to accept a somewhat inconsistent solution to the problem of evil is his statement that monism and dualism "represent the only two wholly consistent solutions that are possible; and unfortunately neither of them is compatible with the basic claims of Christian theology" (21).

4. It is perhaps suggestive of uncertainty in Hick's mind on the connection between creaturely freedom and divine power that he cites both Charles Hartshorne and C. A. Campbell as supporting this notion of freedom as limited creativity. Hartshorne means this doctrine to rule out the possible truth of the traditional doctrine of omnipotence, whereas Campbell holds this traditional doctrine, denying that there can be any "forces independent of God and either actually or potentially hostile to Him." (*On Selfhood and Godhood* [London: George Allen & Unwin, Ltd., 1957], p. 291.)

5. The quotation is taken from T. H. Huxley, *Collected Essays*, Vol. I (London: Macmillan & Co., Ltd., 1894), pp. 192 f.

6. The quotation is taken from F. H. Bradley, *Essays on Truth and Reality* (Oxford: Clarendon Press, 1914), p. 430.

*Chapter* 14. JAMES ROSS: ALL THE WORLD'S A STAGE

1. James F. Ross, *Philosophical Theology* (The Bobbs-Merrill Company, Inc., 1969). All references in the text will be to the pages of this book.

*Chapter* 15. FACKENHEIM AND BRUNNER: OMNIPOTENCE OVER LOGIC

1. Cf. Walther Eichrodt, *Man in the Old Testament,* tr. by K. and R. Gregor Smith (London: SCM Press, Ltd., 1951), pp. 51–66; A. E. Taylor, *The Problem of Evil* (London: Ernest Benn, Ltd., 1929); and the selections by H. H. Rowley, Leonhard Ragaz, Arthur S. Peake, Emil Kraeling, and Hayim Greenberg in Nahum N. Glatzer, *The Dimensions of Job: A Study and Selected Readings* (Schocken Books, Inc., 1969).
2. Richard L. Rubenstein, *After Auschwitz: Radical Theology and Contemporary Judaism* (The Bobbs-Merrill Company, 1966).
3. *Ibid.,* pp. 46, 153.
4. *Ibid.,* pp. 48, 64 f., 153.
5. *Ibid.,* pp. 68, 70.
6. *Ibid.,* pp. 67, 152.
7. *QPF* stands for Emil Fackenheim's *Quest for Past and Future: Essays in Jewish Theology* (Indiana University Press, 1968).
8. *GPH* stands for Fackenheim's *God's Presence in History: Jewish Affirmations and Philosophical Reflections* (Harper & Row, Publishers, Inc., Harper Torchbooks, 1972).
9. All page references to Brunner's writings in the text will be to H. Emil Brunner, *Dogmatics,* Vol. II, *The Christian Doctrine of Creation and Redemption* (T' Westminster Press, 1952).
10. H. Emil Brunner, *The Mediator,* tr. by Olive Wyon (The Westminster Press, 1965), pp. 317–320, 360.
11. Brunner, *Dogmatics,* Vol. II, pp. 351 f., 361 f.

*Chapter* 16. PERSONAL IDEALISM: GOD MAKES A SENSATIONAL IMPRESSION UPON US—MORE UNORTHODOX CONCLUSIONS FROM ORTHODOX PREMISES

1. *D* stands for George Berkeley, *Three Dialogues Between Hylas and Philonous.* References are to the pages of the Library of Liberal Arts edition, edited with an introduction by Colin M. Turbayne (The Bobbs-Merrill Company, Inc., 1954).
2. *PC* stands for Berkeley's *Philosophical Commentaries* (also known as Berkeley's *Commonplace Book*). References are to the numbering of the Luce and Jessop edition. (George Berkeley, *Works,* ed. by A. A. Luce and T. E. Jessop, Vols. 7 and 8 [Thomas Nelson & Sons, 1955–1956]).
3. *P* Stands for *A Treatise Concerning the Principles of Human Knowledge.* This work can be found in Robert M. Hutchins (ed.), *Great Books of the Western World* (Encyclopaedia Britannica, Inc., 1952), Vol. 35. References are to the paragraphs as numbered by Berkeley.

4. LJ stands for Berkeley's letter to Samuel Johnson of November 25, 1729. The references are to the points as numbered by Berkeley in reply to questions raised by Johnson. This letter and two by Johnson are reprinted in *Berkeley's Philosophical Writings,* ed. with an introduction by David M. Armstrong (Collier Books, 1965).

5. Borden Parker Bowne, *Theism* (American Book Company, 1902), pp. 263–290; A. C. Knudson, *The Doctrine of God* (Abingdon Press, 1930), p. 365. In this and the following section, I am indebted to Floyd H. Ross, *Personalism and the Problem of Evil* (Yale University Press, 1940).

6. Bowne, *Theism,* pp. 265 f.; A. C. Knudson, *The Doctrine of Redemption* (Abingdon Press, 1933), p. 215; A. C. Knudson, *Basic Issues in Christian Thought* (Abingdon-Cokesbury Press, 1950), p. 107.

7. Bowne, *Theism,* pp. 272 f.; Knudson, *The Doctrine of Redemption,* p. 220; Knudson, *Basic Issues in Christian Thought,* pp. 104, 106.

8. Rudolf Hermann Lotze, *Microcosmus* (Edinburgh: T. & T. Clark, 1885), Vol. II, p. 717; quoted by Knudson in *The Doctrine of Redemption,* p. 220, and in *Basic Issues in Christian Thought,* p. 104.

9. Knudson, *The Doctrine of God,* p. 259.

10. Borden Parker Bowne, *Studies in Theism* (Phillips and Hunt, 1879), pp. 118 f.; Borden Parker Bowne, *Theory of Thought and Knowledge* (Harper & Brothers, 1897), p. 35.

11. Knudson, *Basic Issues in Christian Thought,* pp. 13–50, especially pp. 15, 41.

12. Bowne, *Theism,* pp. 189 f.

13. Knudson, *The Doctrine of God,* pp. 320–322.

14. *Ibid.,* p. 322.

15. L. Harold DeWolf, *A Theology of the Living Church* (Harper & Brothers, revised ed. 1960), pp. 102, 108, 109, 176.

16. *Ibid.,* pp. 96, 105, 108.

17. *Ibid.,* p. 129.

18. *Ibid.,* p. 152.

19. *Ibid.,* p. 205.

20. *Ibid.,* pp. 120, 122.

21. *Ibid.,* p. 64.

22. *Ibid.,* p. 130.

23. *Ibid.,* pp. 138–140.

24. *Ibid.,* pp. 120 f.

25. *Ibid.,* p. 139.

26. Edgar Sheffield Brightman, *An Introduction to Philosophy* (Henry Holt and Company, 1925), pp. 336, 337. DeWolf's theory of the relation between the mind and the body, which he claims is different from that of Bowne and Brightman, does not affect this point. He still maintains that the body, insofar as it appears to other people, is the direct product of divine activity. L. Harold DeWolf, "The Mind-Body Problem," *The Personalist,* Vol. XXXIV (1953), pp. 15–24, especially p. 23.

27. DeWolf, *A Theology of the Living Church,* pp. 132, 135, 142.

28. *POR* stands for Brightman's *A Philosophy of Religion* (Prentice-Hall, Inc., 1940).

29. *PG* stands for Brightman's *The Problem of God* (Abingdon Press, 1930). *FG* stands for Brightman's *The Finding of God* (Abingdon Press, 1931).

30. *PR* stands for Brightman's *Person and Reality* (The Ronald Press Co., 1958).

31. *PAR* stands for Brightman's *Personality and Religion* (The Abingdon Press, 1934).

32. E. S. Brightman, "The Given and Its Critics," *Religion in Life,* Vol. I (1932), pp. 134–145, esp. p. 136.

33. Rannie Belle Baker, *The Concept of a Limited God: A Study in the Philosophy of Personalism* (Shenandoah Publishing House, Inc., 1934), p. 156.

*Chapter* 17. WORSHIPFULNESS AND THE OMNIPOTENCE FALLACY

1. J. L. Mackie, "Evil and Omnipotence," in Nelson Pike (ed.), *God and Evil* (Prentice-Hall, Inc., 1964), p. 47; H. J. McCloskey, "God and Evil," in Pike (ed.), *God and Evil,* p. 61; H. D. Aiken, "God and Evil: A Study of Some Relations Between Faith and Morals," *Ethics,* Vol. LXVIII (1958), p. 79.

2. Cf. Edward H. Madden and Peter H. Hare, *Evil and the Concept of God* (Charles C. Thomas, Publishers, 1968), pp. 4 f.; Nelson Pike, "God and Evil: A Reconsideration," *Ethics,* Vol. LXVIII (1958), p. 119.

3. McCloskey, "God and Evil," *loc. cit.,* p. 84.

4. Alvin Plantinga, *God and Other Minds* (Cornell University Press, 1967), p. 129.

5. Roderick Chisholm, "The Defeat of Good and Evil," *Proceedings and Addresses of the American Philosophical Association,* Vol. XLII (1968–69), pp. 21–38.

6. Terence Penelhum, "Divine Goodness and the Problem of Evil," *Religious Studies,* Vol. II (1966), p. 107.

7. Madden and Hare, *Evil and the Concept of God,* pp. 4 f.

8. For example, they say: "We believe that some evil clearly is defeasible . . . and hence there is no inconsistent set. Nevertheless the most crucial problem remains, namely: if God is unlimited in power and goodness, why is there so much *prima facie gratuitous evil* in the world?" (Edward H. Madden and Peter H. Hare, "Evil and Inconclusiveness," *Sophia,* Vol. XI [1972], pp. 10 f.) The implication is that, if any of the apparently gratuitous evil were *really* gratuitous, there *would* be an "inconsistent set."

9. Mackie, "Evil and Omnipotence," *loc. cit.,* p. 48.

10. John Wisdom, "God and Evil," *Mind,* Vol. XLIV (1935), p. 20.

11. Austin Farrer, *Love Almighty and Ills Unlimited* (Doubleday & Company, Inc., 1961), pp. 167 f.

12. M. B. Ahern, *The Problem of Evil* (London: Routledge & Kegan Paul, Ltd., 1971), p. 50.

13. Keith Yandell, "A Premature Farewell to Theism (A Reply to Roland Pucetti)," *Religious Studies,* Vol. V (1969), p. 254.

14. Ahern, *The Problem of Evil,* p. 57.

15. Plantinga, *God and Other Minds,* p. 151.

16. Nelson Pike, "Hume on Evil," in Pike (ed.), *God and Evil,* p. 102.

17. Nelson Pike, "God and Evil: A Reconsideration," in Pike (ed.), *God and Evil,* pp. 120–122.

18. Ahern, *The Problem of Evil,* p. xii.

19. Although Charles Hartshorne is noted for developing a number of arguments for God's existence, he has recently said: "All the arguments are phases of one 'global' argument, that *the properly formulated theistically religious view of life and reality is the most intelligible, self-consistent, and satisfactory one that can be conceived.*" (*Creative Synthesis and Philosophic Method* [The Open Court Publishing Company, 1970], p. 276). Probably a majority of those who today accept "arguments for the existence of God" would agree with this evaluation of their status. They would not see them as irresistible proofs, in the strict sense, which no intelligent, fair-minded person could reject.

20. George I. Mavrodes, "Some Recent Philosophical Theology," *Review of Metaphysics,* Vol. XXIV (1970), p. 107.

21. Charles A. Campbell, *On Selfhood and Godhood* (The Macmillan Company, 1957), p. 291.

22. Ahern, *The Problem of Evil,* p. ix.

23. J. N. Findlay, "Can God's Existence Be Disproved?" in *New Essays in Philosophical Theology,* ed. by Antony Flew and Alasdair MacIntyre (London: SCM Press, Ltd., 1955), pp. 51 f.

24. G. E. Hughes, "Can God's Existence Be Disproved?" in Flew and MacIntyre (eds.), *New Essays in Philosophical Theology,* p. 59.

25. Roland Puccetti, "The Concept of God," *Philosophical Quarterly,* Vol. XIV (1964), p. 237.

26. *Ibid.,* pp. 239 f.

27. *Ibid.,* p. 242.

28. McCloskey, "God and Evil," *loc. cit.,* p. 62.

29. Mackie, "Evil and Omnipotence," *loc. cit.,* p. 60.

30. Hick, *Philosophy of Religion* (Prentice-Hall, Inc., 1963), p. 40.

31. Hick, *Evil and the God of Love,* pp. 170 f.

32. Penelhum, *op. cit.,* p. 99.

33. Alfred North Whitehead, *Science and the Modern World* (The Macmillan Company, 1926), pp. 273 f.

34. Charles Hartshorne, *The Divine Relativity: A Social Conception of God* (Yale University Press, 1948), pp. 154 f.

35. Paul G. Kuntz, "Omnipotence: Tradition and Revolt in Philosophical Theology," *New Scholasticism,* Vol. XLII (1968), pp. 278 f.

36. H. D. Aiken is not to be numbered among them, as he says: "I, for one, respect those contemporary theologians who candidly accept the notion of a

finite God. . . . Such finite theologies . . . enable the believer to preserve his moral integrity and his religious devotion to a God who can be regarded with a straight face as a good person. They are possible, however, only to men of great emotional maturity and stability. . . . They are not appealing to those for whom religious piety is possible only to the degree that the needs of emotional dependency are satisfied." (Aiken, "God and Evil," *loc. cit.,* p. 92.)

37. Antony Flew, *God and Philosophy* (Dell Publishing Company, Inc., 1966), pp. 28 f., 41, 43.

38. *Ibid.,* pp. 44–47.

39. *Ibid.,* p. 17.

40. *Ibid.,* pp. 51 f.

41. Puccetti, "The Concept of God," *loc. cit.,* pp. 244, 245.

42. *Ibid.,* p. 245.

43. Dewey J. Hoitenga, Jr., "Logic and the Problem of Evil," *American Philosophical Quarterly,* Vol. IV (1967), pp. 121, 122.

44. *Ibid.,* p. 124.

45. *Ibid.,* p. 125.

46. Mackie, "Evil and Omnipotence," *loc. cit.,* pp. 47, 50.

47. E.g., Ahern, *The Problem of Evil,* p. 15.

48. *Ibid.*

49. Plantinga, *God and Other Minds,* p. 119. Some theologians have indeed suggested that there could not be a world without evil. For example, David Platt in "God, Goodness and a Morally Perfect World," *The Personalist,* Vol. XLVI (1965), pp. 320–326, follows Leibniz in affirming that not all values are compossible, so that the realization of some possibilities always prevents the realization of others. Hence, a plurality of decision makers "guarantees that out of these plural demands some conflict and evil is always bound to arise," so that it is *not* "logically possible that there might have been a morally perfect world" (pp. 323, 325). In *this* sense of the term "evil," I would call it logically necessary in *any* world (not just in a world with human beings), as Austin Farrer comes close to saying (*Love Almighty and Ills Unlimited,* pp. 50–59, 74–76, 104). But the existence of genuine evil as I have defined it does not seem to be logically necessary, since I have not included the foreclosure of possible values that would have been lesser or just equal to the ones actualized. Genuine evil only occurs when the actualization of a lesser possibility eliminates one that would have been better, all things considered. And it seems logically possible that in each instance an event would occur that is better than or at least equal to the other possibilities open then and there.

50. Ahern, *The Problem of Evil,* p. 16.

51. J. L. Mackie, "Theism and Utopia," *Philosophy,* Vol. XXXVII (1962), p. 157.

52. See note 49, above.

53. Haig Khatchadourian, "God, Happiness and Evil," *Religious Studies,* Vol. II (1966), p. 111n.

54. Penelhum, "Divine Goodness and the Problem of Evil, *loc. cit.,* p. 99.

55. Ahern, *The Problem of Evil,* p. 34.

56. I accept Mortimer Taube's definition: "An event A causes event B, when B results partly from some activity or influence originating in A." Mortimer Taube, *Causation, Freedom and Determinism* (London: George Allen & Unwin, Ltd., 1936), p. 17.

57. "Omnipotence," *An Encyclopedia of Religion,* ed. by Vergilius Ferm (Philosophical Library, Inc., 1945), p. 545.

58. Pike, "God and Evil: A Reconsideration," *loc. cit.,* p. 120.

59. S. A. Grave, "On Evil and Omnipotence," *Mind,* Vol. LXV (1956), p. 260.

60. Plantinga, *God and Other Minds,* pp. 138 f.

61. Grave, "On Evil and Omnipotence," *loc. cit.,* p. 261. Geddes MacGregor, *Introduction to Religious Philosophy* (Houghton Mifflin Company, 1959), provides another example of the view that the capacity for self-determination is a divine gift that could have been withheld from the creatures. He believes God could stop sin by divine fiat, but allows it because of the good produced by the freedom that also makes evil possible (p. 257). He says that the Biblical conception did not include the notion of omnipotence in the sense of the ability to do anything (pp. 268–270). Nevertheless, he rejects, on the basis of the "most profound kinds of religious insight and experience," the idea that God is limited in the sense of having to wrestle with evil (p. 271). Such a God would not be free from needs, so that his love would not be entirely untainted by self-interest (p. 275). I regard this as a more serious objection than those which simply say that absolute power as such is essential for a being worthy of worship. However, perfect love need not be free from self-interest as such, but only a self-interest that is in conflict with the good of others. Perfect love can be understood as the coincidence of self-interest and other-interest.

62. Cf. Madden and Hare, *Evil and the Concept of God,* p. 75.

63. Cf. *ibid.,* p. 75; McCloskey, "God and Evil," *loc. cit.,* p. 83.

64. Cf. Plantinga, *God and Other Minds,* pp. 149–51; C. S. Lewis, *The Problem of Pain* (The Macmillan Company, 1965), pp. 122 f.

65. Hartshorne, *The Divine Relativity,* p. 138.

66. Alfred North Whitehead, *Adventures of Ideas* (The Macmillan Company, 1933), p. 220.

*Chapter* 18. A Process Theodicy

1. The following symbols are used for Whitehead's works:

| | |
|---|---|
| *AI* | *Adventures of Ideas.* The Macmillan Company, 1933. |
| *FR* | *The Function of Reason.* Princeton University Press, 1929. |
| Imm. | "Immortality," in *The Philosophy of Alfred North Whitehead,* ed. by Paul Arthur Schilpp. 1941; Tudor Publishing Company, 1951. Pp. 682–700. |
| *MT* | *Modes of Thought.* 1938; The Free Press, 1968. |

| | |
|---|---|
| *PR* | *Process and Reality.* The Macmillan Company, 1929. |
| *RM* | *Religion in the Making.* 1926; The World Publishing Company, 1960. |
| *SMW* | *Science and the Modern World.* The Macmillan Company, 1926. |
| *S* | *Symbolism: Its Meaning and Effect.* 1927; G. P. Putnam's Sons, Inc., Capricorn Books, 1959. |

2. The assertion by process theologians that God's power is persuasive rather than coercive has evoked the following critical response from Edward H. Madden and Peter H. Hare: While process thinkers maintain that "coercive power" is a self-contradictory term, since all actualities have freedom, they also recognize degrees of freedom and, thereby, degrees of coercion. (See "Evil and Persuasive Power," *Process Studies,* Vol. 2, No. 1 [Spring 1972], pp. 44–48, especially p. 46.) Their point is well taken, but it does not affect a process theodicy. This is because there are two different senses of "coercion" or "compulsion" involved. When Whitehead says that God's power is persuasive rather than coercive, he has in mind what can be called "absolute coercion." This would be a form of efficient causation in which the effect is not partially self-determining, i.e., where the change brought about in the affected entity is not in part due to that entity's decision. And it is the denial of this type of divine power upon which a process theodicy depends, because only a being with absolute coercive power could unilaterally prevent all evil. The other sense of coercive power can be called "relative coercion." This would refer to the elements of coercion involved in all persuasive efficient causation. There are indeed such elements in Whitehead's account of the influence of one individual upon another. 1. It is necessarily the case *that* the past occasions out of which a present occasion arises must be felt or positively prehended by that occasion. 2. The past occasions determine *what* can be received from themselves and thereby determine which possibilities are open to the new occasion. 3. The past occasions also determine *how* the new occasion will initially respond to what it receives from them. In reference to this third point Whitehead explicitly says that "the factor of compulsive determinism in the Universe depends on this principle" (*AI* 326). This form of coercion or compulsion is not antithetical to the fact that all individuals have some self-determining freedom so that all power upon them is ultimately persuasive. Even though the power has elements of coercion in it, it is ultimately persuasive, since the individual itself ultimately decides precisely *how* to respond to the data that are forced upon it. Recognizing these elements of coercion is simply another way of saying that there is no absolute freedom. And, since there are degrees of self-determining freedom, since more complex individuals have more than less complex ones, it is implied that there are degrees of (relative) coercion.

Further, Madden and Hare are right in concluding that this means that God's power is a "mixture of coercion and persuasion" (*ibid.,* 45, 46). However, they err in thinking that the reason for God's use of persuasion is moral rather than metaphysical, so that God could at will increase the degree of coercion. They also evidently think of persuasion and coercion as contraries, rather than seeing coercion as an element in all persuasion. In other words, they seem to be thinking of the mixture as a mixture of persuasion and *absolute* coercion. It is on the basis of these errors that they demand that the process theodicist show that "the exercise of *only* persuasive power is morally appropriate" in situations where evil has occurred (*ibid.*, p. 45). This demand is in order in reference to those who maintain that lack of absolute coercion is due to a divine self-limitation, but not in reference to process theologians.

3. Whitehead's usual term for these societies with "personal" or "serial" order is "enduring object"; what endures is the complex eternal object which constitutes the self-identity of the society through time. But he also speaks of "enduring individuals" (*AI* 339, 362, 363). This term is not misleading as long as it is remembered that that which endures is not an "individual" in the strictest ontological sense, i.e., that an enduring individual is not an "enduring subject."

4. Whitehead suggests that that which we call "empty space," such as that between the planets, is really full of actual occasions in a chaotic state. It is only "empty" of enduring individuals (*PR* 141; *SMW* 122, 220–221).

5. The text has "goal" instead of "goad"; but I believe that to be an error.

6. I have interpreted Jesus' message along these lines in *A Process Christology* (The Westminster Press, 1973), pp. 199–205.

7. Farrer, *Love Almighty and Ills Unlimited,* p. 168.

8. Charles Hartshorne and William L. Reese (eds.), *Philosophers Speak of God* (The University of Chicago Press, 1953), p. 277.

9. Charles Hartshorne, *Whitehead's Philosophy: Selected Essays, 1935–1970* (University of Nebraska Press, 1972), p. 139.

10. Charles Hartshorne, *The Divine Relativity* (Yale University Press, 1948), p. 41.

11. Stephen Lee Ely, *The Religious Availability of Whitehead's God: A Critical Analysis* (University of Wisconsin Press, 1942), p. 52.

12. Madden and Hare, *Evil and the Concept of God* p. 124.

13. *Ibid.,* pp. 123 f.

14. *Ibid.,* p. 123.

15. *Ibid.*

16. Incidentally, this deeper beauty or aesthetic enjoyment which Whitehead's God seeks is also distinct from aesthetic enjoyment in the "superficial" sense, by which I mean a limitation to those forms of pleasure which we share with the other animals, which the term "hedonism" usually suggests. For example, Whitehead refers to humans as "a race of beings sensitive to values beyond those of mere animal enjoyment" (*AI* 204). He says that "it is not true that the finer quality [of life] is the direct associate of obvious happiness or obvious pleasure" (*RM* 77). He speaks of our lives as expressing "perfections proper to our finite natures," and thereby including "a mode of satisfaction deeper than joy or sorrow" (*AI* 221). And he indicates that this deeper mode of satisfaction is the aim of deity: "God in the world is the perpetual vision of

the road which leads to the deeper realities" (*RM* 151). Hence, when the deeper sense is distinguished from the simple and superficial senses of aesthetic enjoyment, it is clear that it would be misleading to think of Whitehead's God as either a Divine Aesthete (in the usual sense of that term) or a Cosmic Hedonist.

17. Madden and Hare, *Evil and the Concept of God,* p. 123.

18. Ely, *The Religious Availability of Whitehead's God,* pp. 40 f.

19. Madden and Hare raise this question in relation to the position of E. S. Brightman (Madden and Hare, *Evil and the Concept of God,* p. 111). But the question is also relevant to Whitehead's position.

*Appendix.* Theodicy and Hope for a Future Life

1. "The Possibility of Subjective Immortality in Whitehead's Philosophy," *University of Dayton Review,* Vol. VIII (Winter 1971), pp. 43–56. Reprinted in *The Modern Schoolman,* Vol. LIII, No. 1 (Nov. 1975), pp. 39–57.

2. Griffin, *A Process Christology,* p. 12.

3. See my article "Faith, Reason and Christology—A Response to Father Meilach," *The Cord,* Vol. XXIV, No. 7 (1974), pp. 258–267.

# Index